More P _____ mmunity

"Comprehensive, balance_____ , a Place for Community
is a monumental collection ___ ....e research, experience, data, and policy
guidance on building strong local economies. Essential reading for every city,
county, a_____nce

source to_____

—David

"A breath_____ _____ research on the essential role of strong
community economies in revitalizing American democracy. It contains hundreds of exciting examples of successful policies, businesses, and movements
that demonstrate that localization *is* a viable alternative to the perils of globalization. Every local politician, policymaker, and activist should read, understand, and use this book."
—Michael H. Shuman, author of *Going Local: Creating Self-Reliant*
Communities in a Global Age

Thad Williamson is a doctoral student in the Department of Government at
Harvard University. An editorial board member of *Dollars and Sense* magazine,
he has also written for *The Nation, Tikkun,* and numerous other publications.

David L. Imbroscio is Associate Professor of Political Science at the University
of Louisville. He is the author of *Reconstructing City Politics.* His other scholarly
work has appeared in *Polity, Policy Studies Journal,* the *Journal of Urban Affairs,*
and *Urban Affairs Review.* He currently serves on the editorial board of the
Journal of Urban Affairs

Gar Alperovitz, Lionel R. Bauman Professor of Political Economy at the
University of Maryland and President of the National Center for Economic and
Security Alternatives, has been a leading public voice on behalf of community-
based economic policy for over 30 years. His books include *Rebuilding America*
with Jeff Faux and *The Decision to Use the Atomic Bomb,* and his articles have
appeared in *The New York Times, The New Republic, The Washington Post, The Los
Angeles Times, The Boston Review,* and *The Nation.* He is often invited on television, including *CrossFire, Larry King Live, The Charlie Rose Show,* Sunday *"Today,"*
and *Meet the Press.*

MAKING A
PLACE FOR COMMUNITY

Local Democracy in a Global Era

By Thad Williamson,
David Imbroscio, and
Gar Alperovitz

With a Foreword by Benjamin R. Barber

Routledge
Taylor & Francis Group

NEW YORK AND LONDON

Published in 2003 by
Routledge
29 West 35th Street
New York, NY 10001
www.routledge-ny.com

Published in Great Britain by
Routledge
11 New Fetter Lane
London EC4P 4EE
www.routledge.co.uk

Library of Congress Cataloging-In-Publication Data

Williamson, Thad.
Making a place for community: local democracy in a global era/ by Thad Williamson, David Imbroscio, and Gar Alperovitz; with a foreword by Benjamin Barber.
     p.cm.
Includes bibliographical references and index.
ISBN 0-415-94741-3 (pbk) 0-415-93356-0 (hbk)
Community development, Urban—United States. 2. Community life—United States. 3. United States—Economic conditions. 4. Urban economics. 5. Globalization. I. Imbroscio, David. II. Alperovitz, Gar. III. Title.

HN90.c6 W4665 2002
307.1'416'0973—dc21   2001058939

CONTENTS

ACKNOWLEDGMENTS

We would like to thank the following individuals for their support, help, advice, and criticism. (All errors, of course, are our own.) Alex Campbell, James DeFilippis, Christopher Gunn, Avery Kolers, Christopher Mackin, Rodger Payne, Loren Rodgers, Adria Scharf, Todd Swanstrom, and Jordan Yin were kind enough to read and comment on all or parts of the manuscript. Numerous individuals contributed research, background materials, and other assistance. We would especially like to thank: Matt Berres, Laura Brandt, Jonas Brodin, Wen-Heng Chou, Stephanie Geller, Ted Howard, Michael Jones, Alexandra Kogl, Brendan Leary, Evan Lewis, Byron Lutz, Kathleen Pleasant, Jeff Pope, Preston Quesenberry, Tom Ricker, Jennifer Thangevalu, Matt Weiss, and Donn Worgs. Dwight Haygood and especially Joshua Harris did much of the work of pulling together the appendix. Several passages in Part III drew heavily from *The Emerging New Society* by our colleague Kristen Rusch.

David Imbroscio would also like to thank the College of Arts and Sciences, University of Louisville, the Office of the Vice President for Research, University of Louisville, and Charles Ziegler, Chair of the Department of Political Science, University of Louisville, for supporting his contributions to this project. Thad Williamson acknowledges the support received from the Multidisciplinary Program on Inequality at the Kennedy School of Government; this work benefits greatly from his opportunity to learn from and work with, in particular, Professors Ronald Ferguson, Christopher Jencks, Robert Putnam, and Michael Sandel at Harvard.

The University of Maryland and its faculty have directly and indirectly contributed to the success of this project in many ways. In particular Gar Alperovitz would like to thank the principals and staff of the Civil Society/Community Building Initiative and the Democracy Collaborative. Special thanks to Benjamin Barber for his generous foreword and to Stewart Edelstein, Stephen Elkin, Jessica Gordon Nembhard, and Jon Wilkenfeld for specific contributions and general support of the overall effort.

We gratefully acknowledge the support of the Ford Foundation, the Surdna Foundation, and the Rockefeller Foundation. Related research that contributed to this project was supported by the Annie E. Casey Foundation, the Bauman Foundation, the Cummings Foundation, the John D. and Catherine T. MacArthur Foundation, and the Summit Foundation. Special thanks to Patricia Bauman, John Bryant, Betsy Campbell, Bob Giloth, Charles Halpern, Frances Korten, Lance Lindblom, Julia Lopez, Susan Sechler, and Edward Skloot for their friendship, support, and input.

Our appreciation to editor Eric Nelson at Routledge for his patience and enthusiasm and production editor Nicole Ellis for her hard work with the manuscript.

Special thanks to Ronald Goldfarb for invaluable advice and help.

Finally, thanks to Sharon Alperovitz and Adria Scharf for their patience, love, and support.

FOREWORD

BY BENJAMIN R. BARBER

Democracy, community, place, and work are interdependent terms. From Jean-Jacques Rousseau and Alexis de Tocqueville to Robert Bellah and Robert Putnam, a powerful tradition of social thought has insisted that stable democracies must be grounded in strong communities, which are themselves firmly rooted in civil society. As a consequence, in recent decades the challenges facing democracy have been captured by terms such as "decline of social capital" and "erosion of civic trust." Politics has been reconceptualized in the language of society and citizenship, as political science has been yielding to the powerful analysis of sociology (Bellah is a sociologist, as are influential scholars of America's political sociology such as Seymour Martin Lipset). In the same vein, liberal communitarians such as Michael Sandel, Mary Ann Glendon, and Amitai Etzioni have labored to remind us that individuals—however abstract they may become when regarded as bundles of rights—are in reality embedded in families and associations and generally flourish only as the communities to which they belong flourish. Thus has democratic theory enlarged its dominion from mere state theory to social theory. Thus has politics been rethought in the language of the civic and the social.

As sociological and communitarian analysis has prospered, however, the once fashionable perspective of political economy has wilted. Whether because of Marxism's practical fall from grace with the collapse of the Soviet empire or the rising hegemony of neoliberal theory that accompanied and succeeded it, far less thought has been given in recent decades than previously to how the economy interacts with the twin terms community and democracy. Although neoliberalism treats the economy as trump, it focuses on economics as an independent, indeed autonomous variable that supplants rather than interacts with politics and society. This new study is thus especially welcome, for it not only refurbishes the perspective of political economy for this new age of globalization but does so not at the expense of the communitarian point of view but by offering vital linkages between politics, community, and the economy. Rather than drawing new boundaries, it builds new bridges across old theoretical divides. Neoliberalism has not so much forged as denied linkages, arguing that a laissez-faire free market system is more or less the same thing as democracy—this despite the fact that as ardent an advocate of markets as Charles Lindblom has observed that there is "no convincing evidence or argument that, except in the mind, the market system is necessary to democracy."[1] Indeed, if community stability is a primary condition of democracy, then it may be that the market system is destabilizing rather than nurturing to democracy. Rousseau seemed closer to the mark when he suggested that a pastoral economy, simple economic interests, and frugality helped underwrite the operation of the general will, and alone could sustain democracy in the strong sense. Even leaving aside the Marxist tradition, social theorists and philosophers from Tocqueville to Dewey have wondered whether entrepreneurial capitalism is more likely to undercut than to sustain democratic community.

This vital new study by Thad Williamson, David Imbroscio, and Gar Alperovitz is both a primer in the political economy of local democracy and a strong theoretical and empirical argument on behalf of the position that the stability of democracy cannot be understood without understanding the economics of the community—above all under the conditions of a global market society. In a global economy where the pressures on community come from the top down, democracy as a bottom-up form of political organization is all too easily compromised. In a mobile world where urban and suburban sprawl unknit the fabric of local communities, municipal and regional stability are constantly imperiled. In an era dominated by neoliberal ideology that justifies sacrificing local jobs and economic continuity to shifting markets in labor and capital, the foundations of democracy in place and work are eroded. In the setting of the new information economy, whose capital is knowledge rather than traditional industrial assets, old forms of community based on the linkage between jobs and place are unsettled.

Given these new realities, democracy clearly depends not only on local social capital but also on local economic capital, not only on the kinds of social trust engendered by civic relations but also on the kinds of economic loyalty spurned by global corporatism, not only on enunciating a market rationale for civics but also on developing a civic rationale for markets. From the perspective of economic efficiency in a global market society, "throwing away" cities whose economies have become "obsolete" may be "rational." But from the perspective of democracy, which depends on the stability, continuity, and economic well-being of the real places where real people live and work, it is insane.

As *Making a Place for Community* demonstrates with sharp analysis and careful argumentation, from the point of view of today's constricted ideological doxology, insanity too often passes as reason. The truth is, a full calculation of the costs of throwing away cities—one that includes the cost of lost homes, schools, and community assets—reveals the foolishness of the pure market approach, even from a narrowly economic point of view. Not only are there persuasive democratic and egalitarian reasons for the democratization of the workplace and of capital ownership, there are—as the authors show—persuasive economic reasons as well. Employee stock ownership plans, community development corporations, community financial institutions, land trusts, and other place-based models of ownership have received some attention from progressive social scientists, but these institutions have rarely been contextualized and examined as key pieces not only in a theory of social and economic democratization but also in the demanding terms of a larger perspective that brings together the requirements of place, community, work, and the economy with what the great Canadian political philosopher C. B. MacPherson rightly called the real world of democracy.

The theoretical acumen of the authors, the breadth of their analytic compass, and their focus on the local economy as the keystone of democracy's municipal arch make *Making a Place for Community* a true primer for democratic social science in the new century. Democratic theorists will benefit from its economic and sociological specificity, while sociologists and economists will learn from its preoccupation with the broad democratic consequences of political economy. Students will be introduced to democracy's complexities with a refreshing directness. For by crossing the boundaries between political science, sociology, and economics, the authors compel us to see the world whole. By crossing the boundaries between sound scholarship and thoughtful advocacy, they remind us that the social sciences are configured by values and norms—whether acknowledged or implicit—and that scholars and students are also always advocates and citizens. By crossing the boundaries between theory and practice—how we think about the world and how we behave in it—they recall us to the real purposes of liberal arts education and the engaged university: the cultivation of intelligence as a tool of community living and social comity as well as of personal advance and private satisfaction. And, finally, by crossing the many lines that intersect at the edges of the world of democracy, they restore democracy to its proper place as social science's core subject. In doing all of these things, *Making a Place for Community* lives up to its billing as an indispensable primer for the new century.

PREFACE

TOWARD THE RECONSTRUCTION OF
AMERICAN COMMUNITY AND DEMOCRACY

The past decade has witnessed unprecedented public and academic attention to the decay of civic life and community attachment in the United States. It is a commonplace that community is dying and that isolation, social dysfunction, and cynicism are increasing. Pundits and scholars alike have increasingly used the term community to voice concern over declining political participation, declining membership in civic organizations, a sense of meaninglessness, periodic outbursts of violence such as the 1999 Littleton, Colorado, school killings, and any number of social ills. Other observers put the problems associated with an absence of community in more concrete terms, pointing to environmental damage, huge disparities of income and wealth, the middle-class time crunch, and even traffic snarls. A decade-long Fordham University research project concludes that the overall social health of the United States, as measured by a composite index of nine basic social indicators, has declined since 1973 and is now lower than it was in 1959.[1]

Numerous activists, writers, and political philosophers have attempted to mold a concern for strengthening community life into a broader public philosophy capable of guiding America into the new century. Noting that the "idea that freedom consists in shaping the forces that govern our collective life is difficult to sustain in the modern world," Harvard political philosopher Michael Sandel seeks to resuscitate a vision of "civic republicanism," "a tradition that "reminds us that politics is not only about the size and distribution of the national product. It is also about bringing economic power to democratic account and equipping men and women with the habits and dispositions that suit them to self-rule."[2]

Much can be learned from the research and analysis now being produced by close observers of community life in the United States. There is, however, also something rather odd about the contemporary conversation: Discussions of community and civic decline take place with a background awareness that the U.S. political-economic system explicitly devalues community as a relevant good. Indeed, our policies—as many have argued and as we shall document—often seem designed explicitly to undermine the economic basis of stable communities. While serious observers know this, few want to confront or alter this reality in a direct fashion. Instead, discussions of how to revitalize community (and communities) too often come with this caveat: We want to rebuild community *without* seriously altering the political and economic policies that contradict this goal.[3]

The continued evasion of central political-economic questions is a dead end for those concerned with reconstructing civil and community life in the twenty-first century. Whereas many economists and policy analysts of various political stripes have for decades presumed that preserving and enhancing the economic stability of specific places is an irrelevant or at best secondary policy aim, we argue that it is imperative that our nation make community economic stability a guiding principle for economic and social policy.[4] Such a shift is essential if other problems associated with the decay and decline of community in America are to find a lasting solution. Indeed, while community economic stability is our guiding framework, far more than community life is at stake in this book: We contend that unless a new basis for community economic security can be established, any hope for a rich democracy in which an engaged citizenry can practice meaningful self-governance will remain hopelessly chimerical in the coming century.

The first step is to confront the problem squarely and soberly. By "community economic stability," we refer to a condition in which each geographic entity of significant size (such as cities, towns, and rural counties) possesses job opportunities and a general level of economic activity—that is, reasonably full employment at the community level—adequate to provide a decent standard of living for its population over a sustained period of time. American communities seeking to achieve that goal face a massive triple threat as the new century begins:

- The process of globalization now under way threatens to undermine the basis of economic and social life in local communities by increasing economic volatility and job insecurity, in the process undercutting the capacity of communities to engage in effective self-governance in economic affairs.

- Movement of capital and jobs *within* the United States increasingly and unnecessarily destabilizes communities' social and economic life—while states and cities compete with each other to recapture the jobs lost.

- Suburban sprawl, assisted by powerful public subsidies, undermines community as urban growth is directed away from existing neighborhoods and cities toward newer, less concentrated settlements in haphazard fashion—with many attendant deleterious fiscal, environmental and social consequences.

We shall argue that unless these challenges are met, community economic and social life—and, in turn, the local basis of democracy itself—will continue to erode in the United States.

In any market economy, some local-level economic volatility is a fact of life. The question is not whether communities will undergo economic change over time but whether we will allow communities simply to wither and die when changes take place in market conditions or in the decisions of private economic actors. As we shall suggest, although there are many ways to make the economic position of communities more secure, most American communities are not sufficiently buffered against instability. Many are under increasing stress due to the three overarching forces undercutting the stability of place. Mitigating or reversing the effects of globalization, excessive internal capital mobility, and suburban sprawl requires first and foremost that we recognize that these are not forces of nature or immutable laws given by an omniscient market, but are, in large measure, a by-product of specific public actions and specific political choices (both wise and unwise). This basic insight guides much of the following analysis.*

The following text is not meant to be a detailed academic report on all of

---

* Political philosopher Iris Marion Young and others have voiced important critiques of "community" based on racial or class homogeneity, especially in the context of a highly diverse society. (See Young, *Justice and the Politics of Difference,* Princeton: Princeton University Press, 1990.) Such critiques have in turn led scholars to specify that truly desirable "communities" must be places in which citizens recognize they have a mutual obligation and relationship but also places which preserve liberal norms regarding tolerance and non-exclusion. This is a qualification to the concept of community we accept: in referring to "communities" we are primarily speaking of towns and cities–in short, places–and not a condition of social life in which each person fully identifies with every other member of the locality.

these matters. (We refer interested readers to more detailed work at each step of the analysis.) Rather, it is intended as a primer on the central issues and problems associated with community economic stability, and how they might be resolved.

Part I of the book provides an assessment of how each of the three threats —globalization, internal job and capital shifts, and urban sprawl—undercuts community stability.

Parts II and III shift gears and argue that despite the triple threat to community, a future of chronic instability for American communities is *not* inevitable. There are numerous practical ways to encourage economic restructuring *at the level of local communities* so that geographic areas can be more effectively supported by a stable, long-term job base. In addition, large-scale public facilities can act as such anchors, and expanded public investments could help broaden the number of communities now anchored directly by such public facilities. Tax, loan and other policies can also help. We also suggest that attaining community stability will require finding a way to root more business activity in institutional forms that are inherently locally anchored—and also developing a variety of complementary strategies to stabilize local economies.

In Parts II and III we suggest that building on existing precedents, local, state, and federal community stabilizing policies can be refined in general— and in particular can enhance the impact of such institutional structures as community development finance institutions, worker-owned firms, and community development corporations. A wide range of experience and know-how associated with community-rooted, democratically controlled economic institutions is now available. Decades of hard, quiet developmental work have established a new foundation upon which to build. With adequate policy support, these institutions could become a significant and permanent part of the American economy. Such expansion is desirable for its own sake. But we also believe that building up such institutions over the course of the new century offers important opportunities for achieving community economic stability, establishing a place-respecting political economy, and, ultimately, reconstructing the local basis of genuine democracy in America.

In Part IV we turn to the problem of how to contain threats to community-building work posed by liberalized trade regimes and increasing economic integration across international borders. We discuss a number of alternative approaches to trade policy aimed at lifting community standards of production both at home and abroad, and we explore numerous far-reaching proposals to reform international economic institutions so as to promote greater stability of national economies and the world economy as a whole. Unlike the community-level initiatives discussed in Parts II and III, many of the proposals for altering the rules of the global economy discussed in Part IV are untested, and their possible effects are necessarily uncertain. Even so, we believe it important to think through how "globalization" might proceed in a manner that protects the rights of communities to actively shape their own economies while also establishing a relatively stable global context for local, regional, and national economic and social development.

We have also provided a resource guide as an Appendix for readers who wish to pursue further various practical initiatives and policy possibilities discussed in the main body of the text.

INTRODUCTION

THE CASE FOR COMMUNITY ECONOMIC STABILITY:
ECONOMICS AND POLITICAL ECONOMICS

t he case for making community economic stability a guiding force in the
formulation of economic and social
policies is compelling: Strong, economically secure communities are norma-
tively attractive for a host of reasons, and the effort to build them, on balance, is likely to impose few net costs to society.[1] Contrary to conventional
wisdom, such an objective is achievable in the era of globalization and greater
decentralization of production. Implementing a full-blown policy initiative
to enhance community economic stability would be desirable, efficient, and
possible in the new century. We elaborate upon each of these claims below.[2]

IS COMMUNITY STABILITY DESIRABLE?

To most observers it may seem obvious that it is desirable to preserve, sustain,
and strengthen geographically defined communities over time. Nevertheless,
many economists believe that instead of attempting to support community,
public policy should seek to facilitate individual and business mobility, no
matter the costs. From a different perspective, some sociologists and social
activists argue that geographically defined communities are now less relevant
than communities defined by shared interests, organizational membership,
race and ethnicity, or other forms of association not strictly tied to particular

places. Both arguments suggest that emphasizing geographical communities as a basis for policy is a mistake.

We find such arguments, even stated in their most plausible forms, unconvincing. To be sure, we are not opposed to individual and family mobility, and we agree that forms of community other than geographically defined units are important. But the type of communities we are primarily concerned with in this book are not affective communities, communities of interest, or the feelings of community that arise from membership in clubs, churches, and other associations. Rather, we are concerned with geographically demarcated communities in which a diverse array of citizens join together in self-governance—in short, with the local-level building blocks of democratic practice.[3] And we believe that the cumulative force of a number of considerations converge to suggest overwhelmingly the inherent desirability of policies emphasizing local-level community economic stability.

First and foremost, community economic stability is intimately intertwined with prospects for meaningful local-level democracy. Community economic stability is obviously vital to the nurturance of "civil society" and what has come to be known as "social capital." The strength of a society's social networks, civic associations, religious organizations, and even participation in nonpolitical clubs and groups have been identified by Robert Putnam and a host of other social scientists as an important (and in some cases decisive) determinant of overall institutional performance, including government efficacy, quality of public services, and socioeconomic development. Putnam's study of regional governments in Italy after 1970, for instance, found a striking association between success in twelve separate measures of regional governance efficacy and the degree of civic attachment present in each region. More recently, Putnam has presented an impressive accumulation of evidence showing that, after controlling for a variety of factors, Americans today are less likely to participate in numerous civic institutions—from PTAs to churches to fraternal organizations—while overall measures of social trust and confidence in American institutions have declined.[4]

Not enough is known about the precise relationship between community economic instability and these observed changes in American civic culture. However, the link between long-term stable residence in a community and civic participation has been well established by researchers. The most thorough recent study of American political engagement, conducted by Sidney Verba, Kay Schlozman, and Henry Brady (building on the work of many previous studies finding that long-term residents vote at a higher-than-average level), found that the number of years spent in a community is a positive predictor of both national- and local-level civic involvement, with the effect nearly twice as strong for local involvement. Verba and colleagues go on to note that "those who have educated parents and are themselves well-educated are more mobile and less rooted in their communities. Thus, ties to the community can represent an alternative—indeed, one of the only alternatives— to the dominant force [in predicting political participation] of education and the other socioeconomic stratification variables associated with it."[5] Likewise, a detailed 2000 survey of nearly thirty thousand Americans conducted by the Saguaro Seminar on Civic Engagement at Harvard University shows that both the number of years lived in one's community and the expectation of staying in one's community in the future are positively correlated with greater social trust, civic participation, and formal group involvements.[6]

The nature and strength of the linkage between economic stability and long-term residence has received less attention from researchers. But communities that experience economic displacement and long-term population decline will inevitably lose a substantial portion of their social-capital-enhancing long-term residents.[7] Furthermore, after an economic dislocation, it is the better-educated, higher-income residents who are most likely to be able to leave—the very people who are most likely to be strongly involved in a community's civic life. (This point is often noted in connection with the flight to suburbia of black middle-class residents in recent decades.) Moreover, recent evidence from the Saguaro Survey indicates that the proportion of the workforce in one's immediate locality (the zip code) that consists of either public-sector or nonprofit-sector workers—the part of the workforce that is most insulated from the ups and downs of the market—is positively correlated with long-term community residency as well as several common social capital indicators (such as attendance at public meetings).[8]

Membership in civic organizations, social networks, local grassroots organizations, and simple personal relationships are all threatened when economic decline causes members of a community to lose their jobs, experience increased financial and familial stress, and perhaps move away.[9] Even in relatively good economic times, such as from March 1998 to March 2000, nearly 1.1 million Americans moved because they had lost a job or were looking for work. During this two-year span, another 12 million Americans moved for job-related reasons such as a corporate transfer or relocation; nearly one-third of all moves out of a county are for work-related reasons.[10]

Nearly two decades ago Barry Bluestone and the late Bennett Harrison observed: "Loss of a work network removes an important source of human support. As a result, psychosomatic illnesses, anxiety, worry, tension, impaired interpersonal relations, and an increased sense of powerlessness arise."[11] A recent case study of the effect of Chrysler's closure of an auto plant in Kenosha, Wisconsin, by Yale sociologist Kathryn Marie Dudley illustrates this point, as well as the destruction of tangible social capital involved when plants close:

> When a plant closes, workers lose a social structure in which they have felt valued and validated by their fellows. When they are stripped of their work-place identities, dislocated workers face an external culture that no longer seems to value, or grant social legitimacy to, the kind of work they do . . . and when their plant closes this accumulated cultural capital is lost. Long and respectable work histories are suddenly worthless, and workers are faced with the prospect of starting all over again, from scratch.[12]

A *New York Times* series documenting the effects of downsizing and community instability in Dayton, Ohio, drives the point home:

> Everything, seemingly, is in upheaval: not just the jobs and lives of tens of thousands of people, but also the big corporations, the banks, the schools, the religious and cultural institutions, the old relationships of politics and power, and, especially, the people's expectations of security, stability, and a shared civic life . . . Churches are losing members. So are service organizations; people say they cannot leave work for meetings, even if they only last an hour.[13]

In short, the loss of a community's economic basis leads to the destruction of accumulated social capital. Conversely, communities in which few residents are compelled by economic necessity to move have stronger social bonds.

How widespread are these community-disrupting events? Even in very good times—for instance, the year 2000—there were over 5,622 mass layoffs (measured by the Bureau of Labor Statistics as events when at least fifty employees from the same establishment file unemployment claims after being laid off for at least thirty days) involving 1.2 million workers in the United States. Over 40 percent of these layoffs were seasonal (particularly in agriculture and construction), and in about one-third of the nonseasonal lay-offs, employer recalls were expected. But in 1,572 cases (involving 340,000 workers), the layoffs were permanent, and in 779 cases (involving 188,000 workers), work sites were closed completely. Just over one-half of such per-manent closures were of manufacturing plants. Mass layoffs occur dispropor-tionately in large cities: Forty percent of all layoffs in 2000 took place in the nation's fifty largest metropolitan statistical areas (MSAs). Fourteen of those MSAs had ten thousand or more workers separated from their job in 2000.

Recessions obviously present the potential for much heavier job loss. But even throughout the expansion of the late 1990s, even as unemployment fell below 4 percent nationally, over 2.5 million Americans a year were laid off (including 1.1 to 1.2 million people affected by mass layoffs.)[14] Insecurity of workers and communities—even during relatively good times—has important political consequences. A vast political science literature has established that local democratic governance is compromised (perhaps fatally) in situations where local governments' fiscal prospects (and the health of the local economy in general) are dependent on the decisions of private investors, who may or may not pull out jobs at any time.[15] In such situations democratic choice is sharply circumscribed: Local policy inevitably bends *away* from many publicly favored policies and *toward* meeting the needs of mobile capital, as well as those of existing businesses with a strong stake in local land values.

This body of scholarship also shows that in places with more stable economic bases such as a state capital or a university, or an extremely favorable geographical location, local political regimes that have a broader democratic reach are more likely to be formed. Not only are such local regimes more inclusive of the variety of political interests in localities, but they also tend to pursue policies promoting greater equity. One of the requirements of building up democratically inclusive, equity-oriented local regimes is, accordingly, the development of a stable local economic base capable of supporting such regimes.[16]

When localities are left at the mercy of unrestrained economic forces, local politics either becomes relatively meaningless (lacking sufficient power) or tilts toward the interests of a narrow range of business-oriented constituencies. As University of Maryland political scientist Stephen Elkin observes, an "alliance between public officials and land interests will be at the center of any local politics where capital can move in and out of local boundaries at will. A politics with such an alliance at its center will be unlikely to pursue egalitarian policies of any significant sort and will more than likely work to reinforce existing material differences among the population."[17]

Stable communities of place also have the capacity to impact the character formation of citizens. When the economic underpinnings of a community erode, social networks and institutions—such as families, schools, churches, soccer leagues, and civic organizations—are also weakened, with predictably damaging results. The experiences and lessons learned from growing up in a blighted, depressed neighborhood in which everyone is struggling to get by and sources of social support are scarce are very different from those learned from growing up in a stable neighborhood where institutions are strong and people have confidence in the future. In their work on unstable central-city neighborhoods, John Jakle and David Wilson observe that transiency erodes sociability. When one's neighbors are forever on the move, situated near one for only a few months or even weeks, then neighboring bonds are necessarily weak if not impossible. A constant succession of neighbors almost necessitates mutual suspicion and social distance. As few households are known to one another, people legitimize each other's conduct with great difficulty, always assuming and expecting the worse. Anonymity gives people immunity from moral controls. Missing is the gossip, ridicule, and ostracism by which traditional communities keep members controlled.[18]

We are not here primarily concerned with the relationship of economic class to the character of either a community or the individuals who live in it. On the one hand, in even the poorest areas of America, countervailing, community-building institutions can be found doing amazing work, and on the other, as the Littleton tragedy illustrated, even affluent communities can fall prey to a crisis of meaninglessness and emptiness. We do suggest, however, that relatively stable communities marked by neither boom nor bust and lacking huge inequalities of wealth are more likely than highly unstable communities to nurture positive community values.

Liberty is also involved: Where one chooses to live (to the degree one is able to exercise choice in the matter) is an important way of expressing individual freedom and identity. Some Americans prefer very small towns, some prefer cities of 75,000 to 100,000 people, and some believe New York City to be the pinnacle of human civilization and cannot imagine living anywhere else. When any of these forms of human settlement are allowed (or compelled) to disappear or decay to the point where they become undesirable places to live, the scope of choice available to citizens about what sort of environment in which to live one's life is reduced. If the hometown where you grew up dies out or decays economically and you are *compelled* to leave, a very significant life option has been extinguished.

In his seminal 1983 critique of place-disregarding economic and social policy, geographer and social theorist Gordon Clark articulates the principle of "maintaining community integrity"—a principle akin to our call for community economic stability. Community integrity, he writes, "involves taking jobs to people, thereby building the economy in terms of the locational preferences of residents, not firms." Such a policy recognizes and attempts to realize in practice "the right of individuals to choose where to live and, once a choice has been made, the requirement that governments support this choice by providing for residents' welfare wherever they live."[19]

Clark correctly observes that a variety of federal programs that are consistent with a place-based policy agenda are already in place. But Clark's larger point is that respect for the freedom of individuals requires making a reasonable effort to preserve the places where they have chosen to live, even when this means intervening in economic policy structures and the operations of the market. The late Harvard political theorist Judith Shklar made the related argument that providing work opportunities to all is critical to providing all citizens with a basis for "public respect" as free and equal members of the society. Shklar argued that the "minimum political obligation [owed by American society to its members] must be the creation of paying jobs geographically close to the unemployed."[20] This general principle has been made explicit in several cases in Europe: Regional policy in the Nordic countries of Sweden, Finland, and Norway (for instance) toward outlying towns in the remote, sparsely populated regions of those countries has long been animated by the notion that people have "the right to continue living in the area they were born."[21]

Stable geographic communities also provide a natural site for organizing political action across class, race, ethnic, and gender lines and for developing what some have termed "bridging social capital" that can enhance social cohesion and reduce tension throughout society. To be sure, towns and cities with racially and economically diverse populations are often the site of social conflict and tension. But racial and economic segregation has even worse consequences for local civic life. Princeton political scientist J. Eric Oliver has shown in an important recent study that economically diverse municipalities tend to have higher participation in local politics than homogeneous places.[22] Giving up on specific localities as the site of democratic debate and common social action would consign America to becoming an increasingly fragmented society, with its citizens disconnected from both local decision making and larger-order governance structures. This is a recipe for balkanization and a hardening of boundaries associated with race and other ethnic and class divisions. If meaningful interaction between diverse types of citizens within a public sphere does not take place in the localities where people actually spend their lives, it is not likely to happen at all.

In addition to the benefits it is instrumental in creating, community economic stability is valuable as a good in itself. The uprooting of place represents a tangible destruction of connections with the past and a sense of belonging and shared identity—qualities that help make life meaningful. Lewis Mumford put it this way over half a century ago: "A habitat planned so as to form a continuous background to a delicately graded scale of human feeling and values is the prime requisite of a cultivated life. Where that is lacking, men will fumble uneasily with substitutes, or starve."[23]

Theorists of democracy such as John Stuart Mill, Alexis de Tocqueville, and John Dewey (among many others) have long contended that local democracies are the fundamental schools in which national democratic experience was (or was not) learned and developed. As Tocqueville stressed, "The strength of free peoples resides in the local community. Local institutions are to liberty what primary schools are to science; they put it within the people's reach; they teach people to appreciate its peaceful enjoyment and accustom them to make use of it."[24] Similarly, Mill emphasized participation in local affairs as a means of developing the capacities of citizens. Dewey, too, saw strong local communities as an important check against ignorance and as a mechanism for creating citizens capable of self-governance on a larger scale: "There is no limit to the liberal expansion and confirmation of limited personal intellectual endowment which may proceed from the flow of social intelligence when that circulates by word of mouth from one to another in the communications of the local community. That and that only gives reality to public opinion. We lie, as Emerson said, in the lap of an immense intelligence. But that intelligence is dormant and its communications are broken, inarticulate and faint until it possesses the local community as its medium."[25]

In short, many important political thinkers have argued that the quality of larger-order democracy (and, for some, the moral basis for it) rests upon strong, vigorous local institutions in which citizens learn the art of self-rule. We do not think that the concerns of thinkers such as Tocqueville and Dewey are outdated or irrelevant today. Rather, we suggest that the degree to which the economic underpinnings of local communities can be stabilized—or not —will be inextricably linked with the quality of American democracy in the coming century. A host of indicators—most obvious are national voting trends—have declined dramatically over the last three decades. If Americans do not learn and experience the arts of democracy where they live their lives, we question whether they can ever learn them.

THE EFFICIENCY OF COMMUNITY ECONOMIC STABILITY

No matter how desirable a political economy in which localities are stabilized over time might be in theory, few would urge serious, concerted efforts in this direction if they involved gross, large-scale economic irrationalities and systematic waste. Indeed, the most common argument against place-based development has been that it is "inefficient." Rather than provide subsidies or assistance to places experiencing economic decline, whether cyclical or long-term, or take active steps to anchor capital in place over time, many economists have argued that it is more efficient to allow firms to make their own decisions about where to locate jobs, and then encourage job-seekers to move to areas with employment opportunities. Any restriction on the mobility of capital, it is held, would require firms to keep production running at inefficient sites rather than move to the sites best suited to maximizing profits—which in turn, it is held, means locations with efficient access to transportation, markets, technology, social and business networks, or simply cheaper labor.

The classic statement of this position remains a report issued by President Carter's White House Commission in 1980. *A National Agenda for the Eighties* argued that "the economic health of our nation's communities ultimately depends on the health of our nation's economy. Federal efforts to revitalize. . . areas through [public policies]. . . concerned principally with the health of specific places will inevitably conflict with efforts to revitalize the larger economy." These place-based policies, it went on to argue, have "anti-industry biases" that are "pernicious" because they hurt general economic productivity and impose costs on the nation as a whole. In their stead should be policy efforts that do "not discourage the deconcentration and dispersal of industry and households," because these trends flow from natural workings of the market.[26]

We believe that the traditional efficiency argument against place-based economic policy is fundamentally flawed on two grounds. First, it fails to take account of the costs of what we term "throw-away cities"—namely, the many social costs incurred when people are forced to leave town—as well as the sunk private and public investments in infrastructure, housing, commercial buildings, education, utilities, and other public goods that are left to decay or are abandoned outright (while those very same structures, goods and services must be provided in new communities).

These costs are heightened when we consider that many sophisticated economists have pointed out that when individuals (and by extension communities) *lose* something they have—a job, a steady income, a hometown worth living in—that loss typically generates greater disutility than the utility gained when individuals *gain* goods that may be equivalent in monetary value to what is lost. People are by nature more attached to things they already have than to things they have yet to acquire.[27] It is not simply that economic processes that systematically devalue place concentrate the burdens of the market economy on the "losers," although that is a very important point to keep in mind; rather, it is that the gains from such processes must be very high indeed to outweigh the loss experienced by those who have seen their livelihoods taken away from them.

Second, the traditional view also fails to take account of the fact that optimal firm location is no longer rigidly determined by traditional technical considerations, such as the need to locate heavy industry near transportation networks. With manufacturing on the decline and the tremendous improvement in modern communications, most of the activities of the contemporary American economy can be efficiently located in any number of places.

The Costs of Throw-Away Cities

The costs of "throw-away cities" have not gone unrecognized by thoughtful observers. Economic geographers John Jakle and David Wilson, who have documented the "derelict landscapes" associated with industrial decline, point out that when plant shutdowns occur, "[S]ocial costs are hidden in at least four ways.

> First, infrastructural costs are shifted from entrepreneur to community. Upkeep of streets, sewers, schools, and facilities falls on taxpayers. Second, social costs are transferred from rich to poor. The indigent are least able to participate in a relocation that promises economic benefits. They are left behind to pursue everyday life in a community bereft of opportunities and resources. Third, social costs are transferred from present to future. The degrading of lives and landscapes left behind becomes a social and economic burden borne by future generations. Poverty and decay are problems inherited by future residents. Fourth, social costs are transferred geographically. Regions of economic viability become focal points for capital and resource concentration at the expense of eroding regions.[28]

There have been numerous studies of the general social costs of dislocation. During the 1970s and 1980s, for instance, the deindustrialization of the Midwest and Northeast prompted scholars to examine the impact of plant closures and capital mobility on individual communities. Consistently, researchers found a disruption of community and family life in the form of increased crime and divorce rates. In the wake of plant closings, there were greater demands on social services—at the same time that tax revenues dropped.

Of particular economic significance is the cost of wasted public and private capital. One example: Scott Bernstein of the Center for Neighborhood Technology in Chicago observes that there are nearly four thousand abandoned shopping centers in America's central cities.[29] Similarly, The Sierra Club notes:

> In community after community, we've seen districts. . . shutting schools in existing neighborhood as they build new ones on the fringe. . . Between 1970 and 1990, Minneapolis–St. Paul built 78 new schools in the outer suburbs and closed 162 schools in good conditions located within city limits. In

Maine, though the student population declined by 27,000 students, the state spent a whopping $727 million on new school construction.[30]

Between 1990 and 1999 over one-quarter of the nation's 1,071 communities with more than 25,000 residents saw their populations decline—even as the nation's overall population increased from just under 249 million to 272 million. Between 1980 and 1999, while the national population increased from 227 million to 272 million (roughly a 20 percent increase), some 195 towns with population greater than 25,000—including many major cities—lost 5 percent or more of their residents. Obviously the people in the declining cities went somewhere else—which helps explains why over 150 towns and cities experienced population growth of 75 percent or more over the 1980–99 period. These communities had to rapidly construct new infrastructure to support their bulging populations—while nearly 200 other communities saw a steady drift toward underuse or wastage of their already-built public facilities.

Some states (such as Pennsylvania and Ohio) saw widespread decline of existing towns, while other states (particularly Florida and California) saw dozens of communities arise seemingly from scratch. Still other states, including Illinois and Virginia, saw boomtowns rise even as other places within the state declined. Very few states achieved a balance of stable, slowly growing communities combined with some towns that were growing more rapidly. It is also a mistake to think of very large cities such as Detroit as the only places to experience population losses and thrown-away infrastructure. Most of the communities experiencing decline are smaller cities like Dayton, Ohio and Wheeling, West Virginia.[31]

Several baseline studies have been conducted of the relative infrastructure costs of different kinds of development (low density versus high density). One of the most thorough recent studies of the infrastructure costs of new growth in a locality is planning consultant Eben Fodor's 1998 report, "The Costs of Growth in Oregon." Fodor estimated the per capita costs of adding public infrastructure such as new school facilities, sanitary sewage, transportation facilities, water system facilities, parks and recreation facilities, stormwater drainage, fire protection facilities, library facilities, and electric power generation facilities at $16,301 for each new resident moving into a typical Oregon city. Not included in this figure are the cost of power transmission and distribution facilities.[32] Obviously, this figure should be considered an estimate—the actual cost may vary depending on local conditions (and also on whether new development takes place in a compact or a sprawling fashion).[33] And, of course, to this figure must be added the private costs of providing shops, housing, and workplaces to accommodate the new residents.

Between 1980 and 1990, the 275 American municipalities with population exceeding 25,000 that lost at least 1 percent of their population over the course of the decade saw a net reduction of some 2.05 million residents. Between 1990 and 1999, the 256 communities that experienced population losses greater than 1 percent saw a combined net population loss of over 1.6 million people. Taking these totals together, declining communities experienced a net loss of roughly 3.7 million people during the 1980–99 period. Using an estimate of $17,700 for per capita public infrastructure costs (Fodor's estimate of $16,300, adjusted for inflation), we can make the further estimate that roughly $65 billion (2001 dollars) in new public infrastructure was built over the 1980–99 period to accommodate the needs of new residents who left cities that experienced net population losses—that is, people who left declining cities.[34]

That figure is but an estimate of the *new* public capital costs associated with internal migration from declining places to growing places; it does not even begin to capture the value of the infrastructure wasted in the places left behind when schools, hospitals, roads, public utilities, and housing stock close, fall into disrepair, or are underutilized.[35] Nor, to repeat, does it include the *private* capital costs of new growth, such as the cost of the housing, new businesses, and offices built to accommodate new residents. These costs are even more difficult to estimate, but they are almost certainly substantially higher than the public infrastructure costs; one preliminary estimate by Tom Ricker of the University of Maryland places these costs at roughly five times higher than public costs.[36] If we accept Ricker's estimate of the magnitude of total private capital costs, the estimate of the total capital costs would rise to some $390 billion. But even this last figure does not include costs resulting from the Americans who have moved away from any of the hundreds of declining rural communities and small towns in the past two decades. Also, this figure refers only to mobility-related capital costs and does not include the cost borne by specific communities in lost tax revenues and increased social spending when jobs disappear and citizens leave. Nor are the transportation and other expenses associated with moving itself included.[37]

Such estimates are obviously very preliminary. We find it extraordinary that so little empirical work has focused on measuring these costs—either by economists concerned with efficiency or by public policy analysts. Much more intensive empirical study is clearly needed to gauge total capital costs associated with the rise and fall of population in American cities. Moreover, as Scott Bernstein observes, while there has been significant high-quality work done on the costs of urban sprawl, "there is virtually no analogous research on the 'benefits of reuse.'"[38]

Some scholars have, however, contributed useful, if preliminary, methodological work aimed at developing new evaluative tools to incorporate public (or social) costs into the prescriptive analysis of economic development policy. Policy analyst David Smith's seminal work on the "public balance sheet," for example, builds from the commonsense notion that costs such as those resulting from "throwing away cities"—while external to the private decision-making process—should not be excluded from the public decision-making process. His approach would allow policy makers to compare the *total* taxpayer and public benefits from community stabilization policies against the *total* costs.[39]

The public balance sheet approach evaluates the efficiency or wastefulness of a firm's decision to shut down or relocate a plant from the perspective of the public and of the economy as a whole—not from the perspective of the firm itself. As a result, a public balance sheet factors into the calculation of efficiency a variety of "negative externalities" related to community economic instability. The public balance sheet takes into account several key costs incurred by the public that private firms typically ignore in making investment decisions, including lost public tax revenues, increased government social spending, wasted public capital, and so forth. This comprehensive assessment allows for a more systematic and rigorous cost-benefit comparison between the relative efficiencies of policies oriented to community stability versus policies that exacerbate capital hypermobility and community instability.

Conventional analysis commonly overestimates market economic efficiency while underestimating the efficiency of community stability because it does not adequately factor in the full range of costs.[40] Once such costs are recognized and correctly calculated, the efficiencies associated with community stability, and the inefficiencies of community instability, become increasingly evident. And, to repeat, the public balance sheet still does not include all private costs associated with throw-away cities.

The Efficiencies of Firm Location

There is, however, a second general flaw in the argument that policies aimed at community stability are inefficient: Namely, the assumption that the efficiencies of firm location are inherently tied to technical, rather than socially determined, factors. We find this assumption to be problematic for two key reasons. First, much discussion of the need to allow firms to freely locate in response to technical advantages one place may have over another has rested implicitly on the assumption of a *manufacturing-based economy*—that is, economic activity that historically had to locate near raw material sources and transport hubs, starting with water and evolving to rail and air. But the assumption of a manufacturing-based economy no longer holds: Manufacturing now occupies no more than 14 percent of the American workforce. Indeed, the figure is projected to shrink to less than 10 percent over the next quarter century.[41] Services (including government) now account for over 80 percent of nonagricultural American jobs. In contrast to the situation historically faced by the manufacturing sector, most services need not be wedded to places that happen to provide access to natural resources or to water- or rail-based transportation networks. To be sure, as we note in Chapter 2, there are still important economic benefits to agglomeration today, especially in high-tech sectors (such as the ability of firms in a given area to network with one another or draw upon a shared labor pool of skilled workers). But many enterprises in the service sector can operate in a wide range of locations without sacrificing productive efficiency. As we shall see in Chapter 1, the growth of the service economy has led to an *increase* in the degree to which city economies are localized—despite increased integration with the world economy and despite the fact that many services are now more widely traded outside the immediate locality than in the past.

Table I.1. Distribution of Employment by Sector in the American Economy, 1950–1999

Sectoral shares of nonagricultural employment in the United States

	1950	1960	1970	1980	1990	1999
Manufacturing	33.7%	31.0%	27.3%	22.4%	17.4%	14.4%
Place-specific activities*	7.2%	6.7%	5.9%	5.9%	5.3%	5.4%
Services	59.1%	62.2%	66.7%	71.6%	77.2%	80.2%

*Includes mining and construction.

Source: Derived from *Economic Report of the President 2001* (Washington DC: Government Printing Office, 2001), Table B-46.

If the first major point often forgotten in discussions of the efficiency of economic activities is the decline of manufacturing, the second is that technology itself, especially advances in communications and transportation, has reduced the role played by technical factors in determining the efficiency of firm location in all sectors, including manufacturing. Technological improvements have made dispersal of a firm or industry's operations much more feasible, as individual production facilities, administrative offices, and market outlets can be located in widely separated places. This is true even for manufacturing: Urban economist Edward Glaeser of Harvard University notes that by the end of the twentieth century, "transport costs for goods had declined so much that it was no longer essential for manufacturing plants to be close to customers and suppliers. Indeed, declining transport costs have driven a de-urbanization of manufacturing almost as striking as manufacturing's overall decline."[42] Similarly, there has also been a reduction in the technical need for huge concentrations of capital to be amassed in one place in order to facilitate coordination of production. Again, economic dispersal comes with little or no cost to economic efficiency. Most important is the obvious fact that the Internet now allows coordination over vast distances.

This is not to suggest, however, that place no longer matters in firms' location decisions; the qualities of particular places—particularly, in some industries, the presence of networks—often do matter when capital moves from one place to another.* Moreover, in most cases the decentralization of production has not implied decentralization of control over production, which often remains hierarchically structured, with key investment decisions typically taking place at corporate headquarters, not at the local level. Creating truly stable communities will probably require much more localization of investment decision making than that afforded by large, hierarchical corporations operating multiple production facilities at different locations—and indeed (as discussed in detail in Parts II and III) the development of functional, credible local alternatives to traditional corporate structures.

What is important for our argument at this stage is simply the observation that new communications, transport, and production technology makes place-based decentralization increasingly economically feasible. Purely *technical* determinants of firm location—that is, factors rooted in physical geography, the distribution of natural resources, or the logistical need for centralized coordination—are shrinking in importance and will continue to shrink as manufacturing occupies a decreasing share of the national economy and as communication and transportation technologies continue to advance.

---

* Some analysts argue that the face-to-face interactions and personal relationships that appear to facilitate innovation and networking in certain industries (financial services in New York and information technology in Silicon Valley are commonly cited as examples) ensure that there will continue to be a privileged place for cities and a continued economic function for high density in twenty-first-century economies. We agree, but caution that only a very few cities can be Silicon Valley or New York; most American urban areas are not going to be "global cities."

Instead, the factors that remain important in driving firm location in the postindustrial economy are primarily *socially determined:* labor costs, tax rates, subsidies available to firms, access to universities and technical assistance, access to good public infrastructure (roads, airports, etc.), regulatory policies, quality of education, quality of workforce, and, perhaps most important, presence of a large-scale development anchor (such as a state capital or university) to help stabilize local entrepreneurial activity. In the new postindustrial economy, all kinds of places are capable, *technically,* of being efficient locations for production. On the one hand, this fact illustrates why public policy must play a role in ensuring that the increased capacity of firms to decentralize production does not lead to further destruction of existing communities. On the other hand, it also means that a comprehensive agenda aimed at stabilizing all American communities economically for the sake of enhancing local democracy need not incur overwhelming economic efficiency costs.

THE FEASIBILITY OF COMMUNITY ECONOMIC STABILITY IN THE NEW CENTURY

A third, seemingly powerful objection to nurturing community economic stability is the claim that it simply cannot be done within the context of a modern, postindustrial economy. The market *must,* it is held, control the fate of communities.

In a broad sense, it is true that no economic system has yet blended the goal of sustaining community over time with other economic goals (such as productivity, efficiency, and innovation). But it is false to conclude that there are no successful examples of using public policy within advanced market-oriented societies to sustain communities, or that a disregard for place is the inevitable result of a productive economic system.

Such a conclusion ignores the huge public subsidy and policy system currently operating in the United States to encourage the opposite outcome: mobility and the decline of place. The transient nature of American society is *not* simply a response to market operations but rather in large part the product of political choices expressed through public policies. Urban expert Peter Dreier points out that

> the root causes of the urban crisis are directly tied to federal policy. The flight of industry and the rise of a low-wage American economy, the suburbanization of housing, the siting of Pentagon facilities and contracts, and the redlining by banks and insurance companies can all be traced to federal policy choices, not simply market forces or consumer preferences.

He adds: "Federal aid to cites . . . has served, in effect, to 'clean-up' the problems created by federally assisted disinvestment."[43]

Research by political scientist Jeffrey Lustig on plant closings also documents this point:

> Tax write-offs for plant and equipment losses, liberalized depreciation rules, investment tax credits, and preferential treatment for capital gains all throw disproportionate rewards in the direction of companies engaged in closedowns. . . . The companies benefit from the assumption by the government of the tab for the personal, infrastructure and *social costs* entailed in the closedowns or relocations.[44]

That a contrary policy—one aimed at nurturing community economic stability—is feasible is suggested by the fact that, on reflection, Americans already seem to know a great deal about how stable communities are created and sustained. It is intuitively obvious to most citizens that moderately-sized university towns, state capitals, and even towns near long-established active military bases and prisons have greater economic stability than areas primarily dependent on private investment. (Of course, a university or state capital alone is likely to be inadequate as a stabilizer for very large cities.) Such areas are in many cases recession-proof. Understanding this reality, many struggling localities dream of landing a major public asset or facility as a development anchor. Literally hundreds of communities have bid for the siting of major new federal office facilities or new prison construction, or have attempted to attract retirees and their stable Social Security pensions to town. The practice is only slightly more indirect in the case of military contracts, when politicians go to bat for Department of Defense suppliers within their jurisdiction to try to land weapons contracts or maintain bases.

It is noteworthy that of the 62 state capitals and major public university towns with population between 25,000 and 250,000 listed in Table I.2 above, under 13 percent have experienced population declines of 5 percent or more since 1980—roughly 30 percent less than the nationwide rate of community decline over that period. Even in these cases, population almost certainly would have declined more rapidly than it actually did but for the presence of a state capital or university. Some 66 percent of the towns have experienced stability or moderate growth, while 21 percent have grown more rapidly. It is also worth noting that the unweighted average unemployment rate in these 62 towns and cities in 1999 was just 3.4 percent, compared to a national average of 4.2 percent. Twenty-six of these towns and cities had

Table I.2. Community Stability in Moderate-sized State Capitals and State University Towns, 1980–1999*

Includes all state capitals and all cities hosting its state's flagship public university

Declining (8)	Stable (30)	Moderate Growth (11)	Fast Growth (11)	Boomtown (2)
Albany, NY	Jefferson City, MO	Bismarck, ND	Raleigh, NC	Athens, GA
Jackson, MS	Morgantown, WV	Chapel Hill, NC	Carson City, NV	Missoula, MT
Harrisburg, PA	Lansing, MI	Madison ,WI	Reno, NV	
Richmond, VA	Annapolis, MD	Eugene, OR	Anchorage, AK	
Charleston, WV	Ann Arbor, MI	Concord, NH	Olympia, WA	
Trenton, NJ	Berkeley, CA	Lincoln, NE	Lawrence, KS	
Charlottesville, VA	Little Rock, AR	Norman, OK	Salem, OR	
Hartford, CT	Montgomery, AL	Columbia, MO	Fayetteville, AR	
	Tuscaloosa, AL	Dover, DE	Tallahassee, FL	
	Iowa City, IA	Juneau, AK	Boise, ID	
	Boulder, CO	Bloomington, IN	Santa Fe, NM	
	Gainesville, FL			
	Newark, DE			
	Baton Rouge, LA			
	Springfield, IL			
	Topeka, KS			
	Des Moines, IA			
	Providence, RI			
	State College, PA			
	Knoxville, TN			
	Burlington, VT			
	Salt Lake City, UT			
	Lexington, KY			
	Cheyenne, WY			
	Laramie, WY			
	New Brunswick, NJ			
	Columbia, SC			
	Frankfort, KY			
	Grand Forks, ND			
	Champaign/Urbana, IL			

[1]Derived from Deirdre A. Gaquin and Katherine A. Debrandt, eds. 2001 County and City Extra: Annual Metro, City, and County Data Book. 10th Edition. Lanham, MD: Bernan Press, 2001. State capitals with less than 25,000 or greater than 250,000 (1980) population excluded. Declining cities are those losing 5% or more of population; stable cities are those whose population neither declined by 5% nor grew by 20% or more; moderate growth cities experienced growth of 20 to 40%; fast growth cities grew between 40 and 75%; and boomtowns grew by over 75%.

unemployment rates of 3.0 percent or less, including nine towns with less than 2.0 percent unemployment.[45]

The commonsense perception that places anchored by public institutions tend to be relatively stable is not limited to state capitals and towns with big universities. Consider comments made by residents of Romulus, New York, a small town of 2,065, when New York State cutbacks in the early 1990s led to 601 lost jobs at the Willard Psychiatric Center and threatened to close the facility altogether: "You go into many areas and people say, 'A mental institution—my God, I wouldn't want to live near one,' but that's not the attitude here," said local restaurant owner Ray Sajac. "That facility across the street is a lifeline for the entire community." "If Willard were to close, people just wouldn't know what to do and where to go," said Richard J. Compo, president of the county chamber of commerce. "They've worked there for so long, they would just be lost."[46]

Such illustrations are simply examples of the obvious reality that public policy can help achieve local stability. The fact is, almost 40 percent of the U.S. economy involves direct public financial flows.[47] If we include the impact of indirect public activities that in various ways leverage or constrain private activities (such as regulations, tax programs, loan guarantees, etc.), the figure would be still greater. The possibilities for developing a coherent strategy of using existing levels of public spending to explicitly target community stability are substantial.

In the following pages we explore many widely-accepted traditional strategies to achieve community stability—including, for instance, targeted financial and technical assistance to distressed areas and well-designed human capital initiatives. Also, in Chapter I and again in Part IV, we systematically examine the costs and benefits of international trade—and we review a series of national and international trade-related strategies aimed at helping achieve greater local economic and job security (as well as environmental standards).

In Parts II and III we also examine how local institutions and economic structures that root standard business activities in place can be developed. Thirty years ago, when there was little experience with large-scale worker ownership of manufacturing firms, when institutions such as the community development corporation were in their infancy, and when many other practices (such as establishing community-owned land trusts in downtown areas, using public pension funds to promote local- and state-level economic development, or lending state money to high-tech start-up firms in exchange for equity shares in the new business) were all but unheard of, the idea that local economies could be anchored by anything other than the large-scale private corporation would have struck most observers as unrealistic. Today, however, there is an impressive range of experience with place-rooted institutional forms and little reason why public policy cannot self-consciously seek to nurture the further development and expansion of such institutions. As we shall explore, local initiatives to enhance local economic multipliers can further increase stability.

THE MOVEMENT TO ACHIEVE COMMUNITY STABILITY IN CONTEXT

Our case against American capitalism's tendency to throw away places is not a new one; it rests upon a long tradition of sophisticated analysis and on-the-ground activism aimed at preserving the value of place. Moreover, recent years have seen a resurgence of popular writing concerned with place, often building on earlier work by writers such as E. F. Schumacher and Wendell Berry. Former international development practitioner David Korten, for instance, urges place-rooted strategies as an alternative to corporate-led globalization. In an important treatise on ecological economics, *For the Common Good,* Herman Daly and John Cobb offer a similar vision of local businesses strongly rooted in community. In his book *Going Local!* Michael Shuman presents an array of policy ideas and strategies to help nurture locally controlled economic institutions.[48]

The following primer builds on the evolving discussion of place-centered economics. It takes seriously traditional objections to such policies and provides a realistic assessment of the capacity of different policies and institutional forms to help reroot the American economy. We believe the case for making communities a centerpiece of American economic and social policy is strong, and that—partly as a result of the practical developmental experience and new research of the past quarter century—over the next decade it should be possible to move toward a comprehensive strategy aimed at strengthening communities challenged by globalization, market dislocation and job chasing, and sprawl. Although the idea of community-based social and economic policy cuts against the grain of much traditional economic discourse, we also suggest that the idea of preventing communities from being thrown away has vast potential political and economic appeal. Beyond this, the ongoing shift to a service economy and the advance of new technologies open entirely new possibilities for better stabilizing communities over the next decades of development.

In a more fundamental sense, for many people a community-rooted economic policy is already just plain common sense. Community stability is a uniting value for Americans on the left, on the right, and in the center alike. We agree with the sentiments of former Ohio congressman John Seiberling, who in the wake of several 1978 plant closures in his home state told the House of Representatives:

The people of Akron, the people of Youngstown, the people of Newark, should have a little bit more going for them than the teetering balance in a corporate board room as to whether they are going to stay in a city or move away. . . . It is a lot easier to keep Humpty Dumpty from falling off the wall than to try to put him back together again afterwards. No, this country cannot simply walk away from its investments in its established urban centers where we have billions of dollars invested in public facilities, cultural institutions, universities and schools, factories, offices and stores and, most important of all, where people have invested their life savings to build their homes. We simply cannot walk away from that.[49]

THE TRIPLE THREAT TO
COMMUNITY AND DEMOCRACY

INTRODUCTION

Part I spells out the nature of the triple threat to community and democracy in the United States. Chapter 1 discusses specific mechanisms by which the marriage of free trade ideology to an increasingly integrated global economy threatens the economic underpinnings of community and the possibility for substantial community-level democratic self-governance in the United States—the nation that according to conventional analysis has the most to gain from a globalizing economy. Chapter 2 focuses on the problem of internal capital mobility: Not only do most large-scale shifts in production from one community to another commonly result in social and economic waste, these shifts are actively encouraged by federal policy as well as state and local-level subsidies aimed at attracting mobile corporate capital. The ongoing "war between the states" for jobs is examined in some detail, and we explore possible remedies for the job-chasing phenomena (both short- and long-term). Chapter 3 examines the various ways in which suburban sprawl has impacted the health of American communities. In this chapter we also direct attention to the public policies that have contributed to the growth of sprawl and discuss specific approaches which could help contain or reverse outward, unplanned development.

Each of these problems are complex and daunting and worthy of full-length studies in themselves. Our aims are, first, to examine the main issues and mechanisms at stake, with particular reference to the impact of each on community economic stability and community democracy; and second, to offer an overview of how a range of leading analysts currently think about each issue. In the process, we attempt also to suggest a sense of the depth—indeed, the systemic roots—of each problem. Although the logic of each topic necessarily takes us into quite specific detail, we believe that understanding the impact of globalization, internal capital mobility, and sprawl on communities all point to a common conclusion: The need for a coherent, multi-faceted policy agenda aimed at stabilizing the economic basis of American communities.

CHAPTER 1

GLOBALIZATION AND FREE TRADE

Perhaps the most widely discussed of the major threats facing American communities at the outset of the new century is globalization.

Debate about globalization—what it is, whether it represents something new or is just a continuation of past trends, who benefits from the process, and who loses—has produced a massive amount of literature in recent years, both in the popular press and within academia. It is not our goal here to provide a comprehensive review of each of the various strands of discussion. Rather, the following analysis is intended to serve as a primer on the issues globalization raises for the fundamental topic of this book: how to nurture, sustain, and enhance local community economic stability in the United States. In our view, the direct impact of globalization on community economic stability, though substantial, is as yet not nearly as severe as some activist critics on both the left and the right would imply. However, the current trajectory of globalization contains at least one very grave threat to the future of local community stability—namely, reduced legal capacity of localities to shape their own economic destinies. Describing this threat as well as several other related ways that globalization and international economic volatility may impact American communities is the primary task of this chapter. The discussion necessarily will also touch on other issues, including the link between global economic integration and international economic development and the role of multilateral financial institutions such as the World Bank and the IMF.

What exactly is globalization? How does it matter for communities? Very little academic research to date has focused, directly and explicitly, on the relationship between globalization and community economic security in the United States. Instead, discussion of these questions during the 1990s largely focused on two issues: the impact of increased trade and corporations' new global reach on wages and inequality in developed countries (especially the United States), and whether the globalization process is on balance a healthy development in terms not only of economic well-being but also of environmental and social concerns. The latter question has been the focal point of an often polemical three-way debate among activists and journalists portraying globalization as a uniquely harmful development in world affairs, economists and a handful of serious journalists who insist that the costs of globalization have been overstated and are in any case outbalanced by the purported benefits of an increasingly integrated world economy, and those who argue that both the positive and negative effects of globalization have been overblown and that the chief obstacles to more equitable, egalitarian, social-democratic-style economic policies remain in the realm of domestic politics, not in a shifting global environment.

What effect does the process of economic integration have upon local-level communities?

It is often assumed in popular discussion that increased globalization means that economic activity either no longer is nor can in the future be tied to particular communities. If this were the case, the agenda of this book—stabilizing economic activity in local communities—would face a markedly uphill battle, even if the political obstacles to forwarding a place-respecting agenda could be overcome. But this is not the case. In fact, *more* economic activity in the United States economy is now inherently local—at the same time that more economic activity is tied to trade and global economic activities.

We can begin to grasp this paradox by considering the countless professions and services that remain almost entirely unaffected by international trade in any direct sense: think of carpenters, doctors, schoolteachers, plumbers, local government employees, gardeners, custodial workers, barbers, and construction workers. Economist Thomas Michael Power of the University of Montana calculates that "[A]bout 60 percent of U.S. economic activity is local and provides residents with the goods and services that make their lives comfortable. . . . Almost all local economies are dominated by residents taking in each other's wash."[1] Moreover, this figure has steadily increased, not decreased, in the postwar era, largely due to growth in retail and wholesale sales, services, financial and real estate, and state and local government as a percentage of all economic activity.[2]

Using a different estimation technique, Wim Wiewel and Joseph Persky found that during the 1980s, the proportion of economic activity within communities aimed at serving local markets actually increased in the forty-five American metropolitan areas (MSAs) with population greater than 1 million (as of 1989). Whereas in 1969 42.6 percent of economic activity was local in these MSAs, that proportion rose to 45.3 percent in 1979 and 49.2 percent in 1989. That increase is due to the "deindustrialization of urban areas, a steady expansion of local consumer services, and the considerable growth of the local public and health sectors." Wiewel and Persky add, "The economies of large metropolitan areas in the United States are now more locally oriented than ever."[3]

This is the case *even though*, as Wiewel and Persky acknowledge, some types of services—in particular, producer services, services that meet the needs of businesses—became more tradable over the course of the 1980s. The upward change in services traded outside the locality, however, is more than offset by the baseline increase in services and decline in manufacturing. Wiewel and Persky stress that, in fact, "large cities have long been centers of service employment. The manufacturing city, that strained product of late-nineteenth-century transportation and production technologies, is perhaps more of an historical anomaly than the standard."[4] While follow-up studies to Wiewel and Persky's analysis need to be undertaken, their logic strongly suggests that in all likelihood urban economies continued to become more local in the 1990s as manufacturing continued to decline—even though the percentage of service activity traded outside the locality also very probably increased over the decade. The growing exposure to global trade thus has occurred in tandem with an increase in the degree to which economic activity in the United States has become more localized.

It is thus fair to ask whether the stakes in the free trade debate may have been exaggerated by free trade advocates—even as the negative economic effects of globalization upon American workers and communities may also have been overstated by some activist critics. Only 12.2 percent—less than one-eighth—of the goods and services produced in the United States in 1999 were sold abroad.[5] As Robert Dunn Jr. of George Washington University writes, Americans "should not believe that further trade liberalization will either produce large increases in U.S. incomes or impose large costs on American unskilled workers. U.S. trade restrictions have already been reduced to such low levels that there is not much more to either accomplish or fear in this area."[6] Indeed, a recent rough estimate by Dean Baker of the Center for Economic Policy Research suggests that removing all remaining tariff barriers in the United States would generate at most a $10 billion net gain in aggregate economic welfare—in a $10-trillion-plus economy.[7] From the perspective of this study, the larger point is that the economic loss from reasonable restraints on trade adopted in the interest of sustaining community economies would also not be cataclysmic—and might be a price worth paying in order to nurture democratic self-governance. Given the impact of economic dislocations on community and on community democracy, there is much to the judgment offered by political scientist John Dryzek: "Irrespective of any positive economic benefits of free trade (and even these may appear only in the aggregate, at the expense of large losses to particular categories of people), almost all the implications for democratic control are negative."[8]

CAPITAL MOBILITY AND THE CRISIS OF FREE TRADE IDEOLOGY: THE THEORETICAL CRITIQUE

The conventional theoretical argument for free trade holds that free mobility of goods across borders permits each country to specialize in areas of "comparative advantage," resulting in increased welfare for all. The nineteenth-century classical economist David Ricardo put it this way: "Two men can both make shoes and hats and one is superior to the other in both employments; but in making hats he can only exceed his competitor by one-fifth or 20 percent, and in making shoes he can exceed him by one-third or 33 percent. Will it not be for the interest of both that the superior man should employ himself exclusively in making shoes and the inferior man in making hats?"[9]

Adherence to Ricardo's doctrine of comparative advantage has led many economists to suggest that barriers to trade protecting inefficient local industries are economically foolish and would impose welfare costs on consumers. However, the simple translation of nineteenth-century insights from Ricardo into blind support for free trade ignores how dramatically the world has changed—and in particular, it ignores the mobility of capital. Former World Bank economist Herman Daly and coauthor John Cobb drove this point home with considerable force in their 1989 book *For the Common Good* by carefully examining Ricardo's paradigmatic example of trade between England and Portugal. Ricardo posited a situation in which England required 100 workers to produce a given amount of cloth and 120 workers to produce a given amount of wine, whereas in Portugal cloth could be produced with 90 workers and wine with only 80 workers. Ricardo noted that by concentrating all its production in wine, Portugal could actually end up with more cloth (via trade with England) than it could if it shifted some of its production to cloth—even though Portuguese production of cloth was more efficient than English production.

Daly and Cobb offered the following striking observation about Ricardo's story: As Ricardo himself noted, the comparative advantage principle works only because capital is assumed *not to move across borders*. Given free, relatively costless mobility of capital between England and Portugal, English capitalists could profitably choose to produce both cloth *and* wine in Portugal, making use of the *absolute* advantage enjoyed by Portugal in both goods (and creating massive unemployment in England). Indeed, if capital were totally mobile, there would be no reason in this example for it to remain in England, since both wine and cloth could be produced more cheaply abroad. Ricardo did not have to worry seriously about this possibility, believing that for various reasons capitalists were reluctant to move abroad: "These feelings, which I should be sorry to see weakened, induce most men of property to be satisfied with a low rate of profits in their own country, rather than seek a more advantageous employment for their wealth in foreign nations."[10]

Daly and Cobb thus reach the ironic conclusion that were Ricardo, the apostle of free trade, alive today, he would not be a free trader—or, at least, not nearly so unambiguous about the benefits of comparative advantage as its advocates of today. Simply put, the world today is one in which the input of capital can be and is moved across borders; "trade" does not consist simply of different countries' capitalists competing in product markets on the basis of comparative advantage. Rather, investments are regularly made across borders as capitalists seek not only comparative but *absolute* advantage. When they do so, as Ricardo understood, they weaken the home economy. Indeed, a world of unrestrained capital mobility and free trade in product markets logically implies either heavy unemployment in higher-cost, higher-wage nations or a sharp reduction in wages in such nations so that they can remain competitive. To be sure, as we discuss in Chapter 2, we do not yet live in a world of truly seamless capital mobility—not all forms of capital are completely mobile and footloose. But capital mobility across borders does now take place on a far greater scale and at a greater velocity than the original proponents of the comparative advantage model could ever have imagined.[11]

A second difficulty with unrestricted free trade involves the problem of ensuring that regulations imposed on the domestic production of goods do not lead to unfair disadvantages for domestic producers, especially when imported goods produced under less regulated circumstances are allowed free access to a nation's home market. Adam Smith clearly saw the logic of this problem. In *The Wealth of Nations* he suggested that imposing tariffs on imported goods to compensate for special costs placed on domestic producers would be good economic policy. Having made the argument that protection of certain industries essential to national defense would be legitimate and desirable, Smith went on to urge that

> it will generally be advantageous to lay some burden upon foreign [industry] for the encouragement of domestic industry. . . when some tax is imposed at home upon the produce of the latter. In this case, it seems reasonable that an equal tax should be imposed upon the like produce of the former.[12]

If we extend the logic of Smith's argument beyond tax levies on industry to regulatory requirements, we reach a rather surprising conclusion: Adam Smith would likely have been quite sympathetic to the concerns environmentalists and workers in the United States have voiced about permitting goods produced under regimes that do not enforce environmental laws or workers' rights to have free and open access to the U.S. market.

A third difficulty with the theory of free trade is that it presumes the prices of goods fully reflect the actual costs of production. In fact, as David Morris of the Institute for Local Self-Reliance writes:

> Heavy trucks do not pay taxes sufficient to cover the damage they do to roads. We provide water to California farmers for as little as five percent of the going market rate. We provide huge direct subsidies to corporate farmers. And we allow the costs of agricultural production to be picked up by the society as a whole. Having intervened in the production process in all these ways, we then discover it is cheaper to grow a tomato in California and ship it to Massachusetts than to grow it on the East Coast. We are told this is due to California's climactic advantages, but if we withdrew all our subsidies, it might very well be cheaper to raise produce near the point of sale.[13]

The central point here is that because for various reasons market prices often do not accurately reflect the true costs of goods, there is no reason simply to assume that a policy of free trade will necessarily generate the most socially efficient outcome.[14]

Finally, there is the matter of economic history. For most of its own period as a "developing nation," the United States itself employed protectionist policies. Economic historian Alfred E. Eckes Jr. of Ohio University points out that the first act of Congress under the new Constitution in 1789 was to implement an 8.5 percent revenue tariff. Support for higher tariffs and the

"American System" of Henry Clay spiked sharply upward in the first quarter of the nineteenth century—and generated largely positive economic consequences. Eckes notes:

> From the War of 1812 to World War II, American import duties averaged over 25 percent ad valorem on all dutiable goods in all but six years. In sixty of those years the average rate was 40 percent or higher. . . . In nineteenth-century America substantial tariffs were not simply trade barriers imposed to advance the narrow interests of favored manufacturers. They served a larger national purpose, one intended to secure American independence from foreign interference and to promote national prosperity. Economic data show that the United States achieved high levels of economic growth after the American Civil War, and declining prices for many protected goods suggest that in the context of a large continental market protectionism was not inconsistent with rapid economic development.

Eckes observes: "None of the world's present industrial nations achieved economic success without experiencing a sustained protectionist phase."[15]

CAPITAL MOBILITY AND THE CRISIS OF FREE TRADE IDEOLOGY: THE EMPIRICAL CRITIQUE

There are sound theoretical and historical reasons, then, to question pure free trade arguments if one is serious about the economic prospects of American communities. This is not to say that trade cannot have important beneficial consequences in specific instances; it is to say, however, that a far more balanced and nuanced understanding of the issues is required. It is also necessary to understand empirically the specific ways in which "globalization" can undermine community and local democracy in the United States. The following discussion is divided into four broad topics: first, the direct impact increased globalization and freer trade may have on destabilizing communities and workers; second, the impact of international economic integration on national economic policies; third, the impact of new trade agreements on the ability of localities, states, and even nations to both uphold their own social and ecological standards and take proactive measures to strengthen community stability; and fourth, the impact of globalization upon global economic development and economic stability. Each of these four broad topics is in turn divided into several smaller sections. In each area a balanced understanding helps clarify many hotly contested issues and guards against overstated claims by both supporters and critics of free trade.

Is Globalization Destabilizing American Communities?
We begin by examining the ways in which trade and increased economic integration may directly impact the economic prospects of American workers and their communities, focusing on the issues of job loss, wages and inequality, and increased volatility and insecurity in the labor market.

The General Impact of Trade and Imports on Jobs and Wages
Perhaps the most commonsense understanding of how increased trade can hurt American workers and communities involves new imports entering the American market and directly displacing American producers. The growth of imported Japanese cars in the 1970s and 1980s and the concomitant decline in Detroit, Flint, and other auto-producing communities is a paradigmatic example of how trade can harm American communities. On a related point, politicians and others concerned about the impact of increased trade often point to asymmetries in trade policies among different nations: The United States has often maintained more liberal policies toward trade than most of its partners, including, notably, Japan.[16]

A recent analysis by Robert Scott of the Economic Policy Institute provides evidence that between 1992 and 1999 trade had a net negative impact on employment in the United States. Scott reports that "while rising exports created about 4.1 million jobs, rising imports lost 7.3 million, for a net effect of 3.2 million jobs lost due to trade. While other [statistical] techniques... may yield smaller estimates of the size of the trade effect, there can be no debate about the fact that trade has been a net destroyer of domestic jobs in this period." Noting that even those who find new jobs experience substantial costs (and often losses of long-term income), Scott adds: "A total of 11.4 million workers—8.9 percent of the total labor force in 1999—have either gained or lost a job due to trade. . . . Trade was costly for all workers who were forced to change jobs. The costs include lost wages due to unemployment, retraining and moving expenses, as well as the damage inflicted on their families and communities."[17]

A substantial portion of recent trade-related job loss can be linked to the effects of the North American Free Trade Agreement (NAFTA). Critics of NAFTA point to the more than 260,000 American workers who have been officially certified by the Department of Labor as having lost their jobs due to direct effects of the agreement, and note that a Department of Commerce survey intended to highlight jobs created by NAFTA was shut down after fewer than 1,500 workers could be found.[18] Another recent analysis of NAFTA (also by the Economic Policy Institute, based on data from the

Bureau of Labor Statistics and the Census Bureau) reveals a net loss of 440,000 American jobs due to trade with Mexico and Canada between 1994 and 1998 (1.58 million jobs lost, compared to 1.14 million jobs created), including net losses in all fifty states.[19]

One form of job loss related to globalization results from trade in product markets. A second form of job loss comes when corporations move production from domestic locations overseas. To take one recent example, early in 2001 Matsushita, a Japanese-owned manufacturer of air conditioner compressors, closed down its factory in Mooresville, North Carolina (a factory that had been built only in 1991), and laid off 530 workers, so as to relocate production to China and Malaysia. As one analyst of the state's economy put it, "The Northern states shed these low-end jobs 20 years ago, and they came here. But now technology is replacing a lot of workers, and the cheap labor isn't here anymore—it's overseas."[20]

Other recent studies on the impact of trade on job loss have shown that while trade has had a tangible negative impact on employment, trade in product markets alone does not account for most of the job loss and de-industrialization that took place during the last quarter century.[21] Most economists place greater blame on improved technology, which makes some jobs redundant; related to this, corporate restructuring—"downsizing"—also has played a role, particularly in the 1990s.

But while trade cannot explain everything it does have important, tangible impacts. For instance, Jeffrey Sachs and Howard Shatz at Harvard University estimated that nearly 40 percent of the manufacturing jobs lost in the United States between 1978 and 1990 were due to shifts in international trade.[22] A more recent study by Lori G. Kletzer of over sixty industries in the manufacturing sector finds a positive relationship between job displacement rates and import penetration. Although there are numerous exceptions, the impact of trade on industries such as footwear, toy manufacturing, and watch and clock production is strong enough to lead Kletzer to the conclusion that "workers have good reason to worry about job and income security in the face of increasing foreign competition."[23]

Is increased trade linked to the well-documented rise in income inequality over the past thirty years? Most academic research on this question has concluded that trade is part of the story of rising inequality but probably not the major part. One landmark study by Harvard economists George Borjas, Richard Freeman, and Lawrence Katz found that growth in trade could account for no more than 10 percent of the increase of wage inequality between American college and high school graduates over the course of the

1980s.[24] Although a stereotypical view is that of poor Third World workers undercutting American blue-collar jobs, most U.S. trade, in fact, is with developed (not developing) countries.[25]

Paul Krugman of Princeton has repeatedly urged that since the total volume of north-south trade is still small—imports from developing countries account for just 2 per cent of the Organization for Economic Cooperation and Development (OECD) countries' combined economies—the impact of trade on jobs and wages of competition from low-wage companies must necessarily be small.[26] Moreover, a comprehensive literature review by William Cline has found that "international influences contributed about 20 percent of the rising wage inequality in the 1980s."[27] Jagdish Bhagwati contends that the import prices of labor intensive goods did not fall relative to other goods in the 1980s, indicating that imports from low wage nations were not the primary cause of falling wages for unskilled workers in the United States.[28]

Other economists, however, have questioned this relatively optimistic view of trade's consequences on wages and inequality. For instance, Adrian Wood argues that the evidence on prices cited by Bhagwati and others is in fact ambiguous, and "fails to deliver a clear verdict" exonerating trade of major role in widening inequalities.[29] Similarly, Dani Rodrik suggests that it is a mistake to look at only the direct effects of trade in a vacuum. Rodrik paints a picture of the qualitative changes involved in a more open world economy: "The relevant measures of openness in this context are not the volumes of trade or of investment, but the *ease* with which international transactions can be carried out."[30] Economist Thomas Palley points out that the result of greater openness—the threat of imports—has weakened labor's bargaining position (a point we take up in detail below).[31] The impact on wages in industries sensitive to trade or capital mobility can also have a spillover effect into the economy at large. On a related point, Richard Freeman has calculated that loss of unionized jobs in the United States—the result in part of union jobs being shifted overseas or destroyed altogether—accounts for one-fifth of the increase in wage inequality.[32]

Further, while many economists argue that job-destroying technology has done more direct damage to manufacturing jobs than trade in the 1970s and 1980s, economist Adrian Wood has argued that increased competition from the South may have served as an exogenous stimulus to the implementation of such labor-saving technologies (a hypothesis that has begun to stimulate serious academic investigation).[33] Finally, national-level studies of the impact of trade upon wages may overlook very significant regional variations: For instance, a recent study by Andrew Bernard and J. Bradford Jensen found that several northern states that lost many manufacturing jobs during the

1980s saw much faster rises in wage inequality than states that saw manufacturing gains (mainly in the Southeast). While Bernard and Jensen failed to find a direct connection between import penetration and rising wage inequality, their work suggests that trade might be important in helping explain inequality insofar as it contributes to shifts in the industrial composition of a given state's economy.[34]

In short, trade almost certainly has a substantial impact on growing wage inequality—more than some hold, less than others contend. While the direct effects of trade on wage inequality probably is relatively small (accounting for 20 percent or less of the total increase in inequality), trade also has important indirect effects on inequality through several mechanisms, the full extent of which is as yet incompletely understood by scholars.

Reducing Labor's Bargaining Power

It is now widely recognized that it is increasingly easy for American-based multinational corporations to locate major capital investment outside the United States, in some cases closing down American-based manufacturing. And, as AFL-CIO economist Thomas Palley puts it, capital mobility, "by increasing the options available to business . . . has increased the bargaining power of firms *vis-a-vis* both labor and government. Business in turn has been able to use its increased bargaining power to win concessions from both labor and government."[35]

Two recent studies by Cornell University economist Kate Bronfenbrenner have illustrated how the threat of capital flight plays out at the firm level. Bronfenbrenner examined employers' responses to union organizing drives at plants where a majority of employees had signed union cards, leading to a unionization election. (Many union organizing drives never make it that far.) In the first study, conducted in the two-year period after NAFTA was passed, just over half of firms surveyed threatened to close plants when workers began a union organizing drive. Moreover, Bronfenbrenner found that the percentage of firms carrying through on the threat to close or partially shift production away from a plant increased to 15 percent, up from just 5 percent before NAFTA was passed.[36]

The second study, conducted during 1998 and 1999, found that 51 percent of employers involved in some 407 National Labor Relations Board union elections threatened to close their facilities during the union organizing drives. The threat rate in manufacturing industries was 71 percent in 1998–99 (and much higher in many specific sectors, such as textiles). Equally telling, when employers made threats, union win rates in relatively immobile sectors such as health care and transportation were twice as high

(60 percent) as in manufacturing (28 percent). In just under one-fifth of the campaigns in which employers made threats to close, they specifically threatened to move production to another country (usually Mexico). The union win rate in plants where employers made a specific threat to move abroad was just 24 percent, compared to 51 percent in which employers did not threaten to close the facility. As Bronfenbrenner notes, the very threat of moving, especially in industries where that threat is highly credible, can itself severely undercut union organizing—helping to depress wages in the labor market as a whole.[37]

Increased Labor Market Volatility

Bronfenbrenner's work offers support for Dani Rodrik's claim that the "first-order effect of trade appears to have been a redistribution of the enterprise surplus toward employers rather than the enlargement of that surplus."[38] In addition to weakening labor's bargaining power and undermining nonwage labor standards (a point taken up below), Rodrik argues that a third important consequence of increased economic integration is greater volatility in the demand for labor in high-wage countries such as the United States.[39]

There is substantial evidence of a rise in labor market volatility in the United States in the past generation. For instance, a *Brookings Papers* study by Peter Gottschalk and Robert Moffit found that the variance or instability of earnings increased roughly 40 percent between the 1970s and 1980s, and that instability of earnings for the least-skilled groups almost doubled between the two periods.[40] More volatile ebbs and flows in the demand for labor equate directly to both increased economic insecurity for individuals and increased economic instability at the community level.

The Impact of Globalization on National Economic Policy

The second major way globalization may impact communities and community stability is by hampering national economic policy making. Minimally, no national government can set economic policy in a vacuum. To take one important example, a change in domestic interest rates may affect changes in capital flows into and out of country.[41] The following discussion focuses on two other specific ways globalization may undermine domestic economic strategies.

Leakages Prevent a Traditional Keynesian Strategy

One way increased economic integration may threaten national economic policy is through "leakages." Leakages in national economies, in the form of import purchases, now make a traditional Keynesian demand-stimulus policy less effective, thereby making it more difficult for nations to manage general economic instability and to achieve full employment. Government stimulation of the economy results in substantially higher purchases of imports by consumers, and each dollar leaked out of the economy can no longer be recirculated. Hence, the multiplier effect of increased domestic spending, so central to Keynesian demand-led expansions, is diluted. This is particularly true when fiscal stimulation takes the form of tax cuts: A significant percentage the of new consumer spending is likely to be spent on the resulting imports, leading to greater leakage than if stimulation had taken the form, say, of government investments in infrastructure which directly increase employment in the United States.[42]

Thomas Palley points out that increased dependence on exports "as a source of aggregate demand" also makes the American economy more sensitive to economic downturns abroad. Again, as imports increase and occupy a bigger share of the consumer price index, inflation rates also become "more subject to the vagaries of foreign inflation and movements in the exchange rate."[43] This effect, too, can hurt prospects for a stimulative Keynesian economic policy.

The leakage issue has gained increasing attention in recent years, but the problem itself was recognized as early as the 1930s by John Maynard Keynes, who advocated a pragmatic approach to trade. Keynes warned of the dangers to which protectionist policies could lead, but he saw no need to sacrifice the real economy on the altar of free trade. In the early 1930s he strongly advocated the introduction of a revenue tariff in Britain as a precondition for an expansionary fiscal policy aimed at increasing employment. Such a tariff would help offset the costs of increased public spending, stop leakages abroad ("in so far as it leads to the substitution of home-produced goods for goods previously imported, it will increase employment in this country"), and ensure against a massive trade deficit: "By relieving the pressure on the balance of trade [a tariff] will provide a much-needed margin to pay for the additional imports which a policy of expansion will require and to finance loans by London to necessitous debtor countries. In these ways, the buying power which we take away from the rest of the world by restricting certain imports we shall restore to it with the other hand."[44] As economic historian Barry Eichengreen notes, Keynes' vision of the postwar international economic order "would have allowed countries to change their exchange rates and apply exchange and trade restrictions as required to reconcile full employment with payments balance."[45]

Weakening of Welfare States

Another important consequence of globalization is the impact of increased openness on the capacity of governments to tax capital at a rate sufficient to help provide for a strong welfare state. Peter Katzenstein of Cornell University and other political scientists have shown that many welfare states in Europe also traditionally have had open trade policies; the welfare state served as a way to spread the costs of such trade openness equitably throughout the society. But this situation is changing. As Rodrik observes, due to increases in capital mobility, globalization increasingly "results in increased demands on the state to provide social insurance while reducing the ability of the state to perform that role effectively." Governments find it more difficult to tax corporations that can move elsewhere.

Indeed, Rodrik's analysis of taxation trends in eighteen OECD countries between 1965 and 1991 demonstrates that "taxes on labor respond positively to increases in lagged [trade] openness, while taxes on capital respond negatively. . . . In other words, there is strong evidence that as [global] economic integration advances the tax burden of social insurance programs is shifted from capital to labor." The reason? Nonmobile forces, including especially labor and rooted capital, must pay the full cost of domestic taxes, while mobile factors can avoid them.[46]

There is a burgeoning academic literature on the question of whether globalization undercuts the very possibility of social-democratic-type policies (with particular attention given to the fate of European welfare states).[47] In its strongest form, the hypothesis is that globalization over time will produce a convergence of political-economic arrangements across national borders that will drag down state intervention and welfare policies to a lowest common denominator. Some scholars also stress the fact that increased financial integration decreases the ability of individual nations to pursue independent fiscal or monetary policies.[48] Other scholars, such as Paul Pierson of Harvard University, agree that pressures on the welfare state have increased in advanced capitalist nations, but argue that other factors, such as the slowdown in productivity growth associated with the rise of services-based economies, are more important in explaining these pressures than globalization per se.[49]

A third group of scholars vigorously rejects not only the strongest form of the convergence argument but also the very characterization of the world economy as "globalized." These scholars acknowledge that the world economy has an increasing number of international linkages but argue that it is still primarily dominated by national-level economic units.[50] For instance, Robert Wade of the London School of Economics notes that "national economic borders still define the boundaries of systems of capital accumulation." Wade points out, that most production in the major economic powers remains oriented toward domestic consumption, that most capital investments are domestic investments made out of domestic savings, and that multinational corporations continue to base their strategic and R&D operations in home countries.

A recent assessment by British scholar Andrew Glyn of domestic and external constraints on "progressive economic policy" in the OECD countries judges that domestic political constraints on job-creating Keynesian policies continue to be more important than globalization-related constraints —and that there is still considerable scope for autonomous national economic policy making within the world economy.[51] Echoing this view is Paul Krugman, who holds, "None of the important constraints on American social and economic policy come from abroad. We have the resources to take far better care of our poor and unlucky than we do; if our policies have become increasingly mean-spirited, that is a political choice, not something imposed on us by anonymous forces. We cannot evade responsibility for our actions by claiming that global markets made us do it."[52]

That judgment is particularly appropriate in the case of the United States, where trade continues to be a relatively small sector of the overall economy and most capital investments continue to be made within American borders, not abroad. George Washington University economist Robert Dunn Jr. thus stresses that "the United States still has a national capital market with a considerable degree of independence from those of other industrialized countries," that "there is overwhelming evidence that the Federal Reserve system retains its national independence in managing our monetary system," and that "there is no evidence that the United States is constrained in any significant way in managing its federal budget by what is occurring abroad." Finally, Dunn notes that "the growth of GDP in this country and the cycles through which GDP passes are primarily determined domestically rather than by what is occurring elsewhere." Dunn points out that the United States has witnessed impressive economic growth in the mid- and late 1990s despite continued stagnation in Japan and very slow growth in Germany and the United Kingdom.[53]

Yet while the United States is certainly less impacted by global pressures than smaller nations, it is hardly immune. As many economists have warned, the United States could face economic problems if foreign investors discontinued investments here, which fund the nation's $1-billion-a-day trade deficit. An estimated two-fifths of those investments in recent years have been in "new economy"–type high-tech firms, many of which have now soured. In addition, the establishment of the single currency in Europe may make that continent more attractive to international investors.[54] As numerous economists have observed, large-scale reduction of investment in the

United States would have very damaging consequences for the American economy.

The Impact of Globalization on Democratic Self-Governance

The preceding discussions have dealt with the impact of globalization and trade on jobs and wages in the United States, as well as on economic policy making. This section turns to the third major set of concerns pertaining to globalization: the possibility that the emerging process of globalization and the emerging set of rules governing the international economy could severely weaken prospects for democratic self-governance, both in the United States and elsewhere.

Globalization Can Undercut Established Social and Ecological Norms

Free trade regimes clearly have the potential to undercut established democratically determined norms, especially labor standards and environmental legislation. These norms can be undercut in two distinct ways. First, as noted, allowing imports from countries with substandard labor and environmental protection laws to enter the United States can give those countries a trading advantage based on exploiting either humans or nature. Trade between countries with fundamentally different standards of production can also have the effect of weakening support for higher norms in the nation with better-developed labor and ecological protections. Second, as we will discuss in the next section, free trade regimes may require that a particular nation or regional government's specific rules (for instance, on how beverages must be packaged to prevent ecological damage) represent an unfair restraint of trade.[55] Trade can also increase the competitive disadvantage associated with numerous laws governing the production process that are highly valued in the developed countries (workplace safety laws, environmental laws, workweek length, etc.).

Rodrik points out that there is "little substantive difference" between permitting "blocked exchanges" such as prison labor or child labor to occur in one's home country and in permitting unrestricted imports of goods made under such conditions to undercut local producers. Would those who urge pure free trade accept child labor in U.S. production? Or are norms important?

It is worth noting that some of the most successful exporters in the developing world regularly employ political repression. A 1997 U.S. State Department report, for instance, found that thirteen nations with export growth rates of 7.7 percent or higher between 1990 and 1995 engaged in at least three of the following human rights abuses: extrajudicial killings, torture, restrictions on freedom of speech and religion, government tampering with the judicial system, excessive use of police force, arbitrary arrests, and "significant child labor." These nations include Thailand, Indonesia, Sri Lanka, Kenya, Mexico, China, El Salvador, Bangladesh, Peru, Chile, Turkey, Tunisia, and Pakistan (which engaged in all seven of the abuses). Clearly, production in these countries takes place under very different norms and conditions than in the United States and other developed countries—a discrepancy that no intellectually honest observer can ignore or paper over. Clearly, too, there is no necessary relationship between expanded exports and increased democracy: While some of the high-export-growth nations on the above list (Mexico, Indonesia) have made significant progress toward democratization in recent years, others (Pakistan) clearly have not.[56]

International Trade and Investment Agreements Can Make Industrial Policies and Other Community-Supporting Policies Illegal
A second specific way labor and environmental norms may be challenged is through global free trade rules that potentially override local- and state-level innovations aimed at stimulating local self-reliance, less dependence on outside economic forces, and overall community stability. Except under tightly defined conditions, such rules (enforced in Geneva by a World Trade Organization [WTO] that has only very abstract and indirect accountability to democratic publics) essentially forbid labor and environmental laws at either state or federal levels from being stronger than "international standards" if they restrain trade. Even more suspect from the perspective of the WTO are policies aimed at directly providing preferences to local goods, local producers, and local workers.

Currently most American states have policies on the books favoring local producers in one way or another, such as preferences for local suppliers on bids for state contracts. The emerging trade regime could in principle allow other countries to challenge all such policies; a WTO panel in Geneva would then make a decision on whether the policy in question is acceptable. If the ruling went against the local or state law, the United States would be subject to trade sanctions unless the laws were changed. Each nation retains the constitutional power to keep its own laws, but only at a steep price, in the form of trade penalties. Critics like Lori Wallach of Public Citizen argue that this regime will have a "chilling effect upon progressive sub-federal legislation that often drives effective federal action."[57] Numerous challenges to countries' existing social policies have already taken place under the WTO/ General Agreement on Tariffs and Trade (GATT) regimes and in the

European Union. European restrictions on imports of American beef fed with growth hormones, Puerto Rican milk standards, dolphin protection laws, and fuel efficiency automotive standards have all been challenged under GATT or WTO. A striking example comes from Canada, where the government was sued in 1997 by Ethyl Corporation, an American firm, for $251 million in connection with a regulation banning the import of the gasoline additive MMT, which was deemed by the Canadian government to be a health hazard. As Mark Weisbrot of the Center for Economic Policy Research notes, "Their argument was that the Canadian government's ruling discriminates against Ethyl, and they sued under the provisions of NAFTA that provide for equal treatment of foreign and domestic investors."[58] Canada agreed to end the ban and paid Ethyl $13 million in a settlement. In another example, protestors in Seattle in December 1999 focused attention on the WTO's efforts to compel the United States to modify a U.S. law banning the importation of shrimp farmed without turtle-protecting devices.[59]

More recently, the federal government was sued in 1999 by a Canadian corporation, Methanex, for some $970 million on the grounds that a California law to eliminate the use of the suspected carcinogen MTBE in gasoline violated provisions of NAFTA protecting "investors' rights." Methanex manufactures methanol, a key ingredient in MTBE; its lawsuit claimed that the California law violates its property rights by threatening future profits. (The case stimulated California state legislators to express concern to the United States Trade Representative and to form a committee to critically examine the impact of international trade treaties on state laws.) The Methanex case has yet to be resolved at the time of this writing.[60]

As legal scholar Mark C. Gordon of Columbia University notes, there is a likelihood of many, many more Methanex-type challenges to state law in the United States under the provisions of NAFTA and the WTO as well as the proposed Free Trade Agreement of the Americas (FTAA). Seven specific WTO agreements call into question existing state legislation: the Agreement on the Application of Sanitary and Phytosanitary Measures allows environmental laws to be challenged on the grounds that they may be excessively "trade restrictive" or that they exceed international standards without an adequate scientific basis; the Agreement on Technical Barriers to Trade allows challenges to product certification and testing laws; the Agreemeent on Subsidies and Countervailing Measures allows challenges to state subsidies of firms, industries, or regions; the Agreement on Government Procurement permits challenges to state and local policies that provide preferences to local producers or minorities on procurement, or that use procurement to promote other social goals; the Agreement on Trade-Related Investment Measures restricts the use of "local content" requirements and similar measures governing foreign direct investment; the Agreement on Trade-Related Intellectual Property Rights requires member nations to adopt similar policies governing and protecting intellectual property; and the General Agreement on Trade in Services prohibits market restrictions on the provision of most services—trade in services is to receive most-favored-nation status. Some of these agreements will have greater short-term impact on states than others. But taken together, as Gordon argues, they represent a significant change in the democratic structure of governance in the United States, and indeed "threaten to internationalize many policy decisions which previously fit squarely within States' traditional authority."

American laws that the European Union has already claimed to be inconsistent with the WTO regime include "State environmental standards that exceed federal levels; buy-local, and minority and small-business set-aside laws; State unitary tax laws; and differing State regulations of banking and insurance." Specific laws noted by Gordon that might be challenged include Maryland's ban on phosphates (to stem water pollution in Chesapeake Bay), a New Mexico state law limiting the government's procurement to American-made motor vehicles, a Connecticut law requiring that nickel-cadmium batteries be recycled, Arizona requirements for the use of recycled paper in newsprint, and warning labels in California notifying consumers of the presence of toxic chemicals in food. Some seventy four laws in California alone are estimated to be in potential violation of WTO provisions.[61]

Some observers have pointed out that in particular cases the new WTO agreements could have a positive impact on economic development policy in the states. William Schweke of the Corporation for Enterprise Development thus suggests that WTO "subsidy discipline" policies are a "double-edged sword": New WTO rules could lead to a decrease in state job-chasing activities that involve large subsidies to mobile corporate firms. Unfortunately, the rules also "might restrict the abilities of federal, state, and local governments to achieve other public objectives such as promoting sustainable development, preserving tribal sovereignty in economic development, combating poverty and uneven development, promoting small business, and targeting market imperfections in research development."[62] Schweke argues that activists should seize the opportunity presented by international-level subsidy discipline programs to forcibly impose rationality on state- and-local level economic giveaways—and at the same time fight any restrictions on community-oriented development activities.[63] Schweke thus might endorse the $4 billion in trade sanctions against the United States sought by the European Union in the summer of 2001 after a WTO panel concluded that federal tax credits for large American exporters such as Microsoft and Boeing are in fact an illegal subsidy. (The United States could avoid sanctions by changing the export law.)[64] In our view, however, a consistent critique of WTO intervention into state and federal level policy making suggests that both good policies (restricting suspected carcinogens) and bad policies (providing indiscriminate subsidies to exporters) should be debated and either enacted or defeated by democratic publics, not by distant trade regimes.

Indeed, perhaps the most problematic feature of the WTO, and the one that best explains the passionate grassroots opposition to the institution, is that the procedures through which decisions on these matters are made fail the basic test of accountability to democratic publics. As Robert Kuttner of *The American Prospect* notes, "The WTO is a stunningly undemocratic institution. It operates at several removes from popular sovereignty, much as the pre-democratic deliberative institutions of the seventeenth and eighteenth century operated."[65] The deliberations of WTO's unelected panel are generally conducted in secret, with no presence for critical voices or nongovernmental organizations. Simply put, the guiding purpose of the WTO is the promotion of commerce—not democratic deliberation regarding how international trade should be balanced against the distinctive economic practices and institutions of individual nations.

The Impact of Globalization on Economic Development and Stability

A major argument of those who support free trade concerns its impact on development. Taking account of this argument leads us to the fourth concern raised by globalization: the relationship between the specific unfolding pattern of globalization in recent decades to development and the problem of increased global economic instability.

Do Economic Integration and Free Trade Drive Successful Development?

Many advocates of free trade believe it essential to economic development in poorer countries. Other economists, while admitting free trade has both costs and benefits, urge that protectionism amounts to slamming the door on developing nations, an untenable moral stance for the United States to take.[66] In a critical discussion of the widely cited Sierra Club compendium of antiglobalization activist arguments, *The Case Against the Global Economy,* economist Jay Mandle cites evidence of increased human well-being due to economic growth in the past forty years in China, Indonesia, Pakistan, India, and Bangladesh. The antiglobalization critics, Mandle charges, reject not only the doctrine of comparative advantage but also the "modernization process," which "arguably represents the best hope for ending poverty and successfully addressing threats of environmental devastation."[67] In subsequent work, Mandle (who acknowledges that globalization has some problematic consequenses) has again taken the "antiglobalization left" to task for failing to embrace corporate-led economic development. Mandle shows that there is a correlation between relatively high income and the volume of foreign direct investment; he cites Mexico, Thailand, Brazil, and Turkey as examples of nations with relatively high incomes that also have much higher levels of foreign investment than very poor countries such as Bangladesh. Foreign direct investment, he urges, must obviously be a substantial part of successful development in poorer countries.[68]

There are, however, good reasons to be cautious in accepting Mandle's conclusion that international economic integration and successful development necessarily go hand in hand. Several authors have pointed out that the observed relationship between high levels of foreign direct investment (FDI) and higher income may well be spurious; it may simply be that relatively high levels of income and human capital (as well as, in the cases of Mexico and Turkey, proximity to the United States and Europe) *attract* FDI, not that FDI creates higher income. The critical question is not the relationship between FDI and national incomes, but the relationship between FDI and *increases* in national incomes and living standards over time (i.e., development); the Mexican example, where real wages today are still below 1980s levels despite massive increases in FDI in the past two decades, raises severe doubts concerning the claim that FDI as presently practiced necessarily has a positive impact on development.[69] Moreover, as Dani Rodrik notes, "there is plenty of evidence that financial liberalization [to attract investment] is often followed by financial crash—just ask Mexico, Thailand, or Turkey—while there is little convincing evidence to suggest that higher rates of economic growth follow capital-account liberalization."[70]

Indeed, a recent analysis by Rodrik of the relationship between increased trade and economic performance in developing countries demonstrates that while growing economies usually (but not always) experience a moderate increase in exports, there appears to be no demonstrable link between export expansion in itself and economic growth: Of the twenty-five developing countries with the largest increases in exports as a percentage of GDP between 1975 and 1994, only fourteen countries experienced real per capita GDP growth of more than 1 percent a year, and only seven of these experienced growth above 2 percent a year. Five of these countries actually saw their real per capita GDP *shrink*.[71] Rodrik points out that countries wishing to follow in the footsteps of the successful Asian development stories of the postwar period such as South Korea, Taiwan, and India—countries that restricted imports and/or heavily subsidized exporters—would today "be unable to replicate these experiences without running afoul of the IMF or the WTO." Rodrik thus comes to the following conclusion, with which we concur: "[T]he globalizers have it exactly backwards. Integration is the result, not the cause, of economic and social development."[72]

It *is* important, however, that those who favor modifying trade policy as well as the current model of globalization articulate how such changes might cohere with promoting international development. We reject nationalist approaches to these issues that would deny developing nations access to the U.S. market simply because they are low-wage nations, and we recognize that low-wage industrial development can, in combination with other policies, bring important gains over time to poor countries. The question is how to facilitate a genuine rise not only living in standards but also in respect for basic rights (such as workers' right to organize) and basic environmental standards—that is, how to pull the bottom up and not permit increased economic integration to pull the top down. Fully answering that question is beyond the scope of this volume (although we return at greater length to the issue in Chapter 13). However, we believe Rodrik provides an important clue in emphasizing that the impact of trade and export activity in itself on successful development is routinely exaggerated by both academic economists and policy makers at institutions such as the World Bank. Rather, a long-term viable development strategy must rest on an economic core of increased investments in education and human capital, improved infrastructure, increased domestic investments, and rising aggregate demand as well as a political core of basic democratic rights and effective political institutions.[73] Successful developing nations are also likely to increase exports, but an increase in exports alone hardly guarantees successful development.[74]

*Globalization Increases Global Inequality and Destabilizes Communities
in the Developing World, Leading to Increased Downward Pressure on
Wages in the Developed World*
The Asian financial crisis is an example of what can happen when the inherent instabilities of the global economic system come to the fore. Indeed, the explosive flight away from several Asian currencies in the summer of 1997 helped trigger major dislocations involving millions of people: Unemployment tripled in South Korea in the year following the crisis; the Malaysian economy shrank by an estimated 6.6 percent in 1998; in nearby Indonesia, unemployment more than quadrupled between 1996 and 1998, leaving 20 million people without jobs.

Even during "normal" times, increased economic integration often displaces many thousands of people in poorer nations—and in ways that undercut the capacity of economic integration to deliver its promised benefits (i.e., higher employment and wages) to poorer nations. For instance, American University economist Robin Hahnel argues that even with the best possible reforms, globalization is almost certain to lead to continued increases in global economic inequalities:

> As long as capital is scarce globally, there is good reason to expect that international trade *based on free-market* prices will distribute more of the efficiency gains to wealthier countries than to poorer countries and thereby increase global inequality. And it is even easier to demonstrate that if capital is scarce globally . . . *free-market interest* rates will increase global inequality by distributing more of the efficiency gain from international investment to wealthier lenders than to poorer borrowers.[75]

Such conclusions do not foreclose the possibility of absolute gains in the well-being of the poor even as global inequality increases, but there are good reasons to be skeptical about even this in many lower-tier countries as well. The supply of labor in many developing countries is so enormous that a simple increase in demand for labor, while beneficial, will not lead to anything like a "tight labor market." Moreover, globalization and free trade can worsen this situation, as small entrepreneurs and, more dramatically, millions of farmers making a living through agriculture are displaced. As Hahnel points out, "Before the spread of 'modern' agricultural techniques, the rise of multinational agribusiness, and the emergence of global agricultural markets, large amounts of arable land in the Third World allowed millions of subsistence peasant farmers to produce for their own consumption even though their productivity was quite low."[76]

The fundamental point is that destabilizing agricultural populations in developing nations often generates enormously negative social consequences, as thousands daily abandon the countryside and flock to urban centers to seek paid employment—creating what is in effect a continuous exogenous shock to the labor markets of these countries. While the problems related to the flow of poor rural people to cities did not begin with increased trade, trade measures that expose agricultural producers to new pressures or that permit changes in the patterns of land use aimed at maximizing production for export while displacing previous inhabitants sorely exacerbate the problem.

This inability of developing countries to increase real wages in their labor markets as a result of the continuous inflow of new workers from the countryside may in turn place additional downward pressure on wage rates in the developed world. There is good reason, in short, to reject simple-minded definitions of efficiency gains from increased trade and investment that ignore the human consequences of disrupting and displacing established economic entities.

CONCLUSION

These criticisms of the impact of corporate-led globalization upon communities and workers in the United States and abroad do not span the full range of challenges that have been offered. For instance, we have not discussed the impact of the spreading of Western (and in particular, American) products and culture via the processes of globalization—a subject that has drawn the attention of cultural critics and political thinkers as varied as Benjamin Barber of the University of Maryland and neorealist political scientist Samuel Huntington of Harvard.[77] Similarly, the globalized export of Western consumption attitudes and standards has profound resource and ecological implications that we cannot adequately address here.

Even accepting that trade produces important gains, globalization presents several direct challenges to communities' economic stability and standards of living. To recapitulate the key issues: First, in a world of mobile capital, the old story of "comparative advantage" among nations with rooted capital competing in product markets is no longer adequate; we live in a world where increasingly mobile capital seeks out absolute advantages. Second, social welfare or even long-term economic efficiency are not necessarily enhanced by permitting standards of production, including labor and environmental laws, to be eroded by unrestricted trade among countries with different social standards. Third, the emergent global trade regime threatens to undercut policies in the United States, particularly at the state and local levels, that are aimed at strengthening community and helping local producers and local workers. Fourth, the current institutional arrangements of the global economy often allow or even foster economic instability. Fifth, it is by no means clear that globalization is on balance nearly as advantageous to developing nations as its advocates claim, especially when its destabilizing aspects are accounted for. Finally, from the standpoint of democracy and community, there are important values other than gains in aggregate "economic welfare" or "consumers' well-being" that must be taken into account in formulating international economic policy. Trade-related job loss at the local level not only wreaks havoc on thousands of individuals' lives but also undermines the material basis of meaningful local democracy.

Globalization thus provides an array of challenges to American communities. However, it is also important to bear in mind that not all forms of capital have been loosened from the ties of place and community by globalization processes. Many services—which occupy an increasing share of the American economy—are inherently placed-based, and many corporations may see advantages in locating in particular places, especially places that have particular access to networks of knowledge or other logistical advantages. Saskia Sassen of University of Chicago has persuasively argued that as a result of globalization, some forms of capital will tend to concentrate in a handful of "global cities" (such as New York and London) that act as points of command for the global economy; while Rosabeth Moss Kanter of the Harvard Business School has called on communities to develop long-term strategies aimed at accentuating local strengths so as to become more attractive to mobile capital, as either a "knowledge-based," "maker," or "trader" community.[78] Even in the wake of globalization, communities are not powerless to take effective steps to enhance their local economies—provided there is sufficient public policy support.

Our approach to the question of how to respond to globalization is distinguished from conventional economic discourse in its emphasis on democracy and community as the central frame of reference—not simply economic efficiency. Building the conditions of democracy—and real democratic experience—from the bottom up in the communities where Americans live is an underlying and fundamental value. So, too, is preserving real scope for effective democratic decision making at the national level. We do not deny that trade in product markets can produce important economic gains for trading nations; nor do we deny in principle the social desirability of positive net capital flows from advanced industrialized nations to the developing world (although we are not convinced that sole reliance on the market and private investment decisions is the optimal mechanism for effecting such transfers). But unrestrained trade and increased financial integration also have economic and social costs—and, most importantly, costs to democracy itself. Relatively narrow losses in economic welfare that may accompany managed trade policies can be justified if such policies better promote economic stability and preserve the capacity of states and localities to stabilize local economic life. There are better and worse ways to manage trade and the process of global economic integration. In Part IV we will explore intelligent ways to ensure that globalization does not overrun either economic stability or efforts to reconstruct the local basis of democracy.

CHAPTER 2

THE CHASE FOR JOBS

the second dimension of the triple threat to community is more home-grown, more familiar, and perhaps even more difficult to counter: unnecessary and inefficient mobility of capital within national borders. It would be troublesome enough if market-driven location changes simply failed to take account of the social costs of throwing away communities. But internal relocations are also actively encouraged both by national policies and by state "industrial recruiting" practices that encourage communities to compete with each other by lowering taxes or by offering subsidies, regulatory relaxation, and other special advantages to attract investments from private firms.

Sometimes corporate relocations within the United States make big headlines. When Boeing announced in March 2001 that it would relocate its corporate headquarters, the impact of the move on Seattle's economy became front-page news; analysts debated whether the relocation of some 1,000 management jobs meant that cuts in aircraft production in Seattle would eventually follow. Boeing CEO Phil Condit justified his decision by implying that the company was too rooted in a particular place to make objective decisions. Condit told reporters that getting away from Seattle would allow the company more "flexibility to move capital and talent to the opportunities that maximize shareholder value," a motivation that understandably worried the 70,000 Boeing production workers remaining in Seattle.[1]

Boeing announced that Chicago, Denver, and Dallas were the three "finalists" to become the company's new home base, setting off an intense bidding war as each city wined and dined Boeing executives and offered a variety of financial inducements. Eventually Boeing selected Chicago, which offered inducements estimated at $50 million. The Chicago press celebrated, while the local media in Dallas and Denver alternately discussed "what went wrong" or took comfort in being listed as one of Boeing's three most favored sites for the relocation. As one Dallas official correctly mused: "There will be another corporate relocation and another day."[2]

The Boeing story certainly merited attention. But each month dozens of other, smaller-scale corporate moves take place, most of which are noted only in the business press. In the summer of 2000, for instance, civic leaders in Lincoln, Nebraska, worried that the city needed to improve its "business climate" after the Gallup Organization announced it would relocate an hour away to Omaha.[3] The following spring saw the announcement of a merger of Wachovia and First Union banks in North Carolina, which resulted in a projected loss of 7,000 jobs as well as a shift of Wachovia jobs from Winston-Salem to Charlotte, a move that was considered a very modest boon for rapidly growing Charlotte but a very serious loss for Winston-Salem.[4] A few weeks later, business leaders in Westlake, Texas, celebrated the opening of a new Fidelity Investments corporate campus and expressed hope that future corporate relocations would soon follow.[5]

So far as we are aware, there are no firm numbers available on the number of corporate relocations which take place each year. However, *Site Selection Magazine*, which tracks new corporate projects (including both relocations and first-time investments), reports that the number of new projects undertaken each year doubled during the late 1990s to over 11,000 a year, a finding which may reflect not simply a hot economy but also an increase in the pace of domestic capital mobility. Over twice as many new corporate projects were initiated in 1999 as in 1989, the last full year of the previous economic expansion. While the available data do not allow us to quantify changes in the pace of capital mobility with precision, it is quite clear that the capacity of firms to move from state to state has never been greater. Indeed, a poll of chief executives in June 2000 by the American Management Association found that 42 percent of the CEOs' firms had either recently completed or were "actively considering" a relocation.[6]

Not only factories but also service operations and company headquarters are now moved frequently, as companies seek the best available labor market (a combination of available workers and low wage demands) for their facility and take advantage of available subsidies. As economics reporter Louis Uchitelle of the *New York Times* pointed out in connection with the recent relocation of wood and pulp company Rayonier from Stamford, Connecticut to Jacksonville, Florida, new communications technologies are an important factor behind this growth in mobility: "High-speed telecommunications and fiber optic lines, now available almost everywhere in the country, allow a Rayonier to communicate as easily from Jacksonville as from Stamford, and they also allow a great variety of service companies to link operations in different cities, as if these operations were all in one office."[7] This new technical capacity has removed the brakes from corporations' efforts to find the lowest-cost location—and in most cases local and state governments are there to provide a sweetener. Jacksonville gave Rayonier $1.8 million in cash to move south after twenty years in Stamford and fifty years in the New York City region, and the company is getting additional assistance from the state of Florida.[8]

From the standpoint of community-level democracy, what is important is not simply the quantity of business relocations in a given year, which is likely to fluctuate from year to year, but, to reiterate, the *capacity* of businesses to relocate at the drop of a hat or because a CEO has a flash of "strategic insight." Because it is everywhere understood that corporations can pick up and move to some other location in the United States—and be sure to find a warm welcome—encouraging a favorable business climate is a fundamental goal of most local politicians, Republicans and Democrats alike. This in turn means that business typically enjoys a privileged position in the distribution of local fiscal resources. While many cities are governed by "growth machine" regimes that actively induce new investments by mobile capital so as to boost growth rates and downtown land values, even cities that are content not to grow face the problem of how to hold on to potentially mobile firms already in town. As noted in the Introduction, college towns and other places anchored by stable public or quasi-public investments may at least partially escape this dynamic. However, the example of Lincoln, Nebraska, worrying about its own runaway firms shows that such communities are not totally immune to domestic capital flight and the consequences this has for local politics.

As we have noted in Chapter 1, some economists have argued that overall economic efficiency and hence social well-being are enhanced by unrestricted capital mobility. What these economists commonly fail to consider is the overall public balance sheet—that is, the overall costs to the public—of capital mobility. Within a pure market model, it is often cost-efficient for a particular company to move from one location to another in order to exploit a relatively small cost savings. From the point of view of the economy as a whole, of course, there is no overall gain in genuine productive efficiency if the substance of the cost savings derives from reduced taxes, weakened regulations, or the like.

Genuine efficiency gains from a firm's relocation must also be weighed against the costs to the public of laying off workers and discarding usable facilities, the tax losses and increased welfare costs associated with companies leaving, and the costs of building up new infrastructure and providing new public goods to accommodate the firm's move to a new location (as well as any employees who move to the new location). To be sure, economists have claimed that capital mobility from low-unemployment (high-wage) to high-unemployment (lower-wage) areas may represent an improved allocation of overall resources, but this claim presupposes as given precisely what we wish to question, namely, widespread community economic instability. (Moreover, as we shall see, some economists who have studied job-chasing policies in the United States conclude that there is little or no evidence that such "efficient" relocation is actually being induced by present policies.) Capital mobility to take advantage of cheap labor in high-unemployment areas would be unnecessary in a situation where each community's job base was stabilized and community unemployment was low. Additionally, an important distinction must be made between targeting new investments (both public and private) into higher-unemployment areas, which we favor, and relocating *existing* investments from one community to another.

Perhaps in the past, in certain cases, the overall economic efficiency associated with moving a manufacturing plant to a location with much cheaper transport and communication costs could outweigh the social and economic costs of domestic capital mobility. But in today's economy, there are fewer and fewer cases in which a truly comprehensive assessment of costs and benefits to the public—not simply to an individual firm—would demonstrate that a large-scale relocation of an existing business within the United States is socially and economically rational.

THE WAR BETWEEN THE STATES

It is crucial to understand the basic point that in general, the movement of capital within the borders of the United States is the result not simply of market decisions but of public actions that have often played a decisive role in shaping investment patterns and others. The most obvious are the large scale-military investments documented by Ann R. Markusen. A wide array of federal policies have deliberately accelerated the movement of capital in general —and, too, the particular historical shift of much industrial activity in the second half of the twentieth century from the unionized North to the Sunbelt South. These policies include depreciation rules on factory buildings, which have encouraged discarding older buildings in favor of new business sites; billions of dollars of federal investments in electrification, power, and water projects in the South and West; direct subsidies and protections for numerous Sunbelt industries and ports (including, most spectacularly, sugar, oil, and tobacco); and a range of policies that helped construct America's suburbs and consequently reshaped business investment patterns (as discussed in the following chapter on sprawl).

The federal budget, in fact, acts as a de facto redistributive mechanism, systematically giving southern and western states billions of dollars more in federal spending and benefits than these states pay in taxes, while northern and industrial midwestern states generally pay far more than they receive. The net redistribution of resources away from New York and New Jersey alone effected by the federal government between 1983 and 1998 alone approaches $500 billion. In one recent year, 1997, the southern states of Alabama, Arkansas, Florida, Kentucky, Louisiana, Mississippi, South Carolina, Tennessee, and West Virginia combined received $45 billion more from the federal government than they paid in taxes, while such states as New York, New Jersey, Massachusetts, Michigan, Illinois, Ohio, Minnesota, and Wisconsin paid in over $82 billion more than they received back in federal spending.[9]

One of the most self-defeating uses of public policy to affect the spatial location of firms is the so-called war between the states (and, we might add, the localities). The ongoing competition among states and localities for jobs and new capital investment has never been more heated or more costly. In the past decade policy makers at the state level have shown a willingness to offer extraordinary inducements to corporations in order to attract new jobs:

- In 1992, South Carolina offered BMW $135 million in incentives for a new plant with 1,900 jobs, thus paying $71,000 per job.

- In 1993, Alabama offered Mercedes $253 million for a new plant expected to employ 1,500 people, or $169,000 per job created.

- In 1997, Pennsylvania provided the Norwegian firm Kvaerner some $307 million to open a new shipyard, at a cost of $323,000 per job.

- In 2000, New York offered IBM $475 million in incentives to build a new plant with 1,000 jobs, at a cost of $475,000 per job.

- In 1998, Kentucky gave Williamette Industries over $132 million in potential tax credits for the expansion of a paper mill, requiring the company to create just fifteen new jobs, at an unbelievable cost of $8.8 million per job.[10] Although the company has reportedly in fact hired over a hundred new workers, total incentives still come to well over $1 million per job.

Table 2.1: Common Location Incentives Offered by State Governments

Property tax abatements on land and improvements	Offered by 38 states in 1998	Up from 23 in 1977
Property tax abatements on machinery and equipment	Offered by 42 states in 1998	Up from 28 in 1977
Corporate income tax exemptions	Offered by 37 states in 1998	Up from 21 in 1977
Incentives for new plants in high-unemployment-areas	Offered by 43 states in 1998	NA (36 states also permit city- or county-level incentives for such plants)
Loans for machinery and equipment	Offered by 43 states in 1998	Up from 13 in 1977 (30 states also offer loan guarantees for machinery and equipment)
Loans for building construction	Offered by 42 states in 1998	Up from 19 in 1977 (28 states also offer loan guarantees for construction)
Revenue bond financing	Offered by 45 states in 1998	Up from 20 in 1977 (49 states also permit cities or counties to undertake revenue bond financing)
Research and development tax exemptions	Offered by 38 states in 1998	Up from 9 in 1977
Sales tax exemptions on new equipment	Offered by 47 states in 1998	Up from 33 in 1977
City and county loans for machinery, equipment, and building construction	Offered in 47 states in 1998	Up from 7 in 1977
Accelerated depreciation on industrial equipment	Offered by 41 states in 1998	Up from 25 in 1977

Source: *State Business Incentives: Trends and Options for the Future* (Lexington: Council of State Governments, 1996); *The Book of the States, 2000–01* (Lexington: Council of State Governments, 2000), Tables 11.10 and 11.11, 512–513. *The Book of States, 1998–99* (Lexington: Council of State Governments, 1998), Table 11.4, 486–89. The table is only a partial list of the available financial and tax incentives; the Council of State Governments lists an additional twenty common state incentives to business, eighteen of which are offered in at least twenty four states.

Cities and states have also offered large subsidies to companies already in town to keep them there, as when New York City laid out $600 million in 1998 to retain the New York Stock Exchange, and in 2000 when Michigan persuaded General Motors to build its first new plant in the United States in over a decade with $256 million in incentives (or over $91,000 per new job).[11]

To understand the full scope of the problem, it is useful to review a list of the most widely practiced subsidies (see Table 2.1). Note especially that the number of states offering these subsidies has increased over time. Generalized incentives to business come in addition to specific tax abatements, subsidies, and infrastructure improvements that may be approved for specific corporations in high profile cases, such as the BMW deal in South Carolina. This list does not include anti-labor state laws or relaxed regulatory environments that are also often offered as boons to businesses, especially in the South.[12] Although precise estimates of the total value of state- and local-level corporate subsidies remain elusive, it is safe to say, minimally, that virtually no significant industrial relocation or expansion takes place in the United States without substantial assistance from some level of government.

WHAT DO INCENTIVES ACTUALLY DO?

Clearly, the reasons why private firms locate in one place rather than another are complex. Yet economic development practice has often acted on the assumption that the promise of lower taxation is the single most important factor in determining business location that public policy can impact—overriding not only other important public goods but also place-specific factors (including the presence of business networks and clusters, access to technology, etc.).

Do development incentives—for example, tax breaks given to companies to move to a particular area—make a difference in luring firms to localities? Surveys of employers in the early 1990s found that state and local incentives and tax exemptions ranked seventh and eighth on a list of the top twenty criteria valued in site selection deliberations—below labor costs, highway access, skilled labor availability, construction costs, access to affordable energy, and local crime rate—but ahead of such factors as access to health facilities, availability of land, housing costs, school quality, proximity to suppliers, and climate.[13] A recent comprehensive literature review of the impact of development incentives notes that while overall tax burden does have an impact on site selection, "neither tax incentives, nor non- tax incentives, nor enterprise zone incentives operate to offset the effects of the basic state-local tax systems. The locations that offer the highest returns without incentives are pretty much the locations with the highest returns after incentives are included."[14]

A revealing analysis by Robert M. Ady, a consultant for a firm that provides site selection services to manufacturing companies, shows that at the initial level of site screening, wage differentials, transportation, and specific needs (i.e., access to a research university) generally take precedence over taxes, but that unusually high tax burdens can remove a state or locality from consideration.[15] As the process of selecting a new site goes forward, firms take a close look at the relative tax impact in communities identified as acceptable on other grounds. However, Ady points out, while taxes (and tax incentives) are not entirely unimportant, labor, transportation, utilities, and rent costs are far more important factors than taxes (since they typically represent a much higher percentage of a firm's costs). Moreover, what is important to firms regarding taxes is not simply the amount paid but also the quality of the public services (especially education) provided by those taxes.

There is good reason to think, then, that the usefulness of state and local tax incentives as a fundamental factor in business relocations is rather limited. The cautious assessment of Peter Fisher and Alan Peters, who have studied the issue in great detail, is that tax incentives—other things being equal —have a modestly positive effect on the attractiveness of particular places.[16] Yet localities find themselves in a prisoner's dilemma situation, where they feel they must provide subsidies to avoid being disadvantaged compared to other localities. From a national perspective, this is a lose-lose game in which localities end up subsidizing businesses far more than would be the case if all localities refrained from subsidies.

Some scholars have pushed this point farther to argue that "industrial recruitment" strategies in general are not only wasteful in the aggregate but also, in many cases, damaging to the communities that pursue them. A useful summary is that of economic development expert Scott Loveridge. Loveridge points out that because the odds of landing a new company are relatively long and the competition intense, communities will tend to overbid and "give away the store" in order to beat a competitor. Even if a business does relocate in response to an incentive, it may create new infrastructure costs or increase costs for other businesses already in the area. Further, branch plants established by corporations that relocate are likely to produce smaller multiplier effects (see Chapter 7) than endogenous (locally generated) economic development, largely because branch plants tend to have fewer linkages with local suppliers. Finally, communities following this strategy often end up landing insecure, low-wage jobs, as the companies involved simply seek lower wage costs. Even after the company moves into a new location, there is no guarantee that it will not move yet again to a still cheaper location, perhaps abroad.[17]

Work conducted by Joseph Persky, Daniel Felsenstein, and Wim Wiewel of the University of Illinois at Chicago points to additional considerations that must be taken into account when evaluating the effectiveness of subsidies. Using a comprehensive cost-benefit analysis matrix for studying specific industrial incentives, they point out that from any raw claim of new jobs (or new benefits) created in a locality by a new business, the following subtractions need to be made:

- The number of such jobs that go to newcomers or outsiders

- The number of jobs vacated by local residents who take up employment at the new firm that are not in turn filled by other local residents

- The number of jobs in local businesses displaced by the new, competing firm (as when local retailers close after a Wal-Mart moves in)

- The number of jobs not created by new businesses because of the presence of a new firm (in some cases a business may wish to avoid being in close proximity to another large employer or a competitor)

- Most importantly, the number of jobs that would have been created had the public money not been used as a subsidy but instead spent in a different manner, (such as on education, job training, or nurturance of local enterprise)[18]

In short, Persky and colleagues' analysis shows that the rhetorical claims of economic development officials about jobs and benefits created using incentives demand serious qualification.

Supplementing these theoretical objections to job-chasing policies, a large body of empirical literature now exists on the general question of why economic development policy, in general, commonly doesn't work—where economic development policy means the use of incentives to lure business. For instance, in a 1992 analysis of the flow of fiscal benefits from economic development to some seven hundred municipalities, political scientist Mark Schneider reported that the "actual payoff from economic development in terms of reduced taxes and strengthened tax base were [*sic*] never very large" and that by the mid-1980s, the payoff had declined significantly. Schneider argues that this decline came about because "competition between cities and the changing nature of the global market" forced local governments to "offer more expensive tax abatements and other fiscal inducements to attract business growth."[19] Similarly, Fisher and Peters conclude their analysis of the effect of incentives by commenting: "To the degree that tax and incentive competition results in a redistribution of jobs, our research lends little or no support to the argument that this redistribution has beneficial effects for the nation as a whole, [by, for example] shifting jobs from places with low unemployment to places with high unemployment. . . . Neither are we persuaded that incentive competition improves locational efficiency."[20]

WHY DEVELOPMENT INCENTIVES PERSIST

A puzzle remains: While there are strong reasons to doubt that providing development incentives is a good idea, the practice persists almost universally. Why? One reason may be simply that, compared with alternative development strategies, the provision of development incentives is relatively uncomplicated and (seemingly) inexpensive. Even communities faced with extremely limited resources—both fiscal and organizational—usually have the capacity to dole out incentives.[21] The most powerful explanations for the existence of this paradox, however, lie within the realm of politics and ideology.

The work of political scientist Harold Wolman is especially enlightening here. Wolman demonstrates that even if politicians understand the clear economic irrationalities and ineffectiveness of an economic development strategy built around the provision of development incentives, they still may find it politically rational to engage in this practice: "A politician might well reason that, although it is quite likely fiscal incentives will not affect location decisions, the political benefit that would accrue in the unlikely case the incentives were offered and did work (or the political costs if they were not offered and they were to work for other cities) would be substantial and would indeed outweigh the much smaller political benefit of being fiscally prudent and not offering incentives."[22]

By providing incentives, Wolman adds, elected officials can "claim credit" politically for creating jobs and generating tax revenue, even if such incentives have little to do with positive economic trends. Likewise, such officials can easily "avoid blame" by pursuing this strategy—blame that might arise from the appearance "of standing by and doing nothing while the economy continues to deteriorate or while a firm decides to relocate to another community."[23] The approach has the added political benefit of appearing to show quick results, and thus fits compatibly with the limited time horizons of political officials facing an electoral cycle.[24] (This practice is so common, it has acquired a pejorative nickname: "Shoot anything that flies, claim anything that falls.")[25]

Thus simply imploring lawmakers to be more judicious in the spread of corporate subsidies is unlikely to have a tangible impact on the problem. The issue is largely systemic: So long as states and localities do not have a secure economic basis in rooted capital, the temptation, even compulsion, for politicians seeking reelection to woo mobile capital with special incentives will be overwhelming.

Buried within this political explanation, however, is a deeper ideological one: There exists in the United States a strong bias in favor of the notion that what we call economic development policy *is* the subsidizing and assisting of private firms, a bias nurtured by the fact that most development officials have backgrounds in mainstream state or local politics and/or in business. The American "cultural tradition of privatism" tends to inhibit the ability of state and local public officials to think imaginatively about their economic development problems, leading them invariably back to one solution—the provision of development incentives to private firms.[26]

In a fundamental sense, what has sometimes been called the "war between the states"—or, more evocatively, "smokestack chasing"—is an artifact of an economic system predicated on the notion that private business interests should exercise decisive power over business investments and economic planning, combined with a federalist political system in which states and localities compete with one another for scarce investment.

CLOSING THE CANDY STORE: ALTERNATIVES TO INCENTIVE GIVEAWAYS

The most striking feature of current incentive practices is the aggregate irrationality of hundreds of state and localities bidding against one another for scarce businesses, thereby providing subsidies for jobs that likely would have been created anyway. The phenomenon of states aiming to make themselves "secure" by making their neighbors less secure, and the spiral of competitive bidding that it induces, is like a dog chasing its own tail: The harder the states and local decision makers try to buy economic stability by offering payouts to stimulate investments by mobile capital, the more difficult it becomes for any community to avoid making such handouts simply to keep in place the firms that are already there.

Simply put, the overwhelming majority of city and state policy makers see the creation (and advertisement) of a "good climate for business" as a fundamental goal. The following list of official city slogans compiled by John R. Short of Syracuse University provides a flavorful insight into the image which public officials seek to convey to investors: Dallas calls itself "The City of Choice for Business"; Milwaukee's slogan is "The City That Works for Your

Business"; New York is "The Business City That Never Sleeps"; while Phoenix is "Moving Business in the Right Direction." Even more direct are the pitches of two smaller cities: Norfolk, Virginia considers itself a place "Where Business Is a Pleasure" and Troy, New York, is simply "A Great Location for Your Company."[27] While it is perhaps too easy to scoff at this bumper-sticker boosterism, such slogans are revealing of the extent to which policy makers are oriented toward business—and how subordinate substantive questions about the quality of life of the citizenry are to the attraction and retention of capital. The consequences of this system for local-level democracy are severe. Harvey Molotch of the University of California at Santa Barbara puts it bluntly: "The conventional call is for cities (and states) to be run 'like a business,' which really means being run *for* business."[28]

The challenge, then, is how to stop the community-destabilizing war among localities and states for private business investment, and instead use the available resources to promote community economic stability. Fortunately, as with international trade (and, as we shall see, suburban sprawl), there are important countertrends to the dominant pattern of ever-increasing state and local subsidies to mobile capital. Even as the scale of the job-chasing phenomenon has increased in public visibility, the past ten years also have seen a growing number of proposals intended to dampen or end what critics have labeled the "candy store" approach to economic development.

For example, many analysts and some lawmakers have called on the federal government to legally bar states from using federal development monies for the purposes of luring jobs and companies from other states. Even in cases where there are explicit strings that limit localities from using federal aid to attract companies with subsidies, such as the federal job training programs and grants from the Economic Development Administration, states commonly have played a shell game that in practice indirectly uses the new federal money for job-luring purposes. It has also been proposed that any state engaging in job raiding lose all funding from Department of Labor and Department of Commerce programs for the following year. A precedent is the federal government's requirement in the 1980s that states raise the legal drinking age to twenty-one as a prerequisite for receiving federal highway funds. Representative [Martin] Meehan (D-MA) has introduced legislation under which "no State may engage in the direct or indirect utilization of Federal funds of any kind, in whole or in part, to hire jobs and businesses from another State."[29]

At the state and local levels, additional strategies to dampen the subsidy war have been initiated or seriously considered. Some states and localities have adopted so-called clawback legislation, which requires recipients of development incentives to pay back such monies if they fail to meet job-creation goals. Other proposals on the state and local levels suggest mechanisms through which multiple jurisdictions can voluntarily cooperate with one another to limit subsidy competition. (We discuss these state and local strategies in greater detail in Chapter 5.)

Such strategies, even the most ambitious, are oriented toward the minimal goal of applying brakes on job chasing. However, the underlying reasoning that compels state-level politicians to cut deals favorable to mobile corporations with jobs to offer would remain—even if the federal government did take the minimal step of forbidding use of its funds for job raiding, and even if more states began to attach strings to such aid or began to cooperate with one another to confront the problem. A longer-term view suggests that the most productive way to move toward the goal of stable state and local economies with minimal dependence on private mobile capital is not simply to place performance requirements on subsidy recipients but to slowly redirect who receives such subsidies to begin with. All of the development tools noted above now used to underwrite conventional corporate-based economic development, often with dubious results, could be used instead to nurture, assist, and expand the place-based, community-stabilizing sectors of the economy. The second half of this book will explore some of the specific ways such assistance could (and in many cases already does) take place. Clearly states have substantial resources available to shape the kinds of economic institutions that flourish within their jurisdiction—money that could instead support community reconstruction.

CAPITAL AND COMMUNITY: PAST AND FUTURE

This chapter has focused on the problem of how states and localities ought to respond to the reality of mobile capital investment within the United States. We recognize, however, that some places are more likely than others to be "sticky" with regard to capital investments, that is, better able to retain ongoing private investment over time. Indeed, the assumption that economic activities cannot be rooted in place has been subjected to scrutiny and convincing qualification by economists and economic sociologists. These scholars have demonstrated that even within the context of a capitalist economy with increasing mobility, place matters—and that particular places *do* have the capacity to make political choices to encourage rooted economic activities and hence overall community economic stability. A brief review of the relationship between capital and the characteristics of particular places will be a helpful prelude to thinking about more proactive policies to stabilize communities' economic prospects.

Explaining Concentrations of Capital

One perspective on the relationship between capitalism and geography empha-sizes the political construction of particular places as centers of business activity, particularly through the use of public money, including highway spending, military spending, and other large-scale government projects. Public spending helps shape market patterns, it is argued, and directs investment into some places rather than others. The work of Ann Markusen has been particularly prominent in developing this theme; for instance, Markusen and her colleagues have documented the emergence of the "gun belt" in the United States, as mil-itary spending played a decisive, lead role in creating such communities as Colorado Springs, Colorado. Markusen and her colleagues define the gunbelt as "the stretch from New England down the Atlantic seaboard, across the cen-tral states, and into the lower Mountain and Pacific regions.

> For forty years . . . the growth of manufacturing production and employ-ment in these regions has been strongly and heavily defense-induced. Conversely, the industrial heartland never captured a significant share of cold war aerospace defense contracts, a fact that proved a significant ele-ment in its decline after 1970.[30]

Another important theme of the academic literature in economics involves the tendency of capital to agglomerate in places that offer particular advantages to business. Earlier in American history, access to water transportation was often a major consideration for industrial producers, and hence many port cities (both inland and on the coasts) became major industrial centers. Central cities also offered access to a mass of both workers and consumers. Urban agglomeration theory suggested that choice places with a high density of producers would have important secondary effects. Once a sufficient number of large enterprises has been established in a particular location, a market can be created for local sup-plier firms and producers of services and consumer goods.[31] Today, as scholars such as Saskia Sassen have pointed out, some cities also have certain economic advantages, especially in their capacity to facilitate close interactions among firms and the development of service-based "production complexes."[32]

Indeed, in the past twenty years there has been an impressive outpouring of research demonstrating how business networks and social-capital relation-ships impact industrial development within particular regions. The central argument, as developed by such scholars as Charles Sabel and Michael Piore as well as Anna Lee Saxenian, is that regions marked by nonhierarchical busi-ness networks, large amounts of social interaction and cooperation between firms, and effective transmission of information can develop advantages in economic development, both quantitatively and qualitatively.

Based on their study of firm structure and interaction in northern Italian manufacturing, Sabel and Piore developed the notion of "industrial districts." They argued that the industrial district system represented a healthy mix of competition and cooperation, as firms competed on the basis of technological innovation and product quality but not on the basis of labor costs or cost advantage in general. Moreover, the lives of the firms were rooted in their interactions with one another, and hence the companies were intrinsically rooted in a particular place. Sabel and Piore suggested that it ought to be possible to use state power to construct circumstances favorable to industrial-district-type development as opposed to development dominated by hierarchical firms that place more emphasis on cost savings in their competitive strategy.[33]

Anna Lee Saxenian's classic comparison of the culture of high-tech development in Silicon Valley (California) and the Route 128 corridor (Massachusetts) demonstrated the importance to firms in certain industries of being geographically close to centers of innovation and technology. Saxenian argued that the free flow of information, ideas, and talent facilitated by the networks of small (and a few large) firms in Silicon Valley had allowed the region to leapfrog ahead of the Route 128 corridor as a vibrant engine of high-tech development. The traditionally organized corporate hierarchies in Massachusetts simply could not generate innovation as effectively as networks where knowledge tends to be shared among many researchers whose loyalty may be not to any one corporation but rather to the craft.[34]

This work on networks and industrial districts draws on a broader theoretical literature on "clustering," which attempts to explain why similar types of firms tend to congregate in particular places. Access to transportation, special sources of technological knowledge (such as a major research university or a state-sponsored technical center), a specialized local labor pool, and direct collaboration between businesses may in varying cases play important roles in shaping cluster formation.[35] Both the cluster-formation literature and more theoretical academic literature exploring the implications of a post-Fordist and post-Taylorist economy suggest that these qualities of places remain important in affecting capital investment patterns—even though transportation-related and other technical determinants of firm location have declined in importance.

As a result, even within the structure of a political-economic system that generally devalues place, one can find examples of communities in which capital and place are closely linked. Ann Markusen and several colleagues have usefully sketched out four models of such "sticky" regions—each of which has distinct consequences for long-term community economic stability (as well as other outcomes such as local income inequality). These include industrial districts, hub-and-spoke districts, satellite platforms, and state-anchored industrial districts.

Industrial districts consist of small, locally owned firms that make investment decisions locally and cooperate substantially both through local buyer-supplier linkages and (in what Markusen terms the "Italianate variant") strong trade associations and sharing of risk and innovation. Such districts include a flexible labor market in which workers regularly change firms but only rarely need leave the region. The presence of "patient capital" within the district—local financial institutions willing to make long-term investments in local industry—generally ensures the long-term economic stability of these regions. Perhaps the best examples of such a region is Emilia-Romagna in Italy.

Far more familiar in the American setting are *hub-and-spoke* districts, described by Markusen as "regions where a number of key firms and/or facilities act as anchors or hubs to the regional economy, with suppliers and related activities spread out among them like spokes of a wheel." The classic example of this type of district would be Detroit in its auto heyday; Markusen cites Seattle (with Boeing and Microsoft) as a good contemporary example. In these districts, large firms with high economies of scale have relationships and contracts with firms both within and outside of the region. The presence of the large firms helps stabilize local business. The large firms provide jobs for blue-collar workers, who are committed to the firm and rarely change jobs. Ultimately, Markusen suggests, in this situation the community's long-term economic prospects are tied to those of the relevant industries—as well as the strategies of the firms involved. Changes in the character of the region that raise costs, structural changes internal to industries (such as the development of a capacity to farm some operations out to cheaper locations), and changes in management strategy all may affect the large firms' long-term presence in a region—and hence the region's economic stability. It follows that places fortunate to have large firms in multiple industries may have more security—although even an economically diverse region such as the Seattle area would find disinvestment by Boeing of core production jobs a major economic blow (just as loss of the company headquarters in spring of 2001 proved to be a major psychological blow).

Satellite platforms are communities that are home to one or more branch plants—that is, production facilities owned by a corporation headquartered elsewhere. Platform firms tend to rely on nonlocal suppliers and to have few linkages to the local economy; the more important relationship is that with the parent company. Such communities attract workers from outside the area to take jobs at the platforms (especially highly skilled jobs). Government often assists the platform firms with infrastructure or business inducements. A textbook example of a satellite platform community is Research Triangle Park in North Carolina, home to IBM facilities as well as to operations of numerous other corporations anchored elsewhere. Satellite platform communities are ultimately dependent upon the investment decisions of nonlocal firms to maintain economic stability.

State-anchored industrial districts are communities that (as noted in the introduction) are stabilized by a large public institution, be it a state capital, a university, or a military base. Such state-anchored places have stable local businesses and tend to have a high number of professionals and clerical workers. University and military towns, as well as towns with strong federal government administrative presences, attract a substantial amount of labor from other areas (although few workers leave such regions). Most important for community stability, long-term prospects for these places depend not on private investment decisions but on the political process (i.e., decisions regarding whether to expand or cut back government facilities at a particular location).[36]

Two of these four categories of "sticky" places are relatively congenial to long-term economic stability—industrial districts with many small firms capitalized by local financial institutions, and communities anchored by public facilities. Both hub-and-spoke districts and platform communities are ultimately much more dependent on the exigencies of the market and the investment decisions of private actors to maintain stability—a fundamental fact that drives the job-chasing phenomena explored in this chapter.

To be sure, as Markusen notes, many actual places exhibit a mixture of these traits. For instance, while Silicon Valley has many of the characteristics of an industrial district, it also has been shaped by military spending and the presence of large firms. Similarly, Research Triangle Park in North Carolina is in part a state-anchored district due to its proximity to the state capital and three major research universities, although it is also a platform producer that offers significant subsidies to mobile capital. The key point, from our perspective, is simply that not all forms of "stickiness" are equal. While hub-and-spoke communities may enjoy long periods of relative prosperity as long as the major firms in the region continue to do well, and while platform communities may succeed in luring branch plants (although many would-be platform communities fail), both kinds of places are vulnerable in the long term to market changes and investment decisions.

EXPLAINING THE MOBILITY OF CAPITAL

The question of why capital moves from place to place has been engaged by scholars from a variety of disciplines and ideological perspectives. David Harvey of Johns Hopkins University has described the propensity of capital to shift from place to place as a response to needs created by the perpetual growth and expansion of capitalism itself. For capitalism to expand, new markets must be tapped, which implies an ever-widening expansion of the scope of the market (in geographical terms). Within this context, production shifts can be caused by changes in transportation technology that make new areas more profitable production sites. As growth proceeds, some older places are allowed to die in favor of new production centers. Echoing Joseph Schumpeter's notion of "creative destruction" as intrinsic to capitalism, Harvey writes that "we can expect to witness a perpetual struggle in which capitalism builds a physical landscape appropriate to its own condition at a particular moment in time, only to have to destroy it, usually in the course of a crisis, at a subsequent point in time."[37]

A second broad explanation developed by other scholars sees movements of capital from place to place as intrinsically linked to product cycles. The argument is that regions or districts with high concentrations of technological know-how and a skilled workforce—New England is often cited as a paradigmatic example—will take the lead in developing an industry, including both research and development and production itself. However, as the industry matures, production technology further advances, and competitive pressures increase, it may eventually become advantageous for firms to seek less skilled, cheaper labor. At this point, capital begins to leave the host region and move to cheaper labor regions. The classic example of this in the U.S. context is the shift of manufacturing in industries such as textiles from the unionized northern states to the nonunionized, lower-tax (and, often, higher-public-subsidy) southern states in the postwar era.[38] This argument is now often extended to explain why capital may benefit from seeking still cheaper labor abroad (i.e., abandoning textile plants in the South in favor of those in Latin America).

Product cycle theory has been refined, revised and subjected to sophisticated critiques by numerous scholars.[39] What is important from our point of view is simply the basic point that firms' locational decisions depend on a mix of factors—including access to research and technological know-how, what kind of labor is most appropriate for a given production process (skilled or cheap), and the overall political-economic context of different regions—all factors whose relative importance may shift over the course of the production cycle.

A third set of explanations stresses that firms find it rational to move to states and localities that have the capacity to encourage the formation of clusters and to provide an attractive environment for capital location and/or expansion through the public goods they provide. Capital, then, will tend to flow, other things being equal, to places with a superior stock of public goods. Ronald Ferguson of Harvard University, for instance, speaks of the four "fundamentals" of infrastructure, education, taxation, and regulation as critical to economic development.[40] Infrastructure refers to transportation and communications systems in particular; education refers to the skills present in a given area's workforce; taxation refers to whether a locality's assessments are perceived as rational by businesses; and regulation refers to whether rules are enforced in a predictable, nonarbitrary way and the degree to which there are irrational, time-consuming rules. On this account, locations that can provide an attractive set of public goods combined with a skilled workforce stand a better chance of both generating endogenous economic development and attracting outside investments. One version of this argument, made with respect to the "competitiveness" of the United States in the global economy, has been put forward by former secretary of labor Robert Reich in his 1991 book *The Work of Nations*.[41]

None of these sets of explanations is satisfactory as a sole explanation of how and why capital investment shifts from place to place over time. Nor are the explanations mutually exclusive: Each of these processes (access to markets and shifts in transportation costs, product cycle development, the impact of public investments, social networks and firm clustering, and provision of public goods and/or business climate) can play a role in any nuanced, historical discussion of growth patterns of a particular industry in a particular region. The goal here is not to conduct such an analysis or to ask which theory is best, but to note that all of these processes must be accounted for in constructing policies and institutions intended to securely root capital in communities over time.

As we shall see in Parts II and III of this volume, numerous new strategies that take account of modern academic understanding make this possible—especially as the manufacturing sector steadily declines in importance.

CHAPTER 3

THE CHALLENGE OF URBAN SPRAWL

t he third aspect of the triple threat to community in the United States consists of the complex of issues pertaining to spatial development and land use, usually connoted by the term *sprawl*. Sprawl refers both to the fact of continuing outward development on the perimeters of metropolitan areas and to the specific form such development has taken, namely, construction of freeways, strip malls, and other car-centered uses of space. A recent Brookings Institution analysis of data from the United States Department of Agriculture's National Resources Inventory found that between 1982 and 1997 the rate of outward land expansion outpaced population increases in 264 of the 281 metropolitan areas they examined.

This trend encompassed both urban areas that grew and cities that declined in population. The population of the Pittsburgh metropolitan area, for instance, declined 8 percent, but its land area, as measured by the National Resource Inventory, increased by some 43 percent. In Atlanta, urbanized land increased by 82 percent, even though the area's population increased by only 61 percent—and even though population in the city of Atlanta itself has actually declined since 1980.[1] Nationwide, urbanized land increased by some 47 percent between 1982 and 1997, while population grew only 17 percent. Consequently, average urban density declined by over 20 percent in just fifteen years.[2] In short, with the exception of those few cities that are hemmed in by physical geographical boundaries, the nation's metropolitan areas have become less dense and more spread out in recent decades.

The explosive growth of suburbia in the United States—the "crabgrass frontier," as historian Kenneth Jackson evocatively calls it—is generally dated from the postwar construction boom. As veterans returned from the European and Pacific fronts, politicians accommodated the huge pent-up demand for modestly priced, reasonable-quality housing by subsidizing the construction of new single-family suburban homes. Specific mechanisms included tax deductions for home mortgages and the public construction of roads connecting urban centers with outlying communities (a construction boom that culminated in the late 1950s with the creation of the interstate highway system). At the same time, private developers, following in the footsteps of the first Levittowns, promoted single-family suburban living as the new ideal of American life. They energetically marketed the new suburb (ironically) as a site of strong community cohesion combined with the amenities associated with escape from the city: less crowding, less crime, less filth. (Just under the surface of this marketing effort was the suggestion that suburbs would have fewer racial and ethnic minorities and poor people.) In time, suburban living became synonymous first with privacy, and then with privatism and disregard for public space and public goods—with the exception of the road system, and, often, public schools. Feminist critics such as Betty Friedan noted the isolation of women in suburbia and the community-debilitating consequences of rigid separations between home, work, and market, while others pointed to the characteristic alienation and occasional antisocial behavior of suburban youth.[3]

Historians and policy analysts generally agree that some degree of suburbanization was probably a reasonable response to problems of overcrowding and housing shortages in central cities in midcentury America. In 1950, as today, the most compelling and most frequently cited argument on behalf of outward expansion from cities was the need to provide additional decent, affordable housing. But the suburban housing boom had almost immediate negative consequences for central cities and their remaining residents: As more affluent citizens left, central city tax bases weakened, even as the poorer residents left behind became more isolated. Today, as road construction and further outward development continue to be practiced as the "solution" to the problem of building desirable, affordable housing in metropolitan regions, a wide range of observers have come to recognize that uncontained sprawl also has a negative impact on the quality of life in the suburbs themselves.

UNPLANNED OUTWARD DEVELOPMENT VERSUS PLANNED DECENTRALIZATION

The specific phenomenon of suburban sprawl in the second half of the twentieth century needs to be carefully distinguished from the concept of slowing the growth of cities and encouraging citizens to live in smaller-scale communities. Polls have consistently shown that Americans prefer to live in relatively small communities (100,000 people or less). While there have been few academic studies of optimal city size in recent years, the best extant evidence indicates that smaller cities perform better than large cities with respect to a range of quality of life issues, including environmental quality, crime rates, and traffic congestion.[4] Recent work by Princeton political scientist J. Eric Oliver indicates that smaller cities appear to be more conducive to participation in local politics than very large cities.[5] Such findings in part reflect the damage done to existing big cities by sprawl and associated public policies (as discussed below), but they also suggest that small cities may well be—and be subjectively felt to be—preferable human habitats.

The current form of suburbanization is a distorted reflection of an important line of thinking that originated with Sir Ebenezer Howard and a handful of like-minded thinkers in Britain at the close of the nineteenth century. Howard gave birth to the idea of "garden cities," modestly sized communities organized in circular fashion around the perimeter of large metropolitan agglomerations such as London. Howard's garden city idea helped spawn the "New Towns" movement in Britain and the regional planning movement in the United States of the 1920s and 1930s.

Howard believed garden cities could be the solution to problems of urban poverty and overcrowding. Under his scheme, citizens would leave cities to move to planned new towns located several miles away from the urban core. These new towns would be explicitly designed to accommodate a mix of socioeconomic classes and would be enlivened by visible public spaces and the provision of ecological amenities. Most importantly, in Howard's scheme, land in the new towns would be community-owned, and leased to businesses and residents; as the value of land rose with population growth, the resulting revenue would be used to offset the costs of public goods (thereby also reducing taxes and housing costs). Central to Howard's vision was the notion that the several miles of space between central city and the satellite garden cities would be left undeveloped. Around each garden city, Howard proposed a huge swath of publicly owned, permanent farmland, forests, and pastures, which would demarcate the edge of the city—about 5,000 acres compared with a 1,000-acre town center. Instead of building into this belt, growth would occur only by "jumping over the farm/parklands and "establishing . . . another city some little distance beyond its own zone of country."[6]

British followers of Howard succeeded in getting the government to build over two dozen new towns by 1970. None of the new towns maintained Howard's core socioeconomic institution, local community ownership of land, but observers have credited the towns with helping "[establish] what became a distinctive feature of postwar British planning: the system of towns against a backcloth of open country."7 The new town idea also spread to the United States as well. In the 1930s, New Deal official Rexford Tugwell pushed for the construction of three new "greenbelt" towns in Maryland, Wisconsin and Ohio. In the 1960s developer James Rouse built the new town of Columbia, Maryland, as an explicit attempt to model a multiracial community. The new town experiments in both Britain and the United States enjoyed modest success in providing a relatively high quality of life compared to unplanned suburban development, but even proponents concede that the towns have generally fallen far short of Howard's lofty vision of using local community control over land as a strategy to simultaneously promote social and ecological goals.

The United States in fact never undertook explicit planning aimed at easing urban congestion in a rational manner while also preserving the livability of city centers. Instead, policy makers implemented an array of policies that helped push Americans into suburbia—with little regard either for those left behind in central cities or for the character of the new suburban communities.

THE POLITICAL CONSTRUCTION OF SUBURBAN AMERICA

Let us look more closely at the major policy initiatives and public subsidies driving suburban expansion:

The home mortgage tax exemption. The central federal strategy to encourage home ownership, this policy allows homeowners to take a tax deduction on the interest costs of mortgages. The policy is almost untouchable politically, and most strongly benefits the wealthy. As Kenneth Jackson pointed out in 1985:

> The system works in such a way that a $20,000-a-year bank teller living in a private apartment earns no housing subsidy. But the $250,000-per-year bank president living in a $400,000 home in the suburbs has a veritable laundry list of deductions. All $38,000 in interest payments would be subtracted from income, as well as all $7,000 in property taxes. His $45,000 subtraction would save him approximately $22,500 in taxes, or almost $2,000 per month. . . . Thus, it happens that the average housing subsidy in an elite suburb will exceed by several times the average subsidy to a welfare family in the inner city.8

Importantly, as Jackson also notes, the tax subsidy to affluent Americans is so enticing that remaining in the city as a high-income renter is often economically irrational, given the tax savings forgone. The flight of high-income individuals and families into single-family suburban houses in turn has contributed to fiscal problems in American cities. The annual value of the federal mortgage interest deduction now stands at roughly $66 billion, compared to the $32 billion budget of the federal Department of Housing and Development.[9]

Federal Housing Administration (FHA) subsidies and redlining practices. The FHA is the lead federal agency in promoting home ownership and is estimated to have helped finance nearly 11 million new private homes built between 1934 and 1972.[10] FHA offers mortgage insurance, which allows buyers to purchase homes with as little as 10 percent (or even less) down. As preservationists Richard Moe and Carter Wilkie point out, FHA criteria for eligibility for mortgage insurance was substantially biased against African-American neighborhoods for decades. "A single house occupied by a black family in an urban neighborhood, even one tucked away on an inconspicuous side street, was enough for the FHA to label a predominantly white neighborhood as unfit for mortgage insurance," Moe and Wilkie note. "Areas that failed to meet the test were considered too risky and 'redlined' on confidential maps shared with bankers, whose lack of investment in those neighborhoods doomed many of them to eventual decline."[11] The resulting deterioration and decay of urban neighborhoods hastened the flight to suburbia, first by whites and later by moderate-income African-Americans. Although explicit redlining has now been substantially curtailed, much of America's current spatial development can be traced to the widespread use of such discriminatory practices in the past.[12]

Other federally sponsored institutions that support home ownership via the secondary mortgage market include the Federal National Mortgage Association (Fannie Mae), the Federal Home Loan Mortgage Corporation (Freddie Mac), and the federal Ginnie Mae agency, which guarantees mortgages. Until the 1990s, these federally sponsored institutions had no requirements regarding the spatial distribution of its mortgages, meaning they could ignore city homeowners. These institutions, combined with the Farmers Home Administration and smaller federal programs, have a total mortgage portfolio of $1.8 trillion (as of 1995)—most of which has been used to finance single-family homes in suburbs.[13]

The Housing Act of 1949/urban renewal. This act essentially gave a green light for local officials to break up established neighborhoods in favor of new development, usually involving large-scale commercial initiatives near cities' central business districts. Under this authority, Moe and Wilkie note, "city officials with power of eminent domain could seize property in areas identified as 'slums', purchase it with the help of federal funds, then sell the assembled area to a private developer for redevelopment."[14] Over $13 billion in federal money went to directly support urban renewal between 1953 and 1986. Urban renewal policies brought about the outright destruction of many urban neighborhoods and destabilized many others, causing massive dislocation and overcrowding, and replacing working communities with high-rise public housing projects. All too often, David Rusk charges, "the federal urban renewal program created both dull, lifeless downtown areas that failed to pull suburbanites back into the city and high-poverty, high crime public housing complexes that pushed other households into the suburbs even faster."[15]

Highway construction/National Highway Trust Fund. Hand in hand with the emphasis on establishing middle America in single-family homes in the suburbs was an unprecedented boom in highway expenditures starting in the 1950s. In 1956, the National Highway Trust Fund was established to pay for ongoing highway construction, using revenues generated by taxes on cars and gasoline. U.S. highway construction was thus supported by an autonomous source of revenues not easily touched by other political priorities—a highly unusual mechanism among advanced industrialized democracies. As Pietro Nivola points out, "With a spare-no-expense approach to highway expansions, the size of the U.S. effort became unique. Great distances between cities or states in this country do not wholly account for the magnitude; U.S. interstate plans called for massive expenditures, not just on transcontinental facilities, but also on urban radial and circumferential arteries designed to enhance intra-metropolitan access. These local webs of roadways have sped the dispersal of jobs and housing within metropolitan areas."[16]

Not surprisingly, the percentage of total passenger miles accounted for by public transit in America dropped from 35 percent in 1945 to less than 3 percent today. Between 1977 and 1995 nearly six times as much public funding went to highways and roads as to all forms of mass transit. While critics of Amtrak decry the subsidies needed to keep the intercity rail system in operation, much larger subsidies to highways and automobiles are largely unquestioned politically. Today some 75 percent of federal spending on surface transportation is directed toward highway related projects.[17] Only recently did the 1991 Intermodal Surface Transportation Efficiency Act and the follow-up 1998 TEA-21 legislation begin to take important steps allowing localities some flexibility in promoting mass transit alternatives using federal transportation funds. World Resource Institute economists have estimated that all levels of governments spend over $80 billion a year (1995 dollars) combined on road-related services such as highway patrols.[18]

Low fuel pricing, low taxes on cars, and tax subsidies of parking costs. Suburban growth and sprawl have been driven not only by the massive subsidization of highways but also by direct subsidies to drivers. By international standards, American taxation on gasoline has been exceedingly low: In 1996, gas taxes in the United States totaled 42 cents a gallon, compared with 84 cents in Canada, $2.31 in Great Britain, and over $3 in France, Italy, and the Netherlands.[19] Sales taxes on cars are generally much higher in Europe than in the United States—nine times higher in the Netherlands, thirty-seven times higher in Denmark.[20] American employers are allowed to provide parking as a tax-free benefit, up to $170 a month; the benefit for mass transit users totals just $65 a month.[21] (The parking provision is estimated to cost the United States Treasury over $2 billion a year.)[22]

Tax codes encouraging the discarding of buildings. Other tax laws have also contributed to the decline of cities in favor of new suburban construction and sprawl. On one hand, some observers have complained that building owners receive what is in effect a tax incentive to allow their buildings to decay. Building owners are allowed to depreciate buildings over a period of just 31.5 years. As Moe and Wilkie note, "If property owners could not deduct such losses, they would do more to preserve the value of their property—as well as the value of the surrounding locations that determine the value of their property."[23]

Conversely, other observers have argued that building owners should be taxed *less.* These writers, following the principles of Henry George, have urged a return to land-based, or "site value" taxation. James Howard Kunstler notes that

> our system of property taxes punishes anyone who puts up a decent building made of durable materials. It rewards those who let existing buildings go to hell. It favors speculators who sit on vacant or underutilized land in the hearts of our cities and towns. In doing so it creates an artificial scarcity of land on the free market, which drives up the price of land in general, and encourages ever more scattered development.[24]

Kunstler argues that ending taxation on buildings will encourage the development and preservation of high-quality buildings, while increasing taxation on urban land will discourage speculative activity. This would reduce the costs of urban land by placing more land on the market (as speculators sell) and, by ensuring that all central city land is put to productive use, help undercut pressures toward sprawl. As it is, the existing tax code provides building owners both a disincentive (in the form of building-based taxation) to construct new buildings that appreciate in value over time and an incentive (in the form of accelerated depreciation) to let existing buildings deteriorate. The combined result is increased decay and unattractiveness in center city locations.

High proportion of local property taxes as a source of local revenue. Few Americans realize that in many other advanced countries, such as the United Kingdom and France, national governmental revenues account for the majority of *local* government expenditures. In the United States, only one-third of local government expenditures are funded by federal- and state-level taxes. The reliance of local governments on tax revenues from within their own jurisdictions contributes to the competition between localities for new business investment (as discussed in Chapter 2). However, an additional dimension of the sprawl problem derives from the fact that nearly three-quarters of local taxes are property taxes. As Nivola points out: "Local dependence on property taxation can reinforce a low-density pattern of residential and commercial development. Each jurisdiction acquires an incentive to maximize the assessed valuations of its real estate in relation to the expense of providing local services. One way to defend a favorable ratio [between tax revenue generated and public services provided] is to require through zoning restrictions relatively large parcels of land for buildings."[25] In other words, in order to ensure a strong tax base, suburban localities often seek to bid up taxable land values by promoting not high-density, efficient housing arrangements but large houses and big stores—which in turn implies an auto-dependent design for local communities.

Decreases in federal aid to central cities since 1980. Bruce Katz and Joel Rogers point out that the federal share of municipal budgets declined by over two-thirds between 1980 and 1992 and now stands at less than 4 percent of city budgets. Federal shares of county budgets nationwide have declined even faster, by over 75 percent, since 1980. These cuts in federal aid have taken place at the same time that per capita costs of municipal services have increased. Many state governments also have withdrawn aid for cities. This means local taxes must go up (or city services must be cut back). As Katz and Rogers observe, "The effect of these policies and the resulting income and fiscal dynamics is straightforward. They lower the costs to individuals and firms of living and working outside or on the outer fringes of metropolitan areas, and increase the costs of living and working in the core."[26]

This list of public policies that have contributed to suburbanization and sprawl is hardly exhaustive. It suffices, however, to demonstrate that current spatial patterns in U.S. metropolitan areas are to a substantial degree the result both of political choices and of the peculiar structure of governance in the United States, and not only a result of market processes. To be sure, as Robert Beauregard of New School University has recently argued in detail, the decisions of private economic actors, as well as the overall decline of manufacturing, also played a role in the postwar decline of American cities.[27] In particular, as we have already argued in Chapter 2, corporate decisions to relocate production in a "cheaper" location have imposed large costs on the cities left behind and have compelled citizens to leave town in search of better economic prospects elsewhere. We agree with Beauregard that it is misleading to blame only specific public policy decisions for damage to cities while ignoring the larger pattern of private-sector disinvestment in older industrial centers—but this does not make reevaluating those policies any less important. Indeed, this book is intended to suggest a two-pronged policy response to urban decay and instability: on one hand, changing public policies (such as the ones noted above) that have explicitly damaged central cities and encouraged sprawl, and on the other hand, developing a strategy to contain and ultimately alter the patterns of private sector disinvestment in cities that characterized the second half of the twentieth century.

EVALUATING URBAN SPRAWL

Sprawl, then, is a product of both public policy and private market choices. But were these the right choices? What exactly is wrong with sprawl, especially from the standpoint of a concern with community economic stability (in both cities and suburbs)? Sprawl has been commonly critiqued on six distinct grounds: (1) quality-of-life issues, (2) environmental issues, (3) the waste of public resources via increased infrastructure costs, (4) the effect of sprawl upon cities and their residents, (5) the use of new land to facilitate development of giant corporate-owned superstores, and finally (6) the political consequences of suburbanization. We are concerned about all six dimensions of the sprawl problem, each of which is either directly or indirectly connected to prospects for community economic stability and strengthening local democracy.

Quality of Life and Civic Engagement
When sprawl burst onto the national scene as a potent political issue in 1998, it was largely at the behest of suburban residents themselves. Runaway growth, many suburban residents said, was destroying their quality of life—eating up scenic landscapes, crowding schools, worsening traffic (and lengthening their commutes), and raising taxes.[28] Many rural residents, also, feared losing farmland and rural lifestyles to sprawling development.[29] Loss of open

space, and the loss of the very sense of isolation and quiet that many suburban residents sought when first moving to the outskirts, is an obvious consequence of sprawl. Moreover, the low-density development encourages
automobile dependence—and in fact the number of miles driven per year
has doubled since 1970, with annual growth of over 4 percent a year, a rate
far higher than annual population growth over the same time span.
Consequently, congestion has increased markedly and travel times have
lengthened. The average speed of vehicles on the Washington, D.C.–area
Beltway fell, for instance, from 47 to 23 miles per hour over the course of the
1980s.[30] Since low-density areas are not able to support cost-efficient mass
transit options such as buses, cars are often the only way for many suburban
residents to get around. Hence, there is literally no escaping heavy traffic and
the headaches, lost time, and increased number of accidents it involves.

Such tangible negative effects of sprawl may in time be seen as outweigh-
ing the advantages of suburban amenities such as (relatively) more open
space, larger and cheaper houses, and the like. From our perspective, an even
more important consideration involves the degree to which sprawl also
diminishes the quality of the nation's *civic* life. Low-density development discourages informal interactions between residents, and many planners believe
that such development also discourages residents from joining civic organizations.[31] A recent study by Jack Nasar and David Julian, for instance, found
that mixed-use neighborhoods generated stronger feelings of community
attachment among residents than single-use neighborhoods.[32] Data collected
by Robert Putnam point strongly to a negative relationship between sprawl
and civic engagement: "In round numbers," Putnam reports, "the evidence
suggests that *each additional ten minutes in daily commuting time cuts involvement in community affairs by 10 percent*—fewer public meetings attended,
fewer committees chaired, fewer petitions signed, fewer church services
attended, less volunteering, and so on." This finding, added to the fact that
large places in general (such as metropolitan areas) are in general less conducive to community life than smaller towns, leads Putnam to conclude that
"the residents of large metropolitan areas incur a 'sprawl civic penalty' of
roughly 20 percent on most measures of community involvement. More and
more of us have come to incur this penalty [by moving to suburbs] over the
last thirty years."[33] Finally, it has been widely observed that European cities,
with their more compact form of organization, appear to have more vibrant
public spaces and a stronger sense of place than comparably sized American
metropolitan areas.[34]

The quest for the suburban version of the American dream—including
owning a single-family home in a good neighborhood with good schools—is

also closely associated with the search for status within American society and the use of consumption as a marker for social status. The corresponding political and cultural ethos of prioritizing the search for one's private dream of suburban comfort over provision of public goods and engagement in public affairs is both symptom and cause of the often hollow practice of local-level democratic governance today.[35] Much more evidence needs to be accumulated to document fully the impact of different kinds of spatial design upon civic life and civic participation. But there is already good reason to believe that sprawl, by undermining central cities (and, increasingly, older suburbs as well), negatively impacts not only community economic stability per se but also the quality of community daily life—and that more-compact, less car-centered spatial designs would probably be more compatible with a strong civic community.

Environmental Concerns

It is little surprise that environmental groups such as the Sierra Club have taken the lead in the national antisprawl movement. Sprawl is synonymous with the consumption of open land, including both farmland and forest habitats, as well as with the greenhouse gas emissions and wasted fuel associated with automobile use and traffic congestion.

There are scores of studies of the environmental consequences of sprawl-like development, many of which have been usefully collected in the Natural Resources Defense Council publication *Once There Were Greenfields*. Space permits only a general overview of the picture painted by the drumbeat of scholarly research over the past decade.

Outward development obviously consumes land—lots of land. According to the American Farmland Trust, between 1982 and 1992 alone, over 4.2 million acres of top-quality farmland—and a total of over 13.8 million acres of agricultural land—were lost to development.[36] Land consumption also impacts the overall ecosystem in ways that damage existing wildlife and reduce biological diversity; as existing wildlife habitats are fragmented, they become less capable of supporting a wide variety of species. The phenomenon is especially true of wetlands, which lost a net 117,000 acres between 1985 and 1995, with development responsible for roughly one-fifth of the decline.[37]

Next, there is the environmental impact of suburban driving patterns. A recent HUD report notes that "the average suburban household drives approximately 30 percent more annually than its central city counterpart. That is about 3,300 more miles, which translates to an additional $753 per year per household in transportation costs. Suburban residents spend 110 more hours behind the wheel each year than their urban counterparts—the equivalent of almost 3 full weeks of work."[38] Although many forms of urban air pollution have eased in the past two decades, cars are still a major source of air pollutants, responsible for 62 percent of carbon monoxide releases, as well as 26 percent of volatile organic compound releases and 32 percent of nitrogen oxide releases—two major ingredients in the generation of health-threatening ground-level ozone. A 1998 EPA study estimated that traffic congestion alone generates at least $20 billion a year in health-related costs.[39] While cars have become substantially cleaner in many respects, that gain has been largely offset by the increase in miles driven. Indeed, the trend in Americans' use of cars is negative, not positive—the number of Americans who drive solo to work increased from 64 percent in 1980 to 73 percent in 1990.[40] Moreover, the vehicles now on the road are bigger than ever. Trucks, minivans, and sport-utility vehicles, which are not held to the same fuel efficiency requirements as cars, now account for nearly half of family automobile sales—and, as the NRDC notes, "the 10 most fuel-efficient vehicles in the country today account for only 0.7 percent of all vehicle sales."[41]

A problem potentially even more serious than air pollution is the emission of greenhouse gases by motor vehicles. Mobile sources (i.e., vehicles) now account for 32 percent of all greenhouse gas releases in the United States. Carbon emissions are projected to continue to increase at a rate of 1 percent a year if current habits are maintained, with transportation's share in the total increasing relative to other sources. Simply put, community spatial designs that maximize the amount of driving and gas consumption required to meet the tasks of daily life appear to be fundamentally incompatible with the need to reduce greenhouse emissions in order to forestall or mitigate the potentially disastrous effects of global climate change.[42]

Finally, sprawl increases runoff water pollution. Whereas natural habitats absorb rainfall easily, with runoff into water bodies commonly taking place at a slow, easily absorbable pace, in built-up areas water collects on man-made surfaces such as rooftops and pavements, eventually passing into water sources at higher speeds and in higher quantity. Such runoff causes erosion, generates increased water pollution, and damages underlying water tables. It is estimated that 40 percent of the nation's water bodies are now being damaged by runoff pollution. As sprawl increases the amount of paved area, it contributes more and more to damaging forms of water runoff. Particularly damaging are huge parking lots constructed to service superstores on the suburban fringe. It is little surprise, then, that sprawl-like development has been identified as a causal factor in damage to a number of major water bodies, including perhaps most prominently Chesapeake Bay, along the coast of Virginia, Delaware, and Maryland.[43]

Infrastructure Costs Associated with Sprawl

Quality of community and civic life and environmental well-being have potentially important long-term effects on communities' economic prospects. There are also, however, very direct and immediate costs of sprawl—especially the cost of infrastructure. It is well established that providing roads, water lines, sewers, electric grids, schools, hospitals, police and fire services, and the like to serve low-density development is, in general, more costly than providing such infrastructure to high-density developments. It is also obvious that it is wasteful to allow existing city infrastructure to decay while simultaneously building new developments requiring entirely new infrastructure. Yet that is exactly what sprawl entails. Minnesota legislator and respected scholar Mryon Orfield provides but one illustration of an all-too-common (and understudied) phenomenon: "By 1990, 131,488 acres—nearly one-quarter of [the Twin Cities urban areas served by sewers]—remained undeveloped. Yet between 1987 and 1991 at the request of cities and developers the Metropolitan Council provided sewer access for another 18,000 acres, instead of redirecting new growth into areas with adequate sewer capacity."[44]

A number of empirical studies have been conducted that attempt to estimate the infrastructure and fiscal costs of sprawl-driven development. A 1989 study by James Frank, for instance, compared the public capital costs (including streets, utilities, and schools) associated with different densities of development. Total public capital costs per dwelling unit for a suburban single-family home on four acres (a very large lot) amounted to over $77,000 per unit in 1987 dollars. In the more typical single-family-house neighborhood (three homes per acre), costs per unit came to roughly $31,000. As density increased, costs got progressively lower, including $17,000 per unit for apartment buildings with fifteen dwellings per acre and less than $8,000 per unit for high-rise apartments with 30 dwellings per acre.[45]

Another study, by James Duncan and Associates, based on a detailed study of eight communities in Florida, also focused on the public capital costs associated with different forms of development. Duncan calculated the cost to the public per dwelling unit for providing the following services: roads, education, wastewater, potable water, solid-waste disposal, law enforcement, fire protection, and parks. Two communities with scattered development patterns (i.e., low-density and leapfrog) had costs (in 1998 dollars) of $20,158 and $31,534 per dwelling, respectively. In contrast, the downtown area, featuring compact development, had costs of just $12,177 per unit, and two contiguous developments (moderate-density and built contiguously with existing developments) had costs of only $12,855 and $16,706, respectively.[46]

A third study led by Robert Burchell used computer models to project the future costs to the public associated with different types of development patterns in New Jersey. One development pattern built up central-city areas and increased density rates; the other continued sprawl-like development (low-density and scattered). Public capital costs (roads, utilities, and schools) associated with the sprawl-like development were estimated to total $15.64 billion (1990 dollars) over a twenty-year period, compared to costs of $14.21 billion for compact development. As F. Kaid Benfield, Matthew Raimi, and Donald Chen of the Natural Resources Defense Council observe, if the state had chosen to develop entirely along a compact spatial model starting in 1990, the savings in capital costs would have amounted to $1.79 billion (1998 dollars) over the twenty-year period from 1990 to 2010.[47]

Important qualifications to these studies of the infrastructure costs associated with sprawl have been offered by other researchers, most notably Harvard scholars Alan Altshuler and José Gómez-Ibáñez. Altshuler and Gómez-Ibáñez point out that early studies of sprawl such as the Real Estate Research Corporation's 1973 publication *The Costs of Sprawl* showing higher infrastructure costs for suburban housing did not take into account the fact that suburban housing is often of higher quality and provides more space than urban housing. These scholars also point out that high initial infrastructure costs associated with sprawl may decline if infill development occurs, that retrofitting older areas to accommodate higher density patterns may be more expensive than suburban developments on vacant land, and that in some cases suburban developments can achieve cost-saving economies of scale.

Even so, Altshuler and Gómez-Ibáñez conservatively allow that sprawl developments typically will be about 5 to 10 percent more expensive than well-planned, more compact developments.[48] Moreover, the most recent wave of research by Burchell and other scholars takes account of Altshuler and Gómez-Ibáñez's criticisms of earlier studies and continues to find that compact living patterns are cheaper.[49] Finally, no one disputes that it is almost always wasteful to abandon already-built infrastructure in central cities and inner suburbs at the same time that entirely new developments on metropolitan perimeters are being built.

Central-City Decline and the Costs of Greenfield Development

Advocates of outward growth from central cities often cite the need to provide lower-cost housing as a prime justification for sprawl-like development. But when more affluent residents leave cities (and no one replaces them), they also take their property tax payments with them—thus helping push cities into a fiscal crunch that damages their ability to provide even basic government services. A vicious circle is thus often triggered by suburban flight: As residents leave and the tax base declines, it becomes more difficult to pay for social services to city residents. New small businesses expand to—or even relocate to—suburbia in order to directly serve the affluent populace there, making it more difficult for cities to increase their tax base or provide new jobs through business growth. And as the quality of services such as pothole fixing, police and fire, and (perhaps above all) public schools declines in cities, the incentive to move (for both rich and poor) increases. Finally, as jobs move to the suburbs, more inner-city residents, lacking adequate access to transportation and social networks to take advantage of suburban employment opportunities, fall into long-term unemployment, with devastating personal and social consequences.[50] As we have seen, in some cases the destruction of existing center-city neighborhoods has been quite deliberate, as planners razed perceived ghetto areas under the rubric of "urban renewal," substituting higher-income neighborhoods or commercial development in their place. On occasion, neighborhoods were destroyed to provide the very highways that would carry new residents of suburbia back and forth from city jobs to their new, more spacious homes. The move to suburbia also damages existing social networks within the cities and can lead to a widened income gap between rich and poor within cities when middle-class residents move to the suburbs in force—which in turn heightens social tension.[51]

Many defenders of sprawl-style suburbanization point to the tangible private benefits of outward development, holding that the benefits that accrue to business and individuals outweigh these negative social and public costs. However, the most comprehensive and highly detailed cost-benefit analysis to date of the comparative costs of firm location in greenfields (i.e., undeveloped areas on the suburban fringe) versus firm location in cities tells a different story. The recent landmark study *When Corporations Leave Town*, conducted by Joseph Persky and Wim Wiewel of the University of Illinois at Chicago, demonstrates that the *public* and social *costs* of sprawl-like development are roughly equivalent to the *private benefits* created. In other words, sprawl is a redistributive measure, imposing costs on the public and central-city residents while conferring benefits on suburban firms and residents.

The costs of sprawl include both externalities generated by private actors (but borne by other private and public actors) and direct public fiscal costs. Regarding the first of these costs, Persky and Wiewel carefully take account of six types of externalities associated with sprawl. First, they provide summary estimates of the magnitude of specific sprawl-related costs in the existing literature. Persky and Wiewel then provide their own estimates of such costs in the Chicago metropolitan area, using the expense of building a new electrical equipment plant with 1,000 employees in a greenfield as opposed to an existing urban area as a test case.

- *Traffic congestion.* A number of empirical studies have shown that unpaid costs of driving to work (that is, costs not paid by the driver, such as road upkeep and contribution to congestion) range from roughly 10 cents to 50 cents per mile driven, depending on the setting. Persky and Wiewel estimate that building the new electrical equipment plant in a greenfield location would create $4 million in congestion-related externalities, compared to only $3.5 million for a central-city plant.

- *Accidents.* Based on previous research estimating the costs to the public of traffic accidents, Persky and Wiewel estimate that locating the new firm in a greenfield site would create $1.1 million in accident-related costs, compared to $1 million in such costs for a central-city location. The savings are due to the fact that fewer new vehicles would be put on the road by the central-city plant.

- *Air pollution.* Again using previous estimates of the air pollution generated by automobiles, Persky and Wiewel estimate that a new central-city plant will generate $160,000 in air pollution costs, compared to $178,000 for the greenfield plant.

- *Open space lost.* Persky and Wiewel observe that attempts to quantify the costs of open space lost are inherently problematic because they depend on estimates of citizens' willingness to pay for open space. Nonetheless, based on existing research, they estimate that the value of preserving each acre of open space in the Chicago area to be roughly $180 an acre. Given the expectation that building the new electrical equipment plant in the greenfield site will consume 537 acres of open land (mostly due to new housing and infrastructure built to serve the site and its workers), compared to 156 acres absorbed in the case of a central-city plant, Persky and Wiewel conclude that the greenfield location will create an annual welfare loss of roughly $97,000, compared to $28,000 a year in the case of a central-city plant.

- *Waste of existing housing.* Persky and Wiewel point out that too little is known about the costs of abandoned or run-down housing in central city locations. Such housing is thought to lead to a decline in the property values of neighboring buildings and is also associated with increases in crime and the like, but little empirical work has been undertaken to pinpoint the magnitude of such costs. Assuming that a run-down building leads to a 5 percent annual decline in the capital value of the eight nearest neighboring properties, and that the central-city firm will provide employment to 170 more households who would otherwise be impoverished and unable to maintain their housing than greenfield firms, Persky and Wiewel estimate that a new central-city plant would generate $46,000 a year in "abandonment savings" compared to the greenfield plant.

- *Spatial mismatch.* While numerous researchers have pointed to the mismatch between plentiful suburban jobs and unemployed central-city residents as one of the costs of sprawl, research has not yet quantified the efficiency costs of such a mismatch. Persky and Wiewel estimate that 319 low-wage workers from low-income households would find employment at the plant if it was located in the central city, whereas only 245 such low-wage, poor-household workers would find employment if the plant was located at a greenfield site. That results in an estimated $456,000 less income flowing to low-wage, poor workers in the greenfield scenario compared to building the plant in the central city. (It is assumed that if the plant was built in the central city, the 74 fewer non-poor workers who would not have employment would experience no net welfare loss, since they could likely find other jobs at the same wage. This assumption obviously may not hold in slack labor markets.)

In sum, Persky and Wiewel conclude that the greenfield plant with 1,000 workers would produce $1.1 million more in negative externalities than a similarly sized central-city plant, the great bulk of which is due to increased traffic congestion and the welfare loss of poor workers unable to access the greenfield site's jobs.

But even this is not the whole story. Sprawl also imposes a second set of costs upon the public sector. It might be argued that so long as those who move from cities to the low-density suburban areas pay the full costs of the move, suburbanization places no fiscal burden on the public. Persky and Wiewel examine this issue in the Chicago setting and find a striking difference between the fiscal impact of a typical middle-class household in Chicago as opposed to one in its outer suburbs. Within the city, each new middle-class household brings a net gain to the public coffers of over $1,400 (taxes, fees, etc. generated by the household's presence in the city minus services provided by the city). But within the outer suburbs, where the marginal cost of providing additional public services is much higher, each new middle-class household brings a net loss of over $650. (In inner suburbs, the net loss is just $99.) Based on these findings, Persky and Wiewel conclude that the new central-city plant, by encouraging central-city residency, would create a net fiscal gain for all governments in the metropolitan area of $680,000 (most of which would be captured by the central city). In contrast, the greenfield site would generate a net fiscal *loss* of $20,000 for all governments in the metropolitan region as result of new residents.

The fiscal benefits of increased business activity and business taxes paid also favor the central site location: Persky and Wiewel estimate that the new central city site would yield a fiscal benefit from business of $1 million, compared to $750,000 for the greenfield site (largely due to the higher tax rates within the city). The total positive net fiscal impact of the central city site would be $1.66 million, compared to just $740,000 for the greenfield location.

Finally, the costs of government programs to subsidize highway and housing (such as the mortgage deduction for homeowners) as well as fiscal impacts on the rest of the nation must be considered. Persky and Wiewel estimate that the greenfield site would lead to $210,000 in additional annual spending on highways and $350,000 additional annual spending on housing subsidies, since the greenfield plant creates more homeowners who can claim the mortgage deduction. The greenfield site also imposes $62,000 more in fiscal costs on the rest of the nation than the central-city plant, since more poor households will require subsidies from higher levels of government.

Combining the externality costs of a greenfield site with the public-sector costs, Persky and Wiewel estimate that building the new 1,000-employee electrical equipment plant in a greenfield will produce $2.67 million a year more in social costs than a central-city location. To complete the cost-benefit analysis, however, these publicly or socially borne costs need to be weighed against private benefits from greenfield development. These benefits consist principally of (1) reduced wage costs for businesses in the suburbs, and (2) reduced land, construction, and tax costs for business. Persky and Wiewel estimate that the net *private* benefits overall of locating a firm in the outer suburbs compared to the central city total $2.6 million a year.[52]

Looking at this picture as a whole, Persky and Wiewel conclude that "the costs and benefits associated with the continuing deconcentration of manufacturing are of the same order of magnitude." In subsequent analysis, however, Persky and Wiewel show that deconcentration distributes its benefits in a regressive fashion. [53] Moreover, Persky and Wiewel have also stressed that this analysis is of cities and suburbs as they are—not as "they might be after considerable reinvestment in infrastructure, schools, and public services," reinvestment which would further improve the efficiency of locating plants in cities.[54] As noted above, while the unpaid costs and foregone benefits associated with disinvestment in cities harm the public at large, they tend to impose especially serious hardships on central-city residents. In short, even if *some* individuals gain, their gain is at the expense of other individuals and the public at large—hardly an optimal recipe for good public policy.

Superstores versus Local Business
A fifth dimension of the sprawl problem, not captured by cost-benefit analyses of the kind utilized by Persky and Wiewel or in studies of the infrastructure costs of different forms of development, is the extent to which sprawl-like development has influenced what *kinds* of firms get access to a critical mass of customers and enjoy favorable prospects of success. Specifically, when residents move to the suburbs from central cities, locally owned city businesses are often not well positioned to follow their customer base. Firms with a greater capacity to adjust to changing geographic patterns gain an advantage over firms reliant on a stable, neighborhood-oriented customer base. In practice, this means that large chains—Wal-Mart, fast-food operators, Circuit City, and the long list of ubiquitous corporate chains—have thrived in strip malls, exurbs, and big box-style superstores located on the edge of town. Suburban shopping centers increased from just 100 in 1950 to 3,000 in 1960 and nearly 40,000 by 1992.[55] As Stacy Mitchell of the Institute for Local Self-Reliance notes, Borders Books and Barnes and Nobles alone now account for 25 percent of all book sales, while independent booksellers have seen their market share fall from 58 percent in 1972 to 17 percent (and dropping) as of 1997. Home Depot and Lowe's together control almost 25 percent of the hardware market. Blockbuster Video has 30 percent of the video rental market. Needless to say, locally-owned retailers have not fared as well. Independent office product stores have seen their market share decline from 20 to 4 percent since the mid-1980s, and an estimated 1,000 community pharmacies close annually.[56]

In fact, in a few cases, most spectacularly that of Wal-Mart, chains have deliberately tried to kill off local businesses through predatory pricing, often with the help of state and local subsidies (such as assistance in providing roads and other infrastructure needed to bring large waves of consumers to just-outside-the-city-limits superstores). Developers of new malls and shopping centers often gravitate toward nationally known chains in extending lease offers as a strategy for luring customers as soon as possible. Even in the best-case scenario, where such malls do make homes for local, nonchain businesses, they are commonly anchored by corporate chain department stores. Meanwhile, vibrant downtowns consisting of local businesses owned by local people have become increasingly rare.

What exactly is wrong with chain store development, as compared to locally owned businesses? Certainly the American strip-mall-with-parking-lot scene is often a painful eyesore, an aesthetic nightmare. Moreover, in line with a long tradition of American thought, we believe that the sense of independence and liberty associated with individual or family entrepreneurship is an important value. But local entrepreneurship also has a tangible advantage over the typical corporate chain from the point of view of community economic stability: They are more likely to create purchasing linkages with other local firms, which in turn expands a community's economic multiplier as money gets respent many times in the local economy. Similarly, their profits are not siphoned off to a faraway corporate headquarters, but instead are more likely to be reinvested in the community.[57]

The most detailed studies to date of how superstores affect local communities have been carried out by Kenneth Stone of Iowa State University, who for over a decade has continuously tracked the impact of Wal-Mart on rural communities in Iowa. In a 1997 study, Stone compared thirty-four towns with a Wal-Mart in place for ten years or more with fifteen non–Wal-Mart towns. He found that in a context of overall rural decline, Wal-Mart captured a rapidly increasing share of the shrinking pie—causing damage to independent retailers in Wal-Mart towns. They hurt non–Wal-Mart towns even more by drawing customers away. Overall sales declined by 17 percent in Iowa towns with population between 2,500 and 5,000 in the period between 1983 and 1996, nearly 30 percent for towns with between 1,000 and 2,500 residents, and over 40 percent in towns with fewer than 1,000 people. Shopping at department stores (i.e., Wal-Marts) increased by 42 percent over the same period, whereas drugstores, variety stores, and stores selling automotive parts, groceries, women's apparel, lawn and garden items, hardware, shoes, and men's and boys' wear all suffered significant declines (25 percent or more for all save auto parts and grocery stores) during those years.[58]

These are alarming findings. As Stone concludes, there are strong reasons for seeking to constrict, not accelerate, the growth of superstores—whether the small businesses damaged by the new store are rural or urban. Sadly, it is the fact of widespread economic insecurity that makes low-end retail outlets

—whose rise has been predicated not only on sophisticated distribution systems but also on the use of market power to squeeze suppliers—so attractive to many working-class and poor shoppers anxious to save as much money as possible. But the rise of Wal-Mart-type retail only further undercuts the economic security of small towns and their residents. Nor does Wal-Mart compensate for this negative impact by providing good jobs: The retailer considers a 28-hour week full time, virtually all nonmanagement employees earn less than $10 an hour, and there are few benefits (and no unions).[59]

The Political Consequences of Sprawl

Finally, we call attention to the political culture sprawl has helped generate: namely, a city-suburb divide that has weakened public support for efforts to support community development or to provide other forms of assistance to urban areas. As suburbs grow and central cities lose population, the relative political power of city interests in electoral and legislative politics erodes; presidential and gubernatorial candidates court suburban voters, while urban delegations in both national and state legislatures shrink. More importantly, the creation of largely white suburbs, spatially segregated from lower-class minority groups remaining in central cities, has had an inestimable impact on American political culture and the assumptions of ordinary political debate.[60] It has allowed politicians to define suburban life as mainstream America and central-city residents as a "problem," or what some sociologists call "the other." Lost is the idea that all are in it together. Noted "new urbanist" practitioners Andres Duany, Elizabeth Plater-Zyberk, and Jeff Speck make the point this way:

> A child growing up in [a] homogenous environment is less likely to develop a sense of empathy for people from other walks of life and is ill prepared to live in a diverse society. The *other* becomes alien to the child's experience, witnessed only through the sensationalized eye of the television. The more homogenous and "safe" the environment, the less understanding there is of all that is different, and the less concern for the world beyond the subdivision walls.[61]

Recent research by Juliet Gainsborough of the University of Miami has also demonstrated that suburban residence has a powerful conservative influence on both voters and political attitudes—even *after* controlling for race, gender, age, income, homeownership status, and other standard variables used to predict political orientation. Gainsborough's analysis of National Election Study data found that between 1988 and 1992, living in the suburbs made voters substantially more likely to vote for a Republican congressional or presidential candidate, an effect that cannot be explained by demographic factors. In an even more interesting finding, Gainsborough also found that suburbanites are less likely than others to support aid for cities, government spending, and initiatives to help African-Americans, or to have a sympathetic attitude toward welfare recipients—even *after* controlling for the respondents' party identification as well as other demographic variables. In short, living in the suburbs produces more conservative social attitudes even among self-identified Democrats. Gainsborough's analysis also shows that the strength of this association between suburban residence and conservative social attitudes has intensified in the past two decades—precisely as suburbs have continued to claim a larger share of the nation's population.[62]

We rarely face this issue directly. The problem is not simply that metropolitan areas find it difficult to tax suburbs to pay for the central city—or even to tax commuters enough to pay for the costs of the public goods they themselves consume. It is that our policies systematically create a political-economic reality where inequalities favoring predominantly white suburbs become the rule rather than the exception.[63]

THE TURNING OF THE TIDE?

For years, environmental activists, preservationists, and urban planners who decried sprawl were lonely voices in the political wilderness. Indeed, it was thought all but impossible to do much about the problem in real political terms. In the late 1990s, however—in a manner suggestive of what we believe might be possible with a number of other issues taken up in this volume—a very substantial grouping of state-level politicians "suddenly" caught wind of the widespread public discontent with suburban sprawl, and began to incorporate concerns about sprawl in their political agendas.

Obviously, something quite powerful had already been quietly building below the radar of the mass media. In November 1998, nearly two hundred state and local ballot initiatives on curbing sprawl won approval, as voters set aside more than $7 billion to purchase land or development rights for preservation.[64] In New Jersey, for example—the only state to be technically defined in its entirety as a metropolitan area,[65] and a state that loses 10,000 acres a year to development—a two-thirds majority of voters approved Republican Governor Christine Todd Whitman's proposal to invest $1 billion over a decade to protect one million acres of undeveloped land, half the state's total.[66] Similarly, Florida voters made permanent the state's land conservation bonding authority—which will likely lead to $3 billion in additional financing for land conservation.[67] In Arizona, a measure to spend $220 million over an eleven year period to buy open space won approval.[68] Programs to preserve farmland and open space were also approved in Minnesota, Michigan, Oregon, and Rhode Island.

At the local level, dozens of cities—including seven in California—passed referendums and other ballot measures to impose clear boundaries on future development. Because of a series of such boundaries approved in Ventura County, California, about 80 percent of the county has been preserved from further development. On Cape Cod, voters in the fifteen towns of Barnstable County, Massachusetts approved a "local-option three percent property tax assessment to finance community land banks." In Austin, Texas, voters approved a bond issue of $76 million to support parks and greenways; Austin residents had previously voted to pay $65 million in increased water rates to preserve 15,000 acres of land outside the city.[69] And in New Jersey, in addition to the statewide measure, forty-three cities and six counties approved separate tax increases to finance additional preservation measures.[70]

To date, the most committed anti-sprawl elected official at the state level has been Maryland governor Paris Glendening. During his first term (1995–99), Glendening succeeded in passing several antisprawl measures, including the Rural Legacy program (which "earmarks more than $71 million over the next five years to purchase development rights on environmentally valuable land") and the Smart Growth Areas Act (which "restricts state funding for road and sewer projects to those in older communities and areas already slated for growth").[71] Glendening stressed these polices and continued to spread the antisprawl word during his successful 1998 bid for reelection: "We cannot continue to go on with the old patterns of development," he said. "It doesn't make any financial sense. It doesn't make any environmental sense. It destroys the sense of community."[72] In his second term, Glendening has moved to tie state assistance to counties to how aggressively each county provides open space and curtails sprawl.[73] State funding for school infrastructure has also shifted dramatically in Maryland, as the state now commits 80 percent of the school construction budget to established areas, whereas in the early 1990s over 60 percent of school construction funds were spent in newly developed areas.[74] Other state agencies such as the state Department of Transportation have also undergone major shifts in policy (as well as their internal culture): transportation planners in the state are now encouraged to take into account the needs of pedestrians and the impact of transportation projects on community well-being, instead of bulldozing and laying pavement in every direction.[75]

The antisprawl movement now involves not only environmentalists decrying the loss of habitat and auto exhaust, liberals seeking to stave off inner-city decline, and suburbanites and rural residents seeking to preserve their quality of life, but also members of the business community who believe that sprawl is "bad for business." The Bank of America, for instance, published a comprehensive critique of the impact of sprawl in California in 1996. In 1999 *Governing* editor Alan Ehrenhalt, reporting on Atlanta, noted that antisprawl sentiments there "have spread through [the] entire business community with remarkable speed and intensity. . . . Everybody in Atlanta seems to be against sprawl now—developers, bankers, utility companies, all the interests that have profited from it for five decades. 'You think back two years,' says John Sibley, chairman of the environmentalist Georgia Conservancy, 'and the change in the mind-set is stunning.'"[76] Another 1999 study by the National Association of Local Government Environmental Professionals documented nineteen business-led "smart growth" initiatives nationwide.[77] For instance, the influential Silicon Valley Manufacturing Group has actively promoted high-density development, public transit, and additional low-income housing both in California and nationally.[78]

Former vice president Al Gore also embraced the idea of smart growth during the second Clinton term. The Clinton administration created a Livable Communities Initiative within the Environmental Protection Agency, and established several modest antisprawl policies, such as a home loan pilot program to encourage housing near mass transit, and a $17 million program to buy 53,000 acres of farmland nationwide.[79] The 2000 Democratic platform endorsed the idea of Better America Bonds, which would have provided tax credits to states and localities on bond issues aimed at building "livable communities" (that is, containing sprawl) by preserving open spaces, farmland, and parks and acquiring more land for preservation and recreation purposes.[80]

Antisprawl momentum continued into the 2000 campaign, as Arizona voters considered a statewide antisprawl proposition (which was strongly opposed by the real estate industry), and a similar measure was proposed in Colorado. The Arizona legislation would have established strong growth boundaries statewide, while the Colorado legislation, following the lead of Oregon, would have mandated that localities develop and receive voter approval for comprehensive land-use plans.[81] Both the Colorado and Arizona measures were defeated by wide margins, but activists in both states have claimed that the initiatives helped alter the public debate about growth in each state.

THE IMPERATIVE OF COMMUNITY-CONTROLLED LAND

We are sympathetic to most of the policy measures now being implemented in Maryland and other localities that aim to contain sprawl. But we remain skeptical about the long-term effectiveness of sprawl-fighting policies that fail to address one of the underlying structural realities driving sprawl, namely, control of land by powerful private actors, not only in rural areas but in urban areas as well. As we have already seen, the principle of using public funds to buy undeveloped, often rural, land for conservation purposes is now broadly accepted across party lines. Equally critical is establishing a measure of community control over *urban* land—not as a means of directly stalling outward development but to ensure that sprawl-stopping measures do not perversely disadvantage low-income city residents by raising housing costs.

Here a major problem must be noted: As already experienced in the growth-boundary city of Portland—which has been rated by the National Homebuilders Association as the second most expensive housing market in the nation—over time we can expect urban land values to rise in cases where outward development is curtailed. The rise in land values translates into increased rents, which in turn make city living unaffordable for low-income renters—who are often replaced by higher-income residents in a gentrification process.[82] While some analysts sympathetic to growth boundaries have noted that housing prices have also risen in fast-growing metropolitan areas without growth boundaries— a recent econometric study concluded that Portland's urban growth boundary is "probably not" primarily responsible for rising housing prices in the city—most acknowledge the theoretical point that limiting the supply of available land on which to build housing is likely to place upward pressure on housing prices.[83] The obvious antidote to this consequence of antisprawl public policy is to make direct provision for low-income housing. This might happen by expanding publicly subsidized housing units or by rehabilitating existing housing stock that has fallen into disrepair. Stable low- and middle-income housing can also be secured by means of urban community land trusts. In the latter, units, blocks, or conceivably entire neighborhoods are placed in a trust. Low-income residents can rent or own units on land controlled by the trust, but owners must resell housing back to the trust, not an outside buyer. This effectively takes the units in question out of the private housing market and guarantees that rising land values and urban rebirth do not displace poor residents. As discussed in detail in Chapter 11, there are over one hundred urban land trusts now operating in the United States, and the number is steadily growing.

It is likely that the next decade will see the further development of land trust mechanisms both to preserve open space and to take increasing increments of urban land off the market. Possibly some cities may experiment with site value taxation of the sort advocated by Kunstler, in which land is taxed more heavily than buildings in urban areas, thereby dampening land speculation activities. In the longer term, we also think it makes sense to reconsider the vision Ebenezer Howard laid out at the end of the nineteenth century—cities (be they old cities or new towns) in which the public directly owns both urban land and immediately outlying areas, and can take effective steps to shape land development. Over time, treating land not as a simple commodity but as a community resource that should be under substantial democratic control will be a crucial lever in a serious long-term attack on sprawl-like development. It will also be critical to the restoration of substantive local-level democracy, in which private developers and other land-oriented businesspeople do not have overwhelming political power, especially with respect to urban planning decisions and the use of public resources in economic development.

STRATEGIES AND SOLUTIONS

Urban sprawl clearly will have a lasting place on the national agenda. Leaving aside the long-term goal of bringing more land under direct democratic control, which short-term and medium-term policies and strategies hold the best prospect of actually containing fringe development and preserving existing communities (both urban and suburban)? Following Persky, Wiewel, and Sendzik, the available strategies can be summarized and grouped into four categories: policies intended to stall "deconcentration," redistributive policies aimed at mitigating the consequences of sprawl, policies to develop mechanisms of regional governance, and policies aimed at revitalizing urban centers.[84]

Containing Deconcentration

Policies to raise the costs of deconcentration include a range of approaches that fall under the rubric of growth management. Specific tactics to limit growth through land-use planning include zoning rules intended to constrain new development, impact fees that charge developers for the public costs incurred by new development, and public intervention into land markets to deliberately limit new development. The paradigmatic example of growth management is Portland, Oregon, which has essentially prevented development in outlying areas by establishing and enforcing a growth boundary. As noted above, a number of states have recognized the obvious fact that buying undeveloped tracts of land for preservation purposes (or arranging for nonprofit preservation groups to do so) can help prevent undesired outward development.

More common than direct intervention into land markets is the use of impact fees: Developers and businesses are charged a fee to help cover the estimated costs to the public (roads, sewers, etc.) of new development projects. Various studies suggest that impact fees appear to be moderately effective, but insufficient empirical evidence exists to make firm judgments. Impact fees have been criticized for essentially providing a windfall to existing residents of a community, since by raising the cost of new housing, such fees also raise the value of existing land and buildings within a community.[85] There is also uncertainty over the best method of calculating how high impact fees should be. Impact fees will almost certainly continue to be used as a check on sprawl, but they are a relatively weak tool and unlikely on their own to seriously constrain or reverse outward growth. (Ironically, as more communities adopt impact fees, their relative effectiveness as an anti-growth measure in any particular place is likely to decline, since the competitive disadvantage of developing in an impact-fee-imposing locality disappears if all localities have such fees. Impact fees would still be defensible and desirable in that eventuality, however, as a way to force private developers to pay a larger share of the costs of new growth, and if *all* suburbs adopted such fees and cities did not, that could increase the attractiveness of cities to developers.)

Another available approach is congestion pricing. Congestion pricing simply refers to increased tolls on rush-hour traffic in congested driving areas, to compel drivers to pay more of the actual social cost of using roads at peak hours. In principle such pricing schemes could raise the cost of travel sufficiently so that firms would be compelled to locate on sites that can be accessed without causing additional traffic. Congestion pricing has been attempted only on a limited basis in the United States, although several cities worldwide have implemented such schemes.[86]

Redistributing Costs and Benefits

A second set of policies attempt to redistribute the benefits associated with suburban growth. Such policies include:

- "Reverse commuting" policies, which seek to subsidize transportation for central-city residents to suburban job opportunities

- Constructing low-income housing in the suburbs (which implies overturning often exclusionary zoning practices)

- Tax-base sharing in which cities and suburbs effectively share revenue from property taxes, as has been practiced in the Twin Cities area in Minnesota for the past three decades

- Special regional governance bodies, which have authority over a specific issue involving both urban and suburban areas (such as water supply)[87]

None of these policies is capable of seriously redressing urban sprawl; the intent is to make the best of the current situation through modifications that benefit low-income residents. Unfortunately, such programs face the same political obstacles encountered by other programs to help poor citizens, and tax-base sharing is especially unlikely to be accepted politically, since suburban residents by and large do not want to pay for "urban problems."

Regional Governance Mechanisms

A third antisprawl tactic is the development of formal regional governance authorities, on the model of the Unigov system of combined city and county governance practiced in Indianapolis. Such authorities provide the same benefits as tax-based revenue sharing schemes (allowing suburban tax money to be used to combat urban problems) but may be more efficient in providing public infrastructure and in imposing policies such as impact fees. Regional governance approaches suffer from the same problem of political feasibility that tax-sharing schemes face. Nonetheless, the emergence of regional governance mechanisms would be highly desirable and would make a coordinated antisprawl effort much more plausible. Establishment of such mechanisms, however, would ultimately depend on new city-suburb alliances, based on the realization, as Wiewel and colleagues note, that "suburbs with strong central cities fare better themselves in terms of income and home values."[88] Peter Dreier, John Mollenkopf, and Todd Swanstrom have called upon the federal government to actively promote regional-level governance and cooperation by making metropolitan regions the operational unit for many federal progams.[89]

Revitalizing Cities

A final set of strategies focuses less upon changes in the rules governing suburban expansion than upon making central cities more attractive. These strategies, falling under the broad rubric of community development, will be taken up in much greater detail in Parts II and III of this volume. When urban neighborhoods gain economic stability and become more attractive places to live, some of the distributive effects of sprawl can be countered (such as lack of access by urban residents to suburban jobs). Equally important, there is less impetus for flight to the suburbs on the part of middle-class, high-revenue citizens, as social costs and dysfunctions associated with central-city decline are reduced. As we have noted, making use of existing infrastructure and buildings also has advantages over the construction of new buildings and infrastructure in an effort to escape inner-city decay.

* * *

Consideration of each of the three principal threats to community economic stability in the United States in Part I—the effects of globalization, capital mobility between states, and sprawl—all point in a common policy direction: the need to provide localities with stable economies that will not be blown away by changes in market conditions or in the overall economy, that do not run away when the next opportunity comes along, and that do not relocate to greenfields in order to escape problems at home. There are literally dozens of strategies and tactics that can help achieve the goal of healthy communities resting on stable economic bases, a surprising number of which already have been successfully tried and tested. In Parts II and III we examine such community-building policies. We begin with consideration of the role, both actual and potential, of the federal government in helping to promote local-level economic stability.

PLACE-BASED POLICY ALTERNATIVES

INTRODUCTION

Part I of the book offered an overview of both why community economic stability is important and the challenges to such stability posed by globalization, capital mobility in the United States, and suburban sprawl. Part II takes up the question of how policy makers can respond in ways that encourage greater community stability.

Many federal place-based policies—some well known, others far below the radar of most policy debates—already are in operation. Chapter 4 provides a review of some of the most important and most interesting of these place-based policies, from trade adjustment assistance and procurement policies to brownfield redevelopment. While there is significant room to improve and expand most of these policies to maximize their effectiveness, simply reviewing this wide range of federal initiatives makes it clear that many of the policy pieces necessary to implement a full-blown agenda to stabilize communities are in fact already in place, should the federal government choose to make community stabilization a major policy priority.

Chapter 5 begins our look at state and local policy strategies to enhance community economic stability, reviewing several conventional approaches to promoting economic development and economic health. Among these strategies are job-training programs with direct links to employers, accountability requirements for recipients of economic development subsidies, and local living-wage movements. While these strategies do not typically stabilize jobs in communities in a direct fashion, we believe they have an important role to play in an overall place-based agenda.

Chapter 6 describes how localities can play a more direct role in job creation through the creation and operation of public enterprises. Successful public enterprise at the municipal level is far more common in the United States than is commonly thought, and extends not only to traditional sectors such as utilities but also to cutting-edge industries such as telecommunications and environmental services. Healthy city-owned (and in some cases state-owned) enterprises can help create jobs and generate a positive revenue flow for localities, and should be considered an integral part of a community stability agenda.

Chapter 7 discusses two major ways localities and states can better steward their existing resources in ways that enhance community economic stability. The first is by implementing policies to increase the multiplier effect in local economies—that is, to create local economies that are more diverse and more stable by replacing "imports" into towns with locally produced goods and services. The second is by using public pension funds to help finance investments in economic development within a given city or state. Such economically targeted investments are already widely practiced by many states and large cities in political and economic contexts as diverse as Alabama and New York City. Further encouragement of such investments could be a very important lever for encouraging community economic stability in the years to come.

CHAPTER 4

FEDERAL JOB-STABILIZING POLICIES

much contemporary rhetoric concerning free trade, free markets, and free enterprise systematically obscures—even mystifies—the ongoing reality of widespread government intervention and market making in the United States. From Federal Reserve Board control of the money supply to agricultural subsidies and employment of postal workers, the federal government is a major player in American economic life—and remains so, even after two decades of slowed growth in many federal programs and seven years after a Democratic president declared that "the era of big government is over."

The issue is not whether the federal government will continue to have a role in the economy and in shaping markets. Rather, the issue is whether such intervention will continue to take place in a scattershot, internally inconsistent manner largely driven by special interests, or whether the federal role in the economy might instead serve a coherent objective: securing community economic stability. We believe that a much more coherent and systemic implementation of many of the tools already used extensively by government could play a major role in the reconstruction of community—and local democracy—in America in the new century.

The idea of using federal resources to stabilize local communities economically is hardly unusual or untested. In fact, there is nearly half a century of experience with federal efforts to provide geographically targeted economic assistance. As we document in this chapter, numerous federal programs of substantial scale (as well as many additional smaller ones) provide instructive precedents for how public policy might counteract the triple threat to community.

To date, place-based federal policies have acted as a partial, too often ineffective counter to the many other federal policies that encourage the mobility of capital and people. Historian Alice O'Connor observes that, "having encouraged the trends that impoverish communities in the first place, the federal government steps in with modest and inadequate interventions to deal with the consequences—job loss, poverty, crumbling infrastructure, neighborhood institutional decline, racial and economic polarization—and then wonders why community development so often 'fails'."[1] O'Connor points out that whereas many subsidies benefiting the middle class are beyond political criticism (such as for home mortgage tax deductions and public higher education), policies aimed at poor communities are heavily means-tested and politically contested. Federal place-based policies often have had uncertain political backing, and hence the policies implemented often reflect compromises that conflict with the local community's best interests. Federal policies also often exhibit "administrative fragmentation," with responsibility for action spread over several different agencies, while policy at the local level is managed by a shifting and at times bewildering complex of actors in the private, nonprofit, and governmental sector. All of this so far has worked to keep federal community development policy—as O'Connor puts it—"swimming against the tide."

O'Connor's perspective is a useful caution in the following review of policies. While some federal place-based policies could make important contributions in the future to community economic stability, none are at present adequately funded or supported to achieve such a goal.[2] Moreover, some federal projects intended to help communities, such as the urban renewal program following the Housing Act of 1949, have ended up hurting or even destroying them.

Despite the need to weigh federal policy with care, it is also important not to underestimate the potential role the federal government could play in a reconstructed policy regime. This chapter reviews some of the major federal initiatives that are based at least in part upon the idea of community economic stability. Our review demonstrates that a modern, aggressive, reformed place-based policy need hardly be built from scratch.

TRADE ADJUSTMENT ASSISTANCE

In the era of economic globalization, the Trade Adjustment Assistance (TAA) program is an especially interesting and suggestive precedent for

using the power of the federal government to promote community economic stability. TAA provides federal benefits to workers and firms negatively impacted by international trade, and has a long political lineage
dating to a political the early 1960s. Legislators in Washington have consistently used TAA as a way to demonstrate responsiveness to the concerns of
constituents whose economic well-being has been threatened by expanded
trade. As Ethan Kapstein notes: "TAA, though revisited and revised, has not
been abandoned, despite changing administrations and fluctuations in organized labour's [sic] political power. In short, TAA has proved a low-cost,
non-radical, and politically expedient means of dealing with trade-displaced
workers."[3]

Numerous political economists and journalists who embrace free trade—
including I. M. Destler of the University of Maryland, former DRI McGraw-
Hill economist Lawrence Chimerine, Columbia University's Jagdish
Bhagwati, and *New York Times* columnist Thomas Friedman—also endorse
adjustment assistance as a legitimate, politically essential way to cushion the
costs of a globalizing economy.[4] In essence, then, TAA stands as a clear example of the widely accepted principle that, under conditions of economic disruption and uncertainty, the federal government has an important role to
play in cushioning blows to individuals' and communities' economic
prospects.

The annual budget for TAA has remained stable in recent years, totaling
$342 million in 2001 and an estimated $378 million in fiscal 2002. Total
federal spending on all forms of trade adjustment assistance (including $69
million in NAFTA-specific assistance) amounted to an estimated $498 mil-
lion in 2002.[5]

There are two types of trade adjustment assistance: direct assistance to
workers laid off because of trade-related dislocations (which dates to 1962),
and assistance to firms affected by trade (which dates to 1974).[6]

TAA for Workers

TAA for workers is divided into two parts: benefits and training. TAA benefits
extend unemployment insurance payments up to seventy-eight weeks, provided
certified workers enter a training program. To receive TAA, a petition to the
Department of Labor must be filed by at least three workers (from either the
manufacturing or mining industries), their employer, or their union. To be certified, the workers need to demonstrate not only that sales or production has
declined but also that increased imports have made an important contribution
to those layoffs.[7] A recent academic analysis of TAA recipients in the early 1990s
done by economist Leah Marcal of California State University at Northridge

found that while the recipients were no more likely than other unemployed persons whose unemployment insurance had expired to have higher wages three years after being in the program, they were more likely to be employed.[8]

The other component of the TAA program for workers, job training, is intended to help displaced workers acquire a new skill or start a new career. Recipients are eligible for up to two years of training, which may consist of occupational training, remedial or basic education (including literacy assistance), or English as a second language. The program provides dislocated workers with vouchers that can be used to choose the most appropriate training program.[9] Between 1995 and 2000, over 975,000 workers participated in either the TAA or the NAFTA-TAA program, receiving total benefits of over $1.66 billion.[10] In a typical example of how the program is intended to work, some 200 workers at a Nabisco plant in Niagara Falls, NY will receive benefits after the parent company, Kraft, announced in 2001 that it would close the operation, which had been manufacturing Triscuit crackers, and increase production at a factory in Canada instead.[11]

While the TAA program offers an instructive precedent for how public policy can aid dislocated workers—and, by extension, their families and communities—the federal government now taps a mere fraction of the program's potential. In the face of the economic instability wrought by globalization and the accompanying increase in international trade, the resources devoted to the program remain inadequate. Economist Louis Jacobson notes that TAA "only covers those who are harmed by direct imports. For example, workers in auto assembly plants usually are covered, but workers supplying parts to those plants usually are not. Tertiary declines among service firms dependent on the purchases of manufacturing workers, such as restaurants and retail stores, also are not covered."[12] Moreover, TAA programs are also slow to provide training, even though studies show that early intervention (before or at time of layoff) is most effective.[13] Finally, a recent detailed study of the effectiveness of TAA in six communities impacted by trade faults the program for having inconsistent aid periods for training and income benefits (workers get twenty-four months of training benefits but only eighteen months of income benefits, making it difficult for workers to enter into, for instance, two-year educational programs), unstable funding of training programs, and excessive bureaucratic rigidity in its implementation, flaws that significantly weaken the program's potential effectiveness.[14]

TAA for Firms

While TAA for individuals is, of course, an inherently individualistic program, TAA for firms is an inherently more place-based assistance program.

This version of TAA, administered by the Economic Development Administration, has also exhibited more innovation than the program for workers, even though its budget is much smaller (only $11 million in 2002, or roughly 3 percent of the TAA-for-workers budget).[15] Although federally funded, the effort is administered by a network of twelve Trade Adjustment Assistance Centers (TAAC), each with its own region of operation. To be certified, a firm "must demonstrate that increased imports of articles directly competitive with its products contributed importantly to declines in sales or production and to actual or threatened job loss."[16]

Between 1993 and 1997 about 170 firms a year were certified, with the median company having fifty-four employees and annual sales of $4 million.[17] Once certified, most firms receive assistance, in the form of planning and consulting assistance aimed at specific business-enhancing projects, over a two-to-three-year period. The federal government typically pays for 75 percent of the initial business planning process and 50 percent of subsequent consulting work. To take one example of how the program is intended to work, in the early 1990s Trager Manufacturing, a Seattle manufacturer of backpacks that was struggling to compete against imports, used TAA assistance to help launch a new line of single-strap backpacks. The new product line caught on, allowing the company not only to remain in business but to double its account base within a year.[18]

Firms that received assistance between 1990 and 1995 had a higher survival rate after five years—84 percent compared to 71 percent of unassisted companies that also met certification requirements. Assisted firms also added employees (a 4.2 percent employee increase compared to a 5.3 percent employee decline in unassisted firms) and had stronger sales (33.9 percent average total growth compared to 16.2 percent for unassisted firms). It is estimated that every $3,451 invested by the TAA "created" a new job, and $87 in sales were generated for every TAA dollar invested.[19] However, the TAA-for-firms program has been faulted by the GAO for failing to "formally monitor and track program outcomes of program recipients. . . . As a result, [EDA] does not have the information necessary to systematically assess Center performance in helping firms adjust to import competition."[20]

Unfortunately, this apparently successful program is very small compared with the need. The TAA program lacks adequate resources to assist additional firms. Moreover, firms become eligible after they encounter serious problems, but by this time it may already be too late to save the firm. Speeding up assistance, providing aid more proactively, and, most importantly, dramatically expanding TAA's resources could have a very substantial effect on the lives of workers hurt by the consequences of international trade. A suitably strengthened TAA would also become a model beyond trade-impacted areas for providing much-needed economic stability for small businesses and their communities.

THE NORTH AMERICAN DEVELOPMENT BANK

Another important precedent for using federal policy to stabilize communities is the North American Development Bank (NADBank). Like TAA, this precedent also developed as a response to the economic instability commonly associated with international trade. The creation of NADBank was spurred by the passage of NAFTA in 1993. NADBank is a $3 billion financial institution under the joint operation of Mexico and the United States. Its job is to facilitate the implementation—and soften the impact—of the trade pact; former House member Esteban Torres (D-CA) made creation of the bank a precondition of his needed vote on behalf of the trade agreement.[21]

The NADBank has been criticized for moving into functional operations at a glacial pace, with just $2.3 million in loans and only one concrete project initiated by 1997.[22] However, the bank has become more active in recent years. The bank makes investments in both Mexico and the United States through a number of programs, including an environmental infrastructure fund, a municipal solid-waste fund, a loan and guarantee fund for environmental projects, and a utility management program. By June 2001 NADBank had made some $294 million in loans, loan guarantees, and grants, helping leverage a total of $913 million in investment in some three dozen environmental projects. Closely related to the NADBank is the Border Environment Cooperation Commission, which has allocated over $20 million in technical assistance for environmental infrastructure project in communities along the United States–Mexico border. The BECC also certifies the environmental projects assisted by NADBank; by mid-2001 it had approved nearly fifty projects (not all of which require NADBank involvement), representing over $1 billion in infrastructure investment.[23]

By law the NADBank must devote at least 10 percent of its capital to *adjusting entire communities* to the impact of trade.[24] The bank does this in the United States through the Community Adjustment and Investment Program (CAIP), a loan program linked to other loan programs of the Small Business Administration and the U.S. Department of Agriculture.[25] Through June 2001, some 544 loans worth nearly $370 million had been made; these have created or retained roughly 12,500 jobs, according to bank estimates. (The General Accounting Office has questioned these claims, and also cites numerous administrative problems with the program, including insufficient publicity to possible beneficiaries.)[26] In one of the beneficiary communities—Pacoima, California—small businesses can qualify for SBA guarantees on loans of up to $750,000 by creating at least one new job for every $35,000 borrowed. In Pacoima, the loan funds were made available in the wake of the departure to Mexico of a PricePfister manufacturing plant and other firms with a total of 700 employees.[27] In another representative project, the CAIP provided $180,000 in credit to La Mujer Obrera, a community-based nonprofit in El Paso, to help launch a new restaurant and catering business in the organization's community center. The CAIP also has a grant program, established in 1999, and by October 2000 had made grants of $6.6 million to projects in ten states.[28]

JOB TRAINING PROGRAMS AND THE WORKFORCE INVESTMENT ACT

To help workers and their communities cope with economic instability, the federal government continues to sponsor a variety of job training programs not specifically tied to trade. The 1998 Workforce Investment Act (WIA) was a major step toward rationalization of federal job programs, making the system more manageable for recipients, and facilitating evaluation of the effectiveness of the various programs. For years, a major ongoing criticism of federal job training policy focused on the wasteful, duplicative proliferation of dozens of independently administered job training programs—all operated by the federal government.[29] The WIA, which supplants the Job Partnership Training Act (JPTA), was fully implemented on July 1, 2000.

Total federal outlays for job training amounted to an estimated $5.7 billion in 2001. In 2001, "dislocated worker employment and training activities" sponsored by the Department of Labor received funding of $1.6 billion and were expected to help over 800,000 displaced workers. Funding for dislocated worker assistance is slated to exceed $1.4 billion in fiscal 2003.[30]

Two of the most significant initiatives taken by the WIA involve its new One-Stop centers for workers, trainers, and employers and the creation of Individualized Training Accounts (ITAs). One-Stop centers permit workers to access a variety of job training and job search services and to receive labor market information at a single location. Likewise, employers no longer confront a fragmented federal training bureaucracy, but instead need only to go to one place to post job openings and find unemployed workers whose skills match their needs. Over 1,000 One-Stop centers received approximately $138 million in funding in 2002, and are projected to receive $113 million in 2003. The ITAs are intended to provide more "empowerment" for the unemployed, who can now control how the funds in their own accounts will be used.[31] The WIA also promises universal access: Any individual (not just those demonstrating economic need) can tap some of the core employment-related services available, such as information about job vacancies or assistance with job search efforts or resume writing. The Department of Labor's on-line job bank (America's Job Bank) lists nearly 1 million vacancies a day and is used for an estimated 8 million separate job searches a month.

These changes should have a salutary impact on the federal employment training system. There are, however, real limits to job training as a strategy to stabilize economically troubled communities and ensure a quality standard of living for their residents.[32] In the absence of complementary programs and strategies to create an ample and stable supply of good jobs rooted firmly in these communities, new and improved efforts to increase the skills and aptitudes of the workforce are likely to be hobbled.

COMMUNITY DEVELOPMENT BLOCK GRANTS

While trade adjustment assistance and job training programs focus mostly on helping individuals hurt by economic instability, several federal programs aim explicitly at building local *communities'* stock of jobs, skills, physical capital, and overall economic health. A prime example is the Community Development Block Grant (CDBG) program, run by HUD's Community Planning and Development (CPD) division. Whereas other major intergovernmental transfer and development initiatives, such as revenue sharing and the Urban Development Action Grant program, were completely eliminated during the Republican administrations of the 1980s, the CDBG program survived this period, although its resources were cut in half.[33] The CDBG program, which consists of several different types of block grants and related programs, operates with a total fiscal year 2001 budget of $5.1 billion. The proposed Bush budget for 2003 envisions a cut in the CDBG program to $4.7 billion, just under 2000 levels.[34]

Although the CDBG program is not without its problems, it offers several important precedents for federal policy: First, the program is targeted to benefit low- and moderate-income persons, that is, people who earn less than 80 percent of the median income in their area. By law, at least 70 percent of the grant funds must benefit people with such incomes.[35] Second, the program decentralizes decision-making authority: Within broad limits, communities themselves determine how funds will be used. Third, and related to the previous point, citizen participation is a major element of the CDBG program: The program requires that communities hold an annual public hearing about CDBG allocations; an Urban Institute survey conducted in the early 1990s showed that formal citizen

Table 4.1 Total Federal Spending on Regional and Community
Development, 1960–2002 (in millions of dollars)

	Current dollars	2001 dollars
1962	445	2,610
1965	1,061	5,965
1970	2,134	9,741
1975	3,925	12,920
1980	9,210	19,795
1985	7,715	12,698
1990	6,432	8,715
1995	7,467	8,677
1999	7,443	7,912
2000	8,018	8,246
2001	8,126	8,126
2002 (est.)	8,991	—

Source: Budget of the United States Government, Fiscal Year 2003: Historical tables, Table
3.2; *Economic Report of the President,* Table B-60. Excludes spending on disaster relief.

advisory councils were in place in about half the cities receiving CDBGs.[36]
Although none of these principles works perfectly in practice, they clearly
have had a positive impact. For example, the Urban Institute study indicated that in communities with formalized participation procedures, citizens had more influence than elsewhere in deciding how CDBG funding
should be used. Cities with citizen advisory groups were also more likely
to fund projects that benefit low-income residents, minorities, female-
headed households, homeless persons, and persons who are HIV-
positive.[37]

Though its economic development budget is modest, the CDBG program
has also had a positive effect on job creation. The Urban Institute study in
the early 1990s found that the four-year termination rate of businesses that
receive CDBG assistance was less than 30 percent, compared with the typical
(five-year) small business failure rate of 50 percent.[38] Furthermore, jobs created in these businesses were stable; of the businesses that survive four years,
almost 90 percent of the jobs remain after four additional years. Ninety-six
percent of the jobs were full time, 90 percent were above minimum wage,
and residents who live in the same neighborhood as the business held nearly
one-third of these jobs.[39]

CDBG funding sets a precedent for how the federal government can assist communities without attempting to solve specifically local problems in Washington. As Christopher Walker and colleagues note, the program has "contributed to community capacity to deliver development programs, and in almost every city, local leaders can point to neighborhoods that are demonstrably improved as a result of CDBG spending. . . by engaging a broad range of entities in the delivery of programs, the CDBG program has helped build a network of diverse community agencies and organizations."[40]

Related to the CDBG programs are Section 108 loan guarantees. These loan guarantees allow communities to use federally guaranteed loans rather than CDBG funds to leverage private funds for economic development. Using current and future CDBG funds as collateral, communities can borrow up to five times their annual CDBG allocation. Since such loans are larger than annual CDBG funds, the potential projects the city can fund are of a much more impressive scale.[41] This program is projected to support up to $275 million in loans in 2003.[42]

Another CDBG-related program is the Economic Development Initiative (EDI). EDI grants are used in tandem with Section 108 loan guarantees and are "designed to enable local governments to enhance both the security of loans guaranteed through [the Section 108 loan fund] and the feasibility of the economic development and revitalization projects the Section 108 guarantees finance."[43] EDI grants, established in 1994, are intended to ensure that CDBG grants are not tied up as loan securities but are actually used for economic and community development. Between 1993 and 1999, Section 108 loan guarantees and EDI grants together helped finance 711 projects, generating up to 338,000 new or retained jobs.[44] The Bush administration favors no new spending for EDI grants, however.[45]

LABOR SURPLUS AREAS AND HUB ZONES

Yet another precedent that channels federal resources to localities facing economic adversity is the long-standing place-based preference system for federal contracts. This system is intended to steer federal contracts to areas with higher-than-average unemployment. The practice is a straightforward effort to put federal procurement spending in the service of promoting greater community economic stability.

For many years the primary means by which the federal government accomplished this goal was by designating economically struggling areas with exceptionally high rates of unemployment as "labor surplus areas" and giving contractors in these areas preferences when bidding for federal projects. The Department of Labor each year issues an annual list of labor surplus areas;

the 1996 list contained 1,425 civil jurisdictions so designated.[46] To cite only one agency, the Department of Energy in fiscal 1996 awarded contracts to roughly 260 businesses in labor surplus areas, contracts with a total value of $2.8 billion.[47]

The labor surplus area designation continues to be used. However, greater attention is now given to the HUBZone program as a way to steer more federal contracts to areas with high unemployment.[48] HUBZones (historically underutilized business zones) include those with a high proportion of low-income households or those experiencing a high rate of unemployment. There are over 7,000 urban census tracts and 900 nonmetropolitan counties that qualify as HUBZones; all Indian reservations also automatically qualify.

The HUBZone program is run by the Small Business Administration, which determines whether a business is eligible for a HUBZone contract and also keeps a list of registered HUBZone businesses. The program's goal is to increase federal contracts with HUBZone businesses—in half-percent increments—from 1 percent in 1999 to 3 percent in 2003 (keeping it at 3 percent thereafter). This translates into roughly $6 billion in federal contracts, or an increase of $4 billion compared to 1999 levels. If the program works as intended, the extra $4 billion that will go to businesses in these areas will create thousands of jobs, many of which will go to HUBZone residents.

HUBZone businesses must meet certain requirements to be eligible to compete for contracts. First, to be eligible a business must meet the SBA's criterion as a "small business concern" (usually defined as independently owned and operated businesses that are not dominant in a market). Second, 35 percent of the business's employees must live in a HUBZone. Third, the business must be American-owned. Fourth, the business must have its center of operations in a HUBZone to qualify. Such requirements are designed to prevent businesses anchored elsewhere from taking advantage of the program without actually providing benefits to HUBZone residents.[49]

THE ECONOMIC DEVELOPMENT ADMINISTRATION AND THE APPALACHIAN REGIONAL COMMISSION

The most important federal agency devoted explicitly to assisting relatively underdeveloped areas in the United States is the Economic Development Administration (EDA), established by the Johnson administration in 1965. The EDA's stated mission is to "provide grants for infrastructure development, business incentives and other forms of assistance to help communities alleviate conditions of substantial and persistent unemployment in economically distressed areas and regions."[50] The EDA, which falls under the aegis of the Department of Commerce, is currently funded at the modest level of $350 million a year (expected appropriation for 2003).[51]

Programs are developed by the agency in coordination with six regional offices. The largest program remains public works expenditures such as industrial parks, water and sewer systems, and access roads in poor areas. Between 1992 and 1999, the EDA funded over 1,450 public works projects with grants totaling $1.4 billion. The EDA operates a revolving loan fund program, which has helped set up over 800 local-level revolving loan funds; these funds in turn have leveraged over $1.5 billion in private capital since 1976.[52] The EDA also provides planning and technical assistance to localities and is involved in both economic redevelopment for areas affected by natural disasters and those hurt by government cutbacks such as military base closures.[53] The EDA aimed to help create or retain over 56,000 jobs in 2001.[54]

Another Great Society–era federal initiative designed to assist a depressed geographical area is the Appalachian Regional Commission (ARC). The ARC was established in 1965 after several studies showed that areas in the Appalachian region were experiencing employment reductions at a time when the national economy was growing rapidly. The ARC has funded critical infrastructure investments in the region, with considerable success. "When compared with 'twin counties' outside the 13-State region," a recent report observes, "ARC counties have grown 17 times faster in private sector employment, seven times faster in population, and 34 times faster in per capita income."[55] The ARC now receives a modest $66 million a year (expected 2002 appropriation) in federal funding for 119 development projects over a thirteen-state area. In 2001 it expected to assist directly in creating or stabilizing 22,000 jobs and to deploy a hundred doctors in order to permit an additional 460,000 patient visits to the doctor's office in underserved areas.[56] To extend the ARC concept to the Mississippi Delta region, in December 2000 the Clinton administration established the Delta Regional Authority; the authority will play a similar role to the ARC in coordinating strategic infrastructure investments and overall development policy in over 230 counties in an eight-state region. The authority received funding of $20 million for fiscal 2001 and $10 million in fiscal 2002.[57]

EMPOWERMENT ZONES/ENTERPRISE COMMUNITIES
AND RELATED PLACE-STABILIZING PRACTICES

Since the early 1990s one of the most important efforts aimed at assisting communities facing economic hardship and instability has been the Empowerment Zones/Enterprise Communities program. For areas designated as EZs or ECs, the federal government provides a mix of business subsidies, federal grants, and tax incentives. These involve direct federal expenditures estimated at $185 million for fiscal 2001, plus an estimated $380 million (in 2001) in federal tax breaks to eligible businesses.[58] (Starting in 2003, however, the Bush administration proposes no new direct spending on EZs or ECs.) In addition, EZs and ECs have had priority status in obtaining resources from other federal aid and tax incentive programs. Six urban and three rural areas were designated as Empowerment Zones in 1994 (two more urban areas were added in 1998), along with sixty-five urban and thirty rural areas designated as Enterprise Communities. These designations were for ten-year terms. In 1999, twenty additional communities were named Empowerment Zones (fifteen in urban areas, five in rural areas) and an additional twenty rural areas were designated Enterprise Communities. Legislation passed in December 2000 calls for nine additional Empowerment Zones and forty new Renewal Communities (twenty-eight urban, twelve rural) to be designated by early 2002.[59]

One of the most interesting and potentially valuable precedents coming from the EZ/EC program is its strategic planning process. The goal is to initiate a process of collaboration among local actors who jointly help take stock of a community's most pressing problems and its available resources. HUD guidelines stipulate that EZ/EC development plans should seek to direct economic development toward the strengthening of coherent, identifiable neighborhoods and to balance such development with concerns for noneconomic values, such as respect for human scale. Official HUD documents state that plans "should address how face-to-face interaction at the neighborhood level will be enhanced." Through this planning process, community organizations have input into the direction of economic development. The strategic plan also provides the foundation for evaluation of programs by the federal government. In this sense, the plan is binding: Communities must abide by the strategic plan or risk losing benefits.[60]

Once a community has been designated an Empowerment Zone, it qualifies for a number of additional incentives. First, employers in EZs can claim employee wage credits—a tax credit equal to 20 percent of the first $15,000 in wages paid to qualified employees residing in the zone. Second, businesses are afforded increased tax deductions for property put into service within the zone.[61] Third, businesses can qualify for new tax-exempt bond financing to help acquire property located in an EZ. Fourth, loans or loan guarantees through Section 108 of the Housing and Community Development Act of 1974 are available for community development activities in zones.[62] Finally, One-Stop capital shops are created in each zone with the help of the Small Business

Administration; these provide loans and equity investments for small businesses. Enterprise Communities are also eligible for tax-free bond issues, loan guarantees, and a One-Stop capital shop, although funding levels are lower.

To maximize the impact of EZs and ECs, the federal government has established two additional valuable precedents for stabilizing economically depressed communities: First, the federal government now self-consciously targets the location of public facilities to EZs and ECs. The General Services Administration (GSA) has been directed to "maximize the use of Federal space to provide development and redevelopment anchors for employment of EZ and EC residents" when making determinations about the locations of federal facilities.[63] Targeting of federal facilities has a long history, beginning in 1978 when President Carter issued an executive order requiring the GSA to "give first consideration to a centralized business area and adjacent areas of similar character" in order to "encourage the development and redevelopment of cities."[64] President Clinton reaffirmed the directive in 1996 and also signed a new historic-preservation executive order, requiring federal agencies to give "first consideration" to "locating in historical structures of historic districts, as well as central business districts." In 1999, the GSA established the Center for Urban Development to coordinate its real estate activities in urban areas, with the stated aim of using government buildings to help create "healthy vital communities."[65]

Second, the EZ/EC program demonstrates how the federal government can target places requiring economic stabilization help with a vast array of other federal resources and benefits. Apart from the benefits that flow directly from EZ/EC designation, EZs and ECs also have received preferences (in varying degree) in over a dozen other federal programs aimed at assisting local communities. These include AmeriCorps USA (grants to local nonprofits doing antipoverty work), the Urban Location Program (which also guides placement of federal facilities), CDBGs, Substance Abuse Prevention (an HHS program), the John Heinz Neighborhood Development Program (a HUD program), Planning Program for States and Urban Areas (sponsored by the Department of Commerce), Job Opportunities for Low-Income Individuals (grants given to nonprofits working to help solve long-term unemployment, administered by HHS), School-to-Work Opportunities (a transition program administered by the Departments of Education and Labor), Youthbuild (a construction program that involves youths in building low-income housing, sponsored by HUD), and various programs administered by the Department of Labor.[66]

How much can we expect Empowerment Zones and Enterprise Communities to accomplish? While the first wave of empirical research on the effect of Empowerment Zone–type schemes suggests that designated neighborhoods are likely to benefit from such programs, there is good reason to be skeptical that the current EZ/EC approach can have a dramatic impact on poor communities—and for rather obvious reasons.[67] First, from the point of view of community stability, while the EZ/EC concept may produce net benefits to the extent to which it increases the capacity of existing businesses in poor areas to expand jobs or makes it easier for new businesses to start, gains that come from businesses moving from one community to another to exploit tax breaks are much more ambiguous. (On this point we disagree with economists such as Alan Peters and Peter Fisher, who claim that tax incentives could be justified public policy if it redistributed jobs to poor areas, although they are in fact skeptical that this is likely to be the result of incentive programs.) Second, as Alice O'Connor notes, "even supporters agree that the funding is inadequate given the size of the task," while critics remain

> skeptical about how much investment or job creation can be expected from the private sector and the extent to which community residents will be able to expect corporate responsibility. Like past federal demonstrations, it begs the question of what happens to the thousands of communities not chosen for support, and what happens to the EZ/EC sites once initial funding runs out. It also smacks of symbolic politics at a time when poor urban and rural communities command little more than rhetorical attention on the national agenda. Most of all the plan represents a very modest investment in community revitalization, especially in the face of an overarching policy agenda that encourages footloose capital, low labor costs, reduced social spending, and persistent wage inequality, and that brings about "the end of welfare as we know it" with little thought for the policy's effect on communities.[68]

Put another way: Although many practical precedents have been established, and much experience gained, the programs are very modest, and they are unlikely to make a dramatic impact. While the general strategy of offering businesses inducements to invest in depressed areas stands a reasonable chance of yielding progress in periods of sustained economic expansion (such as the late 1990s), there is good reason to worry that any observed progress in EC/EZs might not survive a recession and that the recipient areas as a whole may experience a community-sized version of the old last-hired-first-fired story.

We are in substantial agreement with O'Connor's assessment of the EZ/EC initiative. Yet, as our discussion above makes clear, there are also several positive elements in the initiative that could contribute to a much broader strategy for community stability under the right circumstances. The attempt to coordinate a range of federal efforts (tax policy, community development, job training, facility siting, etc.) in support of particular places, the emphasis on strategic planning, and the room made for civic participation all are particularly useful improvements in federal policy toward cities—even if the current program is woefully inadequate as a strategy for serious social and economic improvement in depressed communities.

NEW MARKETS INITIATIVE

Related to the EZ/EC program is the most recent federal effort to help economically distressed communities, the New Markets Initiative. The Clinton White House announced the initiative in 1999 during a tour of several depressed communities nationwide. Initially passed by the House in July 2000, the bill was finally signed into law by Clinton in December 2000 after encountering some difficulties in the Senate.

Major elements of the initiative include tax credits of roughly 30 percent for investments in community development banks, venture funds, and other "targeted investment funds," and the creation of ten to twenty New Market Venture Capital Firms, which will make SBA-guaranteed loans to small businesses in low- and moderate-income areas. Expansions of the Empowerment Zone and Enterprise Communities program, the creation of forty Renewal Communities with special tax credits for business, and expansion of the low-income housing tax credit were also authorized under the bill.[69]

However, what was envisioned as the most significant new initiative under the New Markets umbrella, the America's Private Investment Companies (APIC) program, was not authorized in the final bill. Based on the existing Overseas Private Investment Corporation (OPIC) model of providing loan guarantees for businesses making potentially risky investments in foreign markets, each APIC would have used a combination of federal and private funding to make equity investments in businesses operating in low-income areas. Each dollar of private investment into an APIC would have been backed by two dollars of government-leveraged debt; Clinton officials hoped that investments would have totaled $4 billion in over five years.[70]

MILITARY BASE RECONVERSION

Another important precedent for using federal funds to help revitalize localities facing economic shocks is the military base conversion program. The federal experience with base reuse also illustrates what is possible when the federal government recognizes community economic instability as a problem and proactively attempts to counter its effects. Many aspects of the model could be applied more broadly to assist communities facing economic dislocation from less publicized but equally injurious sources.

By the end of 1997, the federal government had provided over $1 billion in specifically targeted redevelopment aid—in addition to general state and federal economic development programs or planning and technical assistance —to help cushion the blow of military base closure.[71] This assistance has had the desired effect: The economic and employment effects of base closures have not been nearly as severe as might have been expected, and many communities have done surprisingly well.[72] Altogether, by 1998 fifteen of the sixty-two bases closed since 1988 had actually created more civilian jobs at the former bases than were lost when the bases closed.[73] More importantly, the experience clearly demonstrates that with proper support, communities that were once largely dependent on a single industry—in this case the military—*can* overcome the equivalent of an industry shutdown and emerge with a more stable and diversified economic base.

Indeed, a base closure can become an economic opportunity for the community, as military bases have a very well developed infrastructure, with roads, airstrips, water and sewage systems, and often on-base housing.[74] Military bases have been converted into commercial airports, ports, technology parks, manufacturing plants, call centers, warehouses, colleges, health facilities, parks, and wildlife preserves. Moreover, property used for education, parks, airports, and for homeless assistance can be transferred to the community at no cost.[75] In another interesting precedent, the FAA provided (through 1997) $270 million in grants to various communities to develop airports at former military bases.[76] Because the airstrips and infrastructure to support an airport are already there, it is relatively easy to turn former air bases into commercial airports. Since the airstrips are larger than those at most local airports, in addition to passenger flights these new airports are able to handle commercial cargo flights. Mather Airport in California, located on what used to be Mather Air Force Base, is now used by Airborne Express, United Parcel Service, BAX Global, and Emery Air Freight.[77] Meanwhile, conversion funds have been used to help open new commercial airports in Austin, Texas, and Myrtle Beach, South Carolina, on former base sites.[78]

Many former military bases have become campuses for colleges or community colleges. By the mid-1990s, over 125,000 students attended schools located on military bases closed during the 1960s and 1970s.[79] Numerous bases closed in the 1990s also were converted to colleges. What was once Fort Ord, on the Monterey Peninsula, is now the home of California State University at Monterey Bay. The federal government turned the land over to the state of California at no cost, and then sold the family housing on the base—would-be dormitories—to the state for just $1 per unit, thus making development of the university much cheaper than it would otherwise have been.[80] The campus, which also received significant assistance from the Economic Development Administration, in 1999 employed over 600 people, with over 1,200 students enrolled.[81]

The most common reuse option is the Economic Development Conveyance, which transfers property to local communities planning to engage in industrial or commercial development and stimulate job creation. In each closure-affected community, Local Reuse Authorities (LRA) have been formed to act as the point of contact between local communities and the federal government. From 1993 to 1999, the Department of Defense negotiated the sale of base property to LRAs, which then implemented the redevelopment plans. In response to complaints that the sale of base property had proven inefficient and time-consuming, in 1999 federal legislation called for EDC property to be transferred to LRAs at no cost at all closed bases, in order to accelerate the redevelopment process. (Such no cost conveyances were already permitted at rural bases.)[82]

Examples of successful conversions to industrial or commercial use abound. Rantoul, Illinois, where Chanute Air Force Base once accounted for 65 percent of the local economy, has created 3,000 new jobs with fifty new industrial and commercial tenants, has increased property values throughout the town, and now has 700 families living in former base housing.[83] After an earthquake forced Packard Bell to close its manufacturing and distribution operations in Northridge, California, the computer manufacturer relocated that production to the Sacramento Army Depot and in turn employed most of the 3,000 depot workers who had lost their jobs as a result of the base closure.[84]

Not all communities possess the fiscal resources required to turn a military base into a commercial or industrial park that will attract new businesses. One way to add resources to the process is to finance infrastructure improvements through state, county, or municipal bonds. Bonds also can be issued by Local Reuse Authorities. The bond issuers borrow capital to convert the base to commercial or industrial use, and then repay the bonds as redevelopment generates revenue. The Economic Development Administration also has credit enhancement grants that allow LRAs to raise the capital to finance infrastructure improvements.[85] In addition, the EDA has provided support for revolving loan funds and infrastructure improvements, as well as technical assistance and assistance with market development and networking. Through the end of 1997, EDA had provided over

$330 million in grants to help communities affected by military base closures develop EDCs.[86]

While the federal government has not provided all the funds needed to rebuild communities hurt by base closures, it has helped ease the pain. The Department of Defense estimates that base closings since 1988 have resulted in the loss of 135,000 jobs. Community redevelopment had already brought over 67,000 jobs to these communities by 2000.[87] At bases closed for two years or more, almost 75 percent of the lost jobs had been replaced by new ones by by 1998.[88] The success achieved by the overall effort with a relatively small expenditure of federal money is an encouraging sign that broader programs aimed at stabilizing other communities experiencing economic dislocation and/or struggling to convert formerly productive facilities would likely achieve an impressive bang for the buck.[89]

UNITED STATES DEPARTMENT OF AGRICULTURE (USDA) PROGRAMS

The federal government has traditionally played an especially strong role in agriculture and in providing assistance of many kinds to farmers and farm communities. Today the United States Department of Agriculture supports a multitude of programs to promote community economic development.

For instance, the USDA gives loans and grants to many rural businesses through the Rural Community Advancement Program (formerly Rural Business Services). About a dozen loan and grant programs, have operated under the aegis of RCAP, some of which have been cut by the Bush administration; total federal spending in 2003 is expected to reach $791 million (a decrease from the 2001 level of $1.1 billion).[90] Most of this money goes for Water and Waste Disposal Grants, which are expected to receive $587 million in fiscal 2003.[91]Among the other programs funded under the RCAP are Business and Industry Guaranteed Loans (fiscal 2003: $733 million in loans guaranteed, down from $2.4 billion in 2001), which provide guarantees for loans made by commercial lenders, giving rural areas greater access to capital;[92] and Rural Business Enterprise Grants (fiscal 2003: $44 million, down from $49 million in 2001), which provides funds to nonprofits and public bodies to assist development of small rural private business enterprises.[93]

Related to RCAP is the Rural Business-Cooperative Service, which helps cooperatives both with development and technical assistance and with financial aid. Assistance under this program includes $15 million in fiscal 2002 spending on rural Empowerment Zones and a proposed $7 million in fiscal 2003 assistance to cooperatives via Rural Cooperative Development Grants.[94] Also, the Rural Housing Service provides the Community Facility

Direct Loan Program, which in fiscal 2003 is expected to make $250 million in direct loans to municipalities and nonprofit organizations for construction, enlargement, or improvement of community facilities, including health care, public safety, and public service facilities.[95]

One of the most interesting USDA programs in terms of structure is run by its Natural Resources Conservation Service (NRCS): the Resource Conservation and Development Program (RC&D). The purpose of RC&D is to improve utilization and development, as well as conservation, of natural resources, and to heighten economic activity in RC&D areas. The program enhances the abilities of state and local organizations (including nonprofits) to effect development and conservation programs, primarily by establishing or improving coordination between different levels of activity. RC&D is organized in bottom-up fashion; local-level councils identify problems or needs in the area that should be addressed, and then develop an Area Plan of action. They also carry out many of the actual projects. Each area has an RC&D coordinator who helps the local community develop and implement the projects developed in its Area Plan and who also is the link between local, state, and national levels. In this way people at the local level do not have to become experts in cutting through red tape, but can concentrate on improving their communities and local resources. This program is expected to receive $51 million in federal funding in fiscal 2003.[96]

The USDA also has several programs to support rural utilities, including the Rural Electrification and Telecommunications Program, Rural Telephone Bank Loans, and Distance Learning and Telemedicine Grants. Like many USDA programs, these are mostly loan and/or grant programs. For instance, USDA's Rural Utilities Service (RUS) gives loans to telecommunication companies and cooperatives, as well as to electrical cooperatives.[97] The RUS also has a number of water and waste loan and grant programs. Water and Waste Disposal Direct Loans fund up to 75 percent of the costs of specific projects, helping to make such development cost-effective for rural areas and towns. In fiscal 2003 these loans are expected to total $814 million.[98]

FEDERAL SUPPORT FOR SMALL BUSINESSES

The federal government also sponsors an array of programs to nurture and support America's small businesses. Although not necessarily geographically targeted to particular communities, support for small business tends to contribute to community economic stabilization because such businesses tend to be more anchored in particular localities—that is, they are somewhat less mobile than larger companies. Small businesses also tend to expand a community's multiplier and often provide more spin-off benefits for the local economy.[99] (See Chapter 7.)

The federal government has long had an entire agency devoted to helping small businesses, the Small Business Administration (SBA). In addition to its involvement in some of the geographically targeted programs previously discussed, such as CAIP and HUBZones, the SBA provides technical assistance, loans, loan guarantees, and venture capital financing for small businesses nationwide and is the nation's biggest single source of financial support for small enterprises. In 2002, the SBA is projected to guarantee some $16.3 billion in new small-business loans.[100] In addition to its activities leveraging business loans, in fiscal 2003 SBA aims to provide up to $1.7 billion in surety bond guarantees for small contractors and make $545 million in direct loans to families and businesses recovering from natural disasters.[101] Additional SBA initiatives under the Clinton administration included funding for Small Business Development Centers at over 1,000 locations in all fifty states; loans to nonprofit microloan lenders; a microloan technical assistance program; direct microloan lending; One-Stop capital shops; and Women's Business Centers.[102]

An additional way the federal government supports small business is through the Small Business Innovation Research (SBIR) program, which provides funding for research and development (R&D). The ten federal agencies that have R&D budgets over $100 million are required to spend 2.5 percent of their R&D budget on small businesses through the SBIR program. All in all, the SBIR program annually distributes over a billion dollars in research funds.[103]

SBIR is only one of many other mechanisms the federal government uses to support small businesses. For instance, every federal agency sets aside a certain percentage of its contracts for small businesses—a policy mandated by the Small Business Act of 1956, as amended. The USDA, for instance, sets a preference goal of awarding more than $2 out of every $5 spent on prime contracts to small businesses.[104]

FEDERAL TRANSPORTATION POLICY AND COMMUNITY DEVELOPMENT

Another federal initiative with important implications for place-based development is the new approach to transportation funding undertaken in the Intermodal Surface Transportation Efficiency Act (ISTEA) of 1991 and the follow-up legislation TEA-21, passed in 1998. The ISTEA legislation marked a major departure by allowing states and localities to use federal transit money for nonhighway purposes, and by reviving metropolitan planning organizations (MPOs) as an important institutional player in state and local transportation planning, with the goal of encouraging transportation planners to consider the broader community-wide implications of transportation decisions.

MPOs were first established and funded in the 1970s (building upon earlier legislation from the Johnson era) by federal law requiring urbanized areas of greater than 50,000 to establish an agency capable of coordinating the use of federal transit support. Although they lay dormant throughout much of the 1980s, often reduced to a rubber-stamp role, since enactment of ISTEA they have gained renewed importance. Under ISTEA/TEA-21, MPOs are charged with exploring multimodal (i.e., not auto-only) local transportation initiatives, and including citizens' groups in local planning. The legislation also forced state departments of transportation, which are typically dominated by highway interests, to cooperate with MPOs in implementing transportation plans.[105] In 2002, the federal government will provide over $60 million in support of metropolitan transportation planning activities.[106]

MPOs, in short, represent an institutional structure capable of undertaking a more rational style of transportation planning that takes into account the social, economic, and environmental consequences of alternative choices. An example of a particularly active MPO is the Wilmington Area Planning Council in Delaware, which in the late 1990s launched an antisprawl transit initiative in conjunction with the rural community of Middletown. The initiative involved rezoning Middletown to promote mixed use, implementing changes in street design, making provision for bicycles and pedestrians a prerequisite for new developments, and allowing trees to be planted curbside on city streets.[107] Other MPOs have initiated programs to redress metropolitan inequities in access to transportation or to assist inner-city residents in getting adequate transportation to jobs, introduced new forms of computer modeling to better inform local transportation planning and involved citizens in long-term land use and transportation planning.[108] To be sure, the new emphasis on giving a role to MPOs in federal transportation policy has not yet revolutionized metropolitan transportation systems. It nonetheless has provided an institutional mechanism through which the primacy of auto-dominated transit planning undertaken with little regard for social and environmental consequences can be challenged—and it has provided a good example of the capacity of the federal government to help stimulate positive changes at the community decision-making level.

THE ENVIRONMENTAL PROTECTION AGENCY AND BROWNFIELDS

The EPA-directed Brownfields Initiative, undertaken in 1997, is one of the most impressive recent examples of coordinated federal action targeted at a single problem: converting America's numerous brownfield sites into productive uses. A brownfield is an abandoned or underused property (usually commercial or industrial) that cannot be readily redeveloped because of contamination. Brownfield cleanup falls under EPA's Superfund program, which is designed to clean up all types of abandoned hazardous-waste sites. Brownfields are harmful from an environmental perspective, but they also hamper economic development, especially in America's inner cities. As the General Accounting Office notes: "Developers' avoidance of brownfields has contributed to a loss of employment opportunities for city residents, a loss of tax revenues for city governments, and an increase in urban sprawl."[109]

The Brownfields Initiative, which has been endorsed in a general way by the Bush administration, focuses on four activity areas. First, the EPA works to clarify liability issues so that lending institutions, municipalities, property holders, developers, and property purchasers all have a clear understanding of the extent of their liability for costs associated with cleanup. Second, EPA has funded over 360 demonstration pilots with up to $200,000 each for a two-year period to "test brownfields assessment models, direct special efforts toward removing regulatory barriers without sacrificing protectiveness, and facilitate coordinated public and private efforts at the federal, state, tribal and local levels."[110] It has also provided grants of up to $50,000 to some forty-three "greenspace" demonstration projects.[111] Third, in the area of workforce development, the EPA works with community colleges, nonprofits, and other organizations to create programs to train and subsequently employ residents of nearby neighborhoods to cleanup brownfields. Thirty-seven job training demonstration projects have been funded since 1998.[112] Finally, in an effort to develop partnerships and promote outreach, the EPA works with nearly twenty other federal agencies and offices in the Interagency Working Group on Brownfields, which is charged with developing a unified strategy for federal efforts addressing the problem.[113]

These general strategies are complemented by a host of additional policies. One of these is the Brownfields Tax Incentive: If a firm is involved in the cleanup of a brownfield, its expenses (site assessment, investigation, and monitoring costs; cleanup costs; operation and maintenance costs; and state voluntary cleanup program oversight fees) are fully tax deductible in that year. Otherwise, these costs would be capitalized (that is, deductible only over a long period), which would be another incentive *not* to clean up the brownfield. According to EPA, the "$1.5 billion incentive is expected to leverage $6.0 billion in private investment and return an estimated 14,000 brownfields to productive use."[114] Another program is the Brownfields Cleanup Revolving Loan Fund (BCRLF), which awards between $50,000 and $500,000 to demonstration pilots to set up revolving loan funds used to finance brownfield cleanups. The pilots may provide loans to public and private parties involved in brownfield cleanups; as with any revolving loan fund, repayments are used to finance new loans. Demonstration pilots seeking BCRLF funds must show both how the local community will be involved and how the BCRLF program will improve community economic development.[115] By September 2001, over 120 pilots had been established.[116]

Finally, there is the Brownfields Showcase Communities program. In this effort, participating federal agencies in 1998 began to direct technical, financial, and other assistance to over a dozen selected showcase communities. The showcase communities are to serve as models for how well a focused and coordinated effort can work.[117] In October 2000 a dozen new showcase communities were designated, bringing the total to twenty-eight communities. The EPA estimates that the first sixteen designated communities have leveraged more than $900 million in cleanup and redevelopment activity and helped create over 2,700 new jobs.[118]

While the EPA already can point to a substantial number of success stories resulting from the Brownfields Initiative, some scholars have questioned whether the program will be effective in more difficult situations where private developers and corporations do not see a clear-cut profit possibility.[119] At a minimum, it should be admitted that the Brownfields Initiative is still at an early stage of development and awaits more thorough evaluations of its effectiveness.

Apart from the importance of the project as a means to revitalize and economically stabilize distressed urban economies, however, there is another significant feature of the Brownfields Initiative: It has demonstrated that the federal government can do some things that cannot be done at any other level and that, despite their poor coordination in other areas (such as, historically, job training), federal agencies are capable of working toward a common goal.

One of the biggest obstacles to coherent federal community-building policies, as many observers have noted, is the fragmentation of related programs. Overcoming this obstacle requires a concentrated interagency effort to define a common goal—an effort that, in turn, usually requires high-level leadership that is clear about overall policy objectives. The Brownfields Initiative is a modest but positive example of such an effort.

OTHER FORMS OF ASSISTANCE TO BUSINESS: A CRITICAL VIEW

To this point we have discussed only federal programs that have established useful precedents for place-based aid—and indeed, our discussion has touched on only some of the most prominent and interesting federal programs that one way or another provide support to communities. There is, however, an entirely different class of federal activities to consider that also sets a precedent, namely, the massive subsidies, tax breaks, and other assistance provided to corporations by the federal government year in and year out.

We believe a substantial number of the programs (and resources) currently used to provide tangible assistance to private firms could profitably be targeted to support community-based economic development, in a manner that would be extremely helpful in stabilizing communities. The point of the following review is less to criticize the various tools that the government now uses to assist private business—although some of these are clearly worthy of challenge—than to question the ends toward which these tools are now directed and, again, to note precedents that might be drawn upon. Some of the most conspicuous illustrative examples of general corporate support that might be retargeted in a comprehensive community strategy include export subsidies and a range of tax breaks.

Export enhancement program. Between 1985 and 1994 the Department of Agriculture provided over $7 billion in cash grants to some 147 firms with the purpose of allowing exporters to "sell U.S. agricultural products in targeted countries at prices below the exporter's costs of acquiring them." No strings were attached to the grants other than evidence of export activity. Some of the subsidies went to foreign corporations that happen to export American agricultural products. Nearly half of the $7 billion over this three-year period went to just three large corporations—Cargill, Continental Grain, and the French-owned Louis Dreyfus Corporation.[120] Exporters are also assisted by the Export-Import Bank (Eximbank) and the Overseas Private Investment Corporation (OPIC). Eximbank provided loans and loan guarantees in support of more than $50 billion in financial deals during the 1990s, over half of which have gone to just ten corporations (headed by Boeing). OPIC provided over $3 billion in co-financing for American firms' overseas investments during the 1990s and also provided loan guarantees for such investments—essentially ensuring that American private investors take little risk when they invest outside of the nation's borders.[121]

Tax breaks. Tax law now allows companies to write off the value of depreciated equipment faster than it actually depreciates, at a cost of $37.1 billion a year.[122] Also, advertising is now completely written off as a tax deduction. If instead one-fifth were treated as a capital cost, the savings to the public would exceed $5 billion a year.[123] And $3 billion to $4 billion is lost each year to the federal treasury due to tax deductions for business meals and other entertainment. As lawyer Robert Benson observes, even though the business meal deduction has been reduced from 80 percent to 50 percent, the public is still paying for "this executive class food-stamp program in which the required vegetable is apparently the olive in the Martini."[124]

Such illustrations represent but a drop in a vast, vast bucket. The Office of Management and Budget, an administrative arm of the executive branch, has estimated that the various tax exemptions available to corporations now total $76 billion a year, and numerous thinktank and independent analyses commonly place the total price tag of corporate support at $125 billion a year, or even higher.[125] In addition to the specific examples noted above, federal support for corporations runs the gamut from federal research and development money for commercial products to free use or use at minimal cost of public resources (such as land, minerals, and the airwaves) to bailouts for failed savings and loans to federal assumption of the insurance risk associated with nuclear power. In 1997, for instance, the Federal Communications Corporation, as part of the implementation of the 1996 Telecommunications Act, simply transferred broadcast licenses for digital television to existing broadcasters—even though it was estimated that an auction for rights to these licenses could have raised as much as $70 billion.[126]

Table 4.2. Summary of Projected Tax Expenditures Exceeding $250 Million That Benefit Corporations Versus Those That Benefit Communities, Fiscal Year 2003

Expenditures Benefiting Corporations	Cost (in millions of dollars)
Accelerated depreciation (total)	40,720
Deferral of income from controlled foreign corporations	7,450
Graduated corporation income tax rates	6,210
Inventory property sales source rules exemption	1,540
Tax credit for corporations doing business in U.S. possessions	2,240
Enhanced oil recovery credit	440
Total	58,600

(Omitted from this total are tax breaks for: corporate research; corporate contributions to child care, health, and pension funds; alternative fuels development; and several other programs that conceivably have a broader social purpose.)

Expenditures Benefiting Communities	Cost (in millions of dollars)
Credit for low-income housing investments	3,460
Exemption of credit union income	1,150
Special ESOP rules	1,420
Empowerment Zones/Enterprise Communities	1,130
Tax incentives for preservation of historic structures	210
Expensing of environmental mediation costs (brownfields)	100
Exclusion from income of conservation subsidies provided by public utilities	70
Exemption of certain mutuals' and cooperatives' income	60
New markets tax credit	190
Total	7,790

Other noteworthy expenditures

	Cost (in millions of dollars)
Charity (combined)	40,700
Exclusion of employer contributions for medical care	99,260
Employer contributions to pensions	112,590
IRA and Keogh retirement plans	25,430

Source: Analytical Tables of the United States Budget, 2003 (Washington, D.C.: Government Printing Office, 2002).

Table 4.3 Projected Tax Expenditures Primarily Benefiting Well-off Americans and Those Primarily Benefiting Low-Income Americans, Fiscal Year 2003

Limited to expenditures totaling $40 million or more. Medical expenditures, public pensions, savings plans, worker's compensation and expenditures to assist the disabled excluded.

Tax expenditures benefiting well-off Americans	Cost (in millions of dollars)
Deductibility of mortgage interest on owner-occupied homes	66,110
Reduced rates on capital gains tax (not including agriculture, iron ore, timber, and coal)	60,200
Capital gains exclusion on home sales	20,260
Total	146,570

Tax expenditures primarily benefiting low-income Americans	Cost (in millions of dollars)
Earned-income tax credit (total program cost)	35,430
HOPE tax credits for college tuition	3,520
Work opportunity tax credits	140
Exclusion of public assistance benefits	400
Welfare-to-work tax credits	40
Total	39,530

Source: *Analytical Tables of the United States Budget, 2003* (Washington, D.C.: Government Printing Office, 2002).

We obviously do not mean to suggest that all corporate incentives are wasteful. However, the question of why the federal government opts to support one type of economic actor (the large corporation) with billions of dollars in aid each year while offering a relative pittance to place-based development or community-oriented economic institutions is of profound policy and normative importance.[127] (See Tables 4.2 and 4.3 above.) It goes to the heart of the issue of power in the United States. Parts III of this book suggests numerous specific ways federal policy might usefully support such diverse community-anchored institutions as worker-owned firms, community land trusts, community development corporations, and community development financial institutions. Even a brief review of the subsidies and tax expenditures now available to corporations reveals that ample resources could be made available to provide such support. And, as our longer review of programs and policies in this chapter illustrates, there is vast accumulated experience and precedent for federal policies to help stabilize America's communities. What has been lacking—a situation, as we shall suggest, that may slowly be changing—is the necessary political will.

CHAPTER 5

CONVENTIONAL POLICY MEASURES
TO HELP COMMUNITIES

m ost community economic development policies discussed by mainstream scholars and policy practitioners do not explicitly and directly aim to root capital in place or to change ownership patterns in local economies. Policy analysts and politicians tend to focus instead either on helping local communities and their residents be more successful in the ongoing competition for jobs and rising living standards or on mitigating the negative consequences of the job-chasing system (discussed in Chapter 2).

Indeed, policy proposals within mainstream economic development discourse too often amount to little more than after-the-fact bandages; they are not designed for—nor do they have the resources for—a systemic program seriously impacting the economic health either of any particular community or of American communities in general. We do not dismiss, however, the relevance of several of the most frequently discussed conventional policy measures for a full community stability agenda. Policies such as improving skills and labor market readiness in low-income areas, holding corporations accountable for the public support they receive, and mandating living wages in urban areas are all important first steps toward fostering community stability. The menu of policies explored in this chapter has an important role to play as a complement to—but not a substitute for—the more comprehensive, longer term strategies discussed in the remainder of the book.

HUMAN-CAPITAL STRATEGIES

Human-capital strategies seek to increase the productivity of a community's workforce through the development of skills and work-related aptitudes. These strategies attract our attention because building a community's stock of human capital tends to enhance its economic stability, albeit in somewhat roundabout ways. On the individual level, workers who are more productive command greater earning power in the labor market, providing community residents with greater incomes. At the community level, a more productive workforce strengthens the locality's overall economic health and its ability to attract, retain and expand business activity.

Efforts to strengthen human capital seek to elevate the quality of both educational opportunities and employment training programs within a community. Most expert studies of human capital have concluded that, in general, investments aimed at helping children and adolescents—the earlier the better—have much greater long-term payoff than attempts to bolster the skills of adult workers.[1] Further, a quality public education system obviously can play a critical role in maintaining a community's long-term economic health, both by developing skills and by attracting stable, long-term residents into the area. Our discussion of human capital, however, will not focus either on early childhood investments or on broader educational issues (although we recognize these issues are critical). Instead, we focus attention on employment training and related programs—programs that are now prominent features of many communities' economic development efforts.

As we have seen in Chapter 4, for decades the federal government has provided a multitude of traditional employment training programs. States have also implemented an array of job training programs, many of which have been directly tied to inducement-oriented efforts to influence the location and/or expansion decisions of businesses. Broadly, states have often combined their desire to build human capital with their efforts to attract jobs.

State job training programs structured to meet those dual goals take a number of forms. Connecticut's Manufacturing Apprenticeship tax credit subsidizes firms that train "skilled craft workers" with tax breaks. North Dakota's New Jobs Training Program provides a loan to firms to cover their training costs, which may be paid off by the income tax withheld from new employees. Other states provide training directly through public institutions. For example, Iowa's Industrial New Jobs Training Program and Missouri's New Jobs Training Program both make use of their states' community college system to meet the job training needs of business.[2]

Such programs are very widespread. But in the judgement of most experts the most notable feature of the array of traditional employment-training efforts—at both the state and federal levels—has been their lack of effectiveness.[3] MIT economist Paul Osterman's comprehensive review of such efforts concludes straightforwardly that "employment and training programs are marginal to the operations of the labor market. Whatever process generates the low earnings of the system's clients is only glancingly affected by the existence of the programs."[4]

Responding to Failure: Bottom-up Innovations of Community-Based Organizations

In response to this failure, the federal government recently restructured its fragmented job training system by supplanting the Job Training Partnership Act with the "streamlined" Workforce Investment Act (see Chapter 4). Several community-based organizations (CBOs) also have taken a bottom-up approach to create more effective job-training programs in their localities.[5]

One alternative approach involves the *direct development of businesses* by CBO training organizations themselves. When these organizations run their own businesses, they are able to provide more intensive skills training or place many of their trainees in jobs within their own business. These innovative efforts propel the human-capital approach beyond the conventional policy framework: As CBOs start and operate economic enterprises themselves, they also create alternative institutions that root jobs firmly in their communities.

A good example of this approach is the Milwaukee-based organization Esperanza Unida. Esperanza Unida runs small businesses in the areas of home repair/carpentry, auto repair, day care, and metal fabrication/welding. These enterprises "provide long-term, on-the-job training to unemployed workers while paying them a wage and providing a service that is sold in the marketplace."[6] Another example is Cooperative Home Care Associates (CHCA), started in the South Bronx in 1985 and replicated in the early 1990s at two sites, Philadelphia and Boston, to form the Cooperative Health Care Network.[7] These three enterprises, established as worker cooperatives, do not exist merely as vehicles to provide employment training. Instead the enterprises try to implement what the Cooperative Network calls a "dual model," which "integrates two distinct components: . . . a profitable business and an on-site, employer-based training program." Steven L. Dawson, president of the organization managing the replication of the CHCA model, notes that the "process is nearly seamless as the participant moves from the training program into the enterprise, for the training program and the enterprise share the same mission, style of management, performance expectations, and even physical space."[8]

A second thrust in the CBO efforts to remake employment-training programs seeks to enhance the community's human capital via the *development of networks*. This strategy addresses the fact that a key difficulty facing low-skilled workers from poor neighborhoods is lack of access to job networks—informal (often social) relationships that provide information about job availability to job seekers, plus referrals to employers.[9] CBOs operating in disadvantaged communities often fill the same role as job networks. By developing ongoing, institutionalized connections with employers, CBOs can be in a good position to gain information about available jobs and provide reliable referrals for prospective employees.

A direct connection with employers is a critical part of the recent efforts of some CBOs to remake employment-training programs. As the late Bennett Harrison and Marc Weiss have noted, CBOs have formed "partnerships, collaborations, and 'strategic alliances'" with many other organizational actors within particular communities to form "Workforce Development Networks."[10] Such networks include not only major regional employers but also other CBOs, community colleges, quasi-public agencies, and state and local governments as well. By "networking across organizational and territorial boundaries"—and thus opening additional doors to jobs—CBOs have become more effective in their employment training efforts.[11]

An example highlighted by Harrison and his colleagues is the San Jose–based Center for Employment Training (CET).[12] Working primarily in the Hispanic community, CET helps disadvantaged job seekers get quality jobs in Silicon Valley by forming networked relationships with other relevant actors in the local employment training system, especially employers.[13] The center has consistently and extensively involved local employers in the structure and implementation of various employment programs. Through its relationships with employers, CET can act as the functional equivalent of an informal employment network for its clients. The center finds out about available job opportunities and provides a credible and trusted reference to employers within its network. As a result, several formal evaluations undertaken over a period of years have found CET to be a highly successful job training effort, and even severe critics of job training programs such as the University of Chicago economist James Heckman have praised CET.[14]

Another interesting project based on network development is the Milwaukee Jobs Initiative (MJI), developed by the Center on Wisconsin Strategy (COWS) under the direction of University of Wisconsin scholar Joel Rogers. MJI works to develop links between businesses and central-city residents in three targeted sectors: manufacturing, printing, and construction.[15] As described by Rogers and Laura Dresser, in each of these sectors the program strives to "improve the organization, integration, and coordination of actors on both the demand and supply sides of the labor market." In the manufacturing sector, MJI works with the Wisconsin Regional Training Program (an older training program also started by COWS) to establish relationships with manufacturing firms that have plans to add new employees. It then works closely with employers to identify the needed skills and to develop customized training programs that prepare trainees to take the jobs. The project also provides peer-advising systems inside participating firms to help support newly hired workers. On the supply side of the labor market MJI taps community-based organizations for recruitment and screening of trainees. Both employer interest and community interest have been strong. As a result, MJI has connected hundreds of central-city Milwaukee residents to jobs.[16]

The MJI nicely illustrates two important attributes of the new generation of network-oriented, locally rooted employment training initiatives springing up in regions all across the country: They are both employer-driven and sectorally focused. "Employer-driven" means that there is a strong emphasis on providing training targeted to and customized for the specific needs of employers seeking to fill jobs, rather than simply imparting to trainees skills that may or may not be demanded in the local labor market. "Sectorally focused" means that programs work closely with sectors of employers—such as metalworking firms, construction firms, and printing firms—which, in comparison to a firm-by-firm approach, allows for increased efficiency through greater economies of scale and scope.[17]

Brenda Lautsch of Simon Fraser University and Paul Osterman of MIT emphasize that such training programs are "more attentive to the local environment," especially the realities of the local labor market, than traditional job-training programs. This attentiveness is clearly demonstrated by the strong emphasis on providing employer-driven, customized training. Moreover, by pursuing a sectoral strategy, they can play a role in reshaping that environment. As Lautsch and Osterman explain, "[S]ectoral programs attempt to combine employment training with interventions among firms. These interventions are intended to alter the hiring and job design patterns of firms and hence act upon the environment as well as upon individuals."[18] Successful programs can provide a crucial source of skilled labor to firms and bring firms together to solve common problems.[19] Sectorally based job training programs can thus contribute to community economic stability by simultaneously helping a local business sector "become revitalized and more rooted in the local economy."[20]

CORPORATE ACCOUNTABILITY MEASURES FOR SUBSIDY RECIPIENTS

In their effort to attract jobs, state and local governments routinely provide generous locational inducements to businesses, such as tax abatements, tax credits, grants, loans and loan guarantees, and industrial revenue bonds (see Chapter 2). In response to the proliferation of these subsidies, and their often unsatisfying results, many states and localities have begun to attach accountability measures to them. These policies represent a second category of conventional stabilization policies employed by states and localities. Rather than eliminating the use of business subsidies in favor of approaches that are more direct and proactive, accountability measures seek to enhance the effectiveness of subsidy programs and protect taxpayers if development deals falter. When properly designed and aggressively enforced, accountability measures can help anchor economic activity and promote community stability by increasing the costs faced by businesses contemplating the withdrawal of their job-creating investments from communities after collecting subsidies.

As John Howe and Mark Vallianatos of the Grassroots Policy Project note, accountability legislation falls into three primary categories: laws that provide the public access to relevant information, requirements that subsidized corporations meet certain standards, and enforcement mechanisms.[21] The first set of laws provides legislators and citizens with the information necessary to hold corporations receiving subsidies accountable for their performance. Included here are "right-to-know" laws and laws requiring public participation in the (often secretive) subsidy-granting process. The second set of laws specifies how corporations must perform. These laws require that corporations receiving subsidies meet job creation and retention goals, and may also require that these corporations pay certain levels of wages and benefits, hire from certain targeted groups of workers, meet environmental standards, and/or refrain from relocating jobs from one area to another. A 2000 study led by economic development expert Greg LeRoy found that at least sixty-six jurisdictions, including thirty-seven states, twenty-five cities, and four counties, now apply "job quality standards" to firms receiving development incentives; the most common standard is specification of a wage standard (such as the $10-an-hour standard attached to one California subsidy).[22] The third set of laws, those involving enforcement, penalize corporations receiving subsidies for failing to meet stipulated conditions and standards.[23]

It is this third set of laws that most interests us. By changing the dynamics driving corporate disinvestment, enforcement mechanisms embody the greatest potential to enhance the economic stability of communities—a fact increasingly recognized by states and localities. By one recent estimate, over three-quarters of new incentive deals involve an accountability provision of some kind.[24] Common sanctions include the cancellation of a subsidy, adjustments to the value of a subsidy, and a variety of other specific penalties.[25] The most far-reaching sanction is the clawback. Because these measures allow governments to recapture benefits already received by corporations, they can help ensure that businesses stay rooted in the communities subsidizing their operations.

The following examples compiled by Howe and Vallianatos illustrate how states and localities have used clawbacks:

- In Vermont companies receiving a tax credit designed to attract financial-service companies must repay all or part of the credit if they significantly reduce employment levels soon after receiving the subsidy. The state imposes the clawback if a company cuts "the number of persons it employs in Vermont below 65 percent of the number it employed when the credit was granted." If this reduction occurs during the first two years, the state recaptures 100 percent of the credit. If a reduction takes place between two and four years after the assistance, the state recovers 50 percent of the credit, and a reduction between four and six years after the subsidy obligates the firm to pay back 25 percent of the credit.

- Nevada included a clawback in its Business Tax Abatement program. If a company receiving the abatement fails to provide health insurance for its employees or fails to pay wages that at least equal the statewide average for industrial jobs, the firm is required to repay the the tax abatement in full.

- Maryland included a similar provision in its Job Creation Tax Credit Act of 1996. If a business receiving the credit fails to create enough jobs (usually sixty) to meet the threshold established by the legislation, the state can recapture the entire amount of the credit. In the event of subsequent job reductions, the law allows for the credit value to be recalculated, and requires businesses to pay an amount in new taxes based on the percentage reduction of jobs.

- Santa Clara County in California also included clawbacks in its Manufacturing Personal Property Tax Rebate program. Provisions are written into the specific subsidy contracts developed between the companies receiving the tax rebate and the county. If a company does not meet specified projected goals regarding job creation, wage rates, or health insurance coverage, the credit is proportionally reduced. A breach-of-contract suit then can be filed against the underperforming company to recapture lost tax revenue.[26]

Numerous other states and localities have clawback provisions in their subsidy programs, including New Haven, Connecticut; Austin, Texas; and the states of Illinois, Ohio, Iowa, Connecticut, New York, Colorado, Texas, Nebraska, Pennsylvania, and West Virginia.[27]

The increased use of clawbacks signals a positive trend in state and local development policy. But for these provisions to be fully effective, state and local governments must overcome the common inclination to yield to the demands of business and demonstrate a willingness to apply sanctions vigorously and recapture forgone revenues when corporations violate the terms of subsidy programs. Existing evidence indicates that the clawback provisions are indeed being taken seriously. One survey of midwestern states identified several programs in which clawback mechanisms are "quite routinely applied."[28] In a specific example of note, New York City in 1996 received a refund check for $60,000 from the Bank of America, which had violated an incentive agreement.[29]

Other states and localities are taking a different approach to ensuring that subsidized corporations live up to their promises. By providing subsidies only *after* corporations have clearly met obligations, rather than doling out large up-front payments, they avoid the need for clawbacks altogether. One example of a state using this "collect-as-you-go" approach is Florida, which refunds tax payments on an annual basis to qualified business after they demonstrate that job and wage targets have been achieved.[30]

VOLUNTARY COMPACTS BETWEEN STATES

The provision of subsidies to businesses is fundamentally driven by the high degree of competition between subnational governments for business investment (see Chapter 2). Some states and localities have begun attacking the problem by attempting to forge voluntary agreements (or compacts) among themselves. Such compacts aim either to limit states' use of subsidies to engage in job poaching or piracy or to combine states' collective economic strength to deter business mobility more generally.

The latter approach is best illustrated by the call for multistate industrial retention commissions (MIRCs), to be formed by agreement of neighboring states in a particular region of the country. As specified in one proposal, a MIRC would work to deter businesses from relocating to lower-wage areas by using the threat of state-level disinvestment. Companies found guilty by the commission of relocations which "lead to layoffs and undermine labor, health and environmental standards" would be barred in all participating MIRC states from receiving state contracts, state development subsidies, and state pension fund investment. (The precedent for this action is experience with widespread pension fund divestment in companies doing business in South Africa in the 1980s.) Legislation to establish such commissions has been considered in at least eighteen states around the country, including many states in the Northeast and Midwest, as well as New Mexico and California.[31]

States and localities also have attempted to develop compacts to stop job poaching or piracy. One example previously mentioned is Maryland's Job Creation Tax Credit Act of 1996. This law also required the state's governor to work with surrounding states, from North Carolina to Pennsylvania, on an "anti-poaching" agreement.[32] The Maryland effort ultimately was unsuccessful—the state continued to spend millions of dollars to lure jobs from other states in the late 1990s—although top officials in the state remain interested in the concept.[33]

Another example of policy makers' interest in compacts to stop job poaching is the Indianapolis Regional Memorandum of Understanding. This agreement, adopted in the 1990s by many central Indiana cities and counties, led by Indianapolis, prohibits signatories from offering subsidies for an economic development project if that project involves the relocation of a firm from another signatory jurisdiction (without that jurisdiction's written approval).[34] Likewise, in south Florida three counties—Dade, Broward, and Palm Beach—recently agreed to a similar truce.[35] New York and New Jersey also have attempted to devise a workable compact to limit job raiding from each other, as have several states in the Midwest. Finally, Ralph Nader has called for federal legislation to facilitate the creation of such agreements; the legislation would "authorize anti-corporate welfare compacts between states, enabling them to enter into binding agreements to refuse to enter into a race to the bottom against each other."[36]

While the development of voluntary compacts among states and localities are an innovative approach to lessening community instability, they remain an inherently difficult way to limit job chasing and capital mobility. To date, no MIRCs have been established, and the state and local efforts to forge antipoaching agreements have as yet been only very marginally successful.[37] Even when states and localities establish such agreements, they tend to be fragile and tenuous, often collapsing over the first disputed action. (The New York–New Jersey truce was "broken by both sides in a matter of months," while the south Florida compact has generated disagreements over "what exactly constitutes poaching").[38] Since states and localities themselves seem unwilling to develop and abide by strong multijurisdictional compacts, federal-level action to encourage such compacts appears to be required if the effective use of anti-poaching agreements is to become a reality.

ADDITIONAL POLICIES

Three additional policy approaches widely discussed in the mainstream economic development literature merit discussion: living-wage ordinances, linked development (or linkage), and metropolitan tax-base sharing. Each of these policies also can contribute to the goal of community stability in real, albeit limited, ways.

Living-Wage Ordinances

Spearheaded by community groups such the Association of Community Organizations for Reform Now (ACORN), labor unions, and faith-based organizations, activists in dozens of communities have engaged in successful "living wage campaigns."[39] According to the Employment Policies Institute (a think tank that opposes the living-wage movement but is tracking it closely), by mid-2001 sixty-five cities and counties had enacted such legislation, and another ninety proposals had been forwarded at the city and county levels (as well as at a number of prominent colleges and universities such as Princeton and Harvard).[40] Generally, such ordinances require local governments and their contractors to pay their employees a wage above the poverty level (variously defined).[41]

Living-wage ordinances contribute to the economic well-being of communities by ensuring that a greater percentage of local workers achieve a decent standard of living. Measures in San Jose, Detroit, Cambridge (Massachusetts), and Ypsilanti (Michigan) have set wage and benefit levels at or above $10 per hour—a level almost twice the federal minimum wage. Santa Cruz, Santa Monica, and several smaller California cities in Silicon Valley have considered proposals around or exceeding the $11-per-hour mark.[42]

The living-wage movement has taken off in significant part because of the economic prosperity of the mid-to late 1990s, which served to sharpen and highlight the incongruity between the affluence experienced by those at the higher end of the income distribution and the continuing struggle of the working poor to earn wages adequate to lift them from poverty. To be sure, the overall impact of living-wage ordinances is clearly (and inherently) limited—by the end of the 1990s fewer than 50,000 people had been directly affected.[43] But like many of the conventional policies reviewed in this chapter, these ordinances (and the social movements behind them) suggest a more consequential means for stabilizing the economies of communities. The basis for living-wage movements is an explicit recognition of the considerable economic power of local governments as major employers and purchasers in local economies. Living-wage ordinances attempt to tap this power to promote a modicum of economic fairness in pay rates. As Chapter 7 will suggest, public procurement dollars can help promote community stability in numerous other ways as well. Moreover, living-wage activists themselves have begun to move the campaign beyond the local level to tap into the enormous purchasing power of the federal government: In November 2000, ACORN launched a campaign to demand a living wage of at least $17,025 a year (equivalent to $8.20 an hour) for full-time workers in firms that receive federal contracts.[44]

Linked Development (or Linkage)

Linkage policies are a type of fee (or exaction) imposed on private investors by a city in exchange for granting the right to develop its prime (usually downtown) real estate. Such policies draw a link between that development and the amelioration of the city's social and economic problems. Using their regulatory powers over land use, cities can obligate developers to help address community needs in areas such as affordable housing.[45] In essence, linkage policies are the mirror opposite of development subsidies: Rather than giving away public revenues to attract private investment, investors seeking public zoning and other help instead must devote private revenues to ameliorate public problems.[46] Policies in San Francisco and Boston date to the early 1980s; each generated several million dollars per year. By the early 1990s, at least fifteen cities had implemented linkage policies, including Seattle, Washington; Santa Monica, California; Cambridge, Massachusetts; Cherry Hill, New Jersey; Hartford, Connecticut; and Palo Alto, California.[47]

Linkage policies help to lessen the uneven nature of urban development patterns in cities, especially central cities. Commonly, downtowns boom with the new construction of office towers, hotels, and sports stadiums, while surrounding neighborhoods experience disinvestment and decline. Such uneven development contributes to urban social problems and aggravates fiscal pressures on city governments, spurring them in turn to intensify their chase for development and jobs. By spreading the benefits of downtown development more evenly throughout the city, linkages enhance the economic stabilization both of neighborhoods and of the community as a whole.

Aggressive policies that require developers to provide public benefits, such as linkage, appear to be most feasible in cities with strong real estate markets, where the demand for land is keen and profit potential great (e.g., Boston,

San Francisco).[48] However, detailed studies by Edward Goetz of the University of Minnesota and Laura Reese of Wayne State University have demonstrated that, contrary to conventional economic wisdom, even cities experiencing economic stress are also obligating developers to provide such benefits.[49]

Linkage policies arise from the understanding that the traditional growth created by mainstream economic actors—the big hotel and convention center deals—often fails to bring about widespread community benefits and economic stabilization. Recognition of this fact opens the door to policies that require mainstream actors to supply some of these benefits to the wider community. That recognition also suggests that other means to develop the economy—such as the kinds of community-based, alternative economic institutions discussed in subsequent chapters—may be more effective vehicles for enhancing the overall well-being and economic stability of local communities than conventional incentive-based economic development strategies.

Metropolitan Tax-Base Sharing

Metropolitan tax-base sharing is an arrangement allowing several taxing bodies within the same metropolitan region, typically neighboring local governments, to derive revenues from a common tax base. These schemes pool a certain percentage of regional tax monies and redistribute it to local governments in a compensatory fashion, providing a greater share of monies to governments with weaker capacities to raise revenue due to their weaker tax bases.[50] Commonly they aim to tax richer suburbs to benefit poorer cities.

Tax-base sharing contributes to the economic stability of communities in a variety of ways. Most obviously, it infuses poorer places with additional fiscal resources, thereby allowing them to better provide public services necessary for a healthy and stable community.[51] Tax-base sharing helps to correct for the fiscal inequities generated by the highly deconcentrated growth patterns associated with urban sprawl: fiscally weak places tend to be central cities and their older, nearby suburbs (see Chapter 3). Less obvious but equally important, tax-base sharing tends to reduce the intense competition among neighboring governments for economic development and jobs because revenues generated by new development are shared among jurisdictions across the metropolitan area.[52]

Urban experts agree that the best example to date of tax-base sharing is found in the Minneapolis–St. Paul region under the authority of its Metropolitan Council.[53] "Established in 1967," explain Wim Wiewel, Joseph Persky, and Mark Sendzik, the Council consists of 17 members appointed by the governor. Its area includes seven counties, comprising 187 local governments and 49 school districts. Under the tax-base sharing system, each city must contribute to a regional fund 40% of the growth in tax revenue from its commercial and industrial tax base. This money then is redistributed in inverse proportion to the amount of nonresidential assessed property in each municipality. At present, about 20% of the regional tax base is shared through this system, and it has reduced tax-base disparities between municipalities from approximately 50:1 to approximately 12:1.[54]

The Minneapolis–St. Paul plan clearly stands as a salutary precedent. Yet even this premier example of metropolitan tax sharing unlocks only a fraction of the concept's potential to enhance community economic stability. The system encompasses only 40 percent of the growth of the commercial and industrial tax base and leaves out residential property altogether.

Many observers see the political viability of tax-base sharing in other metropolitan areas as tied to the ability of central cities to build political alliances with their older, declining, blue-collar suburbs. Myron Orfield, the Minnesota state legislator and urban researcher who has been an architect of such an alliance in the Twin Cities region, believes the formula is politically replicable in other metropolitan areas.[55] Orfield reasons that a substantial majority of metropolitan residents, particularly residents of central cities and inner suburbs, would stand to gain from tax-base sharing, and also might successfully join forces with religious organizations and environmentalists throughout the metropolitan area (including in affluent communities).[56] Other experts are skeptical about the political viability of this approach, since very powerful upper-income suburbs commonly stand to lose in such efforts.

Each of the policies and initiatives discussed in this chapter has the potential to make meaningful contributions to the health and stability of local economies. We are supportive of these initiatives and recognize that many of them have a critical role to play in any comprehensive strategy to strengthen local economies.

On the other hand, none of these policies has the effect of firmly anchoring capital and jobs in place. Achieving that goal would require developing forms of ownership of capital that are inherently place-based and which reduce the structural dependence of localities upon mobile capital. We now turn to more proactive, direct approaches to stabilizing local communities that, through a variety of institutional mechanisms, aim to promote stable, locally controlled investment and thereby enhance long-term economic stability.

CHAPTER 6

STATE AND MUNICIPAL ENTERPRISE

Perhaps the most direct way for local governments to contribute to community economic stability is to go into business for themselves. Locally scaled public ownership anchors economic endeavors and the jobs they generate in specific places. Substantial public ownership in a given locality can reduce the community's vulnerability to economic disinvestment while providing governments with an alternative to doling out expensive incentives to attract new businesses into the community or to prevent current businesses from leaving. The possibility of profitable and efficient state and municipally owned enterprise is rarely discussed in mainstream development literature. Despite this inattention from academics and journalists, locally scaled public enterprise is in fact surprisingly robust in the United States at the beginning of the twenty-first century.

State and local public enterprise has a long and noteworthy history in the United States. Governments have traditionally owned and operated utility enterprises in areas such as electricity, water, sewer, and solid-waste collection, as well as enterprises such as airports and seaports, civic centers, public parking facilities, recreational facilities, public transportation systems, and hospitals.[1] Public ownership of these ventures largely survived the wave of privatization cresting in the 1980s and 1990s. Many cities also continue to be involved in profitable public land development. In recent years, as we shall see, public ownership has been expanded to utilities employing new telecommunications technologies to provide services such as cable television and Internet access.

Traditional forms of public ownership play an important role in stabilizing the economies of communities, generating securely rooted jobs and, especially, providing local governments with a substantial source of revenues. Local government in the United States garners almost half its self-generated revenue from government-owned enterprises and fees (the remainder coming primarily from property and sales taxes).[2] In an era when taxation is fiercely resisted for ideological reasons and out of fear that increases will cause capital and residents to flee, profit-making public enterprise can be an important means to supplement the cost of basic public services.

What is less commonly recognized is that locally rooted state and municipal enterprise can also be expanded beyond the traditional enterprises to other sectors of the economy. Traditional forms of public enterprise tend to have a public-goods character, providing necessary services that the private sector often has failed to provide. In contrast, nontraditional forms of public enterprise involve public entities competing in areas of the economy where private provision historically has dominated. While these nontraditional forms have yet to achieve the scale of traditional public enterprises, there are many interesting examples of nontraditional public enterprise upon which local and state governments can build. Virtually all help anchor jobs, thereby improving local community stability.

Indeed, state and local governments now own and operate businesses in sectors such as real estate, professional sports, banking, insurance, retailing and retail merchandising, training and consulting, fertilizer and soil enhancer production, venture capital provision, methane recovery/energy production, equity investment in commercial development, bottling tap water for sale, auto towing, and more. Like more-established forms of public enterprise, these nontraditional forms are mostly nonideological in nature and have proven politically acceptable to both Democrats and Republicans. In fact, these enterprises are commonly associated with the widespread notions of "reinventing government" or "public entrepreneurialism."[3]

Few people realize how widespread and efficient public enterprise already is in the United States. For many Americans the very idea of public enterprise often calls to mind stereotypes of bumbling government bureaucrats wasting resources. That view is flatly contradicted by a recent detailed assessment of municipal enterprises in the state of Florida by political scientist Gary Paul of Florida A&M University. Paul's study of the use of public enterprise in 216 Florida localities notes that

> Most cities offer enterprise services that (1) have a long tradition of user fee application and (2) a proven record of profitability. Cities seem less inclined to offer a broad range of unproven services. For example, the user fee con-

cept has long been attached to the provision and financing of water and sewer services. The vast majority of ventures either run a surplus or are at least self-supporting. This study finds that a significant 72 percent of all water and sewer funds produced a positive return on investment as did 82 percent of the electric utilities, and 85 percent of the parking. Cities tend to shy away from functions like trailer parks, hospitals, and nursing homes though some were profitable. . . .

Most public enterprise ventures were able to run a profit or at least reach a break-even point. On the whole the broad array of functions, though varied, were more profitable than first assumed.[4]

Such findings give pause to traditional stereotypes about public enterprise. Any effort to expand public enterprise, whether in traditional or nontraditional forms, must meet baseline efficiency criteria. We are not interested here in "lemon socialism," where the public owns and operates a host of grossly inefficient and unprofitable enterprises that serve as a drag on local economic performance and in fact damage long-term community stability. On the other hand, in judging whether a specific enterprise satisfies efficiency criteria, the proper metric for evaluation is the concept of the public balance sheet, which we introduced at the outset of this study (see the Introduction). Some public enterprises might appear unprofitable from the perspective of a purely private balance sheet yet show a very different bottom line once the full public and social costs and benefits of the endeavor are considered. Public enterprise, for instance, can reduce costs imposed on the community through unemployment and underutilized or wasted infrastructure. Taking note of the broader public balance sheet provides a more accurate assessment of public enterprise, allowing policy makers to better identify ventures that are true community assets.

STATE AND LOCAL PUBLIC ENTERPRISE: AN OVERVIEW

In the remainder of this chapter we examine a wide range of existing locally scaled public enterprises, focusing on several sectors where public enterprise is well established. This survey illustrates how municipal enterprises can become an integral part of a broader effort to stabilize the economic bases of American communities.

Public Power
Publicly owned utilities (POUs), the most venerable form of state and local enterprise, were created over a hundred years ago to provide electrification for regions (typically rural) that were being passed over by investor-owned utilities (IOUs) as unprofitable. Municipalities formed their own publicly owned,

not-for-profit electricity companies, the first of which emerged in the 1880s. By 1900, more than 800 communities had constructed their own power companies, mostly in small rural towns. Motivated by the desire to maximize profits, private companies generally shunned these smaller communities, preferring to locate in areas with larger, denser populations.

A century later, one out of seven Americans (a total of about 40 million people) relies on power from one of the nation's 2,000 public utilities. One-third of POUs produce electricity, accounting for roughly 12 percent of the county's total installed generating capacity.[5] (The remaining two-thirds distribute electricity produced elsewhere.) About sixty percent of all public power systems are located in communities with less than 3,000 people, but public utilities are also found in large, urban areas such as Los Angeles, San Antonio, Sacramento, Nashville, Jacksonville, Memphis, and, starting in 1998, Long Island. Public power employs almost 80,000 people directly.[6] Analysts pointed out during the California energy crunch of 2001 that cities such as Los Angeles, served by public utilities with their own generating capacity, were better able to avoid the effects of the state crisis and also to provide lower cost service.[7]

In general, public utilities have been able to offer rates substantially lower than private providers in the open marketplace. According to information reported to the U.S. Department of Energy, the residential customers of IOUs in 1999 paid average electricity rates that were about 18 percent higher than those paid by residential customers of POUs. Commercial customers paid rates 9 percent higher than those paid by commercial customers of POUs. The rate savings enjoyed by POU customers in 1999 was actually lower than the historic average (30 percent lower residential rates for POU earlier in the 1990s), due in part to the weighty inclusion of a new public power system in Long Island, which took over from a high-cost private company. (The Long Island Power Authority, however, slashed residential rates by 16 percent within its first year of operation.)[8] Industry studies have established that most of public power's price advantage is due to the fact of public ownership itself—locally-controlled public utilities can be especially responsive to customers' needs, and do not need to pay dividends to private shareholders.[9]

A noteworthy example of a large-scale public utility that has been successful on a variety of levels is the Sacramento Municipal Utility District (SMUD), the fifth-largest publicly owned utility in the nation. SMUD is recognized across the United States as one of the most dynamic and innovative electric utilities. Established in December 1946, the utility provides electricity and energy services to the 1.2 million residents of Sacramento County and a small portion of neighboring Placer County. SMUD is noted for its application of cutting-edge technologies, commitments to cleaner energy and environmental responsibility, competitive rates, and overall excellent service. In addition, SMUD is a major contributor to gaining and maintaining jobs in the community: In a recent five-year period SMUD estimated that its business recruiting, expansion, and retention programs helped bring 19,000 jobs to the Sacramento area. SMUD also spent $25 million in 2000 on public-goods programs such as energy efficiency and discounts for low-income customers. Finally, SMUD operates the "world's largest distributed photovoltaic systems with more than 600 installed systems." Meetings of the board of directors are held every two weeks by the utility; the meetings are open to the public as well as televised locally (citizens can sign up to make statements of up to three minutes at each meeting).[10]

SMUD is both profitable and efficient. Its 2000 operating revenue was $968 million, $77 million higher than operating costs.[11] SMUD had not raised utility rates since 1990 until the California power crisis forced a rate increase in May of 2001—but SMUD continues to offer lower rates than investor-owned utilities in the state.[12] (SMUD's rates have been about 25 percent cheaper in recent years.)[13]

Another good example of a well-run public utility is Seattle City Light (SCL). Established in 1910 and now the nation's seventh-largest public utility, SCL serves 345,000 customers in a 131.3-square-mile area encompassing the City of Seattle and its seven adjacent municipalities. It also provides full-time employment for about 1,700 people. In 1999 the utility's annual operating revenues were in excess of $372 million, with net operating income of over $55 million.[14] According to SCL media manager Sharon Bennett, "Seattle City Light offers the lowest-cost utilities of any of the U.S.'s 60 largest urban centers." SCL has also been recognized nationally for its strong commitment to environmental stewardship.[15]

Recent reports suggest a new movement to create POUs may be building in reaction to the high electricity rates charged by private providers. From 1980 to 1995, thirty-three new municipal systems were started, and by the mid-1990s twenty-five communities were actively pursuing conversion to public power, while "scores more" were considering the concept.[16] However, Madalyn Cafruny of the American Public Power Association argues that "even though communities may desire publicly owned utilities, established private suppliers are able to bring great resources to bear in order to block new creation of public utilities that compete with their own. For this reason, the number of public utilities has remained static at about 2,000."[17] Nevertheless, the widespread interest in creating new POUs demonstrates that the public ownership option remains a viable and desirable strategy for communities more than a century after the first municipal utilities were formed.

Telecommunications

The telecommunications industry—including landline telephones, PCS service, Internet services, cable television, and the hardware, software, fiber-optic lines, and transmission towers that support these services—continues to grow at an astounding rate. However, the industry's growth has been highly uneven. Echoing the country's experience with electrification in the early twentieth century, private telecommunications companies have focused on building advanced telecommunications infrastructure in lucrative urban markets while neglecting smaller or rural communities. Such "electronic redlining" exacerbates inequality between regions, because an up-to-date technological infrastructure has become vital to maintaining or building a healthy local economy and to giving individuals marketable job skills. As a result, municipal governments—most often the municipal electric utilities—are stepping in to fill the telecommunications void.[18]

Municipal utilities also see Internet, cable television, fiber-optic networks, telephone service, and other telecommunications provision as a way to survive in a competitive deregulated electricity market. Successful small utilities, industry experts believe, can thrive in a climate of deregulation by branching out beyond electricity.[19] Nashville Electric Service, a larger utility, is using its infrastructure to help provide telecommunications, according to Matthew Cordaro, chief executive officer of the 300,000-customer service. The utility has allowed communications access providers to attach fiber-optic cables to its electrical distribution poles. "We can participate in a percentage of their profits and get free fiber for our own use. This is an example where we capitalize on our existing assets to minimize the pressure for increasing rates," he explains.[20] A smaller-scale example is the North Attleboro (Massachusetts) Electric Department (11,000 customers), which has invested $2 million in a fiber-optic network to provide telecom and Internet service.[21] Since the mid-1990s, of thirty-two Iowa cities in which referenda were held, only two community-owned utilities were denied voter approval to operate a telecommunications company offering cable and Internet services. Over a third of the time voters approved establishing these systems by majorities of 90 percent or greater.[22]

By 2001 nearly a hundred other local governments around the nation had constructed their own publicly owned telecommunications network (or a public-private joint venture). These diverse cities include Gainesville,

Florida; Wadsworth, Ohio; Alameda, California; La Grange, Georgia; Braintree, Massachusetts; Chattanooga, Tennessee; and over forty rural communities in the state of Iowa alone.[23] A study conducted in the late 1990s found that of the 270 municipal and cooperative utilities surveyed, 24 percent "planned to compete in the telecommunications industry in the next 5 years."[24]

The telecommunications field offers an arena in which communities can take greater control over their economic fate. By launching their own telecommunications utilities, not only can municipalities ensure that all residents have access to high-quality technologies at affordable rates; they also can strengthen their localities' economic bases by attracting more jobs, capital, and resources to their communities.

The most spectacular example to date of a city of modest means owning its own telecommunications operations service can be found in Glasgow, Kentucky.[25] In 1988 Glasgow's municipally owned utility began construction of a telecommunications network spanning some 120 miles of wire. As a result, the town's 14,000 residents have Internet access a hundred times faster than a telephone modem but pay only $12.95 a month for unlimited use plus access to an intranet linking local government, businesses, libraries, schools, and neighbors. They also are offered a cable television package of fifty-three channels for under $15 a month. By comparison, a private provider, before facing the city's competition, charged nearly $40 a month for standard service. In 2001, the utility bought the competing Comcast system, a move that will double the number of cable customers and nearly quadruple the service area.[26] Even more unusual, Glasgow residents can choose to get local phone service through the utility rather than the local private provider.

Lower cable rates alone have saved Glasgow residents an estimated $14 million since 1989. This is money that can continue to circulate in the local community, helping local businesses and the families they support. The utility itself employs some fifty people and has helped attract (and retain) major industries to the area—bringing further economic stabilization. R. R. Donnelley & Sons, Johnson Controls, Akebono Brake, International Paper, SKF Tapered Bearings, and other firms have relocated or expanded in Glasgow in recent years. The cable television division of the utility has broken even financially every year since fiscal 1997–98, as has the city's Internet division.[27]

Another municipality that recently decided to enter the telecom industry is Tacoma, Washington—a medium-sized city of nearly 200,000 people located thirty miles from Seattle.[28] Tacoma has a long history of municipal enterprises—it established its own water utility in the late nineteenth century when the private provider could not supply enough safe drinking water to support the city's growing population. Soon thereafter the city established its own power utility and railroad beltline. Today, Tacoma Power, through its telecommunications division, Click!, is leading the city's effort to launch a municipally owned and controlled telecommunications network.

Click!'s initial business plan, presented to the Tacoma City Council and the utility board, assumed that if 25 percent of Tacoma's cable customers subscribed, the system could pay for itself. In 1998 the system was connected and by mid-2000 had over 16,000 customers—26 percent of the local market. The city attracted over a hundred high-tech firms within two years of constructing the network. Click! also is working with local telecommunications companies to develop broadband products such as high-speed Internet service.[29]

Other benefits to the citizens of Tacoma include competition in the cable market, which drives down prices and generally raises service levels. (Previously Tacomans had only one choice in cable television: TCI, which upgraded its system in response to the competition from Click!). Today, Click! continues to offer monthly rates $2 cheaper than AT&T Broadband (which has taken over the TCI system).[30] Click! also affords Tacomans access to one of the most advanced information systems in the world, while the telecommunications system generally adds value to the established public utility.

The success and potential of public telecommunications systems have not gone unnoticed. Private providers have organized campaigns in a number of states to get state legislatures to bar municipalities from constructing such systems—measures have passed in ten states so far.[31] There is absolutely no persuasive *economic* argument for banning municipal entry into this market; in most cases, municipalities are either challenging local private monopolists and introducing competition, or introducing service in areas that private firms will not enter unless prodded.

At the heart of the ongoing political struggle is the important question of whether access to the information superhighway is to be regarded as a public good like electricity or as a purely private commodity. An even broader question is whether the private sector should be spared competition from public entities. We believe ideological prejudice against public-sector activity distorts this discussion. Public enterprise can be an expression of collective self-governance, and it can be a bulwark for community stability—which in turn enhances democracy and reduces dependence on private economic actors. On the other hand, efficiency considerations are also important. Unless evaluated with regard to whether or not public-sector initiatives such as Glasgow's improve the quality of life and well-being of the community's residents, the debate about public telecommunications will become nothing less than a political struggle by self-interested private economic actors. The result could be the loss of the possibility of using public utilities in creative ways to enhance both localities' quality of life and local democracy itself.

Financial Institutions

A crucial element in the formula for enhancing community economic stability is provision of locally oriented, democratic control over credit and investment capital. Such control allows economic resources to be directed in ways that help communities maintain a sufficient degree of jobs and economic activity to support the needs of their citizens and governments. As we shall see, several state and local policy initiatives and institutional forms help to democratize credit and capital allocation, including targeted investments by public pension funds (see Chapter 7) and such community-based financial institutions as community credit unions and community development banks (see Chapter 9).

Publicly owned financial institutions—such as banks and insurance companies—offer another option. Leading precedents in this sector can be found on the state level. One is the Wisconsin State Life Insurance Fund (WSLF), created in 1911 at the height of the Progressive movement in Wisconsin. The publicly owned and operated enterprise was started "to give the people of the state the benefit of the best old-line insurance on a mutual plan at the lowest possible cost."[32] Today the fund manages about $70 million in net assets.[33] Because of its low overhead and absence of private profit, WSLF has been able to offer life insurance premiums estimated to be between 10 and 40 percent cheaper than private insurance coverage.[34]

Another precedent is the Bank of North Dakota (BND), which is more than eighty years old. With 2000 earnings of over $32 million, total assets of more than $1.8 billion, bank capital of over $153 million, and loans totaling $1.16 billion, BND stands as an even more impressive example of state-level public enterprise.[35] This state development bank injected more than $200 million into the North Dakota economy in 1998 alone. BND's lending programs offer borrowers lower interest rates and long-term fixed rates, and the bank often takes greater risks in order to achieve socially desirable development goals.[36]

BND directs its development lending to four major categories: business, agriculture, student loans, and residential lending. Working in partnership with private institutions, the bank helped finance over 350 business and industrial projects in the state in 1999 and 2000 alone. The bank also hosts a One-Stop capital center to aid business start-ups or expansions. The center is operated in collaboration with a variety of state and federal agencies such as the Small Business Association. In agriculture alone, BND directly provided or participated in $156 million in loans for 1998, including $30 million to help struggling farmers and ranchers restructure debt. To enhance educational access in the state, BND guaranteed over 31,000 student loans made by other banks throughout the state, totaling $293 million in 1998. Finally, BND funded over $100 million in new home loans in 1998, mostly by providing an aggressive secondary market for VA and FHA federally guaranteed loans, helping "to make home mortgage funding more readily available for smaller towns and rural areas."[37]

Perhaps most remarkably, BND's track record of profitable operation allows it to transfer significant monies back to the state to help fund other public programs. These surpluses, amounting to $50 million for the 1999–2001 biennium, represent the fifth-largest source of money for the state's general fund.[38]

On the municipal level, several governments have flirted with establishing publicly owned financial institutions. There have been serious proposals to open city-owned banks in Detroit, Michigan, and Minot, North Dakota, and to establish a municipal auto insurance company in Baltimore, Maryland.[39] In Detroit a proposal to create a city-owned bank was part of a comprehensive plan to reindustrialize the local economy following waves of corporate disinvestment; in Baltimore, the proposed creation of a city-run insurance firm was seen as a pragmatic response to private insurers' practice of charging city residents exorbitant auto insurance rates (a practice that also helps fuel residential flight to the suburbs).[40]

Venture Capitalism

Another form of public enterprise is state-sponsored venture capitalism. An increasing number of state and local governments have become venture capitalists, using public funds to make equity investments in local firms and becoming a stockholder in return.

In recent years, over twenty-five states have operated venture capital programs that involve direct investments by state agencies in local companies.[41] One of the most interesting is Maryland's Enterprise Investment Fund, which has invested roughly $15 million in over thirty Maryland companies, creating more than 600 jobs and generating an investment portfolio of over $46 million.[42] The fund provides promising high-tech start-ups up to $500,000 in capital in exchange for equity shares and a guarantee that the firm will operate in the state for at least five years.[43] The Maryland fund has performed exceptionally well: From 1994 to 1997, the state realized a 132 percent return on its investments, as the value of its stock held in the various companies rose from $5.25 million to over $12 million.[44] More recently, the fund generated enormous profits when it sold its interests in two highly successful ventures, turning a $750,000 investment into $44 million! These profits are in turn reinvested in the fund and used to capitalize other local companies and generate additional jobs for the state's economy.[45] Similar programs in Connecticut and Massachusetts dating to the 1970s have been credited with the creation of thousands of jobs in their respective states[46], while turning impressive recent profits. Connecticut received about $21 million in returns on its investment in 1999, while Massachusetts expected to make approximately $35 million in 2000.[47]

On the local level, a 1987 survey of 322 cities found that 32 (9.9 percent) used venture capital as an economic development tool in 1986, and over a quarter planned to in the future.[48] Nine years later, a 1996 survey found that one-third of responding city governments had used venture capital funds to help create jobs.[49]

Real Estate

Another important public enterprise activity on the local level is real estate development. Many local governments limit their involvement in this area to managing properties they own through their real estate or asset departments, often simply preparing properties for disposal on the market. However, some cities have chosen a more entrepreneurial path, engaging in public enterprise (in partnership with the private sector) and either retaining land ownership and leasing publicly owned land for private development or receiving partial ownership (equity) in private land development projects in return for public investment.[50] Such efforts contrast with the more typical pattern of public-private collaboration in which the public sector bears most of the risk and the private sector garners most of the reward.[51]

American cities have been involved in entrepreneurial real estate development since at least the 1970s. Under the innovative leadership of city council leader Nicholas Carbone in the 1970s, for instance, the city of Hartford, Connecticut, retained title to the land on which its civic center complex was constructed, leasing the air rights for a hotel, office space, and retail establishments to private operators. The city also took ownership of an abandoned department store and leased it as office space to a major airline. Describing Hartford's strategy in a lecture entitled "The City as a Real Estate Investor," Carbone stated that the city would "try to own property and buildings" to "give the city control over land use and allow [it] to realize the increasing value as land prices increased."[52]

Also in the 1970s, the city of Boston embarked on a joint venture with the Rouse Company to develop the Faneuil Hall Marketplace (a downtown retail complex). Boston not only kept the property under public ownership but negotiated a lease agreement though which the city secured a portion of the development's profits in lieu of property taxes. During the mid-1980s Boston earned $2.5 million per year from the agreement. According to Bernard Frieden and Lynne Sagalyn, "Boston has taken in 40 percent more revenue than it would have collected through conventional property tax channels. . . . If Boston had taken the dollars it invested in the marketplace and put them instead into long-term U.S. Treasury bonds, the return over forty years, after inflation, would have been less than half what the city can expect from Faneuil Hall Marketplace."[53]

Entrepreneurial "participating lease" arrangements for the use of publicly owned property are common around the country. In such arrangements—employed in cities such as New York, San Diego, Los Angeles, and Washington, D.C.—a developer pays the public landlord both a yearly base rent and an additional amount pegged to project performance (e.g., private profits or gross income). As in many private shopping center developments, the principle at work is straightforward: "The more money the developer makes, the higher the rent."[54]

Also dating from at least the 1970s is the joint development of publicly owned land surrounding mass-transit stations. Retaining public ownership in such instances both allows cities to capture the often immediate and dramatic rise in the value of surrounding property that frequently accompanies the opening of a new transit station and also enables cities to plan a mix of development types (retail, housing, office, etc.) around transit stations to maximize the potential public benefits of the investment.

The most well developed example of this activity is the Washington Metropolitan Area Transit Authority in Washington, DC. By the late 1990s, WMATA's twenty-four revenue-generating joint development projects earned between $7 million and $8 million in additional revenue each year for the agency, making it the authority's largest non–fare-box revenue source. Other transit authorities in cities around the country—including Miami, Atlanta, San Francisco, and even Cedar Rapids, Iowa—also have taken or are in the process of taking this approach.[55]

Transit joint development projects and downtown retail centers are only two of the many ways cities have benefited from retaining public ownership over land. San Diego's Real Estate Assets Department holds nearly 700 leases that generate revenues totaling $36 million annually, including Mission Bay Park, Sea World, and sundry other retail, agricultural, and commercial sites.

The city has been continually acquiring property since the 1800s and seldom makes moves to sell land, preferring the benefits of leasing.[56]

Other examples include:

- Portland, Maine, which leases a number of city properties, and operates a twelve-acre naval shipyard, an interisland ferry system, and a pier. In 2001 the city's eight enterprise funds had operating income of nearly $1.5 million.

- The Port of Los Angeles, which controls several retail properties, including Ports O'Call Village, a large retail shopping and dining complex that generates between $650,000 and $1.5 million annually, and another retail/restaurant complex, the West Channel development, which is expected to bring in $1.2 million in leases as well as healthy percentages of gross receipts.

- Alhambra, California, which earns about $1 million a year in rent revenues and profits from a six-acre location it leases to commercial tenants, while requiring the tenant businesses to reserve a majority of jobs for low- and moderate-income community residents.[57]

Some cities have pushed the concept of public enterprise in real estate development even further, moving beyond simply leasing publicly owned property to private interests to become a co-owner of development projects. These equity holdings give local governments a share of project profits or net cash flows. Examples include Fairfield, California (10 to 17 percent of the net cash flow of a regional shopping mall), Cincinnati, Ohio (17 percent of profits from a development project that includes a home office for a local bank and a hotel), San Antonio, Texas (17 percent of net cash flow from a local hotel), and Louisville (15 percent of net cash flow from a project that includes an office building and a hotel).[58]

Equity participation in land development projects clearly sets an important precedent for the further development of state and local public enterprise. It establishes the public sector as a legitimate owner of (and profit-taker from) productive assets. Moreover, profits earned by public enterprise help localities enhance services critical to economic development in general. The establishment of this principle in current practice also opens the door for expanding appropriate public enterprise into other sectors of the local economy.

Commercial Ventures

Over the past several years local governments across the country have launched a wide range of commercially oriented, public firms that generate additional funds to support their programs and services. Such initiatives range from government agencies selling their services or expertise (to other jurisdictions or to businesses) to local governments owning and operating their own retail shops. The strategy became increasingly common in the 1990s in response to local fiscal strain. Largely because California experienced a harsher fiscal climate than most other states, counties and cities in that state (including some very conservative localities) became leaders in this form of local public enterprise.

One popular municipal commercial venture is the city-owned retail store, now found in cities such as Long Beach, Los Angeles, San Diego, Chicago, and Phoenix. These municipal stores sell city-related souvenirs as well as old, unneeded government property. The stores have generated revenues and employment opportunities while boosting community pride and preserving historically significant items (such as old city signs and equipment).

A particularly popular store (both locally and through its mail order catalog) is run by the Los Angeles County Coroner's Office. The store sells a wide range of items, including ID toe tags (used as key chains), beach towels designed with police-chalk body outlines, and mugs decorated with skeletons. The store generates about $20,000 per month in revenues for the department—which in turn helps fund a drunk driving prevention program. Another successful retail initiative is San Diego's City Store. This is a joint public-private venture between the city and a local private contractor charged with managing and operating the enterprise. Its first two shops opened in December 1991, and City Store now has four permanent locations, two of which are in major shopping malls; a fifth site is open only during the holiday season. Through its sales of San Diego souvenirs such as T-shirts, caps, mugs, and postcards as well as salvaged city equipment such as street signs, old parking meters, traffic signals, and fire hydrants, City Store grossed over $750,000 in fiscal 2001, with an operating profit just under $50,000.[59]

Some municipal departments and agencies also sell services and/or expertise to other municipalities, businesses, and other organizations. One example is San Diego's CENTRE for Organization Effectiveness, created by the city in the early 1980s to develop and implement training programs for its own departments. In 1993 CENTRE began to offer its management training, organization development, diversity education, and similar specialized programs to a broad range of municipalities, agencies, special districts, nonprofits, and private organizations. The success of the initiative allowed CENTRE to pay back its start-up loan of $90,000 ahead of schedule and begin funneling profits back into San Diego's general fund. By 1998

CENTRE's revenues had grown to a projected $1 million a year, with $60,000 earmarked for San Diego's general fund.[60]

Not only do local governments sell their expert services; they also have begun to market the products they develop. Journalist Michael Silverstein notes that by the mid-1990s each of Los Angeles County's thirty-four departments engaged in some form of product marketing. For instance, its District Attorney's Office sells crime prevention tapes and court record data to private companies, and its Department of Public Social Services sells food stamp control software it developed to other localities.

In another notable example the Data Resource Center (DRC) of Portland, Oregon's regional government, Metro, developed a desktop version of its Geographic Information Systems (GIS) data and began marketing the product to the public in 1997. This software provides users—such as real estate brokers, transportation engineers, cable and other utility operators, banks, and title companies—with more than fifty map layers of the Portland region that display demographic, economic, and geographical data. In fiscal year 1997–98, Metro's sales of the software generated $302,000 for the Data Resource Center, providing 20 percent of the DRC's operating support.[61]

Professional Sports

Another area ripe for further public enterprise development is professional sports. Over the past decade the prospect of transferring team ownership to the communities they represent has inspired increasing interest. Support for public ownership grew as a number of wealthy major-league team owners used the threat of relocation to obtain huge public subsidies to build lavish new stadiums or remodel existing ones. Many citizens and community activists judged this practice to be unconscionable: The new or remodeled facilities are designed to cater to corporate executives and upscale patrons, while the public dollars funding them are typically generated by regressive taxes disproportionately paid by the poor. Other owners, such as Art Modell of the old Cleveland Browns, after failing to convince their host cities to build new stadiums, made good on the threat and relocated their teams to cities offering a more generous deal.

Uprooting teams obviously disrupts fan loyalty. Given the prominent role played by sports in our culture, runaway sports franchises damage local community life in the United States and weaken a tangible source of community and civic pride.[62] Against this backdrop of financial "blackmail," social inequity, and disregard for community considerations, local public ownership of sports teams looks increasingly attractive. In many cases, buying a local team would not be outrageously expensive—at least not compared to subsidies now given for stadiums, which often amount to three times the market value of the franchise itself. *Governing* magazine's Charles Mahtesian observes that given this context, it is "absurd [for cities] not to at least explore the economics of buying a franchise. If private owners are going to be that expensive, maybe they are a luxury that a smart community can afford to dispense with."[63]

Precedents for publicly owned sports teams abound. "The truth," notes Mahtesian, "is that public ownership of sports teams is not only conceivable —it is actually being done in quite a few communities around the country."[64] Communities that own (or have owned) minor-league baseball teams include Indianapolis, Indiana; Rochester, New York; Franklin County (Columbus), Ohio; Lucus County (Toledo), Ohio; Harrisburg, Pennsylvania; Lackawanna County (Scranton), Pennsylvania; and Visalia, California. On the major-league level, the Green Bay Packers are owned by a nonprofit corporation rather than by a wealthy private individual. This ownership structure, while not technically fitting the public enterprise model, does keep any one person from owning more than a small part of the team and makes it next to impossible for the team to be relocated to another city or purchased by outsiders (see Chapter 10).[65]

Current private owners of sports teams are the biggest obstacle to moving public ownership up to the major leagues. For example, the National Football League bars public ownership (as well as the future creation of a Packers-style nonprofit corporation) by requiring that a single individual own at least 51 percent of each franchise. Major League Baseball has no formal policy against public ownership, but its team owners have consistently blocked it on a case-by-case basis. For instance, former Padres owner Joan Kroc was prohibited from giving her team to the city of San Diego, and the city of Montreal was prohibited from taking an equity stake in the Expos for its investment in the franchise.[66]

One way to get the major leagues to stop discriminating against public ownership is through congressional intervention. Congressman Earl Blumenauer, from Oregon, has introduced legislation (the Give Fans a Chance Act of 1997) that "would override all league rules against public ownership" by taking away something Congress now grants leagues—their sports broadcast antitrust exemption—if a league blocks a community from buying a team.[67] Legislation modeled on the Blumenauer bill would provide localities with a commonsense way to root runaway teams in place and reduce the unfair leverage now enjoyed by wealthy owners.

Other Enterprises

Still another sector in which public enterprises are particularly prominent is recreation. Since the 1970s many state and local governments have extended their recreation programs and facilities beyond traditional neighborhood parks and community swimming pools to own and operate such larger ventures as golf courses. City governments also often provide for-fee classes and programs in such areas as yoga, jujitsu, dancing, dog obedience, and aerobics. In fact, some of these new enterprises are so large that they are not only significant income generators but also major employers for the area.[68]

Many states and localities own and operate golf courses. According to the National Golf Foundation, by the late 1990s there were more than 2,500 publicly owned courses in the United States, representing nearly 16 percent of all courses in the country. Several publicly owned courses are considered to be among the best in the nation. These include Bethpage Black, the site of the 2002 U.S. Open and one of just five courses at New York's Bethpage State Park. Golf courses can be quite a lucrative venture for state and local governments: According to the National Golf Foundation, the median eighteen-hole, municipally-owned course generated nearly $160,000 in net operating income in 1998.[69]

On a quite different level, numerous local governments also have developed moneymaking enterprises that respond to environmental needs. Roughly 1,400 American cities and counties now operate composting systems. Such systems can help localities reduce landfill costs, and in some cases generate revenue from sales of the end product as a soil supplement. Two sewage treatment plants owned by Milwaukee transform 50,000 tons of sludge a year into a fertilizer marketed by the city, yielding about $6 million in annual revenues. An Austin, Texas, facility for wastewater bio-solid reuse saves about $500,000 a year in landfill costs and also contributes to the making of Dillo Dirt, a soil enhancer that earns the city $120,000 per year.[70]

About seventy-five municipalities across the nation are currently involved in revenue-generating methane recovery operations; these collect potentially harmful methane gas from landfills and turn it into an energy source. Glendale, California's program is expected to lead to total savings and added revenues of $2 million per year over a twenty-year period. Glendale has received support from the Department of Energy's Renewable Energy Production Incentive. A methane recovery system at a landfill owned by Riverview, Michigan, produces electricity that is sold to Detroit Edison; royalties covered initial costs in the first two years and now add to Riverview's cash flow. In addition, Raleigh, North Carolina; Jacksonville, Florida; and the state of Rhode Island all operate such systems.[71]

Public enterprise has been successfully utilized in many other sectors. Long Beach, California, owns and operates a towing company. Santa Clara, California, owned and then sold a theme park. Houston, Texas, and Kansas City, Missouri, bottle and sell water from their municipal systems.[72] At the state level, North Carolina purchased a passenger rail company and owns the tracks, trains, and rights of way. Since 1990 the state has offered passenger service from Charlotte to Rocky Mount, and in 1995 it added service between Charlotte and Raleigh. (Both lines are operated by Amtrak staff.) The state is considering eventually expanding passenger service from Raleigh to Wilmington. In 1998 the state spent $71 million to buy out private shareholders in the 317-mile North Carolina Railroad (built in the nineteenth century); it then offered a fifteen-year lease to Norfolk Southern for use of the track for freight service, a deal that will yield the state $11 million a year.[73] A number of other states also own rail track, and Washington State also owns passenger trains.[74]

PUBLIC ENTERPRISE IN PERSPECTIVE

Locally scaled public enterprise has become a logical, direct way to promote community economic stability. Rather than attempting to induce or bribe the private sector to invest in communities as a means of creating jobs (through taxation policies, regulatory schemes, and other incentives), local governments now regularly generate jobs directly by going into business for themselves. Public enterprise has advantages in generating revenue for city operations, too. Instead of remaining dependent on the private sector to produce wealth for the community and using taxes as the sole source of public revenue, local governments can strengthen their fiscal position by utilizing the surpluses produced by public enterprises.

The political, economic, and institutional feasibility of this approach is also evident in the remarkable range of existing, viable, real-world precedents operating today in local economies all across America. It is clear, of course, that no single public enterprise can stabilize and anchor an entire community. But even the examples we have reviewed show that what is possible extends far beyond the old labels of "lemon socialism" and other pejoratives commonly associated with public enterprise, especially if evaluated according to the public balance sheet accounting system. The fact that cities have already succeeded in numerous high-tech areas—from Glasgow's telecommunications system and various cities' ecological initiatives to Maryland's venture capital fund and Portland Metro's GIS software—demonstrates the dynamic potential for developing public enterprises on the cutting edge of the economy.

A word of caution is in order here: Some of the activity that now goes under the broad label of "public entrepreneurship" or "entrepreneurial government" consists not of government providing a marketable product but of the selling off of various parts of the public sphere for a profit. Cities now regularly sell naming rights to sports stadiums (and on occasion naming rights to the city itself), lease advertising space on city buses, grant corporations licensing rights to use the city's logo or name, and the like. In other cases, fees have been charged for services that were previously provided to city residents for free. Some examples of such revenue-enhancement schemes are harmless, but others compromise the integrity of public spaces and the public sphere. The rubric of entrepreneurial government can also be used to justify what are in essence regressive taxes on the delivery of city services. Such forms of revenue enhancement should not be considered municipal enterprise any more than one would call a governor who simply sold a state's forest lands a businessman.

Municipal enterprise consists not in selling off assets or charging new user fees but in earning money by providing a good or service to the public not normally considered a free government provision or in stewarding the public's assets (such as in land development or venture capital funds) in ways that provide jobs and generate a revenue stream while preserving or enhancing the asset.

We believe that municipal enterprise should play a larger role in any comprehensive community stability strategy, in both its job-creation and revenue-enhancement roles. The commonly held myth that public enterprise is either inherently inefficient or ideologically impossible within the context of the United States simply cannot be sustained in light of the rich array of successful public enterprises now operating all across the nation. Many forms of municipal enterprise discussed in this chapter have enjoyed local-level political support from across the political spectrum. It is past time for municipal enterprise to be recognized as a legitimate, rational, and effective way for twenty-first-century communities to help stabilize their local economies.

CHAPTER 7

STRENGTHENING LOCAL MULTIPLIERS

m ost discussions about economic development focus on the question of how to bring in new resources and investments. Relatively little is said about how localities can make the most of the economic activities already present in the community. We believe that strengthening the capacity of communities to use local resources more effectively is a neglected policy tool that must play a crucial role in a comprehensive community stability agenda.

The best way localities can fully capitalize on their existing economic bases is by slowing the leakage of resources out of the community and increasing the degree to which resources circulate internally. Where there is a high level of interdependence among local economic actors, each new local economic activity stimulates significantly more activity as it ripples or spins off through the community. Increasing the size of this spin-off effect—and the degree to which local firms are linked with one another—would make achieving community stabilization more manageable for localities. Simply put, a local economy with rich networks of interaction between local enterprises and higher spin-off effects will be able to stabilize jobs more easily than localities in which every dollar spent flies straight out of the community, and such an economy will be less dependent on attracting new capital investment from outside to maintain economic health.

The critical concept in this policy area is the economic multiplier. Multipliers quantitatively measure the cumulative local economic impact ultimately generated by a given activity. For example, local multipliers measure the extent to which adding or protecting one core job (and income) in the local economy positively impacts the jobs (and incomes) of others. One hundred newly employed workers earning $35,000 annually each obviously will have money to spend on food, clothing, entertainment, and the like, hence creating additional jobs for persons providing those goods and services. If a town or city has a multiplier of 1.5, then for every two new jobs created, a third will naturally spin off of the other two. If, however, this multiplier can be raised from 1.5 to, say, 2.5, then for each two new jobs created, *three more* new jobs also will be added, for a total of five.

The multiplier, as University of Montana economist Thomas Michael Power explains, is determined by "the character and structure of the local economy. The more quickly injected income leaks out of the local economy, the smaller the multiplier." Hence the key to raising community multipliers is to maximize the amount of money local producers and consumers (within both the private and public sectors) spend within the community. The flip side of this dynamic involves minimizing the amount of money flowing out of the community when those same producers and consumers purchase goods imported from nonlocal sources. As Power puts it, "the multiplier is inversely related to the fraction of local spending that goes to importing goods."[1]

Income that is spent and respent locally circulates and recirculates through the community, bringing additional wealth and employment with each transaction. If a local manufacturer buys inputs from a local supplier rather than one located far away, the local supplier will be able to expand its job base and increase its revenues. In turn, if this added business and wage income is also spent locally, other local businesses will be able to expand their job bases and will realize similar revenue increases.[2] So long as expenditures continue to occur locally, the cycle is repeated, multiplying over and over again the economic benefits accruing to the local community. As Power notes, "The more self-sufficient a local economy is, the longer injected income circulates within and the larger the overall multiplier impact."[3] Since the key to increasing local multipliers is to maximize the intensity at which resources (such as income) coming into a community circulate internally before they leak out, communities need to understand how to plug the leaks in their local economies.

To aid communities in this effort, researchers have studied the ways in which resources flow across community boundaries. One tool used in such studies is the Community Income and Expenditure Model (CIEM), recently developed at Michigan State University. The model allows communities to track income and expenditure flows through a comprehensive analysis of "how much money enters the community and how much remains local." Data are collected through community surveys in which "residents, businesses, government offices, and nonprofit agencies are asked to report the size of their expenditures in various categories that apply to them, and what percent of each purchase is bought locally." The surveys also track the source and amount of firms' and households' income. Thus far, the CIEM has been applied to communities such as north Lansing, southwest Detroit, and the Hillman School District (all in Michigan).[4] Historically, the attempt to study how resources flow through a local community's economy dates back at least thirty years. Notable examples of such studies have been undertaken in East Oakland, California; Chester, Pennsylvania; Buffalo, New York; and Minneapolis, Minnesota.[5] Not surprisingly, the methodological basis of these studies has improved over time.[6]

Communities striving to enhance local multipliers can gain a better understanding of where economic leaks occur by conducting or commissioning these studies. Localities (and states) can pursue a variety of policies to plug these leaks. In this chapter, we review the most noteworthy and potentially effective strategies. Import substitution, development of small (and locally owned) businesses, local currency programs, and economically targeted investments (with pension fund dollars) are discussed below. All aim either to increase interdependence among local firms or to increase the degree to which a state or locality's financial resources circulate locally.

IMPORT SUBSTITUTION

Import substitution is the most direct means by which local economic multipliers can be augmented. Because most orthodox economists analyze economic development by focusing their attention almost exclusively on the amount of income injected into the local economy from its export base, many underemphasize the role played by import substitution in stabilizing local economies.[7] Even if a city or region successfully exports products and thus experiences a great injection of income from outside sources, the new income may do relatively little to promote economic vitality if it quickly flows out of the local economy. However, in a city or region that can produce local substitutes for imports, injected income will stay in the community for a longer period of time, boosting local economic vitality substantially.

It may be fairly pointed out that import substitution will hurt other communities' ability to export and that there may be no net gain to the economy as a whole from substituting local goods for non-local goods. (Indeed, prices may rise slightly for consumers.) There are at least three key reasons why such a policy is still desirable. First, as noted, import substitution can increase community economic stability and in turn positively impact local democracy.

Second, as Thomas Michael Power argues, greater local-level economic diversity should imply a higher quality of life for local residents—and also fuel long-term economic health: "The availability of a broad array of local services and amenities makes a community a more attractive place to both potential businesses and residents." Powers adds, "Supporting the establishment and expansion of local-oriented enterprises that make the local economy more diverse and self-sufficient creates the more sophisticated social and economic framework we seek, integrating each of us into a richer and richer social organization."[8] Jane Jacobs made a similar point in describing import substitution as the process by which cities grow and become vital, interesting places.[9] Third, as many environmentalists have pointed out, there may be significant ecological benefit (in the form of reduced transportation and energy costs or, in the case of perishables, less waste) from economies that are more localized. We do not advocate local economic autarky, but we also believe that local economies—and local democracy—can benefit from policies aimed at stimulating a process of import substitution and diversification of the local economy and at keeping money recirculating locally.

Buy-local policies and produce-local policies can promote import substitution in local communities. Buy-local programs seek to encourage local *purchasing* of local goods and services, while produce-local efforts encourage local *production* of goods and services that are currently supplied by outside sources.

Buy-Local Import-Substitution Policies

Efforts to encourage local purchasing come in three primary forms, each targeting a different economic sector. Local buyer-supplier networks attempt to strengthen the economic linkages within a community's business sector by encouraging local enterprises to form purchasing relationships with one another. Households in the consumer sector can be targeted though a variety of efforts to encourage them to buy from local rather than nonlocal sources. The use of procurement preferences by the public sector gives local firms an advantage over nonlocal firms in bidding for government contracts, allowing more public dollars to be spent locally. Each policy attempts to get local purchasers to substitute locally produced goods and services for those imported from outside the community.

Examples and precedents for building local buyer-supplier networks can be found on the local, regional, and state levels. One illustrative attempt to build a buyer-supplier network on the local level is the Buy Chicago program of the 1980s. This program began when several local corporate leaders created the Buy Chicago Committee, with the aim of increasing the inputs large corporations procured from the city's small businesses. The first step was to create a computerized database of the goods and services corporations were willing to buy from a local supplier. Small firms, in turn, submitted product brochures that could be used to find matches in the database. The program later established fairs to match purchasing agents from large firms or institutions with potential local suppliers.[10]

In North Carolina, the state's Mid-East Commission (a development organization serving five rural counties) undertook an effort to build buyer-supplier networks on the regional level. With support from the General Assembly and the North Carolina Rural Economic Development Center, this project, the Rural Local Markets Demonstration, identified "products, services, parts, and raw materials that manufacturers would like to purchase locally" and combined this research with an "analysis of the region's assets and capabilities to produce a list of products and services best suited to [a] . . . local-to-local buying and selling initiative." By enhancing the ties between local suppliers and manufacturers, the project facilitated the local purchase of twenty-five products and services that were formerly imported into the region. "The ties are vital," noted Bob Paciocco, executive director of the Mid-East Commission. "Every dollar that stays within the region helps our local economy, so we must strive to match suppliers' capabilities with manufacturers' needs to ensure that purchasing is done locally."[11]

Two state-level examples of efforts to build buyer-supplier networks are the Oregon Marketplace and Arkansas Matchmaker programs. Oregon Marketplace, established in the early 1980s, contacted local firms to find out which inputs they were purchasing from nonlocal vendors and then circulated a list of these products to local businesses that could potentially meet this demand, with the aim of brokering matches between potential buyers and potential suppliers. The program today is operated (with support from Oregon Lottery funds) by an Oregon nonprofit, the Organization for Economic Initiatives.[12] Similarly, the Arkansas Industrial Development Commission has created the Matchmaker program to bring together the state's manufacturers with potential local suppliers. The program uses one-day "reverse" trade shows held in various Arkansas communities in order to make the matches. At these shows typically ten to twenty manufacturers exhibit the products for which they are seeking Arkansas suppliers. Over one hundred local companies interested in supplying products to the exhibiting manufacturers have attended the events.[13] The commission also maintains a Cross Match database that can be used to identify Arkansas suppliers of goods and raw materials.

A second category of import-substitution efforts attempts to strengthen the economic linkages between household consumers and local businesses. When consumers buy locally produced products or purchase products from local (instead of nonlocal) providers, dollars previously exported out of the local economy remain within it. One example is Good Work Arkansas. In this program, the state provided shops and stores with materials, such as signs, to inform consumers which products are made in the state, and encouraged retailer participation by giving awards honoring the best store displays. It also raised awareness among local consumers during Good Work Arkansas Month by using the mass media in a promotional campaign. Buy-local programs in many other states make similar efforts to help local consumers identify local products. For example, programs in Kansas, Idaho, Ohio, and Massachusetts all disseminate some combination of logos, stickers, decals, or labels to highlight products' local origin.[14] To encourage local consumers to purchase products from local providers, many communities have also started shop-local programs. One example is an effort undertaken by the Central Astoria Local Development Coalition in Queens, New York. The coalition published a guide to familiarize local residential consumers with neighborhood businesses. This guide "[served] as a neighborhood version of the yellow pages."[15]

Third, the public sector also can further the degree of import substitution in the local economy by targeting its procurement spending to local sources. A key way to implement this procurement targeting strategy involves giving local firms a financial preference over nonlocal firms when governments purchase goods and services. Such practices are common at the state, county, and municipal levels; a 1998 study of this activity found that twenty-two of the fifty states, thirteen of twenty-six large cities, and five of eighteen large counties surveyed gave some sort of preference to local firms.[16]

One example on the state level is California, where state small businesses can receive a 5 percent preference, not to exceed $50,000, on bids for a state contract. New Mexico and Alaska offer a similar 5 percent preference, and Louisiana allows a 7 percent preference for products "produced, manufactured, grown, harvested, or assembled" in the state. Counties engaging in the practice include Suffolk County, New York, which gives local companies a 10 percent preference; Riverside County, California, which gives a 5 percent preference; and Multnomah County, Oregon, which gives a 10 percent preference on printing. At the city level, Columbus, Ohio, gives local firms a 5 percent preference on small contracts and a 1 percent preference on larger ones, while Detroit offers sliding scale preferences starting at 10 percent for contracts under $10,000 and declining to 1 percent for contracts over $1 million. New York City, San Francisco, and Washington, D.C., all give 5 percent preference, while Seattle and Chicago give 2 percent preference to local firms.[17]

Aggressively used, public procurement can be a powerful tool for increasing local import substitution. During Harold Washington's tenure as mayor of Chicago in the 1980s, the city instituted a purchasing policy giving a slight (2 percent) preference to local businesses for city contracts, and within two years the percentage of city purchases procured locally increased by almost half.[18] In fact, local-level government purchases, which include the combined spending of city governments, county governments, schools, housing and transportation authorities, and other public authorities and special districts, typically comprise the single largest source of demand for private-sector goods in any state or locality. The modest additional expense to the public entailed in local preference policies can be justified by the many economic benefits to a community from the enhancement of local employment and local multipliers.[19]

Produce-Local Import-Substitution Policies

Import substitution also can be accomplished via policies that successfully encourage the local production of goods and services that formerly had to be imported into the local economy. Here the aim is not only to get purchasers to spend their dollars locally but to increase *local productive capacity* to meet local needs. One type of produce-local strategy derives from the buyer-supplier network concept. Many networking efforts begin by identifying products that local purchasers buy from external sources, and then proceed to link those purchasers with local businesses supplying the same product. Produce-local strategies go a step further by stimulating the production of goods that are currently imported into the local economy for want of a local supplier. Strategies to fill this void in the local supply network can proceed by aiding local firms with the development of new products to meet the demand of local buyers, or by facilitating the formation of start-up firms that would produce products to meet this demand.[20] Specific initiatives can include the provision of worker training, technical assistance (with product development or business administration), and/or financial assistance to local firms capable of producing goods and services that substitute for those currently imported.

A good example of a produce-local strategy is the Wichita/Sedgwick County (Kansas) Purchaser Supplier Support Program. After local businesses were contacted to determine which products they would prefer to purchase locally, this program assisted established local firms with the development of new products and encouraged the formation of new firms to fill the supply gap.[21] Another example is the Rural Local Markets Demonstration in North Carolina noted earlier, where the Mid-East Commission is "providing training and loans to targeted local suppliers and potential start-up firms" that can meet local needs.[22]

The development of more-general business networks, especially among an area's smaller enterprises, can also accelerate import substitution (even when they are established for very different purposes). Business networks allow for individual firms to band together to "carry out some new business activity that the members of the network could not pursue independently."[23] For example, firms may form relationships to assist each other in dealing with shared business problems in such fields as product marketing, worker training, firm purchasing, business management, and technology development. Place-based business networks increase interdependence among industries, as businesses get answers to their problems from relationships with local rather than nonlocal sources. Place-based (or locational) business networks also tend to root firms in communities, since the availability of interfirm assistance depends on firms remaining in close geographical proximity to other firms in the network.

As previously noted, the enormous potential of business networks to bolster sustained local economic development has been confirmed by recent academic research documenting the economic success of industrial districts found in places such as Emilia-Romagna in Italy, Baden-Württemberg in Germany, West Jutland in Denmark, and California's Silicon Valley. These districts "feature spatially-rooted agglomerations of manufacturing firms bound to one another through extensive subcontracting and networking relationships."[24] Such firms are both highly specialized (occupying a niche position in the production process) and also highly interdependent (relying heavily on other firms within the district to supply the goods and services necessary for production). Compared to traditional mass-production methods, networked production enhances productive flexibility by permitting smaller-batch production runs and by making it easier for firms to quickly adjust output through adding or reducing subcontractors.[25] (Hence the catchphrase "flexible specialization.") Other important characteristics of successful industrial districts, as Martin Perry notes, include "shared norms and cultural and social factors that facilitate interfirm cooperation [and] locally embedded industrial know-how and capacity for innovation and information sharing."[26]

Can networked production arrangements be built from scratch, or must they rest on the decades-long evolution of norms in some particularly conducive cultural environment? One attempt to build place-based business networks from scratch is the Vermont Sustainable Jobs Fund (VSJF), Inc. Funded by the Vermont legislature, VSJF provides grants and technical assistance to economic development projects that "encourage cooperative ventures between businesses so individual businesses can produce higher value products and sell them in competitive markets."[27] In one example, the VSJF created a small-grant program designed to develop business networks among small enterprises in the northeastern section of the state. The program awards grants to groups of three or more firms willing to cooperate in a network. Grant applications are evaluated according to the network's ability "to improve the competitive position of the member businesses," create "quality jobs," and "to use Vermont's natural and human resources to gain competitive advantage" in the marketplace.[28] As of mid-2001, the fund had made $700,000 in grants to over fifty projects in a wide range of fields, including wood products, organic barley, apple production, and "agro-tourism."[29]

In Chicago, community-oriented industrial development organizations (IDOs) have facilitated the development of business networks. Joel Rast of the Chicago-based Center for Neighborhood Technology notes that since the 1980s, Chicago's rich nonprofit development community has sought to foster "cooperative and collaborative relationships among manufacturing firms located within close proximity to one another." Rast cites the example of the Jane Addams Resource Corporation (JARC), which pulled together a consortium of some twenty-five metalworking firms in the Chicago area. The networks fostered by JARC allowed individual firms to better cope with industry restructuring by sharing risks and information. Members of the JARC consortium have collaborated on new product development, and also formed reciprocal subcontracting, borrowing, and purchasing arrangements.[30]

The effort to build business networks continued into the 1990s in Chicago, garnering support and funding from the administration of Richard M. Daley. Starting in 1994, the Daley administration began funding the efforts of IDOs to create strategic plans to bolster the economic prospects of the city's industrial corridors while also offering each organization up to $1.5 million in seed money. Some of the resulting plans included proposals to enhance networking relationships among firms within a given IDO's service area. The Greater Southwest Development Corporation, for instance, included a networking proposal in its plan based on a survey finding that "nearly 50 percent of companies [within its corridor] expressed an interest in common warehousing and cooperative purchasing of raw materials or finished goods."[31]

Two other ways to implement a produce-local strategy deserve consideration. The first involves local governments, businesses, and individuals utilizing previously unused raw materials (especially locally generated waste products) to produce previously imported goods locally. This strategy was a central part of St. Paul, Minnesota's Homegrown Economy Project in the 1980s: The city assisted a local business in recycling automobile tires for use as an asphalt supplement at a locally owned asphalt plant. The process reduced the city's need to import raw materials required for asphalt production.[32]

The methane recovery systems now operated by numerous cities across the country represent another way to recover raw materials for local productive use (see Chapter 6). If the energy generated by methane recovery systems is sold to local power companies, locally generated resources can again substitute for energy sources imported from outside the area. Alternatively, it can add to local exports. A good example is the methane recovery system in Riverview, Michigan, which produces electricity sold to Detroit Edison.

Finally, encouraging local food production offers another promising way to expand local production. The past few decades have seen the creation of thousands of community gardens in cities across the nation. Apart from providing fresh and affordable produce to (often underserved) urban residents, these gardens transform vacant urban land, an unused resource, into a tool for keeping dollars circulating in the local economy—dollars that otherwise would be used to pay for imported food. (We discuss urban community gardens and community sustainable-agriculture arrangements in more depth in Chapter 11.)

SMALL-BUSINESS DEVELOPMENT AND THE PROMOTION OF LOCAL OWNERSHIP

Communities also can work to enhance multipliers in their local economies by facilitating the development of a healthy small business sector and ensuring that as many businesses as possible (of all sizes) are locally owned.

Small businesses tend to enhance local multipliers because they require numerous support services from other businesses and hence are likely to be strongly linked to the rest of the local economy through their spin-off purchasing.[33] (Commonly large national corporations purchase inputs centrally, a method that increases imports into the localities hosting a corporate branch.) Communities around the country have provided a range of technical and financial assistance to nurture and "grow" healthy small businesses.[34]

Creating small-business incubators is one common technique. Incubators provide new small businesses with low-rent operating space in a facility shared with other new small businesses, and/or business assistance services. The benefits offered to new companies are both tangible (lowered overhead expenses and increased access to services) and intangible (access to advice, information, and encouragement).[35] During the 1980s and 1990s, use of this economic development tool expanded rapidly, with hundreds of communities establishing business incubators. The National Association of Business Incubators (NABI) reports that over 900 incubators existed by 2001, up from only 12 in 1980.[36] Over half are funded entirely by governments or nonprofit organizations, while another quarter are affiliated with colleges and universities. (About one-quarter of business incubators are estimated to be for-profit operations.) NABI estimates that business incubators have helped create about 500,000 jobs since 1980, and that each $1 of public subsidy of incubators has yielded $45 in additional local tax revenue.[37]

Americans of all political stripes support small business—and there is good reason to think that a rich array of, in particular, *locally oriented* small businesses can be especially helpful to communities seeking to increase their economic multipliers.[38] As noted, compared to absentee-owned corporations, locally owned (independent) enterprises are more likely to purchase local products and services. Moreover, because profits are not siphoned off to a distant corporate headquarters, local ownership facilitates a high rate of profit recirculation within the local economy.[39]

Communities can promote the local ownership of businesses in several other ways. The first, and perhaps most important, is for states and cities to stop subsidizing the growth of absentee-owned corporations with generous development incentives, and instead target these incentives to locally owned businesses (or at least use local ownership as an important criterion for development assistance). Development officials also can promote local ownership by identifying local buyers for established businesses in the community available for purchase and, again, targeting such businesses for development assistance. Another possible approach is to lease municipally owned property exclusively to locally owned businesses, as has been discussed in Boulder, Colorado.[40]

Much of the struggle to promote local ownership focuses on the retail sector, as communities fight to prevent their locally owned establishments from being driven out of business by such corporate chains as Wal-Mart, Home Depot, or Barnes and Noble. Stacy Mitchell of the Institute for Local Self-Reliance's New Rules Project advocates the revival both of federal and state antitrust laws to halt chain stores' anticompetitive practices (such as predatory and discriminatory pricing), orientation of land use plans and zoning laws "to favor locally owned, humanly scaled, diverse businesses," special taxes on chain stores to give nonchains a mild comparative advantage, and the expansion of retailer-owned purchasing and wholesale cooperatives to give smaller merchants increased purchasing power.[41]

Mitchell acknowledges that prospects for a revival of antitrust policy in support of this aim appear remote, as antitrust enforcement "remains passive and no longer infused with a civic concern for decentralized ownership."[42] However, local land-use and zoning policy—an area where courts have consistently given local governments generous grants of authority—is a different story: "Increasing numbers of communities are using this authority to enact rules that defend local businesses and encourage a homegrown retail economy," Mitchell notes. Numerous localities have developed comprehensive land-use plans aimed at strengthening smaller businesses, including the North Beach neighborhood of San Francisco; Kent County, Maryland; and Manchester, Vermont. These plans give local governments protection from lawsuits should the legality of a particular land-use decision be challenged.

Zoning codes, which implement land-use plans via specific land-use rules, also have been applied creatively to forestall and counter the growth of chain stores. Most commonly communities have employed zoning rules to restrict the size of new retail establishments, preventing companies such as Wal-Mart or Borders Books from opening so-called superstores or "big boxes."[43] Other communities, such as Port Jefferson, New York; Carmel, California; Bainbridge Island, Washington; and Coronado, California, have adopted bans or limitations on the number of "formula" businesses they allow. Formula businesses are defined as those that, like Starbucks Coffee, "adopt standardized services, methods of operation, and other features virtually identical to businesses located in other communities."[44] While bans and limitations to date have been restricted to the restaurant industry, Boulder (an acknowledged national leader in promoting small businesses) is considering an ordinance that would place limits on formula businesses in the retail sector as well.[45]

Reviving taxes on chain stores also could play an important role in combating the growth of corporate chains.[46] Such taxes were enacted by more than half the states between 1927 and 1941, helping lead to a decline in the market share of chain stores during the 1930s. Mitchell argues that cities or states could once again impose stiffer licensing fees on chain operations. The justification for the tax builds on the notion that certain types of businesses, such as doctor's offices, should pay reduced licensing fees because they promote the public good. The promotion of locally ownership can be justified on similar grounds.

Purchasing cooperatives can also help local retailers achieve the advantages of scale. Owned by retail businesses themselves, these cooperatives operate through shared decision making and return profits back to their members, the local retailers. Joining such groups enables small retailers to purchase wholesale goods at a much lower cost, given the large buying power of the cooperative and the capacity of these organizations to negotiate favorable deals with manufacturers. Two retail sectors with a long and successful history with purchasing cooperatives are the hardware industry (TruServ and Ace) and grocery stores (Independent Grocers Alliance or IGA).[47]

A caveat: Strengthening local ownership of businesses can increase economic multipliers in local communities, but this positive effect will be still greater when business ownership is not only local but also in one way or another directly anchored, institutionally, in the community. Such enterprises are even more likely than small business to funnel profits back into the community and to purchase inputs from local sources. They also can provide broadly shared economic gains to the community rather than simply create a handful of successful local entrepreneurs. We discuss options for creating community-controlled businesses in Part III.[48]

LOCAL CURRENCIES

Another important way to increase the multiplier effect in local communities is to create local currencies or exchange systems. By definition, local currencies must be spent locally. As author Susan Meeker-Lowry explains, community currencies, in contrast to the national currency, "encourag[e] wealth to stay within a community rather than flowing out."[49] There are more than 300 organized local currency or local exchange systems in the United States today. The initiatives take several different forms, including barter systems, scrip/hours systems, local exchange trading systems (LETS), and Time Dollars systems.

Probably the best-developed of these systems in the United States are local scrip programs. The E. F. Schumacher Society estimates the volume of local scrip in use to be about $1.2 million ($25,000 on average for fifty active programs).[50] Scrip programs are simple to understand and operate because they use a medium familiar to everyone: paper or coin currency. To start a scrip system, a community identifies businesses and individuals willing to trade with each other in local currency and then creates the currency (usually paper money). A baseline value for the currency can be set by estimating the community's hourly "living" wage in national currency. This value, commonly between $10 and $12, becomes the unit upon which the local currency is based. (These units are often called "hours" to connote that for every hour of work at, say, $10, a person can earn one 1-hour note of local currency). To get the currency into initial circulation, small quantities are given to participants who agree to accept scrip for their goods and services. A local currency newspaper or newsletter then functions as a yellow pages or directory, letting people know who will trade with local currency. As the system develops, other mechanisms for currency distribution can be utilized, such as using scrip for employee pay or awarding grants of local currency to community organizations.

The creation of an alternative currency to the U.S. dollar might at first glance seem to be a violation of federal and state law. But, as Michael Shuman has pointed out, such paper currencies are in fact perfectly legal. A study by George Washington University law professor Lewis D. Solomon observes that "[w]ith the possible exception of Virginia and Arkansas, federal or state currency laws would not restrain a system of alternative paper scrip."[51]

The Ithaca, New York, program, HOURS, is probably the most advanced local currency/scrip program in the United States, with more than $60,000 of notes in circulation. "I was sick of watching corporate money come into town, shake a few hands, and leave again without leaving many positive residual effects except maybe a few below-subsistence jobs," reflects the system's founder, Paul Glover.[52] Glover organized some friends and designed a local currency that would complement the dollar but stimulate trade in Ithaca in ways the dollar had not or could not.

Ithaca HOURS are paper currency spent at participating businesses alongside U.S. dollars. Each hour's value is based on a fair hourly wage in Tompkins County, New York (one Ithaca HOUR note is worth $10). Notes are backed not by debt (as the national currency is) but by the faith of its users in the skills and products in Ithaca. In 1991, ninety individuals and five businesses accepted Ithaca HOURS; by 1999, more than 1,500 individuals and 400 businesses were using Ithaca HOURS to exchange goods and services. The program's newsletter, which lists participants, rivals the local yellow pages in size and breadth. With 8,500 Ithaca HOURS ($85,000) in circulation and an estimated multiplier of 6, over $500,000 of trade takes place in HOURS each year.[53]

Ithaca HOURS are spent and circulated in myriad ways. Ithacans use HOURS to buy "plumbing, carpentry, electrical work, nursing, child care, car repair, food, eyeglasses, firewood, and thousands of other goods and services. Credit unions use them for mortgage and loan fees. People pay rent with them. The best restaurants in town take them, as do movie theaters, bowling alleys, two large locally owned grocery stores, and thirty-five farmer's market vendors."[54] John Hanratty of GreenStar, a local grocery, uses Ithaca HOURS to pay vendors for goods and even offers HOURS as part of his employees' compensation. "We just insert HOURS along with the pay stub," he notes. "Anyone who participates informs us via a form how much they will take in HOURS. Our employees actually have turned out to be our major users of HOURS."[55]

With acceptance from a financial institution—the local credit union—faith in the currency has risen substantially. The variety of services and goods that can be purchased with HOURS strengthens its liquidity. All of this makes the local currency a viable supplement to the national currency—and a valuable boost to Ithaca's economic multiplier. By 2001, at least twenty similar programs existed in the United States.[56] Related models, such as Time Dollars, in which members of a Time Dollar network donate one hour of their time toward helping a neighbor in order to earn a one-hour credit, are also gaining in popularity, with over forty Time Dollar programs of varying size in the United States alone.[57]

ECONOMICALLY TARGETED INVESTMENTS (ETIS)
WITH PUBLIC PENSION FUNDS

Perhaps the largest impact policy the fifty states (and some localities) can implement to increase local employment with local resources is to use locally generated (usually publicly controlled) sources of investment capital to fund local economic development. Recirculating the literally trillions of locally generated dollars now held in state and local public employee pension funds in the United States offers one of the greatest untapped possibilities for promoting economic stability in the United States. Directing even a relatively small percentage of available pensions toward investments that promote community-rooted economic development could yield a substantial community stabilization payoff.[58]

That fact has not gone unnoticed. One of the most widely discussed strategies for stabilizing state economies during the past decade has been the use of pension funds (primarily public) to direct investments to companies within a given area (usually a state's boundaries). By the mid-1990s, twenty-seven different state pension funds were managing some sixty ETI programs.[59] Although the Clinton administration did not explicitly conceive of ETIs as a key part of a concerted effort to stabilize communities, it did openly endorse ETIs.

The proliferation of ETI programs has, however, met with resistance, as some conservative interest groups both in Washington and on Wall Street have challenged such investments as an unjustified risk of pensioners' money. The existing evidence tells a different story. In the most comprehensive official review of ETIs to date, the United States Congress's General Accounting Office in 1995 examined seven pension funds' experience with ETIs. It reported that the rate of return earned by such investments is generally comparable to that earned by standard investment strategies.[60] Similarly, a survey conducted by the Center for Policy Alternatives found that when retirement systems carefully chose their ETIs (ensuring that these investments fill identifiable gaps in capital markets and have the capacity to generate risk-adjusted market rates of return) and utilized a diversification strategy while carefully monitoring their investment performance, these systems "were rewarded by solid performance on their ETI investment portfolio."[61] Moreover, the Institute for Fiduciary Education's poll of over a hundred of the largest public pension funds found that, according to the funds' investment managers, ETIs "do not entail higher risks or lower returns," and a majority of managers were "either satisfied or very satisfied with the results of their ETIs' investments."[62]

This is not to say that ETIs are incapable of failure. In the most spectacular example, Kansas abandoned its ETI program after experiencing some $236 million in losses on investments starting in the mid-1980s. Likewise, Alaska experienced losses when it too heavily financed in-state mortgages and the state's real estate market declined.[63] Yet, as former Assistant Secretary of Labor Olena Berg points out in defense of ETIs, private failures in the market are even more common. As Berg put it in 1994 (shortly after IBM underwent a painful downsizing), "Is the recent experience with IBM a reason not to invest in equities?"[64]

Many critics use anecdotal accounts such as the Kansas and Alaska examples to undermine the credibility of ETIs. A recent review of critical academic studies by Monique Morrissey of the Financial Open Markets Center concluded that the body of evidence attempting to demonstrate that pension funds with ETI programs perform poorly is "extremely small" and that the findings are "contradictory," "ambiguous," "methodologically flawed," and "inconclusive." For example, many of these studies reach conclusions about the inferiority of funds using ETIs without adequately controlling for risk. That is, funds not using ETIs have tended to produce somewhat better returns, but these funds have done so by placing the monies of pensioners in higher-risk investments.[65]

Part of the controversy stems from a general state of confusion over what ETIs are and what they are not.[66] To clarify the concept, Ronald Watson—a former chair of the U.S. Department of Labor's ERISA Advisory Council—contrasts ETIs with "the 'social investing' concerns of the late 1970s and early 1980s, which sought to discourage investors from holding assets associated with politically incorrect behavior . . . regardless of any underlying financial merit." In contrast, he continues, ETIs "focus on the positive aspects of investing—especially investing in projects that benefit the investor's community. Job-creation, small-business development, low-income housing, and tax-base expansion can be benefits associated with an ETI."[67] Michael Calabrese, former general counsel for the Congressional Joint Economic Committee, adds: "Few if any ETIs result from [the] wooly-headed do-gooderism" associated with "below market social investing." Instead, Calabrese observes, "[m]ost result from the hardheaded self-interest of pension managers trying to maximize the multiple and very long-term interests of both current retirees and the young workers contributing to the plan who may be 30 or more years away from drawing benefits."[68]

It is important to keep in mind that pension investment mangers have an affirmative obligation to maximize these varied, long-term interests. As Watson explains, managers must "consider both the financial attributes of an investment and its multipliers and externalities—positive and negative." Because multipliers (or ripple effects) of an investment create, either directly or indirectly, wealth for pension plan participants, "these effects should be factored into the investment allocation decision."[69] Managers need to consider the possibility that investing pension money back into the local communities where participants live and/or work can yield higher overall returns for these participants compared to traditional investment strategies. The kinds of positive externalities flowing from ETIs that might boost these overall returns include an increase in the value of other local investments held by participants (such as owner-occupied housing), better-paying and more abundant job opportunities for those participants still in the workforce, and a reduction in participants' tax burden.[70] Moreover, the health of a pension fund does not rest solely on its income from investments; also important are the contributions from current workers and the economic strength of the sponsoring institution. In the case of public pension funds, their ability to pay generous benefits depends on the fiscal health of the state or locality, not just the direct return on investments. Insofar as ETI investments not only provide an investment return but also expand the tax base by stimulating local economic development, a strong case can be made that the economic interests of plan participants are significantly advanced by ETIs.[71]

Unfortunately, the evidence currently available to evaluate the capacity of ETIs to stimulate local economic development is limited. Most public pension funds have little systematic data on the economic impact of their ETIs, and the information they do have is of restricted value.[72] Nevertheless, a brief review of the direct effects of ETIs demonstrates their potential to stabilize the employment base of communities. The 1995 GAO study of ETIs, for instance, showed that job generation reported by individual states was considerable for the period of the early 1990s under review. In Massachusetts, for example, $52 million in ETI investments contributed to the creation or retention of 4,800 jobs; in Pennsylvania, investments of $89.6 million created or retained 6,850 jobs; in Minnesota, investments of $11.9 million created or retained 2,115 jobs; in Colorado, venture capital investments of $41.5 million created or retained 4,603 jobs.[73]

More precise studies of the comprehensive economic impact of ETIs—including both direct job creation and indirect effects resulting from the multiplier effect—will be needed to gauge the success and future potential of this strategy. But, as the following review of particularly active ETI programs in all parts of the country shows, there is considerable case-by-case evidence that ETIs can be used in innovative ways to help stabilize America's communities. The various precedents also demonstrate political viability in both conservative and liberal political environments.

Alabama. Retirement Systems of Alabama (RSA), which manages the pension money of teachers and state employees, has aggressively invested in a wide range of local industries, from aerospace to tourism development, over the past twenty years under the bold leadership of David G. Bronner. The investments have been of substantial scale—$100 million was invested in the Alabama Pine Pulp Company, for example. RSA also has built downtown office buildings in Montgomery, invested $60 million in a statewide golf course network (maintaining a 33 percent ownership stake), and in the early 1980s invested $250 million in Alabama-backed Ginnie Mae mortgages.[74] Probably the most innovative RSA investments have been its formation of two media conglomerates. The fund has financed the formation of Community Newspaper Holdings (involving over 330 local newspapers) and RayCom Media (which holds thirty-four television stations and a number of radio stations). RSA estimates these media holdings also provide Alabama with some $40 million a year in free advertising for the state.[75] RSA formed these companies, established their headquarters in Alabama, and set the companies up as joint public- and employee-owned corporations.[76]

California. The California Public Employee Retirement System (CalPERS) has been among the most active state pension funds in its use of ETIs, investing 12 percent of its almost $151 billion investment portfolio within the state (about $20 billion as of May 2001).[77] Another California fund, the California State Teachers' Retirement System (CSTRS), with assets approaching the $100 billion mark, also has been an active ETI investor. Both funds have invested substantially in California housing construction and mortgages and in venture capital pools for small and expanding California firms. In addition, CalPERS has made individual ETIs of substantial scale, including the financing of a $55 million office building in the state capital. It also has illustrated how pension fund resources can be effectively targeted geographically to stabilize communities. In the wake of the uprising sparked by the Rodney King case, the fund initiated some $75 million in direct investments in South Central Los Angeles.[78] Similarly, when the state faced economic woes in the early and mid-1990s and traditional sources withdrew from financing housing construction, CalPERS stepped in to fill the capital gap by committing hundreds of millions of dollars, single-handedly financing about 4 percent of the state's single family-housing market.[79] Most recently, in an effort to help boost economic development statewide, in 2001 the fund announced investments of $475 million in private investment firms within the state working in underserved markets.[80]

New York City. Among local government funds, the New York City Employees Retirement Systems (NYCERS), as well as the city's other four pension funds, has been a leader in ETIs since 1981. NYCERS provides another important precedent for how pension money can be used for community investment. By working with a financial intermediary, the Community Preservation Corporation (CPC), NYCERS invested more than $400 million to finance the rehabilitation and construction of more than 10,000 affordable housing units (mostly apartments) over a ten-year period. Even more importantly, the funds have worked closely with Ginnie Mae to finance home loans for areas of the city historically redlined by traditional finance institutions. This program has provided thousands of mortgages in minority and mixed-race neighborhoods in Queens and the Bronx. NYCERS also invested $100 million in a nonconforming mortgage program that gave low- and moderate-income New Yorkers the opportunity to buy homes with as little as 5 percent down. NYCERS' targeted investments yielded a 7.6 percent return between 1993 and 2000. Taken together, New York City's public pension funds have helped finance over 30,000 housing units and invested over $700 million in the city to date.[81]

Colorado. Another state active in ETIs is Colorado, with its Public Employees' Retirement Association (PERA). PERA's investment policy gives explicit preference to in-state investments, "all other things being equal," and permits such investments to be up to 20 percent of its aggregate portfolio. As of the end of 2000, PERA targeted over $1.28 billion to in-state investments, of which $700 million consists of venture capital investments.[82] In one of its notable targeted investments, the fund had by the early 1990s invested about $50 million through an intermediary state development agency, the Colorado Housing and Finance Agency (CHFA), buying CHFA bonds that finance long-term, fixed-rate small-business loans.[83] These have gone to a host of in-state small businesses, ranging from a pharmaceutical manufacturer to a

Dairy Queen.[84] PERA also has invested over $40 million in several aggressive venture capital partnerships based in the Denver area. These investments led, by the mid-1990s, to the creation of over 4,600 Colorado jobs, mainly in the technology, manufacturing, and communications sectors. It also has engaged in ETIs of significant scale by making a $33 million loan to finance the construction of a gas-powered cogeneration plant, which serves as an energy-efficient source of electric power and steam.[85]

These examples show that states and localities have only scratched the surface of what is possible in using public pension funds to enhance local economic multipliers and stabilize their communities. It is estimated that as of 2000, the funds managed $2.7 trillion. If all states and localities committed just 10 percent to ETIs, $270 billion in capital would be available for local, multiplier-enhancing investment. Such investments could have a major impact if directly and explicitly targeted toward community economic stability.

California state treasurer Philip Angelides has urged, further, that rather than sending public capital abroad (public pension funds in 1999 held $242 billion in foreign stocks), the state's monies (and other infrastructure funds) should be invested in strategic ways "to rebuild its decaying older cities and curb wasteful and environmentally risky sprawl development at the urban fringe" (aptly labeled by Angelides as "Smart Investments").[86] Observing how the CalPERS pension fund has suffered negative returns from some of its investments in so-called emerging markets, the California state treasurer found it "amazing . . . how American investment in volatile overseas areas is a 'given' of our capital markets, even while our own emerging markets—inner cities, minority small businesses—are so often written off as risky and troublesome."[87]

Plainly the potential for using public pension funds to enhance local economic multipliers and stabilize America's communities is enormous. However, an impediment to tapping this potential is current federal law (as expressed through the Employee Retirement and Security Act [ERISA]) and parallel state laws governing state and local government funds. The restrictive language of ERISA and the state laws based upon it requires pension fund managers to invest with diligence, prudence, skill, and care in ways solely in the interest of plan participants. While the Department of Labor ruled in the mid-1990s that ETIs are permissible under ERISA so long as they earn a return equal to or greater than that of nontargeted investments, potential ambiguities in the fiduciary standards of ETI investments remain.[88] If ETIs' full potential is to be tapped, probably the ERISA rule and the parallel state laws would have to be clarified to provide specific, binding assurances that ETIs may be used.

MULTIPLYING MULTIPLIER POLICIES

Strengthening local multipliers is clearly critical to achieving the goal of community stabilization. Many of the policy options we have reviewed either have only begun to be exploited, or have been implemented only on a modest scale. Nevertheless, the record shows that there are numerous ways communities interested in increasing local multipliers can proceed—and that these policies should be seen as an integral part of a deliberate and comprehensive effort to stabilize American communities.

Attempts to increase local multipliers may face other obstacles, however—including most seriously the possibility that international trade agreements may prohibit and override local policies offering special assistance to local (as opposed to nonlocal) enterprises. As we have seen, one of the most powerful tools for increasing the degree of local import substitution, targeted public procurement, is threatened by trade agreements (and WTO rules) that aim to restrict the use of procurement preferences. Given that these trade agreements also conceivably could be used as a vehicle to forbid many of the other multiplier-enhancing policies described above, citizens' groups struggling to control the economic destinies of their communities may need to launch parallel efforts to fight trade agreements that undercut localities' ability to implement buy-local and produce-local strategies.

We turn in Part III to a discussion of the variety of new community-oriented and -controlled economic structures now operating around the nation, such as employee-owned businesses, community development corporations, community development financial institutions, and community land trusts. The local multiplier policies reviewed in this chapter should be seen as a complement to each of these institutions. Effective steps to raise local multipliers would increase the economic payoff of new community economic institutions—and thereby further ease the path to effective community economic stabilization.

PLACE-BASED ECONOMIC STRUCTURES

INTRODUCTION

Part III of the book assesses the capacity and potential of innovative forms of ownership—such as employee ownership, businesses operated by community development corporations, nonprofit-owned businesses, and community land trusts—to contribute to community economic stability. There has been striking growth in each of these institutional innovations in the past thirty years. With appropriate policy support, ownership strategies that root capital directly in communities can help stabilize the economic base of localities.

Chapter 8 examines perhaps the best-developed of these institutional forms, employee ownership. Employee stock ownership plans (ESOP) encompass millions of Americans—in fact, the number of employees at firms with ESOP plans now exceeds the number of private-sector employees in unionized firms. This chapter examines the successes and limitations to date of employee ownership as a vehicle to expand employee participation, improve economic outcomes for workers, and contribute to community stability by offering a plausible alternative to plant shutdowns. We also examine in some detail the range of existing and proposed policies at the state and federal levels that support employee ownership in the United States.

Chapter 9 turns to discussion of another well-established institutional form, the community development corporation (CDC), as well as a new institutional form that has taken on greater importance in recent years, the community development financial institution (CDFI). While CDCs have tended to focus primarily on housing activities, a number of CDCs, operating in very different contexts (from Newark to rural Mississippi), have directly created and operated businesses that both create jobs and help fund further community-building work. In part because of support from the federal CDFI Fund, community development financial institutions of various kinds have also flourished in recent years. These funds help provide critical access to credit for individuals and businesses in low-income areas that typically have been undeserved by mainstream financial institutions. This chapter notes both the accomplishments and shortcomings of CDCs and CDFIs and discusses the ways in which public policy can support their further development.

Chapter 10 takes up three less well known ownership forms that are also intrinsically rooted in particular places: consumer cooperatives, community-owned corporations, and nonprofit-owned businesses. While these ownership strategies will probably not play a lead role in stabilizing American communities, they can play a supplementary role and might prove to be very important indeed in particular localities.

Chapter 11 turns to urban land trusts, conservation land trusts, community-supported agriculture, and community gardens. While many of these land-based initiatives are small in scale, they are of potential long-term importance: For instance, the growth of urban land trusts might in time make a major contribution to affordable housing in the United States. In the long term, developing alternative forms of land ownership, especially in urban contexts, could greatly ease the formation of progressive local political regimes and enhance the ability of the public to deal with pressing problems such as unchecked suburban sprawl.

CHAPTER 8

SUPPORTING EMPLOYEE OWNERSHIP IN AMERICA

e
mployee ownership of firms is the most-discussed and best-developed modification to traditional corporate structures in the United States. The possibility of worker ownership within a market economy has had long-standing appeal, for reasons that were spelled out quite clearly in the 1860s by the English philosopher John Stuart Mill. In successive editions of his massive treatise *Principles of Political Economy,* Mill endorsed worker cooperatives as a way to develop the talents and capacities of working people. Mill suggested that there is a deep connection between habits learned at work and the development of morally autonomous individuals capable of making good use of the liberty permitted by modern constitutional regimes. Wrote Mill: "Eventually, and in perhaps a less remote future than may be supposed,

> we may, through the co-operative principle, see our way to a change in society, which would combine the freedom and independence of the individual with the moral, intellectual and economical advantatges of aggregate production; and which . . . would realize, at least in the industrial department, the best aspirations of the democratic spirit, by putting an end to the division of society into the industrious and the idle, and effacing all social distinctions but those fairly earned by personal services and exertions.[1]

Mill also thought that having a stake in their own associations would serve as a "vast stimulus" to workers' productivity, but added that this "material benefit" was "as nothing compared with the moral revolution in society that would accompany it":

> The healing of the standing feud between capital and labour; the transformation of human life, from a conflict of classes struggling for opposite interests, to a friendly rivalry in the pursuit of a good common to all; the elevation of the dignity of labour; a new sense of security and independence in the labouring class; and the conversion of each human being's daily occupation into a school of the social sympathies and the practical intelligence.[2]

The moral force of Mill's argument for democracy in the workplace remains attractive to a range of political thinkers.[3] But contemporary practitioners and advocates of worker ownership have tended to focus more attention on the immediate practical benefits of employee ownership. These benefits include, first, saving jobs that might have been destroyed but for either a worker buyout or a trade by labor of wage and rule concessions for shares of stock, and second, providing workers with additional material benefits compared to workers in conventional private firms. A third benefit stressed by many academic economists who have closely studied worker-owned firms is the substantial boost in productivity and sales generated when meaningful worker participation in management decisions and worker ownership of a firm are combined.

Today, employee ownership in America falls into two broad categories: cooperatives and employee stock ownership. (In addition, stock option and profit-sharing plans are widespread, although these are less significant as mechanisms to promote community stability.) Worker cooperatives are firms privately held by worker-owners. Each worker is entitled to an equal share of the firm's profits. Management decisions (including both day-to-day governance and long-term strategy) are made either directly by the workers or by managers hired by and directly accountable to the cooperative members. Co-ops first appeared in America in the 1830s but owe their modern existence largely to the Wagner-Lewis Relief Act of 1933. During the New Deal some 250 cooperatives received nearly $5 million in government assistance.[4] In the postwar era, plywood cooperatives in the Pacific Northwest enjoyed particular success for several decades before experiencing a steep decline. (One plywood co-op that has survived is Hoquiam Plywood in Hoquiam, Washington, which has ninety-seven "working owners.")[5] Today, there are approximately 200 wholly owned worker cooperatives in the United States.[6]

Looking abroad, the Mondragon network in the Basque region of Spain has been the most spectacular example of successful cooperative structures in the modern capitalist world. The Mondragon system now involves over 160 cooperatives, with roughly 30,000 worker-members and annual sales estimated at $5 billion, although, according to some observers, there has in recent years been a weakening of the network's original egalitarian ideology.[7] A similar story can be told about the Israeli kibbutzim, which for decades were an overwhelming economic success, typically enjoying higher productivity rates than comparable private producers of both agricultural and manufacturing goods, but which of late have tended to shift away from communal economics (in part due to reduced government support).[8] Cooperatives also remain robust in northern Italy: In Emilia-Romagna, cooperatives account for approximately one-eighth of the regional economy.[9]

Worker cooperatives, in addition to providing a more egalitarian distribution of wages and resources within firms and increasing the tangible power workers have over their work lives, have one obvious benefit from the standpoint of community economic security: Most are by their very nature rooted in a particular geographic locality and extremely unlikely to move to a location different from that of the local worker-owners. Some authors also argue that worker cooperatives should be more efficient users of natural resources and other material inputs than conventional firms; Marquette University economist Douglas Booth notes that worker cooperatives will have greater incentive to use materials and resources as efficiently as possible in the production process than conventional firms, which often focus primarily on increasing the intensity of workers' efforts or on expanding an enterprise's scale as profitability strategies.[10]

In the United States today, employee stock ownership is a far more common vehicle for worker ownership than the cooperative. The best-developed form of employee ownership is the employee stock ownership plan (ESOP). ESOP companies are corporations in which bundles of stock are held by a trust on behalf of employees; although ESOP firms can be either privately held or publicly traded, 90 percent of ESOPs are in privately held firms.[11] Employee stock ownership (and even majority stock ownership of a company) does not inevitably imply control over management decisions or commitment to a particular locality. Nevertheless, this form of employee ownership has the potential to make a substantial contribution to community stabilization.

That potential flows in part from the fact that employee stock ownership is already so widespread in America. Millions of American workers now participate in some form of stock ownership plan. The National Center for Employee Ownership (NCEO) has estimated that total worker holdings came to 8.3 percent of all U.S. corporate stock by the late 1990s, for a total of $800 billion. As of 2000, NCEO estimates that about $500 billion in company stock is owned by the 8.5 million participants in some 11,500 ESOPs in the United States. (Significant holdings by employees, estimated to run to hundreds of billions of dollars, are also held in both company stock owned by employees through 401(k) plans and stock options granted to employees.)[12]

FEDERAL SUPPORT FOR EMPLOYEE OWNERSHIP

Important advocates for employee stock ownership, starting with San Francisco lawyer Louis Kelso in the 1950s and continuing through contemporary writers such as Jeff Gates, have urged stock ownership as a way to broaden the benefits of capital ownership and create a more inclusive economic system. Kelso, a pioneer in the field, reasoned that giving more Americans a "second income"—that is, income derived from capital holdings —would be a boon to individual liberty. Kelso sketched a concrete program for gradually transferring capital ownership stakes over time to a larger and larger number of Americans. Kelso proposed that banks loan employees the capital to buy newly-issued corporate stock; these loans would be paid back out of dividends earned on the new shares. After the bank was repaid each employee would begin receiving dividends.[13]

Kelso's ideas directly influenced the creation of the original federal ESOP legislation in 1974. The ERISA legislation of 1974, sponsored by Louisiana senator Russell Long, established ESOPs as an employee benefit fund with unique authority to borrow money and invest in company stock. The major assistance to the new ESOP form came in the tax deductibility of employer contributions to repay the principal of ESOP loans; this incentive, along with Section 1042 deductions allowing company owners to defer taxes on the sale of stock to ESOPs, has played the lead role in stimulating the growth of ESOPs.

Subsequent federal legislation and programmatic initiatives have provided additional assistance to ESOPs—and illustrate, too, the well-established precedents for using federal policy to nurture worker ownership. In 1980, for example, the Small Business Administration was authorized to provide loan guarantees to ESOP firms. SBA assistance to ESOPs continues today under the Qualified Employee Trusts Loan Program. In most cases, maximum loan to ESOPs under the program is $1 million, with the SBA guaranteeing $750,000 of that.[14]

Additional federal assistance was provided to ESOPs through the Job Training Partnership Act (JTPA). This legislation, which was in effect from 1983 to 1998, provided direct federal assistance to start-up worker-owned companies. Moreover, JTPA funds have been used by states to conduct worker ownership feasibility studies in the event of plant closures or substantial layoffs at existing firms. Over a dozen states used these funds to underwrite feasibility studies, and roughly one in six studies resulted in an actual employee buyout that saved a plant. New York has made the most extensive use of the provision, authorizing over fifty studies of alternative ownership possibilities at threatened facilities in fiscal 1997 alone.[15] The Workforce Investment Act, which superseded the JTPA in 1998, does not provide specific assistance for feasability studies, however.

Of the 86 studies for which there is complete data, there have been fourteen successful employee buyouts, and another twenty plants were kept open by other means. (The feasibility study may justify the purchase of the company by another buyer, or justify the original owner keeping the business open. That so many firms turned out upon close scrutiny to be economically viable is a stunning indication of the many plants that might be saved or refurbished but are regularly closed by corporate owners, especially those seeking higher returns or responding to special incentives.) In Ohio some eighteen feasibility studies resulted in the preservation of 415 jobs. The eighteen studies cost a total of $185,000; hence, the public needed to invest just $445 per job to save these jobs—pennies on the dollar compared to the massive subsidies often given to lure new firms to an area.[16]

Apart from direct subsidies, the federal government continues to provide very substantial tax deductions to ESOPs, despite recent changes in federal law. (In 1996 the Small Business Job Protection Act repealed provisions allowing lenders to ESOPs to claim a tax deduction on 50 percent of income earned from ESOP loans.) Employers can still deduct contributions to ESOPs in an amount equivalent to 25 percent (or less) of the payroll. Employers are also permitted to deduct dividends paid on ESOP stock if such dividends are either paid to workers directly or applied to repay ESOP loans. Finally, under Section 1042, company owners can defer capital gains taxation on stock sold to the ESOPs if workers hold at least 30 percent of the total value of the stock and the stock sale proceeds are immediately reinvested in "qualified replacement property," such as another U.S. company's stock. This provision provides an incentive to, commonly, retiring business owners to sell their company to their employees.[17] In 1998, provisions allowing ESOPs to own S corporations became law. (S corporations do not pay corporate taxes; rather, stockholders pay taxes on earnings as part of their individual tax returns.) S corporations that are 100 percent owned by ESOPs can avoid taxation altogether.[18]

Apart from ESOP legislation, federal law also allows 401(k) retirement plans to invest in employer stock. By 1996, 401(k) retirement plans held over $200 billion in company stock. In the vast majority of cases, total stock held by 401(k) plans is less than 10 percent of total firm stock, although there are prominent exceptions, such as United Parcel Service, which is majority-held by a 401(k) plan. It is also possible for companies to combine ESOP and 401(k) forms of employee ownership.[19]

STATE SUPPORT FOR EMPLOYEE OWNERSHIP

The bulk of state-level legislation related to worker ownership passed during the early 1980s, when political concern about deindustrialization was at a high. Overall, twenty-eight states have offered some form of support for worker ownership, and seven states—Washington, Massachusetts, New York, Oregon, Hawaii, Michigan, and Ohio—have had active state ownership programs. By far the most impressive of these efforts is located at Kent State University in Ohio. The Ohio Employee Ownership Center, with a staff of seven and an annual budget of $400,000, conducts feasibility studies of both potential worker buyouts and transitions from retiring owners to ESOP structures. By the end of 2000, the center had helped orchestrate fifty-one employee buyouts of Ohio firms, stabilizing over 11,000 jobs in the process. A bill to renew funding for the Ohio program passed with wide bipartisan support in January of 2001.[20]

Michigan, New York, Oregon, and Washington have also had particularly aggressive policies in support of employee ownership in the past two decades, including state-sponsored programs to directly assist ESOPs.[21] In addition, the Michigan Economic Development Authority has been authorized to provide loans of up to $100 million for large-scale worker buyouts. New York instituted a similar provision during the 1980s with a cap of $10 million. Washington State has given employee-owned companies preferential treatment for economic development loans. Other states authorize technical assistance to employee-owned firms and public promotion of the companies.[22]

By the late 1980s, with concerns about deindustrialization fading, state-level employee ownership programs began to fall on harder times, and in the past decade new state initiatives to support employee ownership have been sporadic. In 1997, the state of Washington's once-active employee ownership office was closed, and in New York, under Republican governor George Pataki, the name of the Center for Employee Ownership was changed to Ownership Transition Services, signaling a shift in focus to assisting retiring business owners, with employee ownership as just one among many possible outcomes.[23] In Massachusetts a $1.2 million initiative to support worker ownership was approved in 1990 but was never adequately funded.[24] On the other hand, the Massachusetts Office for Employee Involvement and Ownership has been taken over by the Economic Stabilization Trust, which uses state and federal Economic Development Administration money to provide loans and technical assistance to state companies. Employee-owned firms are eligible for such assistance. For instance, in 1992 the trust contributed a $100,000 loan toward the buyout of Marland Mold, a thirty-employee firm in Pittsfield. The Pittsfield plant was almost closed in 1991 by its corporate owner before the International Union of Electric Workers mobilized support for an employee buyout. Today annual sales at the ESOP firm total $11 million and employment has tripled to 90.[25]

While state-level initiatives have had some tangible success, they have not yet succeeded in bringing worker ownership to the critical mass of political momentum needed to sustain large-scale efforts over time. Instead, the relative economic health of the latter half of the 1990s has helped erase the image of closing steel plants from the public eye. As a result, in most states the political commitment to aggressive promotion of employee ownership has weakened. Still, state interest in worker ownership has not ebbed entirely—due to the interest of a single legislator who had attended a seminar on employee ownership, in 1997 Maine passed legislation to fund loan guarantees for employee buyouts, and more recently it established a commission to examine ownership patterns in the state that is expected to issue policy recommendations for broadening employee ownership in the state.[26] Overall, however, we agree with the assessment of the Ohio Employee Ownership Center's John Logue: At this point, states are still missing a proven cost-effective opportunity to stabilize jobs in their states by failing to more vigorously support employee ownership.[27]

ARE ESOPS EFFECTIVE?

For nearly two decades economists and other scholars have compiled impressive evidence demonstrating that employee ownership combined with workplace participation can lead to substantial productivity boosts, especially in closely held firms.[28] The past decade has also seen a vibrant debate among scholars and advocates regarding the extent to which ESOPs actually promote either increased worker participation or increased equality of rewards in the workplace. Recent studies of ESOPs support the claim that middle-level and lower-middle-level workers see a tangible, modest financial benefit from employee stock ownership, and there are a handful of cases in which blue-collar workers have retired as near millionaires.

Meaningful worker participation in management is less common but not at all unknown. The National Center for Employee Ownership in Oakland now lists twenty ESOP firms as exemplary instances of substantial change in management practices.[29] Examples of ESOP firms in which workers have substantial voice include Carris Reels, a Vermont-based firm; Mobile Tool International, a Denver company; and Parametrix, a Washington-based firm. At Carris Reels, where the ESOP began as a an ownership initiative in 1995, workers have cast votes on how stock is allocated among employees (a critical decision made at most ESOPs by management, and which often reinforces wage hierarchies by giving better-paid workers more stock than lower-paid employees). Workers at Carris Reels have also voted on company-wide health benefit plans. Worker representatives (one for every fifty employees) sit on the company's steering committee, which meets twice a year to set broad policies. With the company expected to become a majority worker-owned firm within several years (workers now have 43 percent of the stock), further moves to democratize the workplace are expected.[30]

Mobile Tool International became an employee-owned (and unionized) firm in 1995 after a worker buyout from a subdivision of Penn Central. At Mobile Tool, which has just under 1,000 employee-owners, the stock allocation formula includes a maximum ratio of 3 to 1 in the shares given to the best compensated as opposed to the least compensated employees. Three representatives from the International Brotherhood of Electric Workers sit on the nine-member governing board; the company's CEO is a former shop-floor worker. Parametrix, a Washington State–based, 350-employee environmental engineering firm with an annual growth rate of 11 percent, is a 100 percent ESOP firm with very high employee participation in management decisions. For instance, a recent major decision about how to restructure the ESOP to accommodate new employees at the growing firm was put to a vote among employees. Employees have input into more routine management decisions through an eleven-member ESOP committee. The ESOP Association named Parametrix the 2001 national ESOP Company of the Year.[31]

Despite such success stories, which set important precedents, ESOPs have been sharply criticized, not unfairly, by such authors as Seymour Melman for regularly failing to produce substantial changes in corporate management.[32] Indeed, the National Center for Employee Ownership acknowledges that even most ESOPs in which workers are given full voting rights are in practice often governed much like other private corporations.[33]

However, it is also clear that under certain circumstances the ESOP structure could help stimulate substantial changes in workplace management. John Logue and Jacquelyn Yates' survey of ESOPs in Ohio found that in the vast majority of ESOPs employee participation had increased, that voting rights had been given to employees in about half of majority-owned ESOPs, that 63 percent of Ohio ESOPs have "formal mechanisms for employee participation in shop decisions—up from 37 percent before the ESOP was put in place," and that a significant minority of majority ESOP-owned firms in Ohio have nonmanagerial employee representation on their boards. Logue and Yates also argue that ESOPs in Ohio have become more participatory and more democratic over time.[34] A major strategic question for the future is how best to encourage more ESOPs to combine workplace democracy with stock ownership—especially as many more ESOPs move to majority worker ownership. Logue and Yates strongly advocate establishing "learning networks" among ESOP firms that are attempting to implement broadened workplace democracy.

ESOPs have a more clear-cut track record in improving material outcomes for workers. The best study to date on the financial benefits of ESOPs was conducted by Peter Kardas, Adria Scharf, and Jim Keogh, who compared employee-owned firms in Washington State with a control group of comparable companies. They found that ESOPs surpassed the control groups in providing retirement benefits: The average value of all retirement benefits for ESOP companies amounted to approximately $32,000 per employee, while that of the comparison companies was approximately $12,500. (Most of the comparison companies had no retirement plan at all.) The ESOPs also paid higher wages: The median wage for the ESOP companies was $14.72 per hour, while the median for non-ESOP companies was $13.58—an 8 percent difference. The average wage for the ESOPs stood at $19.09 per hour, while that of the comparison companies was $17, a 12 percent difference. On the other hand, nonunionized ESOPs also had larger disparities between low-wage and high-wage workers than nonunionized non-ESOP firms—indicating that in some cases an ESOP actually reinforces disparities in the wage structure. Still, ESOP companies also paid out an average of over $1,350 more in stock options, cash bonuses, and other fringe benefits than did the control companies.

As Kardas, Scharf, and Keogh conclude:

> The sum of all these findings is that, on average, the ESOP companies in this study provide a significantly higher total compensation to their

employees than do their competitors. However, the increased inequality within non-union ESOP firms (represented by the ratio of 90th to 10th percentile wages) suggests that ESOP companies are not establishing new standards for compensation equality within the firm.[35]

In general, since ESOPS provide higher overall worker compensation, they contribute to a reduction of inequality in the economy as a whole and are likely to continue to do so as they grow in number.

EMPLOYEE OWNERSHIP AND COMMUNITY STABILITY

How well worker ownership can foster more participatory workplaces and more equal incomes is an important question, and the findings of the Kardas-Scharf-Keogh study are encouraging in suggesting that ESOPs do improve outcomes for workers. The debate to date, however, has largely overlooked another question central to the concerns of this volume: Are ESOP firms significantly more likely to enhance community economic stability than other corporations? Obviously, when an ESOP-structured worker buyout of a firm that would otherwise have closed or moved takes place, ESOPs make a concrete contribution to community stability. John Logue estimates that no more than 2 percent of ESOP firms have been established through a worker buyout, however—far more common are conversions to ESOPs in closely held companies when an owner retires. In this case, too, the ESOP plays a community-stabilizing function. Even so, firm data do not exist indicating just how many ESOP companies are tied to a single community or region. It is clear that much more research is needed. We are skeptical that simply having an ESOP structure, divorced from substantial worker control over management decisions, is likely to make a large impact on the planning priorities of large corporations. But ESOPs can be used to save firms—and communities—that otherwise would have faltered economically.

Can an ESOP Move? The Case of Krause Publications
One interesting example of an ESOP company that has played a critical role in preserving a community's economic health is Krause Publications, a 550-employee magazine publisher that by the late 1990s was 62 percent worker-owned. Based in Iola, Wisconsin, Krause is a major community institution—and odds are long against the majority worker-owned firm ever leaving the Iola area. A look in detail at the mechanics of Krause's ESOP provides insight into the capacity of ESOP firms to stabilize communities.[36]

A strong commitment to advanced technology and employee training as well as the strategic acquisition of smaller firms has permitted Krause to thrive as a midsized publishing firm. Founded in 1952, Krause specializes in hobby publishing (comics, coins, antiques, etc.)—it prints fifty-five hobby-related magazines and offers some 700 hobby-related books.[37] Located in a town with a population of 1,000, Krause prides itself on strong community roots. The company is so much a part of life in Iola that "not much happens here that Krause doesn't have a finger in," according to vice president of human resources Buddy Redling. Head of photography Ross Hubbard characterizes himself and his fellow employees as placing a great deal of importance on "where we live and our neighbors." "The people we work with are the people we see in church, at the doctor, and in the supermarket," says Hubbard. From participating in food and toy drives to volunteering as emergency medical technicians and firefighters, employees demonstrate a commitment to civic life. Satisfaction with the quality of life in Iola has reinforced the employees' strong desire to keep their jobs and their company rooted in the area.

By all accounts, Krause and its workers have a strong link with the surrounding community. But is it possible the firm could be sold an outside buyer, who might require employees to relocate or else lose their jobs? Company officials acknowledge that the ESOP structure, established in 1988, does not guarantee there will not be a takeover. If Krause was offered an outstanding buyout proposal, there is no assurance that the trustees, whose first obligation is to make decisions in the best interest of shareholders, would not sell. In ESOP companies, the trustees, not the board, determine how shares would be voted if there was a buyout offer. At Krause, the three trustees are senior managers who also sit on the board of directors.

Neither the board nor the trustees have a hand in day-to-day operational decisions. But trustees do have the final say in the most consequential decision of all—whether or not to accept a buyout offer, which could mean relocation of the company. Obviously, in companies where employees control the majority of shares *and are able to vote their shares,* the workers themselves would determine the fate of the company in any buyout decision. At Krause, employees own 62 percent of the company; of this portion, 85 percent is owned by the ESOP and senior management holds 15 percent. (The rest of the shares are held by Krause family members and will eventually be sold to the ESOP.) Within the ESOP, only 54 percent of these shares are allocated to individual employee accounts. The other 46 percent remains unallocated. Under ESOP law, employee owners have the right to direct trustees how to vote all allocated shares on major issues directly affecting the company's future, such as a proposed sale. The trustees, who at Krause are the three management employees on the board, vote the *unallocated* shares at their discretion. (ESOPs, if management wishes, can be structured to allow employees to vote both the unallocated and the allocated shares, however.)

In the event of an acquisition attempt, management would vote its 15 percent and also the portion of shares within the ESOP that remain unallocated; nonmanagement employees would vote their allocated shares within the ESOP. At present, if all nonmanagement employees were opposed to a buyout offer but management favored it, it would still succeed because management shares outweigh those of the rank and file. Each year, however, more unallocated shares are placed in individual ESOP accounts. As Krause moves toward 100 percent employee ownership, still more shares will come under employee control. Although any decision regarding a takeover attempt is now in the hands of management, gradually this authority will shift to the majority of employees. Over time, the risk of something happening that would be contrary to employees' wishes will diminish.

There is always the possibility that a buyout could mean early retirement for the majority of employees and that they would vote to sell. However, a very generous offer sufficient to produce this is unlikely. Indeed, Krause employees have much to gain economically from the continued good health of the firm. An employee who has been with Krause for ten years will accumulate the equivalent of five times his or her yearly salary in an ESOP account.

Additionally, as company vice president Redling stresses, a scenario in which management voted for something that the majority of employees opposed is also unlikely. "Quite frankly it [a takeover] is highly unlikely even now because I would find it highly unlikely that management would vote contrary to our employees," states Redling. (Another possibility—less likely in this instance—is that an outsider buyer could take over Krause, terminate the ESOP, introduce new management, and change the company name but retain production in Iola.) Instead of needing to relocate to remain competitive, Krause can continue to take advantage of publishing technology that enables it to remain in a small town. Because employee-owners appreciate their small-town life and the fact that, as Hubbard puts it, "there is no sitting in a traffic jam" on the way to work, as their ownership grows there is every reason to believe company identity and success will be increasingly shaped by desires of local employees.

What can be learned from this review of Krause's situation in the community and its potential for providing a permanent stabilizing presence as an ESOP firm? Three observations are in order. First, even though the firm's ESOP plan has been in place for over ten years and the percentage of shares held by workers has steadily increased, workers still lack the *formal* power to block a buyout and prevent the jobs from being lost. Second, as time goes on and the share holdings of workers increase, eventually workers will acquire the formal capacity to block any buyouts (although, as noted, there is no guarantee that workers would pass up the chance to become millionaires if an especially lucrative offer was made). Obviously the pace of an ESOP firm's move to majority ownership will vary widely from case to case. Third, there is strong reason to believe that when ESOP firms inhabit a single community or region, management itself is highly likely to be opposed to moving—especially when a community has other attractive features such as a high quality of life and good schools. This suggests that an ESOP structure, together with more traditional place-stabilizing factors such as high-quality public goods and local amenities, may add stability to a community, even when workers lack formal control over fundamental management decisions. This relatively optimistic conclusion should not blind advocates of employee stock ownership to the need to restructure ESOPs in order to maximize worker oversight and participation in management decisions; nor does it necessarily apply to larger ESOP firms with holdings in many communities that may lack the overriding commitment to one particular place that characterizes Krause. But it does suggest that in many cases, even the imperfect existing ESOP firm structure can provide far more stability to a local community than conventional private firms.

Even so, it must be stressed that majority-owned ESOP firms represent a relatively modest percentage of the companies now involved in employee ownership. Of the 11,000 companies now utilizing ESOPs, about 30 percent are majority-owned by workers, and most ESOP firms in fact have less than 10 percent worker ownership.[38] (Only twelve publicly traded corporations are majority worker-owned.) More importantly, as Dan Swinney of the Center for Labor Research cautions, no one should mistake contemporary forms of worker ownership as a radical break from conventional capitalism.[39]

On the other hand, there is growing evidence that long-skeptical labor unions are beginning to embrace ESOPs as a strategy to further enhance worker benefits and security within already unionized firms, as well as seeing the need to push for unionization in firms with established ESOPs. One striking case is that of United Airlines, an ESOP company where the International Association of Machinists successfully organized thousands of previously non-unionized employees in 1998. As Christopher Mackin of Ownership Associates in Cambridge, Massachusetts, points out, "The choice to bring in a union was in part fueled by the interest of employee owners in achieving a platform to express their ownership interest, through the union."

While United has had several well-publicized difficulties in recent years (as have other airlines), the governance structure of the company has been fundamentally altered, with workers having much more power (including the power, effectively, to veto the appointment of a CEO) than at most ESOPs.[40]

A subsequent analysis by Adria Scharf noted, "A strong union may actually be a precondition for an employee stock ownership program that gives workers increased control over company decisions."[41] Scharf also cites the case of cement manufacturer CXT in Spokane, Washington. After the company was bought out by the United Steelworkers of America, three union members were placed on the eight-person board of directors. Union presence on the board derailed one management proposal for layoffs; instead of cutting workers, the company diversified its product line and successfully found new markets. (CXT was subsequently sold for an undisclosed amount in June 1999 and is now a subdivision of L. B. Foster, Co.; workers received 80 percent of the proceeds from the sale and management 20 percent.)[42]

We agree with Scharf's conclusion that labor organizing and the continued struggle to win worker representation within the management structures of ESOPs are indispensable to a long-term strategy for making existing forms of employee stock ownership truly supportive of community economic stability. While many ESOPs today do little to foster such stability, in different ways the examples of both Krause Publications and CXT illustrate that, at their best, ESOPs can play an important role in stabilizing jobs and communities.

EXAMPLES OF BUYOUTS

Most ESOPs begin life as management initiatives. Management may start an ESOP intending to raise productivity, gain tax benefits, or continue the firm when an owner retires; often it may be done out of a belief in giving employees a fair stake. However, there also have been numerous interesting examples of employees coming together to buy their companies. For our purposes, some of the most interesting are those that were facilitated by local, state, and/or federal government support. The 1990 employee buyout of GenCorp Polymer Products of Toledo, Ohio, for example, was facilitated in part by a $800,000 loan from the Ohio Department of Development. The company, now known as Textileather Corporation, employs about 280 workers, and although the company has not remained employee-owned, it has remained in operation in Toledo thanks to the buyout. (In 1995, it was sold to Canadian General Tower for 60 percent above the listed stock price. As a part of the deal, the workers received a 10 percent pay raise, guarantees of new capital investments in the plant, and right of first refusal if the company is again put up for sale.)[43]

Weirton Steel

Weirton Steel was at one time the largest employee-owned company in the country. When National Steel announced in 1982 that it might be closing its Weirton plant, shock waves were sent throughout the community of Weirton, West Virginia. The plant was the state's largest private employer and the lifeblood of the town that had grown up around it. Tragedy was averted when National Steel agreed to turn the plant over to the employees and management, saving the plant's 8,000 jobs. Overwhelming support from local community institutions and the support of local politicians were crucial in putting the buyout together.

Weirton is no fairy tale, however. Management retained effective control over workplace decisions even after the ESOP was founded; of late the company has been struggling to survive, and workers' holdings of firm stock have been diluted.[44] The plant incurred a large load of debt because of a $1 billion modernization effort. Modernization dramatically increased efficiency, but it also reduced the number of full-time employees required for plant operation (to around 4,000).[45] Another significant new threat has emerged from the recent surge of cheap imported steel. In response, Weirton has filed several antidumping cases against the offending countries. In the meantime, the plant has had to reduce its workforce, laying off about one-quarter of its employees for several months, and the company ran an operating loss in 2000.[46] Not surprisingly, employee ownership, for all its admirable attributes, cannot protect a company from the effects of either fair trade competition or unfair trade practices. (Indeed, several employee-owned and formerly employee-owned steel companies in the Ohio area had to close or reorganize in 2000 and 2001 due to industrywide problems, including dumping. Nationwide, over a dozen steel companies ceased operations in 2001.)[47]

Nevertheless, nearly two decades after the initial threat of closure, the steel plant at Weirton is still open. People are still working—and there is still a possibility that the workforce might again be expanded if conditions in the international market improve.

Brainard Rivet

Due in significant part to the catalytic role played by the Ohio Employee Ownership Center, Ohio boasts numerous examples of successful employee buyouts of struggling firms. The story of Brainard Rivet in Girard, Ohio, is illustrative. When Textron, a Fortune 500 company, announced it would be closing down Brainard Rivet in 1997, workers and community members were surprised. The plant, which employed sixty-eight skilled workers, had earned more than $2.2 million for the company in 1996. It soon became clear that the company was shutting down the plant simply because of an antiunion policy. As John Logue of the Ohio Employee Ownership Center remarked, "I've seen a lot of shutdowns. . . . But I've never seen a company shut down a plant that was profitable just because it was their only union plant in the U.S. This really took the cake."[48]

The workers put together a buyout committee, received help from the Ohio Bureau of Employment Services to fund a feasibility study, and enlisted the support of the governor, the mayor of Youngstown, and other local elected officials. Textron refused to sell the plant to the employees and instead shut the plant down. When it was revealed that Textron was directing former customers to its former competitors rather than doing the work at its other plants, as had been claimed, pressure from elected officials such as Congressman Jim Traficant intensified. Finally, Textron backed off its stance against selling to the employees. The buyout committee found a partner in Fastener Industries, an employee-owned company. The employees of Brainard now operate the factory as a wholly owned subsidiary of Fastener and receive Fastener stock annually. The plant, which had been closed for eleven months, finally reopened during the summer of 1998 and has been operating successfully since.[49]

POLICY PROPOSALS TO EXPAND EMPLOYEE OWNERSHIP

Public support for employee ownership, both through the ESOP legislation itself and through various forms of support for buyout efforts, has played a crucial role in the institution's ongoing development. A comprehensive program aimed self-consciously at broadening ownership and facilitating worker takeovers would likely yield a dramatic expansion of worker ownership in America. There is no shortage of proposals to further expand employee ownership. In 1992 candidate Bill Clinton embraced the concept of employee ownership as part of his Putting People First campaign, and his postelection transition team commissioned ESOP expert Joseph Blasi to develop a detailed plan for increased federal assistance to worker ownership in December of 1992.

Blasi advocated establishing a central point person in the administration to oversee employee ownership and coordinate the work of appropriate officials in the Internal Revenue Service, Department of Labor, Office of Management and Budget, Small Business Administration, and Economic Development Administration. He also proposed numerous changes in federal law to further assist employee ownership, including allowing ESOPs to buy stock from deceased owners' estates; giving employees more time to organize a counteroffer in the case of business takeovers; giving 50 percent of investment tax credits to employees in the form of stock ownership; promoting employee ownership at the SBA; and allowing employees to partner with other entities in undertaking leveraged buyouts.

To encourage greater worker participation, Blasi urged that federal law be rewritten to give employees more power to shape how employee ownership plans are used (e.g., giving them full shareholder rights), that ESOP corporations be required to "develop an employee participation plan" to qualify for tax benefits, and that employee advisory groups be established in all new privately-held ESOPs in which workers hold at least a 10 percent stake.

Finally, Blasi proposed a $1.36 billion program to directly assist employee ownership. The funds would be used to provide federal matching support to create state employee ownership centers; to allow retiring private firm owners to avoid capital gains taxation by turning the firm over to workers; to allow public corporations to avoid 50 percent of capital gains taxation on sales of subsidiaries to workers; to allow workers earning less than $30,000 a year to get stock equivalent to 35 percent of their salary, up from 25 percent; and to restore the capacity of banks to deduct half of their interest income on ESOP loans from taxes.[50]

Unfortunately, Blasi's comprehensive effort to spell out what a sympathetic federal government could do to promote employee ownership full throttle did not come to fruition during the Clinton presidency. In 1993 the Office of the American Workplace was established to help coordinate employee ownership efforts, but this lost its funding and was closed in 1996. The rest of the Blasi agenda remains relevant as a (partial) guide to what could be done in an all-out effort in support of employee ownership.

A proposal for state-level assistance for new employee ownership efforts comes from OEOC director John Logue and Jacqueline Yates. Logue and Yates propose establishing friendly equity investment pools at the state level using public pension funds. These pools would "have a strong preference for various local and broader ownership structures, including employee ownership." Logue has also urged federal support for state-run efforts: "While the U.S. Government sinks billions in tax breaks in ESOPs, it doesn't support the relatively cheap programs like the OEOC and Steelworkers Worker Ownership Institute that promote democratic ESOPs, support co-ops, and train employees for the risks of ownership. A federal matching grant of $3 million would probably triple the public, nonprofit and union infrastructure supporting employee ownership in three years."[51]

Perhaps the most thorough recent statement of what a concerted effort to boost employee ownership would look like was made by Jeff Gates, the former counsel to the U.S. Senate Committee on Finance and a close advisor of former legislator Russell Long (author of the original ESOP legislation). Gates has laid out a ten-point plan to reform tax policy so as to encourage more rapid growth of employee ownership. Gates' proposed mechanisms include:

- Reduced capital gains taxation when such gains are reinvested in worker-owned firms, or when such gains come from the sale of ESOP stock

- Tax incentives to banks that make loans to ESOP firms

- Reduced estate taxes on holdings in ESOP firms, and tax deductions on business assets sold to ESOPs (as when a family-owned business is sold to its workers after the proprietor's death)

- Cutting the current tax-exempt status of pension funds that do not invest at least 25 percent of their assets in employee-owned firms; funds failing to meet this standard would face taxation on the value of the fund's growth

- Tax deductions for individuals who buy stock in their own companies

- Limiting the tax credit for American-based multinational corporations for taxes paid abroad to those corporations with significant worker ownership in their overseas holdings

- Preferential treatment on commercial loans to employee-owned firms[52]

Gates also advocates the institution of a wealth tax, a crackdown on the use of the United States as a tax haven by foreign investors taking advantage of tax loopholes for outside investors, and the development of affordable and accessible financial services for worker-owned firms. In general, Gates insists upon the importance of broadening access to credit—the idea at the heart of the original Kelso plan of loaning money to workers and citizens to purchase stock, using the flow of future dividends as implicit collateral. Like Blasi and Logue, Gates also strongly advocates state-level employee ownership programs as "a modern counterpart to the agricultural extension service."[53]

Gates' agenda is shaped by his personal experience on Capitol Hill working with legislators on both the left and the right; he believes the idea of expanding ownership has the potential to forge very broad, unprecedented political alliances. Indeed, significant bipartisan legislative support already exists for active steps to further employee ownership.

The most ambitious legislative initiative now on the table at the federal level is a dramatic proposal put forth by one of the most conservative members of Congress—Republican representative Dana Rohrabacher of California. Rohrabacher's proposal urges a concerted federal effort to increase the amount of corporate stock held by ESOPs to 30 percent by the year 2010. Even more impressive than that bold figure is Rohrabacher's proposal to define a new legal category—the employee-owned and -controlled corporation" (which he calls "ESOP plus plus"). Such corporations (EOCCs) would be required to ensure that over 50 percent of all stock is held by employees, that 90 percent of regular employees are enrolled in the plan, and that all employees vote their stock on a one-person, one-vote basis. (An EOCC with 60 percent employee stock ownership would have its workers vote on how that 60 percent would be voted on management and corporate issues in the larger corporate meeting.)

Rohrabacher's proposed legislation—the Employee Ownership Act of 1999—would confer an unprecedented array of tax incentives on EOCC firms, including relief from all corporate income taxes, a three-year tax-free period on stock provided to employees in lieu of other compensation, no taxes on sale of stock by EOCC employee-owners back to the company or another employee, a tax credit for EOCC stock transferred to an EOCC trust by estates (allowing the estate to avoid inheritance taxes), no capital gains taxes on sales of stock to EOCC trusts, and no taxes on the first 25 percent of dividends claimed by outside investors in EOCCs. Rohrabacher explains that "what we are trying to do now is expand . . . . The home mortgage deduction, expand on the Homestead Act, expand on the idea that people have a right to own their own home but they also should have an incentive in the tax system to own and control their own company. They will control their own economic destiny. This is the ultimate empowerment."[54]

We strongly support the thrust of the agenda spelled out by Rohrabacher and Gates, but we are less certain that expanded ESOP ownership in itself will lead to greater worker participation and workplace democracy, or that aggregate gains in ESOP ownership shares will necessarily yield greater community stability. Provisions ensuring one-person-one-vote governance in employee ownership are important in connection with the former. In connection with the latter, we believe that additional steps to expand employee ownership should give special attention to the use of worker buyouts that stabilize jobs and local communities directly—either when corporate owners plan to shut a plant down or when retiring owners of private firms decide to sell. There is also a clear rationale for new investment in state-level employee ownership centers to conduct feasibility studies of worker buyouts and to help secure financing for buyouts. Indeed, given that some feasibility studies have convinced private owners or investors that there is no need to close a plant, we believe there is also a strong rationale for legally requiring *all* plant shutdowns affecting fifty or more employees to be subject to a feasibility study of the site's future potential. Related policy measures to support employee ownership should include a federal law to provide employees with the right of first refusal to buy a plant in the event of a shutdown, and federal provision of temporary financing support for employees who wish to engage in a buyout.

Tax measures of the sort advocated by Gates can also play an important role—provided they are especially targeted to ESOP firms that are rooted in specific communities. Majority-owned ESOP companies that also grant workers sufficient power to block any proposed shutdown or corporate relocation deserve significantly more favorable treatment than ESOPs that are not majority-owned or, if majority-owned, give no effective control over management decisions to workers. More research is needed to begin to sort out how many ESOPs would qualify as what might be termed a "category A" ESOP (ESOPs that genuinely stabilize community) as opposed to a "category B" ESOP (ESOPs that simply hold stock on behalf of employees without yielding control or committing to specific communities), recognizing that the boundaries between category A and category B ESOPs may often be permeable over time.

ENRON

The recent experience of the Enron Corporation, in which thousand of workers in a 401(k) retirement plan saw their savings evaporate when the company bankrupted, has raised concerns about all forms of retirement plans involving employee stock ownership, including ESOPs. While there is certainly room for improvement in the structure of ESOP firms, there is no basis for claims that employees in ESOP (or indeed, in most 401(k) plans) are made worse off by virtue of the ESOP. In fact, ESOP firms are more likely than other firms to offer other forms of retirement plans, and as we have seen, the average value of retirement benefits for employees in ESOP firms has been shown to be more than twice as high as employees in comparable non-ESOP firms. In less than 10 percent of ESOPs, workers have given up wages in exchange for ownership stakes, and wages have been shown to be higher at ESOP firms than in comparable firms. Further, ESOP law requires that employees aged 55 with ten years' experience and five years' tenure at the same firm be allowed to diversify up to 25 percent of their holdings of company stock, and that employees aged 60 with fifteen years experience and ten years' tenure be allowed to diversify up to 50 percent of their holdings. As Corey Rosen of the National Center for Employee Ownership stresses, employee ownership plans should be thought of as part of a retirement plan, "but not as retirement plans in themselves." But in most cases, ESOPs add substantial material benefits to workers.

Moreover, the risk associated with those benefits in existing ESOPs are quite modest (especially in comparison with, for instance, a small business owner whose entire savings are invested in the business). According to a 1995 Department of Labor study of ESOP performance over a ten year period, less than 1 percent of ESOP firms went bankrupt, and researchers have found that privately held ESOPs are less likely to sell out or go bankrupt than comparable firms. Indeed, in contrast to Enron, the overwhelming majority of ESOP firms are credible businesses involved in making tangible products, not speculative operations based on manipulation of markets or exotic financial instruments. Above all, the strongest lesson taught by the Enron case for ESOPs is the importance of expanding more democratic governance within firms in which employees have substantial stock, so as to ensure that the abuses of management power seen at Enron cannot be repeated and that employees' assets are protected.[55] The Enron case might also usefully inspire ESOP firms to explore other ways of reducing risk, such as cooperatively forming "pooled insurance" schemes, to ensure against unexpected adverse events.[56]

EMPLOYEE OWNERSHIP IN PERSPECTIVE

From the standpoint of a comprehensive community stabilization policy, we believe employee ownership is a uniquely important tool. ESOP laws allow a gradual transfer of assets of *existing* firms to workers. Most of the other institutional forms discussed in this book—such as municipal enterprises or firms owned by community development corporations (CDCs)—involve the generation of new, start-up businesses. Employee ownership is now an established institutional form for stable, community-based manufacturing enterprises. Employee-owned manufacturing firms have a proven track record of success as well as a vast accumulation of knowledge and experience. While municipal enterprises and community development corporations also have impressive accomplishments (see Chapters 6 and 9), neither has extensive experience in manufacturing.

On the other hand, in the new century, manufacturing is not—and will not be—the end-all and the be-all of the economy. To reiterate, manufacturing will at best occupy under 10 percent of the nation's workforce by the year 2025 and already employs just 14 percent of all Americans. Even if every local manufacturing enterprise in the country could somehow be brought under the control of worker-owned firms, community economic security would not be guaranteed for communities in the United States.

The relevance of ESOPs, however, is not limited to manufacturing: It is estimated that fewer than half of current ESOPs are involved in manufacturing, and worker ownership has worked well in a number of service sector settings. ESOP structures may in time also prove to be the most advantageous available structure for bringing larger-scale service operations (such as supermarket chains) under some form of democratic control. But ESOPs can't do the job of stabilizing communities alone. Other, complementary institutional forms also need to be nurtured in support of economically secure communities in the coming decades.

COMMUNITY DEVELOPMENT CORPORATIONS AND COMMUNITY DEVELOPMENT FINANCIAL INSTITUTIONS

C ommunity-controlled economic development in dilapidated, deteriorating urban neighborhoods has been inextricably linked with the emergence of community development corporations (CDCs) as viable economic entities over the past thirty years. In this chapter, we examine the record and accomplishments of both CDCs and their capital- and credit-providing cousins, community development financial institutions (CDFIs).

CDCs are nonprofit organizations dedicated to bringing about the revitalization of a clearly defined geographic area—often an urban neighborhood scarred by decades of disinvestment and concentrated poverty or an isolated and underdeveloped rural area. Governed by boards of directors composed primarily of local residents and other citizens with a strong stake in the community, most CDCs engage in some form of economic development within their service areas.

CDCs were originally conceived as institutions that could catalyze and direct urban economic development, while at the same time offering more control and power to local residents over the development process. Robert Kennedy, who played a lead role in establishing the first major CDC in Bedford-Stuyvesant in 1967, believed that CDCs could be powerful weapons in the fight to overcome inner-city poverty by combining "the best of community action with the best of the private enterprise system."[1] From the out-set, supporters of the CDC movement argued that the new institutions merited major governmental backing—and many elected officials agreed.

Even after Kennedy's death and Richard Nixon's election in 1968, CDCs quietly continued to grow throughout the 1970s, 1980s, and 1990s. According to the most recent survey by the National Congress for Community Economic Development (NCCED), the CDC trade association, at least 3,600 CDCs now operate in the United States. With this expanded capacity has come an expansion in tangible achievements, particularly in housing development: It is estimated that through 1998, CDCs produced well over half a million units of affordable housing. CDCs have, however, done significant work beyond the housing realm, developing over 71 million square feet of commercial/industrial space and loaning some $200 million for business development. All told, according to the NCCED, CDCs have (as of 1998) created roughly 247,000 full-time jobs.[2]

Thirty years ago, when the first serious community development efforts got off the ground in most cities, CDCs were in many cases the only game in town. Today, however, CDCs are but one part of what Ronald Ferguson and William Dickens term the "community development system."[3] Another increasingly important player in that system is the community development financial institution (CDFI), hundreds of which are also now active in American communities.

CDFIs have emerged as a localized, grass roots response both to the redlining of minority communities by traditional banks and to the broader delocalization of the U.S. financial system. (The ascendance of larger and larger megabanks and the rise of "parallel bank" institutions—mutual funds and pension funds—have pulled local savings into regional, national, and even international markets.)[4] The term "community development financial institution" refers to a variety of institutional forms aimed at funneling credit to communities underserved by traditional commercial lenders, including community development banks, community development credit unions, community development loan funds, microcredit/microenterprise programs, and community development venture capital funds.

Bill Clinton's 1992 campaign manifesto *Putting People First* envisioned federal aid to help establish a national network of community-rooted development banks. Federal support for such institutions has indeed increased tangibly during the past decade. With the establishment of the federal CDFI Fund in 1994, the Clinton administration made CDFIs part of a three-pronged approach to improve credit access and capital for low-income communities. (The other initiatives emphasized by Clinton were strengthened enforcement of the Community Reinvestment Act, which requires traditional banks to serve all areas from which they draw deposits, including low-income communities, and the Empowerment Zone/ Enterprise Community program, discussed in Chapter 4.) With the help of such public support, CDFIs have grown impressively in number—an estimated 500 were in operation by 2001.[5]

Contemporary commentaries on the effectiveness of CDCs and CDFIs vary widely. Practitioners and support groups often point to their numerous tangible achievements and see CDCs and CDFIs as a success story.[6] But numerous journalistic and academic critics are quick to point out that most CDC-led development has been limited to housing and that these institutions have largely failed to bring about significant broad-based neighborhood revitalization. Still others point to tensions and contradictions inherent in the model that often prevent these organizations from achieving community revitalization while also remaining democratically controlled by the community. We see merit in each of these positions but remain cautiously optimistic about the ability over time of properly structured and funded CDCs and CDFIs to make a serious, salutary contribution to the economic stability of poor communities throughout the United States.

As will be seen below, some CDCs have been surprisingly successful in development activities far beyond housing. Still, too few CDCs engage in the type of comprehensive economic, social, and political development activities their original founders envisioned, and the development activities of CDFIs are similarly modest. We believe that the key to tapping the full community-stabilizing potential of CDCs lies in a revival of the spirit of this earlier vision —and we are heartened to note that some CDCs are beginning to move their development agendas toward greater comprehensiveness. Of particular importance, we believe, is community-owned and -controlled business development and commercial revitalization that creates jobs for local residents—whether this is undertaken by CDCs directly or in partnership with the traditional private sector. Also important is a renewal of advocacy and community organizing capacities.

But it is also clear that CDCs and CDFIs, in any form, cannot do the job of stabilizing the economies of poor communities alone. The question is not whether CDCs and CDFIs can do the whole job, but whether they can make a critical contribution when combined with the other types of community-rooted institutions and community-supporting policies reviewed throughout this volume.

POSITIVE TRENDS: THE GROWTH OF CDCS

Both CDCs and the larger community development system of which they are a part have enjoyed increased recognition, visibility, and legitimacy since the early 1990s, thanks in part to the Clinton administration's interest in community-based economic development in poor areas. Although that interest did not translate into a full reversal of the budget cuts of the Reagan years, increases in federal backing of community development have occurred. Federal funding (most commonly from Community Development Block Grants and the low-income housing tax credit) is currently CDCs' largest single source of support. There also has been a major expansion in support for CDCs over the last decades from corporations, foundations, private banking groups, nonprofits, and local and state governments—a change reflecting both CDCs' increased recognition and the increased acceptance of community-based development strategies. CDCs, their intermediaries, and other funders/supporters have clearly evolved into a viable industry. CDCs' growth is reflected by the dynamic expansion of the National Congress for Community Economic Development (NCCED), which grew from 250 members in 1989 to 700 members in 1996.[7]

A key factor in the accelerated growth of CDCs is the expanded number, increased capacity, and broadened focus of the support organizations providing CDCs with technical assistance, financing, training, and information. One of the most important support organizations has been the New York–based Local Initiatives Support Corporation (LISC), now under the presidency of former Clinton treasury secretary Robert Rubin. In the 1990s, LISC increased its grants, loans, and investments in CDCs, established more offices across the nation, and widened the scope of its work beyond its traditional focus on housing development. During these years, LISC launched its Community Building Initiative to help fund community-based social-service programs (e.g., child care services, health care facilities, block clubs, etc.), its Retail Initiative to invest funds in inner-city supermarket-anchored shopping centers developed/owned by CDCs, and its Community Security Initiative to help foster partnerships between police departments and CDC-based citizen-led crime prevention efforts.[8] LISC also attracts investors to purchase equity in community-based housing developments, plays a role in the secondary market for CDC housing and economic development loans, and directs programs related to the provision of job training and the development of CDCs' management and operational capacity.[9] In total, LISC is credited with marshalling over $3 billion in assistance, plus leveraging another $3.5 billion in private and public funds, to assist some 1,700 CDCs.[10] Other important support organizations for CDCs include the Enterprise Foundation, the federally created Neighborhood Reinvestment Corporation, and the NCCED itself.

A major development in CDC activity since the 1990s has been a move away from a narrow focus on housing and a return to a comprehensive community development agenda aimed at attacking multiple economic and social problems in urban neighborhoods simultaneously. Many CDCs now are directly involved in community-building and social-capital-oriented activities such as community policing efforts, leadership development workshops, day care programs, and neighborhood cleanup initiatives; they also often take part in community organizing and advocacy, as well as a variety of economic development initiatives. Part of this sea change is attributable to steering done by foundations and other funding sources. By the mid-1990s, as Pierre Clavel and his colleagues have pointed out, "after 20 years of funding predominately bricks-and-mortar projects, foundations began to recognize the shortsightedness of such a narrow approach and poured millions of dollars into comprehensive experiments. Almost every major foundation involved in community development had a comprehensive initiative under way in 1996, as did several intermediaries such as LISC and the Enterprise Foundation."[11] While funds available for these types of endeavors remain small relative to resources available for physical development projects, they have enabled CDCs to operate a much broader range of services and programs in recent years.

CRITICAL EVALUATIONS OF THE CDC MODEL

Despite these positive trends, a generation of experience with CDCs also provides reasons for caution and pointed criticisms. Many street-level activists (and some academic observers) have faulted CDCs for too often being run autocratically as personal fiefdoms, and for allying more with a corporate worldview than with community needs. These observers question the amount of democratic control and accountability present in the CDC format. As Dan Swinney of the Center for Labor and Community Research puts it:

> The "community" in community development is typically a token relationship with relatively little grass roots participation on the Boards of CDCs and weak consultation and education with a broad pool of community residents. Many CDCs as seen in the Board structure are business development organizations that receive tax breaks, yet are not accountable to truly protect the assets of the community.

Swinney faults many CDCs for being nonentrepreneurial, taking a passive approach to development, and lowering "their sights to generally marginal types of business activity in light of what really drives the health or decline of a community."[12]

Indeed, although reports highlighting CDCs' tangible achievements in the 1990s have generally been laudatory, many scholars argue that CDCs have failed in realizing their original objectives. Sigmund Shipp, for example, examined CDCs' ability to strengthen and transform African-American communities and concluded that "many CDCs succumbed to the profit-making ethos that was intrinsic to the capitalistic environment in which they operated." As a result, Shipp argues, CDCs have helped only a few black entrepreneurs rather than the broader community.[13]

Most recent critiques emphasize that the model itself commonly involves two basic flaws that hinder CDCs from achieving their traditional goals—inadequate funding and insufficient scale.[14] As organizations aiming to affect meaningful change in distressed areas, CDCs clearly need significant resources and funds. This need places CDCs in a dependent situation, requiring them to rely on outsiders' support and assistance. CDCs are consrained in their capacity to act autonomously (i.e., initiating the activities most in line with residents' needs); often they must alter their agendas to reflect funders' priorities rather than their own. A common experience is that many intermediaries, foundations, and governments want to appear successful to their sponsors, supporters, and/or constituents—and may pressure CDCs they fund to emphasize measurable physical development projects over other long-term, more difficult community-building goals.

Many observers believe that to effect meaningful change, CDCs will have to become large enough to produce a broad range of projects at a significant scale. This was the original idea behind the Bedford-Stuyvesant CDC, for instance, but this brings additional problems. As CDCs grow, they almost inevitably become less tied to the community, and often become less participatory as well. Hence larger CDCs often tend to lose the characteristics essential for them to realize other critical goals, such as resident empowerment and civic involvement. Similarly, the need to produce "to scale" often requires CDCs to turn to outsiders (including intermediary institutions) that possess critical technical skills/knowledge. This again is problematic, as it can reduce community participation and opportunities for residents themselves to acquire relevant technical skills.

CDCS AND OWNERSHIP

Despite the high ambitions of the founders of the CDC movement, in practice substantial limitations have become evident. The conventional scholarly wisdom about the history of CDCs is that although these organizations have performed the quasi-public function of affordable housing provision reasonably well, CDCs have not been a particularly effective vehicle for revitalizing the economies of poor communities.

We believe this common view should not be overstated or taken as the last word on CDCs. Indeed, three decades of development and trial-and-error learning have set the stage for a potentially important move forward both in scale and in community-building capacity. The fact is that many CDCs have become successful economic developers, generating place-based jobs that benefit local residents and illustrate future possibilities. There is substantial evidence that CDCs, even in their current form, can be important vehicles for community ownership and stable job creation in a variety of contexts. Consider the following examples:[15]

- For 17 years, Asian Neighborhood Design (AND) in the Bay Area (Oakland–San Francisco), operated a successful nonprofit business, Specialty Mills Products, which makes custom furniture. Its annual revenues were over $5 million, with seventy full-time employees, most of whom were people of color.[16] The company was sold in 2001 to its long-time general manager, but continues to operate with the same staff.

- The original flagship CDC, Bedford-Stuyvesant Restoration Corporation in Brooklyn, New York, is two-thirds owner of the Restoration Supermarket Corporation, which provides 126 part-time and 46 full-time jobs and earns profits of roughly $300,000 to $400,000 a year. Revenues at the RSC's Pathmark grocery store exceeded $28 million in 2000.[17] BSRC also operates a 200-seat theater, a revolving loan fund and revolving equity fund for local start-up businesses.

- Bickerdike CDC in Chicago operates the Humboldt Construction Company, which employs eight to fifteen carpenters at union wages, depending on demand, in addition to its permanent staff of fifty-five; annual contracts for the construction company have exceeded $10 million in recent years. Bickerdike also provides lead removal services. Over 90 percent of employees at Bickerdike (and 75 percent of those in the construction company) are local residents.[18]

- Dineh Cooperatives, a CDC serving the Navajo nation in Arizona, New Mexico, and Utah, operates a shopping center employing a total of 170 people, as well as a manufacturer of precision machine parts for General Motors. Total employment at DCI is now over 350, and expansion plans are under way.[19]

- Esperanza Unida, a CDC primarily serving the Hispanic community in Milwaukee, employs roughly a hundred local residents in seven businesses in a range of fields, including auto repair, construction, printing, child care, customer service skills, and welding. The CDC also recently opened a coffeehouse/bookstore called ¿Que Pasa?, which offers books and periodicals in both Spanish and English and hosts numerous community events. The CDC has also trained nearly 2,000 residents in its businesses since the mid-1980s. Some 50 to 70 percent of the CDC's annual revenues come from its business activities.[20]

- Ganados del Valle, based in the rural community of Los Ojos, New Mexico, has in the past two decades created a weaving cooperative (which now operates as an independent worker cooperative), a lamb-marketing cooperative, a wool-washing plant, and a tire-recycling firm. The various employment and educational programs of Ganados have provided employment or other assistance to some 500 families in the region.[21]

- The New Community Corporation (NCC) in Newark is the largest private employer of local residents in the city—60 percent of NCC's 1,750 workers live in Newark. (Over 90 percent are minorities.) In addition to a variety of job-training services and a two-thirds stake in a Pathmark supermarket and shopping center, the CDC also operates eight day care centers, a nursing home, a medical day care center for seniors, two other grocery stores, a restaurant, a newspaper, and a credit union. Corporate interests are not allowed on the board, which has an unusually high degree of direct community participation. NCC owns each of the stores in its shopping centers, including several franchises of national chains. NCC's total real estate holdings have an estimated value of $500 million, and NCC generates some $200 million in economic activity each year.[22]

- The Quitman County Development Organization in Mississippi operates a small shopping complex, a credit union, and a housing development program, as well as a day care center. In 1998 it started a microloan program, and since 1985 it has made seed grants to African-American churches statewide engaged in economic development.[23]

- The East Los Angeles Community Union has assets of over $300 million and revenues of $100 million annually. It provides financial services, makes loans to low-income residents, and operates two development companies, a real estate company, a construction management company, a telecommunications firm, a roofing supply provider, and a restaurant, as well as an array of social services. The fourth-largest Hispanic business in California, it employs 700 to 1,000 people annually.[24]

- Coastal Enterprises in Maine, formed in 1977, has been involved in providing over $300 million in financing, including both direct loans and investments and leveraged financing, to over 1,000 businesses, helping to create over 10,000 jobs. In addition to loans, the CDC makes equity investments in growing local companies through its subsidiary, the Coastal Ventures Limited Partnership.[25]

- Kentucky Highlands Investment Corporation (KHIC) has invested over $77 million in some 175 enterprises helping create or retain 7,400 jobs in southeast Kentucky, including one in three manufacturing jobs in the region. In 1998 it was estimated that 10 percent of the households in KHIC's nine county service area had "at least one bread-winner in which the CDC has invested."[26]

These examples demonstrate the range of current activities. Some are modest; others are dramatic. Newark's New Community Corporation in particular demonstrates the capacity of CDCs to play a serious role in helping bolster a community's economy. Perhaps most remarkable is that this sample of CDCs successfully involved in economic development and community ownership activities are predominantly located in some of the nation's poorest communities.

The practitioner community is divided on the question of whether CDCs should get involved in ownership on a substantial scale. Newark Community Corporation's director of development, Raymond Codey, points to lack of capital and an inability to take risks as major obstacles to CDCs getting involved in ownership; other practitioners point to the administrative costs involved in ownership and prefer to use CDC funds to leverage creation by private businesses.[27] Moreover, as the discussion later in this chapter of programs providing support for CDCs indicates, to date most public money targeted at CDCs has focused on low-income housing and broader development concerns, not ownership initiatives. Nonetheless, the NCC's experience in inner-city Newark with direct community ownership and the Kentucky Highlands Investment

Corporation's experience with equity investments in rural areas of the state illustrate that it is possible for CDCs to successfully act as a significant institutional vehicle for job creation and stabilization via ownership strategies.

In each of the examples noted above, local-level practitioners have demonstrated the imagination and vision to create businesses and related programs appropriate to the skills, resources, and culture of their particular communities. Most also have demonstrated the ability to engage in long-term business planning and to link job creation to meeting human needs. Although increasing the numbers of CDCs involved in these kinds of comprehensive economic development activities will be a significant challenge, there is good reason to think that with committed policy support, CDCs can assume a larger economic role (beyond housing) in more communities over the coming decades.

Similarly, CDCs can also contribute to the community organizing and advocacy activities that were so central to the early CDC vision. As the resources available to CDCs increase—especially to the degree that such resources are self-generated—the capacity of CDCs to sponsor community-organizing and community-building activities of various kinds should increase. Columbia University political scientist J. Philip Thompson has described the potential for community development groups with significant economic independence to play an important role in the formation of a politically progressive political coalition in New York City.[28] But just as CDCs are no longer the only game in town when it comes to community development, there are now many other actors active in community organizing in American cities, such as congregation-based community organizations built on the Saul Alinsky model. As Carmen Sirianni and Lewis Friedland have recently shown, there is tremendous potential for the development work undertaken by CDCs to be linked with these broader community organizing efforts in interesting ways, with the aim of developing a twin capacity within communities to both build up economic assets from within while seeking additional resources from outside the community, and in particular from state and federal government.[29] Indeed, closer linkages between community organizing efforts and community development efforts can be one mechanism for improving the accountability of CDCs and ensuring that their development initiatives meet the needs and match the vision of neighborhood residents.

CDFIS: GROWTH AND COMMUNITY STABILIZATION

CDFIs confront many of the same dilemmas of accountability, inadequate funding and scale that CDCs face. Yet as the brief survey below demonstrates, a variety of community-based finance mechanisms also have demonstrated their capacity to make important contributions to stabilizing economically troubled communities.

Community Development Banks

Community development banks in many ways are like traditional banks, except that they are designed especially to facilitate economic revitalization in poorer communities. South Shore Bank in Chicago—now a subsidiary of the Shorebank Corporation—became the nation's first genuine community development bank after its purchase in 1973 by four investors determined to show other lenders that profits could be earned in redlined areas. Its parent corporation, Shorebank, now holds over a dozen operating companies, each of which is oriented toward community development. These subsidiaries— located in Cleveland, Michigan, and the Pacific Northwest, as well as Chicago—provide real estate management, technical assistance and job training, equity investments, and economic consulting. Shorebank, which boasts assets exceeding $1 billion, invested nearly $150 million in disadvantaged communities in 2000 alone.[30]

Since 1988 over a dozen new community development banks have been launched, starting with the Southern Development Bankcorp in Arkadelphia, Arkansas, which focuses lending in the rural western part of that state.[31] Other areas with new development banks include New York, Kansas City, Cleveland, Detroit, Louisville, and Oakland; a 10 percent stake in the Community Bank of the Bay, which opened in 1996, is held by the city of Oakland.[32]

Community Development Credit Unions

The last two decades have also seen the proliferation of community development credit unions (CDCUs), defined as credit unions serving neighborhoods in which over half the residents have incomes below the regional median. According to a recent Brookings Institution study, the number of CDCUs quadrupled during the 1990s, with over 530 in operation by 1999.[33] The priorities of CDCUs vary from case to case—in some instances the emphasis is on affordable banking services, while in others it is on using deposits to foster local economic development. Although there are prominent exceptions, the low average deposit ($500) of credit union members and current federal restrictions on the amount of development lending (no more than 15 percent of reserves) have often made it difficult for CDCUs to undertake significant scale development activities.

Probably the most widely emulated model of a CDCU strongly oriented toward community development is the Center for Community Self-Help

Self Help) in Durham, North Carolina. Established in 1980 by two activists seeking to create a pool of capital to help workers affected by textile layoffs in North Carolina, Self Help's credit union now has assets of over $40 million and branches in five other North Carolina cities. To date it has provided over $1 billion in assistance to poor people, minorities, rural residents, and women, including $352 million in 2000 alone, mostly through business loans, mortgages, and loans to nonprofits. Self Help also has a venture capital fund that undertakes commercial and real estate investments. Through 2000, Self-Help had loaned over $100 million to more than 1,500 small enterprises, helping to create or stabilize over 2,200 jobs in 2000. Most capital for Self Help is raised from socially conscious investors, typically at a lower-than-market rate of return. Perhaps most impressively, Self Help has maintained a broader political agenda: Self Help played a leading role in helping create the Coalition for Responsible Lending, which in 1999 persuaded the North Carolina legislature to pass a landmark law restricting predatory mortgage lending. Self Help is now advocating new legislation to fight predatory lending at the national level.[34]

Another successful institution is the Santa Cruz Community Credit Union, with assets of $40 million and over 7,600 (mostly Hispanic) members. Lending is guided by the question "How can we improve the social and economic condition of an area and address the needs of the people who live there?" The credit union has provided funding to construct an AIDS hospice, a free dental clinic, and women's shelters, as well as to assist local organic farmers and worker-owned businesses. At the same time, it offers standard deposit services and administers a small-business loan program for the nearby city of Watsonville.[35]

Other localities with community credit unions operating on a significant scale include Ithaca, New York, where the Alternatives Federal Credit Union utilizes part of its $34.5 million in assets (2000) to assist worker-owned businesses and co-ops, using the Mondragon (Spain) system as a model,[36] and Brooklyn, New York, where the Central Brooklyn Federal Credit Union, launched in 1993 as "the world's first hip-hop credit union," holds (as of 2000) $3.8 million in assets and serves 2,600 low- and moderate-income members.[37]

Community Development Loan Funds

Another example of community-based finance is the community development loan fund (CDLF). CDLFs are formally defined as nonprofit financial intermediaries focused on community development and "empowering low-income people and communities through access to credit, technical assistance, and mutual accountability." According to the National Community Capital Association, there are now over 200 community development loan funds in the United States.[38]

The oldest and most successful example is the revolving loan fund operated by the Institute for Community Economics (ICE) in Springfield, Massachusetts. The fund, launched as an arm of ICE in 1979, had by 2001 loaned some $35 million, with over 400 loans going to community organizations in thirty states. These funds facilitated the development of over 3,850 units of housing. Through 1999, less than 1.5 percent of the fund's loans had to be written off. The vast majority of the loans (88 percent) have been made to land trust and housing groups (including over $11 million to assist community land trusts), but loans have also been made to worker-owned firms, nonprofit business, co-ops, and community service organizations. Examples of ICE's loan fund activity include $3,500 to help a community-owned laundromat replace its washing machines, $20,000 to a Mississippi group aiming to start their own loan fund, $285,000 to rehabilitate a sixteen-unit housing co-op in Washington, DC, and $500,000 to help a Cincinnati group establish a community land trust.[39]

Microenterprise Loan Funds
A fourth major form of community development finance is the microenterprise loan fund.

Microenterprise funds are broadly patterned after Bangladesh's Grameen Bank, an innovative antipoverty initiative started in 1976 by Dr. Muhammad Yunus. The basic concept behind the original Grameen Bank is to make very small loans ($50 or less) to women organized in peer groups, enabling the loan recipients to make otherwise unaffordable investments in, for instance, a new sewing machine—a tool that can sharply increase the recipient's earning potential. No new loans can be made available until all the women in a peer group have repaid the initial loan. To date, Grameen has realized a default rate of just 3 percent on loans using this strategy.[40]

In the past decade, the Grameen model has gained prominence in the United States, and there has been an explosion of microlenders in this country. According to a recent survey, at least 340 microenterprise programs were operating in forty-six states in 1998 and had helped start over 40,000 businesses.[41] Such programs generally both provide access to credit and entrepreneurial training for disadvantaged persons striving to start their own (often home-based) businesses. The idea in the United States is similar to the Grameen model—make small, usually short-term loans to poor people (usually averaging under $5,000) that will allow them to undertake some form of entrepreneurial activity, often in the informal economy. Many such organizations also use the peer group concept, although the specific lending guidelines and practices vary widely among these organizations. According to the author of a recent comprehensive study of U.S. microenterprise programs, the "single common denominator" of such programs "is that they serve as lenders of last resort, providing credit to people who want to be self-employed but who cannot obtain credit through traditional channels."[42]

Two prominent organizations that have supported microloan programs in the United States and abroad are Working Capital, based in Cambridge, Massachusetts, and Acción International, based in Somerville, Massachusetts. After many years of extensive work as separate organizations, Working Capital merged in September 2001 with Accion's domestic initiative, Acción USA. Acción now has five United States affiliates, located in San Diego, Chicago, New Mexico, Texas, and New York City, and by mid-2001 had made $29 million in loans through these organizations to some 4,600 small-business owners.[43] In a typical case, Acción's San Antonio affiliate made a small loan to a self-employed Tex-Mex chef to allow her to meet increased charges for vendor's booths at local street fairs. Fifty-five percent of Acción's U.S. loan recipients are impoverished (according to federal standards) and 85 percent are minorities.[44]

Prior to the merger, Working Capital offered loans to individual entrepreneurs. Many prospective borrowers join an "entrepreneur alliance" composed of at least five business owners; these groups elect a credit committee that approves loan requests from members, and no new loans can be issued unless all members are current on payments. Working Capital made over 3,000 loans (in ten states) of $500–$20,000 each to small and start-up entrepreneurs. Total loans disbursed exceeded $4.4 million, with an average size of roughly $1,500. A survey by Working Capital of its customers in January and February 2000 found that loan recipients on average saw sales in their ventures increase by some 88 percent, from $14,000 to $26,000 a year.[45]

Community Development Venture Capital Funds

Two other financial institutions with the potential to make substantial contributions to place-based development are venture capital funds and savings and loan associations (S&Ls). The Community Development Venture Capital Alliance now counts eighty members, forty of which are venture capital funds, including the Kentucky Highlands Investment Corporation (profiled above in the discussion of CDCs). Another successful venture fund is the Northeast Ventures Corporation in Duluth, Minnesota, which through 2000 had invested $11.4 million in 27 firms in the region. Northeast Ventures, which has a target return rate of 25 percent on each investment, has helped create or save 695 jobs. Other model venture capital funds—all created since 1996—include the Boston Community Venture Fund ($10 million in assets), Community Development Ventures in Baltimore ($8 million in assets), and the New York Community Investment Company ($47 million in assets).[46]

TAPPING THE FULL POTENTIAL OF CDCS AND CDFIS

The two most important keys to tapping the full potential of the CDCs and CDFIs to contribute to a community stability strategy are, first, obtaining adequate policy support from governmental actors and, second, ensuring that community development practitioners maintain a broad vision of comprehensive community improvement that extends beyond mortar-and-brick projects.

CDCs and CDFIs have benefited and continue to benefit from a number of supportive policies and programs at the federal, state, and local levels. Expansion of these programs would generate badly needed additional resources for local-level practitioners and allow CDCs and CDFIs to play a more prominent role in community economic stabilization efforts.

Policy Support

Federal Assistance for CDCs
At the federal level, Community Development Block Grants (CDBGs) distributed through HUD are the most widely used source of federal funds for CDCs. (It has been estimated that over three-quarters of operating CDCs receive CDBG or other federal funds.)[47] The program distributes $4.7 billion annually to assist a wide range of community revitalization efforts. After being initially disbursed to state and local authorities, a significant portion of the funds are used to support community development corporations. The Urban Institute estimates that in 1995 over $600 million in federal aid assisted urban CDCs or other housing nonprofits, roughly 10 percent of total federal spending on housing subsidies.[48]

As we have noted, the majority of CDC projects have been focused on housing—and a significant number of the federal programs that support CDCs also focus on housing initiatives. Key programs include the HOME Investment Partnership Program, legislated into existence in 1992, which "approximately doubled the amount of housing subsidies available for invest-ment by local governments."[49] Administered by HUD, the HOME program provides grants to states and localities for affordable housing projects. These funds, which require that states and localities provide matching funds equiv-alent to 25 percent of the federal contribution, are used in partnership with local nonprofits. (Distressed communities may receive full or partial relief from this matching requirement.) In fiscal 2003, the HOME program is expected to receive over $2 billion, leading to the creation of over 104,000 affordable housing units.[50]

CDCs also benefit from the Federal Home Loan Bank System, which consists of twelve regional banks established in 1932 to support housing finance. Owned cooperatively by their member institutions, the FHL banks make loans or cash advances to members. With nearly 7,800 mem-bers and $700 billion in assets, the FHLB has helped finance the construc-tion or rehabilitation of over 270,000 housing units between 1990 and 2000 through its Affordable Housing Program.[51] This program helps non-profits finance the purchase, construction, or rehabilitation of housing units (by providing funds that serve as private matching funds for CDBG and other government funds). Likewise, the FHLB's Community Investment Program (CIP) provides loans at a reduced rate to nonprofits involved in community economic development; during the 1990s, nearly $23 billion in CIP-funded loans helped create roughly 430,000 housing units, and the program also contributed over $1.4 billion to broader eco-nomic development activities.[52]

A related source of support for CDC housing activity is the low-income housing tax credit—the primary tool for financing new affordable housing throughout the nation. The tax credit will amount to over $3.3 billion in 2002. This credit allows developers of affordable rental housing to apply for an annual federal income tax credit of a percentage of qualified development costs each year for ten years. This credit, established in 1986, makes it much easier for nonprofits such as CDCs to attract private capital into partnerships to develop affordable housing. Intermediaries such as LISC and its offshoot, the National Equity Fund, have played a key role in making the most of this credit by brokering deals between local CDCs and private investors (who often invest in multiple housing projects with different CDCs in different cities simultaneously). Many housing advocates as well as LISC itself adamantly support a substantial increase in the value of this credit, which has already played a role in financing over a million affordable housing units.[53]

Another federal agency that provides smaller but noteworthy support for CDCs is the Office of Community Service (OCS), located in the

Department of Health and Human Services. The OCS administers the Urban and Rural Community Economic Development grant program to CDCs for projects aimed at providing "employment and ownership opportunities for low-income people through business, physical or commercial development."[54] The $23 million allocated to the program for 2001 includes $17 million for operational grants for CDCs, $2.1 million for projects developed by historically black colleges and universities in conjunction with a CDC, and $750,000 for development grants to newly created CDCs that have not previously received OCS funds. (Such CDCs are subsequently eligible for funding from another $2.5 million pool of set-aside grant money.) In 2000, the program provided assistance to sixty-five new businesses, leading to employment for 1,600 low-income people.[55] Prominent community development organizations that have received assistance from OCS include New Community Corporation in Newark, Coastal Enterprises in Maine, and the Kentucky Highlands Investment Corporation.

Many other federal programs (reviewed in more detail in Chapter 6) also provide modest assistance to CDCs in the course of supporting economic development in general. The Economic Development Administration, for instance, has provided $1.8 million to assist the New Community Corporation's modular housing factory project, which will eventually bring 200 new manufacturing jobs, located on the site of an abandoned milk processing plant, to downtown Newark.[56] Another federal program that interacts with CDCs is HUD's Office of Community Planning and Development, which operates both the Loan Guarantee Fund and the Economic Development Initiative (EDI). These programs have also provided significant assistance to several CDCs. For instance, the Anacostia Economic Development Corporation in Washington, DC, received EDI funds in its development of Good Hope Marketplace, a shopping center providing badly needed services such as a pharmacy to local residents.[57]

State and Local Level Assistance for CDCs

Numerous state programs also offer significant assistance to CDCs. Model programs recently identified by NCCED, for instance, include the New York's Neighborhood Preservation Companies Program (NPC) and Rural Preservation Companies Program (RPC), aimed at urban and rural CDCs in New York State. The urban program (NPC) offers annual grants of up to $100,000 to CDCs for use in housing development. The program supports over 160 CDCs a year, with annual funding of roughly $11 to $12 million.[58] The rural program (RPC) provides funds to approximately 70 CDCs a year; its annual funding is roughly $4 to $5 million a year.[59]

The North Carolina Community Development Initiative (NCCDI), begun in 1994, "offers financial help directly to mature CDCs across the state of North Carolina to enable them to strengthen their operations, retain top-notch staff, and pursue development projects."[60] CDCs are eligible to receive up to $150,000 for operating grants, and $50,000 to assist new programs. In addition, they are eligible for project and emergency cash-flow loans. Through 1999, NCCDI had provided $19 million in assistance to CDCs, helping generate some $100 million in economic activity. Annual funding for the program is roughly $2 million a year, with additional funding from private and foundation sources.[61]

In Massachusetts two programs are worth noting: The Community Economic Development Assistance Corporation (CEDAC) offers technical assistance to CDCs, including staff training programs, and offers loans to help CDCs undertake development projects. CEPAC has now lent over $32 million to help create or preserve 15,000 housing units.[62] The state's Community Enterprise Economic Development (CEED) program also provides funds and technical assistance to CDCs in economically depressed communities. The program, which disbursed over $2 million in grants in 2000, supports economic development and housing development, as well as education and neighborhood organizing.[63]

The Ohio Community Development Finance Fund (CDFF), a private nonprofit that receives state funding, helps Ohio CDCs obtain financing for projects in low- and moderate-income neighborhoods. CDFF operates a "linked deposit" fund by recruiting "benevolent investors," matching their investments with state dollars, and depositing funds in participating lending institutions that in turn provide more favorable financing to nonprofit developers. The program has resulted in some $2 million in linked deposits in banks to promote local community developments. In addition, the program provides predevelopment grants and loans to assess the feasibility of specific projects. The fund also focuses on development of child care facilities. In one recent year it provided $250,000 in predevelopment grants, $350,000 for economic development projects, $150,000 for Head Start, and $100,000 for childcare programs.[64]

Local governments also have been involved in actively supporting CDCs. Of the 1,160 community-based development organizations responding to a 1991 survey by the National Congress for Community Economic Development, 413 reported receiving support from local government, in addition to pass-through money from the Community Development Block Grants. More recently, the Urban Institute reported that "support for CDCs among city governments and other local institutions has grown substantially," as large cities around the nation are making CDCs leading partners in neighborhood revitalization strategies. The Urban Institute notes that almost half of the twenty-three cities surveyed—including Indianapolis, Baltimore, Cleveland, Portland, New York, Seattle, Boston, Philadelphia, Washington, DC, Newark, and Kansas City—give CDCs a "central role in the delivery of government programs in low-income neighborhoods." The Institute also notes that nine of the twenty-three cities had "registered large gains in public support" in the 1990s, including Indianapolis, Portland, Seattle, Philadelphia, Newark, Los Angeles, San Antonio, Detroit, and Columbus.[65]

Federal Support for Community Development Finance Institutions
Federal support for CDFIs got a major boost in the first Clinton administration, with the establishment of Community Development Financial Institutions Fund in 1994. This fund provides assistance in a variety of forms to certified CDFIs, including equity investments, deposits, loans, grants, and technical assistance. Another provision of the law, the Bank Enterprise Awards Program, provides grants to commercial banks which assist or invest in CDFIs or directly assist distressed communities. Initial capitalization of this fund was $382 million over four years. An additional $118 million in capital was provided under the fiscal 2001 federal budget. (However, the Bush administration has proposed cutting new funding to just $68 million in fiscal 2003.)[66]

To be eligible for support under the program, a CDFI must have as its primary purpose the promotion of community development within an investment area or on behalf of an underserved target population, and must provide development services along with financial services while maintaining accountability to the served area through community representation on its board. The CDFI must also demonstrate through a comprehensive plan that it will be properly managed and operated, that it has a strategy to meet the needs of the target population, and that it will coordinate assistance from all available sources—federal, state, local, and private. (It also must secure matching funds from sources other than the federal government.)

Awards can be up to $5 million over three years, except in cases where the CDFI is moving into a new area of activity, in which case the ceiling is $8.75 million. Normally, federal assistance must be matched on a one-to-one basis from nonfederal sources, with the same type of funds matched (e.g., equity for equity).[67] By the end of 2000, the CDFI Fund had issued some 245 grants totaling nearly $230 million for core CDFI assistance,

225 grants totaling $10 million for technical assistance, and 395 grants to banks and thrifts totaling $121 million via the Bank Enterprise Awards Program. Early studies conducted by the fund indicate that 1997 core funding recipients were able to increase loan activities by over 75 percent and expand total assets by nearly 50 percent in the first two years after receiving a grant.[68]

The Coalition of Community Development Financial Institutions has made several additional proposals for strengthened federal support of CDFIs, including permanent authorization for the CDFI Fund and preserving the 2001 funding levels. The coalition also suggests that government-sponsored enterprises aimed primarily at housing finance—the Federal Home Loan Bank, Fannie Mae, and Freddie Mac—be required to "develop customized secondary market programs for housing and business loans originated by CDFIs." The coalition urges that a shift in such agencies from simple housing provision to a broader vision of economic development would lead them to view CDFIs as a natural partner, since their "success is based on their knowledge of local markets," making CDFIs "the most efficient vehicle for the system to reach resource-poor communities."[69]

Another means of strengthening CDFIs involves expanded use of the Community Reinvestment Act (CRA). The CRA, which requires banks to serve communities from which they draw deposits, dates to the late 1970s. Importantly, community organizations can use the law to challenge bank merger and acquisitions if a bank has not adequately met its CRA obligations. Better enforcement of the law, often lax until the 1990s, has recently produced a major increase in the amount of CRA-related money invested in urban neighborhoods.[70]

The CRA legislation itself was significantly overhauled in 1995 to meet criticisms of banks in regard to administrative problems and to address the need for clarity and objectivity in requirements. The most significant part of the new CRA is the strategic plan option: A bank can choose to forgo being evaluated by regulators on its CRA record by developing a "strategic plan detailing how it plans to meet the credit needs of the community."[71] Public participation in development of the plan is required. The bank must informally seek input from members of the community while developing the plan, formally solicit public comment on the plan for at least thirty days three months prior to the effective date of the plan, and make copies available to the public at no charge. A plan may cover up to five years; annual performance goals are required.[72]

The new CRA has proven to be a dramatically more effective tool than the earlier legislation. Hundreds of banks have negotiated reinvestment agreements with community groups, while many others have made voluntary commitments to reinvest in underserved communities. Alex Schwartz of New School University notes that by the end of 1999, "more than 300 negotiated and voluntary agreements had been launched, amounting to *more than $1 trillion* worth of investment commitments."[73] Former LISC president Paul Grogan and journalist Tony Proscio have also documented the recent increases:

> The National Community Reinvestment Coalition . . . has kept a tally of banks' CRA commitments over the years. In the fourteen years between 1977 and 1991, they reported a total of $8.8 billion in aggregate commitments. In the next six years, new commitments added more than $388 billion to that total—enough, for example, to put nearly 4 million people in the new or renovated homes (though it will surely be used for more things than housing). But then, that entire twenty-year amount was instantly dwarfed by the announcements made in just the first *six months* of 1998.[74]

Many observers believe that the CRA and CDFIs can and should be used in combination more systematically to foster a more efficient means of supplying capital to communities. Simply put, additional amounts of CRA funds should be funneled to CDFIs. Legal scholar Christopher Heisen, for instance, argues that CDFIs can be more efficient in supplying capital because traditional banks do not have either the orientation or the expertise required for effective low- and moderate-income market development; or for flexible small-business lending. In addition, the trend toward consolidation in commercial banking makes these institutions less responsive to community needs, as large banks begin to "specializ[e] in particular market niches rather than providing comprehensive banking services to the public at large, which would make them less able to provide broad-based solutions to community development problems."[75] Dan Immergluck of the Woodstock Institute also points out that new performance-based evaluations adopted in 1997 clarify the CRA credit banks receive for investing in CDFIs (something that in the past was often murky).[76]

State and Local Support for Community Development Finance Institutions and Local Lending

States have an array of tools at their disposal that can be used to support CDFIs (and more local lending in general). States can set aside a percentage of deposits to be made in community banks, target loan guarantees to community-oriented projects and firms, and use public resources in many other ways to support community-based banking. At least twelve states (including Oklahoma, Missouri, and Texas) now have linked deposit programs, which place a portion of the state's bank deposits in lending institutions that provide low-cost capital for local investments by small businesses and farms. State-level revolving loan funds are widespread, and nineteen states now have capital access programs (CAPs), in which states essentially provide a subsidy (by contributing to a loan loss reserve fund) to encourage banks to make higher risk loans to small, local businesses or other targeted groups.[77]

Localities can help, too. Michael Shuman, for instance, has pointed out that "one of the most difficult requirements facing a new commercial bank that seeks to qualify for federal insurance of its deposits is to secure at least $2 million in capitalization." Shuman suggests that "local government could help the bank clear this threshold" by issuing tax-exempt bonds to benefit the bank or by depositing city or pension funds into the community bank.[78]

Expanding the Vision of CDCs and CDFIS

Strong financial support from all levels of government is important to achieving the full community-stabilizing potential of both CDCs and CDFIs. Only when these institutions are adequately funded do they have the capacity to undertake comprehensive community revitalization projects. When funds are scarce, CDCs and CDFIs are often forced to simply broker deals with private financial institutions and other outside sources in order to get tangible projects off the ground. Their capacity to deal with the challenges of community development in a sustained way is often thereby severely limited.

Financing and policy support alone, however, will not suffice to tap the full potential of CDCs and CDFIs: Vision is also critical. One area of innovation is ownership and operation of businesses directly on behalf of the larger community (possibly with financial support provided by CDFIs). As previously discussed, important precedents in which CDCs have played a direct role in creating jobs (and in recycling profits back into the community) include, among many others, the Pathmark supermarkets and various stores and businesses operated by the Newark Community Corporation, the furniture production firm operated by Asian Neighborhood Design in Oakland, and the multiple businesses (and associated job-training programs) operated by Esperanza Unida in Milwaukee. As CDCs continue to mature, we believe there will be a real opportunity for more CDCs to engage in such profitable, innovative business development in the coming decade.

A second important element in a positive vision for CDCs involves advocacy, community organizing, and a broad view of development. Judy Meima, a longtime community development practitioner in Chicago, observes:

> I am always suspicious when people in community development start using the term "deal." It almost always means they have moved their priorities from empowerment and community development to straight housing production which doesn't work for poor communities. For CDCs that remain true to their mission, the "deal" is never the important thing.[79]

Meima goes on to suggest that "at some point, many CDCs will have to decide if they're part of the establishment or part of the grassroots movement," a movement that would collectively advocate for more resources for community development.

Meima also makes the important point that there is an internal connection between sufficient resources and expansiveness of vision. Many CDCs that got off the ground during the 1980s, when community development funds were especially scarce, have been forced into the position of cutting deals to make anything happen. Adequate resources, on the other hand, permit CDCs to pursue goals more in line with the original mission articulated by Robert Kennedy and the first generation of CDCs in the late 1960s.

CHAPTER 10

OTHER PLACE-BASED OWNERSHIP MODELS

Who owns capital matters for community economic stability. Whether a community's core job base is predominantly owned by entities that are inherently local or whether it is controlled by a distant headquarters has profound consequences for the long-term economic security of communities. In this chapter, we discuss four additional models of alternative ownership: consumer cooperatives, community-owned corporations, nonprofit corporations, and nonprofit business enterprises. Each of these alternative ownership models tends to ensure that business enterprises and the jobs they create remain firmly rooted in communities they serve, and hence each is capable of making important contributions to community economic stability in the United States.

CONSUMER COOPERATIVES

Cooperative business enterprises are jointly owned, financed, and democratically governed by groups of persons united voluntarily to meet their own economic, material, or social needs. Although rarely recognized as such, this form of business organization plays a major role in the U.S. economy: According to the National Cooperative Bank, more than 48,000 cooperatives generate over $120 billion in economic activity yearly and directly serve one-third of the country's population in one way or another.[1]

The cooperative form of business organization has appeared twice in our discussion thus far. In our chapter on strengthening local multipliers we noted how producer-owned cooperatives can help local (independent) retailers in their struggle against large corporate chains (see Chapter 7). We also discussed worker-owned cooperatives as a form of employee ownership (see Chapter 8).

Producer-owned co-ops allow businesses to aggregate their purchasing power to buy in bulk the inputs necessary for the production of commodities or goods and/or collectively market and sell their products. By establishing a significant presence in the marketplace, these co-ops have the ability to save money through volume discounts, to negotiate favorable credit terms, and to attract purchasers. Producer co-ops are most prominent in the agricultural sector. Formed by small farming operations as a way to compete with larger agribusinesses while maintaining their individual independence, these co-ops accounted for 30 percent of all agricultural commodity sales in 1998.[2] Worker-owned cooperatives, on the other hand, are the rarest type of co-op in the United States. As noted, there are probably no more than 200 worker-owned co-ops in the United States, located mainly on the West and East Coasts.[3] Worker-owned co-ops are typically small-scale service and retail operations, such as bakeries, cab companies, and house-cleaning businesses.

In this chapter we wish to bring attention to a third type of cooperative, the consumer-owned co-op. Consumer co-ops, found mainly in the retail grocery industry, housing, health care, and rural electricity distribution, are self-help economic structures that provide goods and services to their members. They also are rooted strongly in local communities. As Christopher and Hazel Dayton Gunn observe: "Consumer co-ops serve those who can get to the store, live in the housing, or visit the clinic. . . . The income they generate, members they serve, and accumulation they create . . . tend to be geographically defined."[4] While co-ops have been operating in the United States since the nineteenth century, in the 1960s and 1970s the emergent counterculture's quest for developing alternative forms of business organization spawned a resurgence of consumer cooperatives.[5]

Most consumer co-ops follow the Rochdale Principles. These principles were developed in mid-nineteenth-century Rochdale, England, when, in response to the unreasonable prices charged by local merchants, twenty-eight tradespeople in the town pooled their resources to establish a store they owned and operated as a group. The principles specify operational guidelines such as open and voluntary membership (usually for a nominal fee), the return of surpluses (profits) to co-op members (based on member usage of the co-op), and democratic control (based on one member, one vote).[6] The latter is particularly significant: Each co-op member is entitled to only a *single* vote in the affairs of the business. This contrasts with investor-owned enterprise, which distributes votes to shareholders in proportion to the amount of equity each holds in the company—a system that translates financial power into decision-making clout. Co-op members typically elect representatives to serve on the co-op's governing body—the board of directors—and participate in co-op-wide referenda or other democratic decision-making activities.

The consumer cooperative form of business organization plays a strong role in the utility sector of the U.S. economy. According to the National Rural Electric Co-operative Association (NRECA), 865 electricity distribution co-ops serve 35 million people—12 percent of the country's population—in forty-six states. Electric co-ops own about 44 percent of the country's electricity distribution lines, spanning three-quarters of the landmass of the United States. In addition to the distribution co-ops, there are sixty generation and transmission (G&T) co-ops owned by member distribution systems. NRECA emphasizes that electricity co-ops operate at cost to provide the least expensive electricity to their customer-owners, and they return any surplus above expenses, investments, and reserves to the membership proportional to members' individual use.[7]

Another area of the economy where consumer cooperatives have a strong foothold in significant numbers is the retail grocery industry. A 2000 survey of retail food cooperatives published in the industry journal *Co-operative Grocer* estimated the number of U.S. food co-ops at 300, with total sales estimated at $700 million in 2000.[8] The survival of these co-ops has become increasingly challenging, however, in light of competition from investor-owned grocery chains that have lured customers away from co-ops as "natural" and organic foods have gone mainstream.

One successful retail grocery cooperative is the Park Slope Food Coop in Brooklyn, New York. While the co-op generates traditional jobs—Park Slope employs twenty-six paid staff who generally function as managers in the co-op—it primarily relies on the labor of its members (an alternative form of employment where compensation comes in the form of membership privileges). The cooperative's nearly 6,000 members, mostly drawn from the neighborhood, perform an astounding 80 percent of the co-op's work. Each member is required to work a 2¾-hour shift once every four weeks. In return for this unpaid service, members are able to purchase high-quality organic and conventional produce and other groceries for 10 to 25 percent below market prices. (A comparison in Park Slope's newspaper, *The Linewaiter's Gazette*, showed that in about seven out of eight cases, prices were more expensive at the local Pathmark national grocery chain store than at the cooperative.) Membership requires only a one-time $25 fee of each adult member in a household. Members must also contribute a $100 investment, payable in installments and refundable upon leaving the cooperative (reduced to $10 for food stamp recipients). Eric Schneider, secretary of Park Slope's board of directors, explains that the co-op has a tradition of governance based on the New England town meeting system. Six directors, elected from the co-op's general membership, make up the board. The cooperative's bylaws require allowing general members to attend and participate in every meeting of the board.[9]

Not all successful modern co-ops are small scale—consider Recreational Equipment, Inc. (REI), an outdoor equipment retailer and producer. REI, which employs over 7,000 people and had revenues of nearly $700 million in 2000, is owned by its 1.6 million members, who each receive annual refunds on their purchases in the previous year. Named as one of the "100 Best Companies to Work For in America" by *Fortune* magazine, REI has taken part in a number of joint ventures with local environmental groups and regularly funds recreation clubs and conversation groups.[10]

One of the most formidable barriers confronting the proliferation and growth of co-ops is access to capital, as traditional financial institutions are often unwilling to lend to an enterprise with an unusual structure. Over the years, however, a few alternative financial institutions have emerged to provide financial support. These institutions provide possible precedents for building the financial infrastructure necessary for the future expansion of cooperatives.

Most prominent is the National Consumer Co-operative Bank, commonly known as the National Co-operative Bank (NCB). Established though an act of Congress in 1978 as a mixed-ownership government corporation, the bank was fully privatized in 1981 after President Reagan took office. Today, the NCB is set up as a private cooperative, with a membership of individual co-ops around the country. Its development arm, the NCB Development Corporation (NCBDC), was also created by the 1978 act to provide technical assistance to start-up co-ops. In 2000, the NCB provided some $615 million in capital in the form of commercial and real estate loans to a wide range of cooperative enterprises (such as insurance mutuals, wholesalers, ESOPs, nonprofit cultural institutions, and housing co-ops).[11] Among the many co-ops the NCB has aided is the Park Slope Food Co-op, discussed above, which has relied on NCB capital to help finance expansions.

Another alternative financial institution providing financial support for co-ops is the Co-operative Development Foundation.[13] CDF was established as part of the Co-operative League of the United States of America (later to become the National Co-operative Business Association) to help international co-ops recover after World War II co-ops. CDF's work remained international in scope throughout the 1970s and 1980s, but since the late 1980s its mission has focused on developing co-ops in the United States. In the 1990s, CDF distributed $5 million worth of grants and loans to domestic co-ops. The bulk of CDF's work has focused on rural co-op development, and in particular, senior housing and retirement communities; in the 1990s, CDF created over 1,000 units of senior cooperative housing.[14]

A interesting model operating on the regional level is the Northcountry Cooperative Development Fund (NCDF) in Minnesota.[15] After finding it difficult to receive financing from banks, several Twin Cities–area cooperatives decided to pool their money and make loans to themselves. Starting with just $4,500 in initial funds in 1978, today the NCDF boasts assets of over $3 million and supports retail, agricultural, housing, and worker-owned cooperative efforts in ten states of the upper Midwest. NCDF is itself a cooperative, owned and controlled by its member cooperatives and individuals. About one-third of NCDF's loan capital comes from deposits by these member cooperatives; one-half comes from institutional investors, including foundations, community groups, the National Community Capital Association, and the National Cooperative Bank Development Corporation; the rest comes from individual deposits and the fund's own equity reserves. In 1999 NCDF made a dozen new loans of nearly $1 million, 80 percent of which went to borrowers in low-income communities, with consumer food co-ops typically being the largest borrowing sector. The fund has grown steadily (6.4 percent in 1999) over time and turned an operating profit in six of the seven years between 1993 and 1999.[16]

COMMUNITY-OWNED CORPORATIONS

Another form of alternative ownership strongly rooted in place is what might be called the community-owned corporation. Community-owned corporations are similar to traditional corporations save one crucial factor: They are owned primarily by citizens living in or strongly connected to the local community. Although usually not as democratic or egalitarian as consumer cooperatives, they nonetheless are generally structured in ways that distribute ownership and control of the business enterprise broadly and are strongly rooted in the communities where they are owned.

In recent years there have been several examples of groups of community members joining together to buy a business providing an important community service (and hence contributing to the community's economic stability), especially in smaller towns experiencing economic decay. For example, after the last privately owned coffee shop in town closed, the citizens of Scranton, North Dakota, "formed Scranton Community Café, Inc., sold shares in the corporation, and raised $90,000 by canvassing the surrounding school district for funds."[17] Numerous other community-owned cafés dot the Midwest, while other communities have considered pursuing this approach to reopen bakeries and grocery stores. In fact, as Ellen Perlman of *Governing* magazine reports, of late "the basic idea is beginning to sprout a whole new set of experimental ventures." The residents of Rushville, Illinois, saved the only movie theater in Schuyler County by forming a community corporation and selling stock at $100 a share to more than 200 people, generating some $53,000 for the project. In Bonaparte, Iowa, citizens saved a whole downtown shopping block by creating a community corporation, as "fifty townspeople came forward to invest the limit of $2,000 each."[18] In another example, the people of the tiny village of Hebron, New Hampshire, formed a community corporation to save their local general store, "a sacrosanct symbol of small-town New England"; a group of residents (from seventeen local families) purchased twenty-three shares at $12,000 apiece, raising $276,000 for the enterprise.[19]

The most celebrated example of a community corporation is Wisconsin's National Football League franchise, the Green Bay Packers. The Packers are owned by about 110,000 shareholders, more than half of whom live in the state.[20] Its corporate bylaws prevent any one individual from owning more than twenty shares, ensuring broadly based ownership. They also make it almost impossible for the team to be sold and moved to another city because, as a nonprofit corporation, shareholders would receive no capital gains upon resale. The bylaws require all proceeds from a sale to be donated to the local chapter of the American Legion "for the purposes of erecting a proper soldier's memorial."[21]

The professional sports world offers many other examples of community corporations. Two minor-league baseball teams in upstate New York, the triple-A Rochester Red Barons and the Syracuse SkyChiefs, are owned by their fans (the Red Barons are owned by about 8,000 shareholders, with most owning less than five shares; nearly 4,000 shareholders own the SkyChiefs). Both clubs, operated as for-profit community enterprises, sold stock to their respective communities back in the 1950s after their major league affiliates cut financial support. The single-A Wisconsin Timber Rattlers, a baseball team organized as a nonprofit corporation, has also raised capital through sales of nontradable stock to local investors.[22]

Many community-owned businesses are community-owned strictly by happenstance: Nothing *technically* precludes non–community members from owning a controlling interest in them (for example, almost half of the stockholders of the celebrated Packers reside outside of the state of Wisconsin).

Accordingly, Michael Shuman suggests the creation of "a new kind of business structure" where "*only members of the local community would be allowed to own voting shares of stock.*" Shuman proposes that "shareholders could exchange or sell stock freely, but voting shares could only be sold to other community members. Whenever such a shareholder decided to move out of the community, she would be obligated to sell off her shares to other community members or back to the company."[23] To expand the possibilities for generating capital investment while maintaining local control, Shuman advocates that these businesses create different classes of shareholders, as conventional corporations often do: those shareholders with voting rights, who must be community residents, and those holding nonvoting shares, who could live anywhere.

As a precedent, Shuman cites Ben & Jerry's ice cream, which "restricted its first stock issue to residents of Vermont" (although, as he points out, "subsequent issues dropped this restriction and diluted local control").[24] Shuman also notes that hundreds of community development credit unions (discussed in Chapter 9) usually place such residential restrictions on their member-owners. Residential restrictions on ownership appear to be legally permissible in most cases.[25]

From the standpoint of community stability, Shuman's proposal for how to structure community corporations is commendable. As Shuman argues, "with all voting shareholders residing in the community, it's unlikely that the firm would move operations elsewhere (unless relocation were clearly in the interest of the community)." Moreover, although this form of ownership does not guarantee that all the corporation's actions will necessarily be in the broad community interest, Shuman points out that "it enables [corporate] regulation to proceed without today's fear that the firm automatically will skip town. No longer would higher labor and ecological standards have to mean a less attractive business environment."[26]

NONPROFIT CORPORATIONS

Traditional nonprofit corporations are a broader category of organizations that also have the ability to stabilize jobs and economic activity in communities. Nonprofits, which account for over six percent of the American economy and over seven percent of total employment, are often referred to as the "third sector" in the United States, after private firms and governmental entities.[27] About a third of the economic impact of nonprofits can be attributed to religious institutions, arts and civic groups, foundations or charities. Health services, education and research account for the remaining two-thirds.[28] Universities ("eds") and medical facilities ("meds") are especially powerful job producers for America's large cities: In the twenty largest U.S. cities, 69 of the 200 largest private firms (35 percent) are eds and meds; in four of these cities—Washington, Philadelphia, San Diego, and Baltimore—eds and meds supply over 50 percent of all jobs.[29]

While far from perfect, nonprofit organizations tend to be more responsive and accountable to their communities than traditional for-profit corporations. The boards of directors that govern nonprofits often feel a strong mandate to be sensitive to broader community concerns and needs. Nonprofits also tend to be strongly rooted geographically. Although some very large nonprofits are national in scope and not necessarily wedded to a particular community—the National Collegiate Athletic Association, for instance, moved its headquarters from Kansas to Indianapolis—the overwhelming majority of organizations enjoying formal nonprofit status are local in orientation, explicitly created to meet local needs and inextricable from their local context.

ENTERPRISE ACTIVITIES OF NONPROFIT CORPORATIONS

A newly emerging trend—the proliferation of nonprofit-owned and -operated business endeavors—is helping make the nonprofit sector even more important as a source of stable community jobs.

In order to be recognized by the IRS as a nonprofit, organizations must issue a mission statement that explains what they aim to accomplish. Mission statements may be broad enough to allow nonprofits to partake in for-profit activity so long as such monies are allocated primarily toward a set social objective. Many nonprofits historically have generated revenues through the sale of publications, user fees, and the like. In the past twenty years there has been dramatic growth in more aggressive entrepreneurial activity. As the Surdna Foundation's Ed Skloot explains, this activity was a response by nonprofits to "a changing environment characterized by tighter budgets, diminishing governmental funds, increased competition for donated dollars, a more receptive national attitude toward enterprise, and the gradual acceptance by some nonprofits that commerce and charity can safely co-exist."[30]

From the standpoint of the nonprofits, the motivation for generating a stable revenue stream is obvious: organizational stability and less dependence on outside funding sources (many of which, such as foundations or governments, may have priorities or expectations in tension with the nonprofit's core work). From the standpoint of community, what is interesting is the notion of taking profits earned through business activity and recycling the money back into programs and initiatives that directly benefit local community members—while also offering a source of employment to local residents. As nonprofit enterprise expert Bill Shore notes in his book *The Cathedral Within,* successful examples of enterprises (some of which are highlighted below) have "proved that nonprofits can do more than just redistribute wealth, which they are typically good at. They can also create wealth, though it is a different kind of wealth —community wealth—that is used to directly benefit the community."[31]

Entrepreneurial activity undertaken by nonprofits can take varied forms. One version involves the creation of partnerships with traditional corporations, through activities such as cause-related marketing, licensing, and sponsorship arrangements. (Bill Shore's own organization, Share Our Strength, which supports antihunger and antipoverty efforts, generates over 80 percent of its operating budget in this way).[32] Given our concern about community stability, of greatest interest to us are entrepreneurial activities that provide significant numbers of rooted jobs for the communities in which nonprofits operate. The Roberts Foundation defines the concept in a manner compatible with our more focused concerns: Such an enterprise, the report states, is a "revenue-generating venture founded to create jobs or training opportunities for low-income individuals, while simultaneously operating with reference to the financial bottom-line."[33]

Following the criteria of this definition, we highlight several examples of nonprofit enterprises below—examples demonstrating the institutional form's potential as a source of community-rooted employment and training opportunities, especially for the economically disadvantaged.

- The Greystone Foundation in Yonkers, New York—dedicated to transforming and uplifting the inner-city community of southwest Yonkers—operates the Greystone Bakery as a for-profit subsidiary. The bakery, a $3.5-million-per-year food production business providing permanent employment for fifty-five people (most of whom were formerly considered unskilled or unemployable), markets gourmet tarts and cakes to top Manhattan restaurants and stores, and is the sole supplier of the brownies used in Ben & Jerry's ice cream and frozen yogurt.[34]

- Minnesota Diversified Industries—dedicated to providing jobs for persons with disabilities—operates in four Minnesota cities (Hibbing,

Grand Rapids, Minneapolis, and St. Paul) and employs over 650 people, collecting annual revenues totaling more than $65 million. These revenues, most of which are generated through its manufacturing and distribution-and-fulfillment services contracts with clients such as 3M and the U.S. Postal Service, allow MDI to be 99 percent self-sustaining.[35]

- The Bidwell Training Center in Pittsburgh—dedicated to helping Pittsburgh's inner-city residents develop employment skills—developed and spun off a for-profit subsidiary that provides food service and catering to several major institutional clients around the city, including the Carnegie Science Center. By the late 1990s, the venture generated over $3 million in annual revenues; 15 percent of Bidwell Food Services employees are graduates of the training center.[36]

- Housing Works in New York City—dedicated to providing housing, health care, job training and placement, and other critical support services to homeless persons living with HIV and AIDS—operates four upscale thrift shops, a used-book store/café combination, and a food service company. These enterprises generate approximately $3–4 million annually and employ over fifty persons. That money in turn has helped the organization's efforts to provide housing for 2,500 people over the past decade, and services to an additional 5,000 people.[37]

- Rubicon Programs in Richmond, California—dedicated to assisting persons with disabilities, the homeless, and the economically disadvantaged through the provision of housing and employment services—generates nearly half of its $14 million annual budget from its three enterprises: a wholesale bakery, a home health care agency, and a landscaping service. These businesses are a source of both vocational training and job placement for the participants in Rubicon's programs.[38]

Perhaps the most celebrated example of nonprofit enterprise activity is Pioneer Human Services (PHS) in Seattle, Washington. Founded in 1962, PHS assists addicts, homeless people, parolees, and others on society's margins to attain economic and social betterment by providing housing, job training, and rehabilitation services. Today the organization, a $55 million operation, serves more than 6,000 clients per year and employs about 1,000 people in its programs. Its revenues are generated primarily through the sales of its services and products.[39]

PHS operates a total of eight enterprises. The largest and most interesting is Pioneer Industries, a precision light-metal fabricator. This enterprise is Boeing's sole supplier of sheet-metal liners for the cargo bays of its aircraft, and it also has contracts with more than thirty other manufacturers in the telecommunications, medical, and power-management industries. Twenty-five percent of Pioneer Industries' 300 employees are experienced workers hired from the surrounding community; the other seventy-five percent are inexperienced workers recruited from PHS housing and work-release programs. The latter category includes mostly convicts, parolees, and others who, because they lack training or have large gaps in their employment history, commonly have difficulty finding employment. Pioneer Industries offers all full-time employees a competitive, living wage. Inexperienced employees participate in an eighteen-month career training course, earning a slightly lower wage, and they are paid for their time in the classroom as well as in the shop. Trainees learn metalworking, mathematics, basic shop theory, blueprint analysis, metal filing, welding, punch pressing, and similar skills.

Other PHS businesses include the 150-seat Mezza Café and its satellite, the Pronto Deli; the Food Buying Service, a wholesale food distribution enterprise that distributes over 7 million pounds of food to nonprofit organizations in twenty-five states; the 132-room St. Regis Hotel, which serves both Seattle tourists and recovering substance abusers; a full-service mail production house, Greater Seattle Printing & Mailing, serving area businesses; and a real estate enterprise administering a wide range of property and asset management services for its over 750,000 square feet of commercial and residential properties.[40]

Faith-based economic development efforts are yet another type of nonprofit enterprise. An increasing number of churches, especially African-American churches in large cities, have either initiated new businesses or worked in collaboration with other community development actors to bring new jobs into their neighborhoods. One influential large-scale example is the 11,000-member Allen A.M.E. Church in Jamaica, New York, which under the leadership of the Rev. Floyd Flake, a former member of Congress, has become a major economic force in South Jamaica. The church, which has a $29 million annual budget, 850 employees, and nine nonprofit or for-profit subsidiaries, has, among other accomplishments, built a 300-unit apartment complex for senior citizens, constructed over 170 affordable homes for first-time buyers, and started a private school. The church operates a federal credit union and a small transportation company and owns a retail strip as well as office space; its real estate management company hosts over twenty-five businesses and boasts over $2 million in assets. Allen operates a social-services center, a resource center for battered women, a senior-citizens center, and a home care services.[41] While Allen A.M.E. is perhaps the most visible example of the role large churches might play in place-based development, many other church groups nationwide have been involved in affordable housing development or in securing access to credit in their communities, and some denominations have invested part of their pension funds into low-income economic development.

As PHS, Allen A.M.E., and the other examples show, nonprofits enterprises offer an institutional mechanism to create rooted jobs (and job training opportunities) and provide a revenue stream supporting the social missions of community-based nonprofits. Both of these outcomes enhance the stability of the communities in which these enterprises operate.

Beyond their employment and revenue effects, nonprofit enterprises provide additional benefits for their communities, such as being more employee-oriented than traditional corporations. Often they can afford to pay higher wages because of their tax-exempt status and because they are not required to pay owner-investors profits. Moreover, most offer full benefits and have a compelling interest in investing in the future of their employees. Minnesota Diversified Industries, for example, spends twice as much on worker training per employee than the average private corporation. The employee orientation of nonprofit enterprises also often leads them to be sensitive to employees' personal and family circumstances. At PHS, for example, management will schedule workers around the timetable of their families, particularly in the case of single mothers.[42]

Other advantages for communities can be identified as well: Like the non-profit sector as a whole, these nonprofit businesses are relatively responsive to community needs and accountable for their actions. In addition, research suggests that such enterprise activities yield positive returns to their communities: a cost-benefit analysis of the businesses of Rubicon Programs, one of the entrepreneurial nonprofits highlighted above, found that over a recent ten-year period these businesses were projected to generate almost $6 million in net social benefits.[43]

Notwithstanding their many advantages, nonprofit enterprises face numerous challenges. In particular, such enterprises need to balance carefully their objectives and goals, taking care not to let the profit motive override their social missions. Nonprofits going into business also need to ensure that their organizations possess sufficient business experience and training, especially in areas such as management and marketing.

Other difficulties confronting nonprofit enterprises are political in nature, as their increasing significance and maturity have begun to arouse criticism and resistance from traditional for-profit competitors. Interest groups representing for-profits have raised numerous objections to their tax-exempt status, claiming that this gives nonprofit businesses an unfair advantage. What this criticism misses, however, is that nonprofit businesses also possess an inherent competitive *disadvantage* "because they're trying to do something more significant, such as house the homeless or train the untrained, than merely run a business." Bill Shore thus observes: "You don't see these [private businesses] saying, 'We're going to train poor people for jobs in the food industry.'"[44]

Perhaps the greatest difficulties confronting efforts to expand the number and scope of nonprofit enterprises derive from a lack of imagination within the nonprofit sector itself. As Shore notes, while nonprofits, like all enterprises, face significant obstacles when moving into entrepreneurial activity, "the limitations on nonprofits starting businesses have by and large been self-imposed."[45]

CHAPTER 11

COMMUNITY LAND TRUSTS
AND COMMUNITY AGRICULTURE

a t the end of Chapter 3 we noted that a lasting solution to the phenomenon of urban sprawl must include a forth-right confrontation with the problem of land use and the issue of control over land. Private control of urban land not only makes land-use planning in the public interest more difficult but also commonly tilts the power structure of urban politics in favor of downtown landowners (who typically lobby for policies that increase the value of that land, whether such policies are on balance beneficial for the community as a whole or not).[1] As we have seen in the rural and greenbelt context, land set aside by the public or a nonprofit institution for conservation purposes counters this thrust and is an important check on unplanned, decentralized urban sprawl. Other applications of the concept are also important in a long-term community-building program.

The notion of community ownership of land is relatively unfamiliar to Americans. But many other cultures worldwide have embraced the notion that land should not be treated simply as a private commodity. We need only consider Scandinavia, where community ownership of land has a long history; Native American practices surviving to this day regarding land stewardship; the pre-enclosure institution of the commons in England; or the garden city proposals of Ebenezer Howard. The most well known historical challenge to the exclusively private control of land in the American context was the single-tax economics proposal espoused by Henry George at the end of the nineteenth century. George reasoned that since the community as a whole played a central role in increasing the value of land over time, the value of that increase should be captured by the community, not private landowners. While Georgist ideas were implemented in two small towns, one in Alabama and one in Delaware, with lasting success, the approach never caught on widely.

It might be considered surprising, then, that in the past fifteen years the concept of community ownership of land has been revived in the United States via the institution of the community land trust. Community land trusts (CLTs) are nonprofit organizations that hold parcels of land on behalf of the larger community. In this chapter we explore the CLT concept and discuss some relevant precedents and trends in the development of this institutional form. We also explore two other land-oriented institutions, community-supported agriculture (CSA) and urban community gardens (CGs). Both CSAs and CGs help bring the production and distribution of food more directly under the control of local communities.

COMMUNITY LAND TRUSTS

Community land trusts aim to preserve the long-term affordability of land by removing it from the control of market forces and actors and placing it under the direct control of the local community. Land trusts have steadily expanded in the United States since the mid-1980s: The Institute for Community Economics listed some 114 trusts active in the United States in 2001, up from fewer than 40 in the mid-1980s.[2]

One source of the land trust concept is the Indian *gramdan* (village gift) movement, in which two followers of Mahatma Gandhi, J. P. Narayan and Vinoba Bhave, traveled the countryside asking wealthy landowners to donate land to the community. Narayan and Bhave first simply turned over land parcels to poor people, but they soon discovered that most poor recipients lacked the tools and equipment to earn a living from the land and were forced to sell out. As an alternative, Narayan and Bhave began placing donated land in a community-wide trust that in turn leased parcels of land out to individuals, with the requirement that leaseholders work the land.

During the 1960s, Bob Swann, now of the E. F. Schumacher Society, started the first modern U.S. land trust in Albany, Georgia. Swann undertook this effort as part of civil rights activity in Albany, helping local African-American farmers secure a stable land base. To promote and expand the CLT concept thereafter, Swann and several colleagues formed the Institute for Community Economics (ICE) in 1967.[3]

ICE refined the land trust model by establishing two formal principles to help ensure that the interests of both individuals and communities would be respected.[4] First, all land within the CLT is to be "held perpetually for the community's benefit," although homes (and other structures built on the land) can be owned by residents. Second, CLTs would be governed by their membership, which would be open both to those who reside on the trust land and to other members of the local community.

Typically, a CLT acquires land either by gift or by purchase and, after soliciting input from residents of the community, develops a land-use plan for the property. The land trust then leases sites for the purposes agreed upon by local residents and CLT planners—including, for instance, affordable housing and business development. Leases typically run for ninety-nine years and are inheritable and renewable on the original terms. As noted, the leaseholder may own the physical structure on the land, but the land itself remains in control of the community. Additionally, leaseholders may not sublet or sell the land, as it is not theirs to sell, but rather belongs collectively to the community. When leaseholders resell their property (for instance, a house built on the land), they receive a fair but limited price calculated on the basis of a formula set in the lease agreement—usually the purchase price plus cost of major improvements, adjusted for inflation and real depreciation. The land trust structure thus eliminates home (and business) ownership as a vehicle of speculation but not as a way to build equity, as the trust "distinguishes between that portion of the real estate's market value that is created by the individual home or business owner through investment of labor or capital, and that part that is created by the community or the general public through community development or improvement efforts, public investment, or broader economic forces."[5]

Community land trusts are thus structured to allocate the benefits of real estate development more equitably, allowing the community—rather than private landholders—to capture the full value of the wealth arising from general increases in land value. The institutional bulwark CLTs provide against land speculation is particularly useful within the urban context as a way to prevent gentrification and ensure long-term neighborhood stability. Under the land trust structure, increases in local land values need not result in higher rents for residents nor drive low-income people from the neighborhood.

The Burlington Community Land Trust

One of the country's earliest, largest, and most influential CLTs is the Burlington Community Land Trust (BCLT) in Burlington, Vermont. The impetus for the BCLT was an early 1980s economic boom, which caused housing costs in the lakefront city of 40,000 to spiral out of the reach of many long-term, low- and moderate-income residents (rents doubled between 1980 and 1985).[6] During this period, the city's last affordable housing stock in a working class neighborhood on the banks of Lake Champlain was in danger of being gentrified and becoming a waterfront enclave for the wealthy.

To forestall gentrification, the city's administration proposed a community land trust, providing a $200,000 seed grant for the effort. The trust, established in 1984 with widespread bipartisan political support, has since built up a membership of more than 1,000 people and acquired or built nearly 500 units of affordable housing—including apartments, moderately priced single-family homes, multifamily co-ops (including an artists' co-op), special-needs housing, and transitional housing for women and families.[7] Recently the trust became involved in redeveloping blighted industrial and commercial properties into, among other things, affordable apartments, a legal-aid office, and an emergency food shelf. On the commercial front, the trust is working with the state and city to develop a public market on the waterfront for area farmers.

Governance of the trust is vested in a twelve-member board, including leaseholders, representatives of public community development agencies, and community members at large (including at least one financial-industry employee). Board members are democratically elected by the membership. BCLT member-residents devote no more than 30 percent of their income to rents or mortgages. By contrast, lower-income renters in the area can commonly see half to three-quarters of their paycheck going to rent because of extremely high housing costs. Moreover, the more than 200 homeowners in the trust are building equity rather than merely paying rent. The price of a single-family home on the land trust is about one-third less than the average market rate in Chittenden County as a whole, according to land trust officials. Income caps are set on who may buy a land trust home, and the trust has generally been able to afford to sell to those in lower-income brackets. "We've been selling houses to families making half the median income and below, which is rare, to the say the least," observes BCLTS director Brenda Torpy. Homeowners who sell are entitled to keep only 25 percent of the increase in the value of the home from the time of their initial purchase. Nevertheless, home sellers still have been able to build equity: "In the 30 to 40 resales we've had, almost all of the owners have walked away with something," Torpy reports.[8]

Expanding Community Land Trusts

The current development of land trusts in diverse parts of the country owes much to the lead role played by the Institute for Community Economics. ICE provides technical assistance and training, as well as financial assistance through its revolving loan fund. It assists land trusts in negotiations with larger financial and housing authorities when needed, and produces educational materials about the CLT idea for the broader public. Government support has also been critical to the emergence of CLTs. Federal money from the CBDG and HOME programs has been used to help boost CLT production and enable CLTs to develop affordable housing units on a much larger scale. The state of Vermont, too, has been particularly supportive of CLT endeavors, agreeing to fund the Vermont Housing Conservation Board (a group of housing and conservation advocates who work together to make grants for housing and/or preservation projects).[9]

Most existing urban land trusts are modest in scale, usually providing fewer than 150 units of low-income housing, and the movement as a whole has not yet expanded its focus beyond affordable housing to undertake broader community economic development initiatives. The land trust movement as currently constituted is clearly too small to make a substantial dent in either the preservation of stable affordable housing neighborhoods or in the control of city land generally. On the other hand, there is enormous potential for the land trust form to grow. While no land trust is ever established without overcoming significant obstacles, with sufficient public support there is no reason why locally controlled land trusts cannot become an important community-stabilizing force throughout the neighborhoods of urban America.

One way to build on the existing momentum would be to extend the land trust model to the commercial sector. Land trusts can be used as a base to launch community-owned business endeavors, or a portion of land trust acreage can be leased to private commercial ventures, whose rents can in turn be used for broader community revitalization projects. CLTs already are beginning to develop partnerships with other community development groups to expand their activities and impact. One example of such collaboration involves the New Columbia CLT of Washington, DC. New Columbia works closely with the grassroots organization WISH (Washington Inner-City Self-Help), which itself helped found New Columbia in 1990. WISH helps low-income tenants develop co-operatives, and then New Columbia purchases the land beneath the buildings to ensure they remain affordable. Julie Orvis of the Institute for Community Economics points out that while most CLTs initially focus on affordable housing, as these groups mature they tend to adopt a more holistic view of their community. Recognition that their localities' difficulties extend far beyond the housing realm can provide land trusts with a powerful incentive to collaborate with other community groups on broader initiatives.[10]

Another institutional form that attempts to stabilize urban housing prices is the limited-equity co-op. In limited-equity co-ops, members buy a share of the cooperative, which owns a housing unit or units (such as a multifamily row house or an apartment building). In exchange, members receive a long-term lease. When members leave, they sell their share in the co-op to the replacement resident; capital gains on the sale of the stock are limited. While limited-equity co-ops exist nationwide, with the help of enabling state legislation they have become increasingly common in Massachusetts and particularly the housing-starved Boston area.[11]

CONSERVATION LAND TRUSTS

A second and more common form of land trust focuses on conservation rather than development. Conservation land trusts typically consist of undeveloped land, either forest or open, which a nonprofit organization buys up for conservation purposes. According to a 2000 survey, there are now more than 1,260 local and regional conservation land trusts nationwide, a 42 percent increase since 1990; these trusts help protect approximately 6.2 million acres of land from excessive development.[12] Conversation land trusts can be established by a landowner donating acres to a conservation trust or by land trust groups raising money to buy land from private owners. As noted in Chapter 3, an increasing number of public authorities (including the state of New Jersey) have begun buying undeveloped land as a way to keep development in check. While conservation land trusts lack the same community development aspirations as active urban land trusts, activists who envision a broader land reform movement in the United States consider them an important ally. And, as already noted, conservation land trusts are of obvious importance in developing a comprehensive strategy to substitute planned development of human settlements for unchecked sprawl.

COMMUNITY-SUPPORTED AGRICULTURE

Although government aid has helped increase the stature of the land trust movement in recent years, community land trusts are notable in part because they began life as a civil society initiative, with minimal direct government support. Another land-oriented institutional structure emerging from civil society in the past twenty years is community-supported agriculture (CSA).

CSAs are cooperative partnerships established between producers/farmers and consumers to produce food in a manner that helps stabilize small- and midsized farms, reconnect consumers with farmers and the source of their food, promote sustainable agricultural practices and land stewardship, and strengthen local economies and regional food systems. CSAs share the risks and rewards of food production. While there are many variations on the theme, in typical arrangements consumers are shareholders who "invest" each year in a farmers' production by purchasing "shares" of the seasonal harvest. Shares represent a financial commitment to support the farm and cover the operating expenses of the farm (seeds, soil preparation, equipment, water, rent on land, labor costs, etc.) in exchange for a portion of the seasonal produce (called a "harvest share"). The arrangement guarantees small and midsized farmers a market for their produce, thus reducing the risk of loss in a poor growing season. The arrangement also directly connects consumers with the source of their food and provides them with a weekly supply of fresh, locally grown produce.

The CSA concept originated in Japan in the 1960s as a strategy to support local farmers and secure land for organic food production. In response to diminishing local farmland and increasing reliance on food imports in 1965, a group of Japanese women and a local farm family introduced a new way to share the costs and risks of production. The farmers agreed to provide fresh fruits and vegetables to families in exchange for direct financial support of the farm. The contractual partnership was called *teikei*, or "putting the farmers' face on food." *Teikei*-focused purchasing clubs in Japan now involve thousands of people and support hundreds of farmers.[13] During the 1970s, the movement expanded to Europe as a means of organizing individuals to provide food security and support organic farmers.

In 1985 Indian Line Farm in Massachusetts dubbed the concept "community-supported agriculture," and an American movement was born. The CSA movement expanded outward from Massachusetts into the northeast of the United States. Today the majority of American CSA farms are located in New England and the Mid-Atlantic states. However, an increasing number of CSA farms have been established in the Great Lakes region, in the Midwest, and on the West Coast.

By 1999, there were over 1,000 operating CSAs in the United States, according to the Massachusetts-based organization Community Supported Agriculture of North America (CSANA), with more growth expected.[14]

While the exact number of individuals benefiting from CSA is unknown, CSANA's Elizabeth Keen estimates that food produced by CSAs directly benefits approximately 100,000 to 150,000 families across the United States. Thousands more benefit from CSA food donated to food banks, homeless shelters, and other charity organizations.[15]

Roxbury Farm Community-Supported Agriculture

One noteworthy illustration is Roxbury Farm CSA, a 140-acre farm in Kinderhook, New York. Like most CSAs, Roxbury sells "shares" of an upcoming season's harvest. One Roxbury share entitles a member to ten to fourteen pounds of produce a week, intended to feed two to four people. To determine the price of a share, a Roxbury co-manager meets each winter with a core group of CSA members to calculate operating expenses for the coming season. This cost is then divided by the number of shares the farm can reasonably fill. Shares for the coming year are then sold; as the year progress, the weekly harvest is divided according to the number of shares sold. The quantity of food each share buys will vary with the success of the growing season.[16]

Roxbury Farm produces about 250,000 pounds of organic food each season and delivers to its supporters seven to ten different types of fruits and vegetables each week from the first week in June to December. The weekly newsletter *Notes from the Farm*, written by one of the three co-managers, arrives with the produce at each pick-up site, offering a page of news, notes, and educational items, with a recipe on the back. The farm's $210,000 annual operating expenses are met almost entirely with the support of three distinct communities who purchase a total of 650 shares, making it one of the largest CSAs in the nation. Besides paying the farm, each of the three communities has its own operating expenses. Budgets differ according to administrative expenses, distribution arrangements, and other factors such as newsletter production and special events. Accordingly, each Roxbury Farm community determines its own exact price per share, but members pay around $300 per share (slightly more if they live in New York City, to offset delivery costs). The share price reflects the true costs of food production; the farm makes no profit.

Purchasing food months ahead of time is obviously risky for consumers, but Roxbury CSA members have not had to bear any significant losses. In one recent year, for example, the parsnips failed, but since the farm delivered about fifty-nine other types of fruits and vegetables to members that year, missing parsnips did not upset the balance of anybody's diet. While no one wants to lose food or food money, with a CSA losses are less likely to be drastic than losses commonly experienced under monocropping or conventional farming methods, in which a farmer enters into huge debt early in the year betting that one or two crops will pay off later.

Three full-time employees, four apprentices, and dozens of volunteers complete all planting, harvesting, animal care, and daily chores at Roxbury. All Roxbury community supporters are asked to put in two to three hours of work a season, making phone calls, bringing leftover food to emergency food services, unloading the delivery truck at a pickup site, helping with the harvest, or performing other tasks that keep the system operating smoothly. Roxbury's Columbia County community offers "harvester's shares" to members who want to work off up to 50 percent of their food costs by putting in four hours each week helping farm hands harvest labor-intensive crops. By sharing the workload, volunteers contribute a valuable service to the farmers and to their communities and also gain hands-on experience with the realities of food production. Roxbury Farm co-manager Betsy Cashen says one of the best things about operating a CSA is that "I can experience how people get connected to the farm."

The security provided by a CSA arrangement allows the three co-managers to farm in an ecologically sustainable fashion. Released from market pressures, they shun pesticides and rotate crops each season without risking financial ruin. Further, they are able to make decisions not economically feasible for conventional farmers, such as to allow some fields to lie fallow in order to restore nutrients. The farmers, in fact, use only twenty-five acres each year for raising vegetables. Though their available acreage is obviously reduced by such methods, their actual crop yield per acre has increased over time. While Roxbury could potentially support more members, it has set a limit—and reached it—so that the farm can maintain sustainable agricultural methods. After Roxbury's first decade as a CSA, crop loss is down, soil fertility is up, and its members can look forward to even greater quality and quantity of produce in years to come.

Community-Supported Agriculture in Context

CSAs such as Roxbury represent a tangible response to the community-damaging by-products of the dominant food production and distribution system in America. As Don Villarejo of the California Institute for Rural Studies points out, in 1964 the largest 100,000 farms produced just one-third of the nation's agricultural goods and earned one-sixth of the nation's net agricultural income. By 1996, the largest 100,000 farms accounted for approximately 60 percent of farm production and net income.[17] David Orr of Oberlin College observes that "concentration throughout the foods system . . . means that formerly self-reliant communities, consisting of owner-operated farms and local markets, have lost control over their economies."[18] Most American states now purchase between 85 and 90 percent of their food from outside their borders. On average, produce travels 1,300 miles from the field to the table.[19]

This system generates an extraordinary amount of ecological damage and sheer waste. For instance, farmers spent nearly $8 billion on pesticides— equivalent to 4.6 percent of total farm production expenditures in 1995.[20] An estimated 300,000 farm workers suffer from pesticide-related illnesses each year in the United States.[21] Soil erosion rates, exacerbated by monocrop practices associated with industrial agriculture, exceed the tolerable soil loss rate on some 108 million acres of cropland (29 percent of the nation's total).[22] The extensive transport associated with the current system is a major factor in food wastage due to spoilage. A study conducted by USDA's Economic Research Service found that in 1995 "about 96 billion pounds of food, or 27 percent of the 356 billion pounds of the food available for human consumption in the United States, were wasted at the retail, consumer, and food service levels." The disposal cost of waste food for municipalities exceeded an estimated $1 billion per year by the mid-1990s.[23]

Additionally, the restructuring of food distribution channels brought on by the consolidation of supermarket ownership and precipitated by urban flight to the suburbs has left urban areas noticeably underserved. Many national chains have closed urban markets in favor of suburban areas with larger stores, more consumers, and lower overhead.

Most practitioners of CSAs locate their work against this backdrop of increasing concentration over farm resources, agricultural pollution, pesticide-laden food, food waste, and uneven distribution of food. Simply put, the overall intent of CSAs and allied movements is to reintegrate consumers with producers into a more functional food system. Consumers who buy shares in CSAs provide the farms with the economic stability needed to make smaller-scale production of (often organically grown) food economically viable. The transaction and transportation costs associated with the corporate distribution of food are bypassed, and CSAs typically donate excess or unsold food to local organizations for distribution to the needy. In a very concrete sense, CSAs see their work as community-building—contributing to community stability by encouraging cooperative efforts in classic civil society networking fashion.

CSAs have also succeeded in advancing their agenda by helping develop the politically active Community Food Security Coalition, an advocacy network of over 350 organizations concerned with hunger, sustainable agriculture, the environment, community development, and other food-related issues. The coalition was founded in 1994, and in 1995 it crafted a multitiered legislative initiative to fundamentally reorder federal food and agriculture programs. The Community Food Security Empowerment Act called for a restructuring of existing food and agricultural policy to reflect a systems approach. In 1996 farm legislation, Congress approved a portion of the Community Food Security Act, titled "Assistance to Community Food Projects." The legislation established the USDA Community Food Projects Program, authorized to provide $16 million in funding over seven years to locally initiated food security projects. The Community Food Projects Program will help to provide significant stimulus for community-based food security projects. In its first year, the program awarded $1 million in seed grants to thirteen organizations around the country. From 1997 through 2002 the USDA is awarding $2.5 million per year to small-scale food projects. The Community Food Security Coalition continues to be an active advocate for linking hunger relief with sustainable agriculture: In 2001 it launched a campaign to include reauthorization of the Community Foods Project Program as well as new federal spending (totaling $70 million) on related initiatives.[24]

COMMUNITY GARDENS

Another land-related, community-oriented institution that has gained increasing visibility in recent years is the urban community garden. Community gardens became a national cause *célèbre* in the spring of 1999 when the singer Bette Midler headlined a consortium of groups that agreed to pay over $4 million to New York City to preserve over a hundred community gardens operating on city-owned vacant lots, in response to Mayor Rudolph Giuliani's original plan to sell the lots to developers.[25] Community gardens provide a way to simultaneously counter visible scars of urban decay, such as vacant lots, while also rebuilding community connections and networks of social capital, improving urban ecological environments, offering a sense of respite and meaning in the lives of urban dwellers and—not least—providing affordable, quality food to urban residents.

Karl Linn, a pioneer and close observer of the U.S. community garden movement, reports that "During the 1990s community gardening has become more and more widely acknowledged as an integral part of our urban existence."[26] The American Community Gardening Association (ACGA) estimates that over 550 citywide gardening programs are operating nationwide, up from less than 20 in the early 1970s. Citywide programs range in size from 10 to 1,000 garden sites, each with five to fifty individual plots. One vibrant example of a citywide program is Philadelphia Green, which has worked with over 700 community groups to establish more than 2,500 community gardens or related greening projects throughout the city.[27] Another is Boston Urban Gardeners (BUG), which converts vacant public spaces into community gardens. Boston now has 140 community gardens producing 1.5 million pounds of food annually.[28]

The nation's largest and most vibrant municipally operated gardening program is GreenThumb in New York City. This program licenses vacant public land to hundreds of community groups who maintain vegetable and sitting gardens that green and beautify their neighborhoods. Sponsored by the City of New York's Parks Department, GreenThumb has since 1978 provided technical and material assistance to groups dedicated to transforming abandoned, trash-filled lots into green community resources. GreenThumb now boasts over 650 member gardens serving 20,000 residents.[29]

Community gardens also present opportunities for job training and local employment for urban youth and adults. Through its Youth Garden Internship program, in one typical year the San Francisco League of Urban Gardeners (SLUG) in San Francisco, California, provided employment to a hundred teens, 70 percent of whom lived in San Francisco's low-income neighborhoods.[30] The Homeless Garden Project in Santa Cruz, California, employs homeless men and women in three-year job training and transitional employment gardening programs, with more than 120 participants over the period 1990 to 1997.[31] The Veterans' Garden in Los Angeles, California, provides part- and full-time jobs for twenty-five to thirty-five veterans in horticulture and landscaping on its fifteen-acre urban farm.[32] The Garden Project in San Francisco has employed over 3,500 former prisoners since 1992. Studies show that program participants have recidivism rates less than one half of the state average.[33]

The deindustrialization and depopulation experienced by many older industrial cities, and the resulting demolition and removal of deteriorated structures, have as a side effect created opportunities to expand the scope of urban community gardening. Many cities now contain a high percentage of vacant land within their boundaries. Philadelphia, for example, has an estimated 31,000 parcels of vacant land; Detroit, 46,000 vacant parcels; Chicago, 70,000 vacant parcels.[34] Portions of this available land can be reused for community gardens, thereby helping communities recoup some of the devastating costs of urban deindustrialization and simultaneously contribute to the rebuilding of a sense of community.

Explicit public support can play an important role in underwriting the expansion of community gardens (and CSAs). Localities can provide seed grants and loans for land purchase, offer organizational and technical assistance, pass ordinances that ease the transfer of vacant lots to community organizations, and even use city-owned bulldozers to clear land for new gardens. At the federal level, although community gardens and CSAs have already benefited from USDA assistance, the overwhelming bulk of food-related government spending now consists of large-scale subsidies for large landholders and corporate farmers—not assistance to locally scaled, community-oriented production. Even a relatively modest shift in the Department of Agriculture's assistance priorities would have enormous leverage in undergirding the stability of existing community gardens and CSAs and in accelerating the growth of new ventures.

THE POTENTIAL OF COMMUNITY LAND ALTERNATIVES

Surely community gardens, land trusts, and community-supported organic farms are nice things to do—but do they really contribute to a serious response to the triple threat to community economic stability identified in Part One of this book?

Our answer is in the affirmative—but with several caveats. First, it is important to see beyond the relatively small scale to the broader implications of each of these institutions: the possibility of large-scale land reform. Each of the institutions concretely demonstrates the feasibility and advantages of community control over land and sets a precedent for broader-based, larger-scale efforts to put land in direct service of the community. Second, by directly involving citizens in community-building cooperative economics, community land trusts, community-supported agriculture projects, and community gardens all help foster a new ethic within civil society of community building and economic cooperation. Land trusts, CSAs, and community gardens all give ordinary Americans a direct, personal way to participate in community economic reconstruction. Importantly, most of the citizens involved are not community development professionals but hold other jobs, have other commitments, and may have little prior ideological commitment to community-oriented economics. Third, each of these institutions is capable of making a substantial contribution to the economic security of lower-income and middle-income Americans. By stabilizing long-term housing costs and/or ensuring a stable supply of quality food, these institutions can help relieve some of the everyday stresses faced by millions of Americans, especially in urban areas. Finally, there is enormous potential for the dramatic expansion of each of these institutional forms—at relatively small financial cost—in the foreseeable future.

But the most fundamental reason for paying serious attention to these land-based initiatives is this: Community control over land is a key step in the long-term restructuring of local-level power relationships—and this in turn can substantially bolster the prospects of redistributive and community-stabilizing policies at the local level. Such shifts in power, experience, and consciousness at the local level—combined with the formation of new coalitions and political organizations explicitly focused on promoting community—can in turn help stimulate increased popular support for the more ambitious regional, national, and even international policies entailed in a comprehensive, community-stabilizing agenda.

THE GLOBAL CONTEXT

INTRODUCTION

n Part IV, we return to the issue of how to deal with the potential threats to community stability posed by free trade policies and economic globalization. While we believe that much important work can be done to advance the policies and institutions described in Parts II and III of the book even in the absence of substantial progress on trade- and globalization-related issues, the potentially damaging impact of the current trajectory of globalization on both community stability and the ability of communities to introduce and implement an innovative, place-based agenda cannot be ignored.

Chapter 12 examines several comprehensive proposals for restructuring key international financial institutions, such as the World Bank and the IMF, and/or creating new institutions to promote both global economic stability and greater fairness. We argue that managing the global market in ways that prevent economic turmoil and promote balanced worldwide development would protect American communities as well as the people of developing nations. The more difficult question is how to achieve those goals. This chapter provides an overview of some of the best-thought-out proposals to date on this problem.

Chapter 13 engages the debate over appropriate U.S. trade policy. Here we point to the false dichotomy within this debate between those favoring unrestricted free trade and those favoring protectionism. Acknowledging the potential benefits of trade for both the poorer, developing world and the United States alike, we argue it is nevertheless imperative for trade policy to promote the upward harmonization of social, labor, and ecological standards among trading nations. Such harmonization is necessary if trade is to contribute to community stability rather than community instability, both here and abroad. At the same time we argue that modifications in current trade policies that might affect developing countries should go hand in hand with a broader agenda aimed at offering poorer countries viable opportunities for economic development. In short, we accept the need to modify trade policy in ways that encourage basic rights and standards both in the United States and in the developing world while also rejecting nationalist positions on trade that would close the door on all imports from low-wage countries.

CHAPTER 12

RESTRUCTURING GLOBAL ECONOMIC INSTITUTIONS

Since the Asian financial crisis of 1997–98 there have been numerous proposals to alter, reform, or restructure the global financial system and key multilateral governance institutions. At first blush it might appear that discussion of international-level governance mechanisms and questions pertaining to exchange rates, international central banks, and financial bailout terms are far removed from the question that has occupied most of this volume: how to stabilize the economies of local-level communities. It would indeed be easier if an approach to helping stabilize capital in local communities could proceed without regard to the fate of the world economy—but that is not the world in which we live. International economic volatility is harmful to the majority of the world's population who live in developing countries—but it can also be deleterious to community stability within the United States.

Far more is at stake than whether economic instability will harm the development of American export markets and the investments of American financial institutions—the concerns that usually dominate American media discussion of world economic events and American policy itself. Economic instability and insecurity drive down standards of production, reduce attention to labor rights and human rights, and pit American workers and communities against workers and communities in the developing world in ways that are beneficial to the neither "winners" nor the "losers." Economic instability also weakens environmental protection and democratic systems, from fragile democracies in the developing world to local communities in the United States.

It is thus appropriate—indeed, absolutely essential—that those concerned with stabilizing local communities in the United States also consider the question of how to reduce instability in the global economy. Toward that end, this chapter provides an overview of several of the most comprehensive, far-ranging, and innovative long-term approaches to international-level reform yet articulated—those of economists John Eatwell and Lance Taylor, Thomas Palley of the AFL-CIO, Vermont representative Bernard Sanders, and American University economist Robert Blecker—with special attention to the detailed review and analysis of possibilities for global economic reform offered by Blecker.

FROM MARKET VOLATILITY TO MARKET MANAGEMENT:
EATWELL AND TAYLOR, PALLEY, AND SANDERS

One response to the form of globalization now ascendant—and to the specter of worldwide economic volatility—consists of a series of proposals to create new institutional mechanisms for the rational coordination and management of international financial markets and to apply brakes to the dizzying flow of largely speculative international capital flows. John Eatwell of Cambridge University and Lance Taylor of New School University propose a multipronged set of institutional reforms, including:

1. Establishment of a World Financial Authority (WFA) to formally regulate international financial markets, help coordinate national monetary policies, oversee the activities of the IMF and the World Bank, and help the IMF establish itself as a lender of last resort to developing countries while also ensuring that the recipient country's financial markets are properly regulated. Eatwell and Taylor envision the World Financial Authority as a logical extension of the Financial Stability Forum established in 1999 by G-8 nations and based at the Bureau of International Settlements (BIS). They suggest that the regulatory functions of the authority—authorization, information, surveillance, enforcement, and policy—be carried out by BIS staff in conjunction with national-level regulators.

2. Reform of the IMF so that it acts as a lender of last resort, as noted, and reorientation of the World Bank to emphasize expanding credit in poor countries. Particularly critical would be the establishment of a mechanism for long-term investments in developing countries, as

opposed to short-term, in-and-out investments. To this end, Eatwell and Taylor propose a new closed-end investment fund for emerging markets. Such a fund would provide a measure of long-term financial stability to the recipient countries, and would also be a means of providing more accurate information about market conditions to other private investors.

3. Increased national-level oversight over all financial institutions—especially offshore institutions—and the establishment of tougher capital reserve requirements, in particular, as a hedge against major speculative losses.

4. Adoption of capital controls, particularly on short-term flows, through tax measures (i.e., the Tobin tax on international monetary transactions, described below) or other means. Such controls would be managed in coordination with the World Finance Authority.

Viewed in its entirety, Eatwell and Taylor's package of proposals constitutes an effort to save globalization from itself, first by attacking its worst side effects—the financial volatility and contagion that have the capacity to destroy entire national economies—and then by encouraging coordinated national policies aimed at high growth rates and full employment.[1]

Eatwell and Taylor base their proposal on an analysis of the consequences of the collapse of the Bretton Woods international financial system in the early 1970s. Once public authorities no longer guaranteed exchange rate stability, a chain of events was set in motion in which the private sector sought to diversify its own (greatly magnified) risk through the creation of more exotic financial instruments (such as derivatives) and governments typically shifted from expansionist policies that prioritized employment to more cautious policies aimed at maintaining "credibility" with market actors. The result, Eatwell and Taylor argue, has been an increase in international economic instability and a decrease in average growth rates worldwide.[2]

A second set of strategies, championed by respected AFL-CIO economist Thomas Palley, urges a shift away from export-led growth to a renewed focus on increasing domestic-demand-led growth both in developing countries and in the United States. A critical first step for Palley would be debt relief and the provision of credit for poorer countries, a move that he believes would also bring "benefits to developed economies in the form of increased demand for exports of capital goods."[3] A second step would be a coordinated effort to expand workers' rights globally—above all, to prevent a "race to the bottom" and to encourage competition based on product quality and input-output efficiency rather than cutting wages. A third step for Palley would be harmonization of tax rates to the extent possible across national borders. A fourth step would be Tobin taxes (described below) on capital flows or requirements that cross-border investments be held for a minimum period of time. Palley also calls for strengthening central banks worldwide so as to increase their capacity to protect the value of national currencies against speculators.[4]

Another set of proposals for dealing with the global economy is contained in Vermont Representative Bernard Sanders' Global Sustainable Development Resolution, introduced on the House floor in March 1999. The proposed bill is an ambitious attempt to lay out a comprehensive progressive agenda for dealing with globalization; it pays particular attention to ecological issues. Also of special interest is the fact that it was developed in close contact with (and subsequently endorsed by) numerous leading Washington-based activist and research organizations working on globalization issues. Indeed, the Sanders document can be viewed as a summation and exposition of how many progressive activists and economists now think about how to deal with an increasingly integrated global economy.

The Sanders bill holds that "unregulated economic globalization" is associated with the following ills (many of which have been noted in our initial discussion of globalization in Chapter 1): international financial volatility; a "race to the bottom" in production standards; economic stagnation due to excess capacity and insufficient aggregate demand; increased poverty and economic inequality; damaging impacts on women, minorities, and indigenous people; and "degradation of democracy" due on one hand to increased corporate political power and on the other to growing economic decision making by unaccountable international institutions. The bill urges that the United States adopt the goal of strengthening democracy, human rights, environmental sustainability, and living standards throughout the world as the basis for its economic policies. The ultimate intent is to construct "a democratic multilevel global economy that strengthens the capacity of governments to expand the capacity of their people to meet economic needs" while also promoting human rights, international cooperation, and the subsidiarity principle of decision making in economic life.[5]

Sanders puts forward a number of policy proposals to meet these broad goals. In order to reduce "financial volatility and meltdown," he endorses capital controls and taxation of international financial transactions, currency stabilization (via an unspecified mechanism), coordinated international efforts to increase aggregate global demand, and measures to ensure that speculators bear a larger share of losses (instead of being bailed out by national or international financial authorities). At the same time, his proposal suggests that national-level policies should pursue what is essentially a traditional progressive agenda: raising wages for low-income workers; long-term public investments in health care, education, and the like; expansion of credit for small business; progressive taxation; and "channel[ing] resources to locally controlled development." Sanders further stipulates that trade and other international agreements should not be allowed to supersede the capacity of local governments to "set minimum standards [ecological, etc.] and to pursue economic self-reliance." At the international level, debt of the poorest countries should be written off, and multilateral organizations such as the IMF should be democratized to give more voice to poorer countries as well as to NGOs, labor unions, and other grassroots organizations. Additionally, Sanders urges that reducing global inequality should become a stated, explicit goal of international policy.

The Sanders document spells out many of the specifics of how such policies might be implemented. Among the most interesting and innovative ideas contained in the bill are:

- The creation of at least one "public international investment fund." The fund or funds would serve the dual purpose of making long-term investments in developing nations that would not be subject to market-driven volatility, and also serving as a lever of Keynesian countercyclical spending policy on a global level.

- Immediate cancellation of all debt owed by the world's poorest countries to the United States, and American advocacy for relief of debt owed both to private creditors and to multilateral institutions such as the IMF—with no structural-adjustment strings attached.

- Making respect for labor rights a precondition of financial assistance from the IMF and World Bank—and in turn making U.S. funding for these institutions conditional on the adoption of such a policy.

- Systematic assessment of the ecological impact of all projects and policies implemented by the IMF and World Bank, as well as the employment of natural-resource economists to assist in properly accounting for the ecological costs of such policies.

- Investment of 20 percent of the World Bank's energy portfolio in energy efficiency alternative- and renewable-energy projects, while reducing the carbon-based emissions of energy producers in the bank's portfolio by 10 percent a year. The bank would make meeting the energy needs of the world's poorest 2 billion people a strategic aim and shift transportation spending away from automobiles toward public transportation. The bank would also invest in sustainable forestry and agriculture and water efficiency projects, and it would refrain from projects likely to cause substantial ecological damage.

- As a condition of aid from the IMF, no decreases in credit availability to small business or in per capita social spending by recipient governments would be permitted.

- Open publication of all financial and policy decision-making records of the World Bank and the IMF.

- Establishment of an international Code of Conduct for Transnational Corporations. All transnational corporations would be required to (1) disclose the amount and location of pollutant emissions and the location of all production sites (including those of subcontractors), (2) report all international transport of hazardous material, (3) recognize worker rights and comply with environmental laws, (4) provide advance notice and severance pay when plants are closed, and (5) disclose all relevant financial data as well as "information on policies of the corporation that affect stakeholders other than shareholders, such as employment practices, worker health, tax payments, and receipt of government subsidies."[6] Corporations not meeting the code of conduct would be subject to sanctions (by an as yet unspecified legal body), and both governments and citizens could "initiate complaints of noncompliance" by transnationals.

In addition, the Sanders bill lays out an alternative approach to trade policy (see Chapter 13 for further details) and calls for the appointment of two commissions aimed at generating a wide-ranging public dialogue on the global economy.[7]

It is worth adding here that Sanders is not the only member of Congress to call attention to the negative aspects of globalization and the way that existing policies tend to favor corporations over communities. Democratic Senator Byron Dorgan of North Dakota, for instance, has challenged policies giving tax deferrals on income earned abroad to American corporations that move plants overseas: "This reward system for runaway plants, and other assets, costs federal taxpayers some $3.4 billion a year and rising." Dorgan also has attacked the practice of "transfer pricing," which allows transnational corporations to adopt an accounting procedure that assigns distorted price values to its internal international transactions with the aim of avoiding taxation in the United States. A 1999 study by finance economists Simon Pak and John Zdanowicz estimates that this practice costs the United States Treasury $43 billion a year. Dorgan has proposed replacing the transfer pricing system of evaluating transnationals' assets with the "unit rule" used by states to evaluate the assets held by corporations operating in multiple jurisdictions.[8]

FROM MARKET VOLATILITY TO MARKET MANAGEMENT: BLECKER AND FRIENDS

The proposals of Eatwell and Taylor, Palley, and Sanders are representative of a burgeoning literature on how to correct the flaws of the global financial system. A steady of stream of proposed alternatives has been generated in the past five years by academics, activists, and policy researchers.[9] A comprehensive assessment of significant proposed reforms of the global financial system has been provided by Robert Blecker of American University and the Economic Policy Institute. Following Blecker, we organize the discussion below by distinguishing five kinds of reform measures: first, proposals, promulgated largely by G-8 governments themselves, to make modest changes to the existing financial institutions to further rationalize the process of financial market liberalization worldwide (such as greater disclosure requirements for international financial institutions); second, proposals to regulate international flows of capital; third, measures to directly alter the mission and practices of the World Bank and IMF (and perhaps create new international institutions with new roles); fourth, strategies to stabilize exchange rates; and fifth, measures to improve coordination of macroeconomic policy from country to country.

Rationalizing Financial Market Liberalization
The first set of proposed reforms, while reasonable in itself, only marginally comes to grips with the failure of neoliberal policy models for international development. Even if implemented, they would fall far short of promoting stable economic development and the goal of avoiding economy-wrecking financial meltdowns in poor countries—the negative effects of which can also impact the health of G-8 countries themselves, including the United States). Specific proposed mechanisms include:

- Tougher accounting requirements for both firms and central banks (including publication of central banks' foreign exchange holdings)

- Improved surveillance by the IMF of member countries' economies

- Regulations aimed at reducing risk in developing countries' financial institutions, such as capital reserve requirements and deposit insurance

- Steps to increase the flow of reliable information about economies to overseas investors (to help forestall the herd phenomenon, in which investors rush into a country armed with little information other than that other investors are doing the same thing)

- Improved crisis management aimed at preventing large-scale investor withdrawals from a developing nation's economy

Advocates of these kinds of proposals have included the United States Council of Economic Advisers, former Secretary of the Treasury Lawrence Summers, and some staff members of the IMF itself. For the most part, the proposals take the goal of open capital markets for granted and focus simply on getting the financial institutions and practices in less-developed countries "up to speed."[10] Left untouched by the official proposals is the ongoing volatility generated by short-term capital flows across borders, and the fact that even with much stronger accountability and transparency measures, investors may continue to engage in highly speculative investments. Second, the official proposals presume that liberalization of capital markets and full integration into the world economy are in the best interests not only of the most advanced developing countries but of all countries at all times, regardless of local conditions. Finally, the official proposals do little to expand the capacity of developing countries to adopt expansionary strategies aimed at increasing domestic standards of living.[11]

Capital Flow Regulation
The second set of reform proposals addresses the issue of capital flows. Some observers have suggested the use of taxation strategies to provide more stable regulation. One of the best-known and most widely discussed measures for discouraging damaging financial speculation is the so-called Tobin tax, first proposed by Yale economist James Tobin in the 1970s. The tax would be a small levy applied to all international financial transactions, probably less than 0.5 percent of the value of the transaction. Such a levy would discourage purely speculative transactions without unduly penalizing returns on long-term investments in legitimate economic activities. Other economists have estimated that such a tax could raise $100–200 billion a year, which might be used by a multilateral organization to combat specific global problems (such as the AIDS crisis in Africa or persistent hunger and malnutrition) or simply

distributed among national governments. Even if the tax was too small to discourage all forms of speculative activity, it would at least represent a brake on current speculative practices (and a not insubstantial source of revenue for the world's governments).

Two major problems with implementing the Tobin tax immediately present themselves: The first is how to get multiple countries to agree to such a measure; the second is the need to close off escape valves (such as offshore locales) through which speculative activity could be funneled in order to escape the tax. To address these issues, an alternative version of an international transactions tax has been forwarded by French economist Jacques Melitz. In Melitz's scheme, instead of levying a tax at the point of sale, profits from foreign exchange transactions would be taxed at a rate of 100 percent by an investor's home country. This special tax would apply only to transactions involving funds held less than one year. Such a scheme, Melitz believes, could be effectively implemented by a handful of countries and still retain effectiveness, since no matter where a particular sale is made—via the London Stock Exchange or the Cayman Islands—tax liability (for investors of the country which implemented the tax) could not be avoided.[12]

Others suggest a more direct approach to regulate capital flows. Blecker describes the economic management problems faced by national governments in terms of a "policy trilemma": In the new global economy, governments cannot simultaneously maintain autonomous control over the value of their national currency, exercise control over monetary policy, and also liberalize capital markets.[13] Only two of the three policies can be maintained at the same time. As Blecker explains, "A country with open capital markets can still control its interest rates if it is willing to let its exchange rate float freely —but if such a country wants to manage its exchange rate it must then give up control over interest rates and set them at levels that are consistent with exchange rate targets." Simply put, if a country lowers its interest rates and capital is allowed to flow freely, capital will exit the country in search of higher returns (via higher interest rates) elsewhere, but this exit of capital will cause the country's currency value to fall. A country may attempt to counter this fall by buying up its own domestic currency and selling off foreign reserves, but this strategy invites a speculative attack. Moreover, the bank will be unable to maintain the policy indefinitely if downward pressure continues to be placed on the currency (eventually there will be no foreign exchange reserves to convert to domestic currency). A country wishing to maintain a stable exchange rate, then, is obliged to keep its interest rates in line with changes in interest rates in other countries and to match international interest rate increases if it also wants to keep open capital markets.[14]

Given this trilemma, Blecker argues that national governments should be willing to sacrifice liberalized, fully integrated capital markets rather than give up control over either their exchange rate or monetary policies. Hence the justification for capital controls—even though, as Blecker hastens to point out, no capital control policy is foolproof against evasion, and such policies are unlikely to be a cure-all. They can work, however, to guard against rapid, destabilizing disinvestment in a developing country and thereby help fortify national (and in turn global) economic stability. Princeton economist Paul Krugman has also endorsed capital controls as an appropriate measure for some developing nations. Krugman, generally a pro-free-trade economist, shares Blecker's assessment that a country cannot simultaneously stabilize exchange rates, run an expansionary monetary policy, and also maintain unregulated capital flows. Krugman believes regulating capital flows may be preferable to abandoning expansionary policies in developing countries.[15]

Three types of capital controls have gained the most attention from scholars and policy advocates. The first, following the example of Chile's policy in the early 1990s, involves establishing a reserve requirement for short-term investments from abroad. Starting in 1991, a portion of the value of investments in Chile held for less than one year was required to be placed in a restricted, non-interest-bearing account; the reserve requirement provides a disincentive to short-term flows of capital both in and out of the country. While Blecker faults the Chilean policy as excessively geared toward stabilizing the Chilean peso within a broader strategy of austerity (not full employment and expansion), he notes that in Chile the ratio of direct investment (investments in new productive activities) compared to portfolio investments (shares held in existing companies) was "relatively high," which helped Chile cushion the blow of the 1997 Asian downturn.[16] Chile began reducing its controls on capital in 1999, and newly elected president Ricardo Logas of the Socialist Party has phased out the remaining restrictions.[17]

A second approach is that adopted by Malaysia in 1997 in the wake of an attack on its currency. The government instituted a temporary ban on repatriation of profits from foreign portfolio investments held for less than a year, placed restrictions on the amount of Malaysian currency that could leave the country, and required exporters to convert foreign exchange earnings through the central bank, all in an elaborate effort to prop up the value of the Malaysian ringgit. The policy largely worked, and having defended the value of its currency, Malaysia was able to cut interest rates and stimulate the domestic economy—at least in the short term.[18]

A third approach, and the one most relevant to American policy makers, calls for controls on foreign investment from industrialized countries to the developing world, with the goal of ensuring adequate risk protection on investments so as to avoid a rapid pullout from a given country when overexposed investors panic. Analyst Jane D'Arista of the Financial Markets Center, for instance, proposes "risk-weighted capital requirements" that would require American mutual funds and other institutional investors to make cash deposits in commercial banks to offset the riskiness of investments held abroad; the required cash deposit would vary according to the magnitude and riskiness of an institution's overseas portfolio. While reserve requirements are already in place for banks, mutual funds currently have no such requirements, giving them a competitive advantage over banks and increased incentive to make risky investments abroad. D'Arista also proposes as a complement to new reserve requirements the creation of a closed-end mutual fund (in which the number of shares cannot be increased but the value of the existing shares fluctuates) specifically targeted to investments in developing countries.[19] Such a fund, envisioned as operating under the aegis of an international institution such as the World Bank, would not need to liquidate its investments to meet cash requirements when stockholders sold their shares, as is the case with open-ended funds, and hence would be a better source of stable, long-term investment in the developing world than existing mechanisms such as private mutual funds.

An additional proposal—offered by (among others) George Soros—is for "credit insurance." Soros's proposal, which might be seen as an extension of the logic underlying the loan guarantee program of the U.S. Overseas Private Investment Corporation, would create a new global public institution to guarantee international loans up to a given ceiling. For investors who purchased insurance, such a plan might also forestall rapid withdrawals of capital from economies in times of crisis. Blecker notes, however, that it is unclear why investors would agree to a scheme in which cautious, "good" lenders essentially bail out less cautious, "bad" lenders.[20]

Blecker's own recommendation is to use both a form of taxation on international transactions as well as changes in the rules governing short-term international investments from industrialized countries—and also permit developing countries to impose their own more direct controls on short-term capital flows. But this last proposal in turn presumes a change in the character of multilateral governance institutions such as the IMF and World Bank, which have made adoption of capital market liberalization a precondition of financial assistance.

What to Do about the IMF and the World Bank

A somewhat unusual group of free-market economists, on one hand, and antiglobalization activists (including the Bangkok-based Focus on the Global South), on the other, have called for abolition of the IMF and the World Bank.* One group holds that such institutions interfere with the natural workings of the free market by bailing out failed investors, the other that multilateral institutions inevitably serve the purposes of global corporate interests, not the needs of the world's majority, let alone local communities.[21] We have previously argued that sacrificing community economic stability, let alone entire national economies, to the ebb and flow of the unrestricted market is undesirable from the point of view of democracy and likely to be inefficient in any comprehensive balance sheet of costs and benefits to the public. Furthermore, the gradual elevation of living standards, conditions of production, democratic practices, and human rights in general in developing countries would have a positive impact on general trading relations and thus on the economic stability of communities within the developed world. Effective multilateral institutions surely would be needed to achieve those goals.

A more troubling question is whether multilateral institutions that do not give pride of place in setting policy to the interests of international corporations and investors are in fact achievable within the context of global capitalism. Even relative optimists on this question, such as Blecker, concede that progressive political parties committed to expansionary economic policies both at home and abroad would need to come to power simultaneously in several major industrial nations before the necessary reforms could become even a remotely practical possibility.[22] It is nonetheless worth discussing just what such institutions might look like in broad outline, even if prospects for meaningful near-term restructuring of entrenched institutions such as the IMF and the World Bank appear limited at the moment.

Three levels of proposals to redress deficiencies in the existing institutions have been forwarded by activists and policy scholars: reforming the IMF, replacing it with a new world central bank, or replacing it with regionalized monetary funds. Blecker endorses the first option with some gusto and lays out a plan for reconstructing the IMF. His first move—after placing the fund in temporary receivership of "the major governments of the world, including developing countries as well as industrialized nations"—would be to dismiss the current leadership (including both top political and top economic advisors) and replace much of the senior staff as well. Governments would next

---

*   For a summary of the most common criticisms of the IMF and the World Bank, see Chapter 1.

appoint a respected financial leader to assemble a diverse "board of overseers" representative of a variety of ideological and geographical viewpoints. The IMF would then move through a transition to a new institutional structure operating in accordance with the following procedures: open publication of IMF documents and decision making, increased voice in governance for developing countries via a permanent board of directors, formal reviews of IMF programs, and more input from constituencies (such as NGOs and trade unions) within member countries other than national treasury departments. Perhaps most importantly for Blecker, the mission of the IMF itself should be formally changed:

> The IMF needs to redefine its overarching mission as promoting sustainable global growth with full employment and an equitable distribution of income in its member countries. Its interventions in countries with balance-of-payments problems should be designed with these larger objectives in mind, rather than having these objectives sacrificed to serve financial interests that want to salvage the value of their investments while imposing the costs of their imprudent lending on debtors.[23]

In practice Blecker's revitalized IMF would seek to oversee "the global level of aggregate demand." Instead of being biased toward contractionary austerity programs for countries with balance-of-payments problems, the objective would be to maintain full employment to the extent possible while also supporting basic human rights and freedoms (such as the right to organize unions). Bailout packages would shift much of the burden to creditors, requiring them to assume some losses when a country defaults on its loans and/or loans while also giving them incentives not to exit the country and worsen the crisis. Equally important, receipt of financial assistance would be tied to the enactment of policy measures—not long-term structural reforms in the economy—that are country-specific and adopted with the larger social mission in mind. Under such an approach, requiring capital market liberalization or massive cuts in domestic social spending or public investment as a condition of assistance would be all but ruled out. While on occasion currency devaluation or fiscal tightness might be recommended, Blecker urges that full-scale austerity programs are never appropriate and that, in general, austerity measures should be offset by other policies intended to maintain a country's aggregate demand and employment rates.[24]

Advocates of a new world central bank tend to have goals similar to those articulated by Blecker in his vision of a reformed IMF—namely, establishing a worldwide lender of last resort that acts to manage global demand and thus forestall worldwide economic crises or collapses. Jeffrey Garten of Yale

University thus argues that "a global central bank could provide more money to the world economy when it is rapidly losing steam" by buying government bonds of struggling countries or buying out debt from a country's creditors.[25] Financial Markets Center and former government economist Jane D'Arista's proposal for an international central bank puts a twist on the basic idea by suggesting that the bank also act as a clearinghouse through which all international debts could be settled. The bank would be able to buy bonds of any member country and thus stabilize the country's currency, with the aim of putting an effective end to speculation on currencies.[26] More importantly, nations would be able, as D'Arista explains, "to pay for cross-border transactions in its own currency and so bar speculators from raiding the world's currency reserves. People could then create wealth in their own currencies within their national economy and be able to have equality of interaction with the rest of the world." Export-led development to earn foreign exchange to pay for imports or pay off debt would no longer be mandatory for developing nations since each country could pay its debts via the clearinghouse bank in its own currency.[27]

The most obvious objection to a new world central bank is its political implausibility. Proposals along the lines of D'Arista's and Garten's—which recall proposals made by Keynes and others at the very outset of the modern post–World War II era—threaten established financial interests and are also open to the charge of ceding too much national sovereignty to distant powers with uncertain accountability. A third set of proposals—those calling for new regional financial institutions—mitigates this political difficulty somewhat by demanding only that a group of countries within a given region agree to form an overseer bank. An important existing example of such a bank is the European Central Bank. (As many note, however, the European Central Bank has been committed to fighting inflation as a priority, not full employment or economic expansion, and also is excessively shielded from democratic accountability.) In line with this regional approach, London School of Economics economist Robert Wade and international financial consultant Frank Veneroso endorse creating an Asian Monetary Fund (AMF), as first proposed by the Japanese government in 1997. The AMF would allow Asian countries to organize their own system of bailout assistance and oversight of national economies freed from the IMF/World Bank commitment to a neoliberal agenda, thereby facilitating policies more tolerant of capital controls, government intervention in the economy, and other characteristics of Asian-style capitalism. A successful AMF might also create pressure on the IMF to re-evaluate its own policies.[28]

Exchange Rate Stability

Any revamped set of international institutions would need to address the fundamental problem of how best to stabilize national currencies. Traditional approaches have fallen into two broad categories: those based on the judgment that exchange rates should "float"—that is, be allowed to fluctuate according to the market's evaluation of a particular currency's worth—and those based on fixed exchange rates. Many economists argue there are flaws in both rigid positions and advocate a middle way in which exchange rates are allowed to fluctuate within set parameters.

The case for floating exchange rates as now employed by the United States, Japan, and the European Union is that countries facing economic slowdowns or shocks can improve their export position by devaluing their currency (making their goods cheaper for others to buy) and need not raise interest rates to high levels to defend a currency's value. The major problem with this approach parallels the problem with export-led strategies in general: It doesn't work when every nation tries to devalue its currency in order to improve exports. Instead of giving one country in isolation export benefits, currency devaluations in developing countries tend to be matched by other countries, leading to no net competitive gain. Additionally, currency devaluations increase the costs of imports (adding to inflation) and make debts owed to foreigners more onerous. There is also little evidence that developing countries with floating exchange rates actually employ expansionary monetary policies.[29]

Fixed exchange rates also present problems in that they sacrifice monetary policy autonomy to the need to defend a currency's value. Several scholars, for instance have advocated "dollarization" of Latin American currencies—that is, directly tying a nation's currency to the value of the American dollar at a 1:1 ratio (as now practiced in Panama)—as a solution to currency instability. By definition, such a policy would make Latin American economies dependent on the monetary policies of the United States and effectively end the possibility of autonomous national monetary policy.[30]

A "middle way" alternative to either fixed rates or freely floating rates is a system of target zones for currencies. In this scheme, national currencies are allowed to float within, say, 10 percent in either direction of a given target or "peg," but when a currency reaches the limit of its target zone, aggressive action is taken to keep the currency value within the zone. Research by John Williamson has sought to specify a formula for calculating the value of such pegs; under his approach currencies would be pegged at a level allowing national current account values to match the underlying flow of capital in or out of the country over the course of a business cycle. John Grieve Smith has modified this proposal to allow for the currency pegs to "crawl" over time—

that is, to be frequently adjusted in order to account for differential inflation rates among countries, changes in economic growth rates, and other structural changes. Smith recommends that an International Stabilization Fund be established to put teeth into a system of crawling target zones, with sufficiently large resources to buy and sell national currencies so as to ensure that participating nations' currencies stay within the proper target zones and are defended from speculative attacks.[31] This general approach of holding currency values within a set band is also a key part of Eatwell and Taylor's vision for international financial reform under the aegis of a World Financial Authority.[32]

Such schemes need not be adopted on a universal basis in order to get off the ground: Regional blocs in the developing world and/or the G-8 countries could implement such a system among themselves, then in turn negotiate exchange rates with other regions. A limited system would likely be more politically viable, and probably more desirable on its own terms, since Asian countries, for instance, may face quite different structural conditions than those obtaining in the G-8 or Latin America.

Arjun Makhijani of the Institute for Energy and Environmental Research in Takoma Park, Maryland takes up a deeper question: the *justice* of existing exchange rates. Makhijani points out that there is a significant discrepancy between the domestic purchasing power of many developing countries and the value of what such countries can import. For instance, the per capita GNP of Mexico, converted to U.S. dollars based on prevailing exchange rates, was $3,940 in 1994. But the actual amount of per capita purchasing power in Mexico was equivalent to $7,239. To take one example, bread, rice, and tortillas are cheaper in Mexico than in the United States. Hence, the per capita GNP monetary figure grossly undervalues the real productivity of the Mexican economy. Simply put, existing exchange rates do not accurately reflect the underlying productivity of developing nations.*

This undervaluation, as Makhijani shows, has two serious detrimental effects. First (as D'Arista has also noted), it means Mexico has to pay nearly twice as much for goods from the United States as it would in a system based on the actual productivity of the economy, making it more difficult for the country to earn foreign exchange. Second, it creates an artificial incentive for American capital to move to Mexico to take advantage of cheap labor, a cheapness nearly doubled by the weakness of the peso relative to the Mexican economy's actual productivity. Mexico is one of the most striking examples of

---

* International organizations and economists have long been aware of this discrepancy, and have responded by creating "purchasing power parity" indexes to measure the real buying power of national currencies.

a phenomenon common to the entire global South: Currency values often do not reflect productivity levels, and as a consequence poorer nations are, in essence, shortchanged in trade with richer nations.

Makhijani urges a strategy to tie currency values to actual labor productivity, not to the flows of supply and demand on the highly speculative currency market. Exchange rates would be determined based on the "relative prices of basic consumer goods in each country."[33] A new international currency unit with a fixed purchasing power wherever used would be established; each country then would be required to maintain a reserve of core commodity stocks. Above-average labor productivity increases would make currency values rise.

Makhijani argues that this system would increase real purchasing power on the global market for the world's poor countries, permit countries to pursue development policies without fear of being constrained by the currency markets, and lead to a much more stable system of international trade, benefiting both rich and poor countries.[34]

In the context of the broader long-term discussion over how best to stabilize exchange rates, Makhijani's proposal merits serious consideration. Indeed, a modified Williamson-Smith approach to exchange rates involving crawling target zones would still need to make an initial calculation of what a given nation's currency value should be—a process that obviously cannot rely on technical analyses alone but necessarily involves normative judgments (about, for instance, the desirable growth rate of a given economy). Makhijani's suggestion of tying baseline currency pegs to the actual productivity of nation's economies as reflected in purchasing power parities may be viewed as a useful complement to the crawling target zone approach to exchange rate stabilization.

Macroeconomic Coordination

Perhaps the most important step in stabilizing the global economy is sustained international coordination of macroeconomic policies. Such coordination should aim at sustaining global aggregate demand and at eliminating shocks and speculative attacks that exploit inconsistencies in national economic policies. A new approach might permit a group of countries to undertake coordinated cuts in interest rates without fear that capital would flow out of one country in search of greater returns in higher-interest-rate nations. In principle, of course, such general ideas are commonly supported by many nations. The real issue is how these goals can be achieved.

One approach to making macroeconomic coordination more effective is what Blecker calls the "modified Williamson-Miller plan," building on the work of John Williamson and Marcus H. Miller. Once a group of countries had agreed on a target zone for their national currencies (as in the plan noted just above), they would also agree to peg their average interest rates over time so as to match the exchange rate pegs. For instance, a country would not be permitted to raise interest rates to a level that raised the value of its currency above its target zone or to cut interest rates to a level that caused the currency to fall below its target zone.

The key to making this system work would be coordination of differences in interest rates across countries; the absolute value of interest rates would be set at a level designed to maximize growth and employment in each country. Whereas Williamson and Miller believe that this target should be a given level of aggregate demand (which includes both real output plus inflation), Blecker believes that targeting real employment directly would be preferable in such a system—both because it would bias the system in a Keynesian, expansionist direction and because data on employment are more likely to be available in real time than aggregate demand data. Specific macroeconomic policies to produce full employment and stable economic growth would include reductions in worldwide interest rates to stimulate demand, significant reductions in American interest rates to reduce the value of the dollar and correct America's trade deficit, and the pursuit of expansionary monetary and fiscal policies in Europe and Japan (with the lead to come from the fiscal side in Japan, where interest rates have been at or near zero in recent years).[35]

Such a system of coordinated interest rate setting presumes a return to fiscal stimulus policies at the national level, including, when necessary, expansionary government deficits. With interest rate setting largely out of the hands of national monetary authorities, national governments would need to adopt other tools, such as the use of reserve requirements, to manage internal financial flows. Thus, if the Federal Reserve increased the amount of reserves financial institutions were required to maintain, the effective money supply would shrink, and if reserve requirements were cut, the money supply would increase. But reliance on reserve policies in turn implies that such requirements must be applied to all financial institutions, not just banks, to avoid evasion of requirements through use of nonbank institutions or through loans and deposits held in foreign currencies.[36]

Blecker is forthright in noting that a system of coordinated macroeconomic policies would be a dramatic step away from the notion of national autonomy over economic policies. That step can be justified, he urges, given that the alternative to partial political control over a nation's economic policy via an international consortium is even *less* national autonomy as the decisions of national policy makers gradually become more and more subordinate to the swings of international financial markets. Still, such a historic shift would almost certainly face serious political opposition, as Blecker makes clear:

> Any country agreeing to target its exchange rates and to coordinate its macroeconomic policies with other countries is, of necessity, surrendering some measure of autonomy. It may, for example, have to set its own interest rates higher or lower than it would otherwise in order to reach agreement with other countries. The hoped-for advantage is that whatever policy results from this type of coordination is more effective and more sustainable than a similar policy carried out by a single country. But from a strictly national viewpoint, there are likely to be situations in which a single country could do better on its own (e.g. because it would adopt a larger interest rate cut, and is willing to either let its currency depreciate or close its capital market) than if it had to coordinate with other countries. One cannot start down the road of policy coordination without recognizing that it may require compromises of some national objectives in the interest of promoting a generally more stable and prosperous global economy, in which all countries are ultimately better off.[37]

THE PROSPECTS FOR REFORM

Americans conditioned by conventional policy discussions within the United States may be surprised by the degree to which ideas similar to the policy menu laid out by Blecker and to the proposals of Eatwell and Taylor, Thomas Palley, and Bernard Sanders are acceptable, even commonplace, outside the shores of the United States. A number of world leaders share major aspects of the critique of unfettered global financial markets noted here, and many representatives of both Asian and European countries reject the "Washington Consensus" on international development policy and the broader American model of minimally regulated capitalism. French prime minister Lionel Jospin, for instance, has remarked that the "crises we have witnessed teach us three things: Capitalism remains unstable, the economy is political, and the global economy calls for regulation."[38] Similarly, United Nations secretary-general Kofi Annan has declared that the "spread of markets far outpaces the ability of societies and their political systems to adjust to them."[39] International financier George Soros adds that the problem with markets is "that they are not always stable. They frequently swing to excesses. That is why I can say that markets, instead of swinging like a pendulum, can sometimes act like a wrecking ball, knocking over economies."[40]

While there has been some movement in American public discussions toward acceptance of possible structural changes (especially in the area of capital controls, which has won grudging approval as a possible least bad solution for some countries from pro-globalization economists such as Jagdish Bhagwati), many feel, with Paul Krugman, that "the policy ideas that the community of respectable opinion can allow itself to discuss are at best marginal, at worst irrelevant."[41] The dissent of Krugman, Bhagwati, and other mainstream economists from IMF–World Bank orthodoxy represents what John Cavanagh and Robin Broad have described as "cracks in the Washington Consensus."[42] Criticism of the austerity orientation of the IMF and World Bank has also become respectable in some mainstream political discourse. On the other hand, however, more thoroughgoing proposals to radically overhaul the governance structure of the international economy continue to be marginalized in American public debate and in the media.

The difficulty is not simply ideological narrowness and unwillingness even to entertain alternatives. As Robert Wade points out, American-based transnational corporations and Wall Street benefit from and bolster capital market liberalization and the adoption of American-style capitalism worldwide. "It is in the U.S. interest to have the rest of the world play by American rules for both international finance and multinational corporations," Wade observes.

> The goal is to make the rest of the world adopt the same arrangements of shareholder control, free labor markets, low taxes, and minimal welfare state that U.S. corporations enjoy at home. U.S. firms could then move more easily from place to place and compete against national or regional firms on a more equal basis. This goal is especially important in Asia because the Asian system of long-term market relationships and patient capital (investors that are more willing to wait for returns) has put U.S. firms at a significant disadvantage.
>
> The United States sees free capital movement as a wedge that will force other economies to move in its direction. Indeed, the Asian crisis [of 1997] is a dreadful confirmation that financial liberalization and capital account opening make it more difficult to sustain the long-term relationships and national industrial-policy arrangements that have prevailed in the Asian political economy.[43]

Wade suggests that so long as American financial interests continue to be an important driving force behind American international economic policy, serious moves toward capital controls—and, we might add, other items from the reform agenda—are likely to be resisted in Washington. We suspect that Wade is largely correct—at least until a point is reached where global economic instability threatens American prosperity in a much more tangible way, and perhaps forces new institutions into existence. Unfortunately, the institutions generated in response to such a crisis are unlikely to be as well thought out or as thorough as the comprehensive approach of Blecker and the other scholars noted here.

From the standpoint of Europe, Asia, or the developing countries, a prolonged American resistance to altering the neoliberal policy framework will likely shut off many of the most far-reaching solutions for a considerable period. There may, however, be some limited room for regional action—including national-level capital flow controls, the creation of an Asian Monetary Fund as an alternative to the IMF, or regional alliances aimed at establishing crawling target zones for currencies—which might buffer some of the instability generated by the present international financial architecture. Additionally, the United States has expressed a willingness to accept at least partial debt relief for the poorest nations, a move that would lift an enormous burden from those nations and remove a drag on the global economy as a whole. But it would probably take another round of Asian crisis-scale systemic shocks to the global economy combined with a deep American recession to open the way for more dramatic reform.

That cold political fact is unfortunate for the prospects of community economic stability in the United States itself. Obviously there is an ongoing risk of extreme economic dislocation if global economic shocks should ever reach the point of significantly damaging American financial interests, and it is all but certain that any new global crisis would exacerbate the length and scale of the next American recession. It is important, too, to recognize that the American financial position itself—which rests upon heavy borrowing from abroad to finance a chronic balance-of-payments deficit—is a potential source of global instability: There is no guarantee that at some point foreign investors will not sell off their holdings of dollars and stimulate a speculative attack on the American currency. As Eatwell and Taylor warn, in the absence of effective mechanisms to stabilize currency values

> a sell-off of the dollar would produce sharp falls in U.S. bond prices and hence a rise in interest rates. . . . The potential disequilibria—portfolio shifts away from the U.S., bigger interest obligations on its debt, and growing financial stress on the household sector—could begin to feed on one another and on the views of the markets. At that point with an expecta-

tional run on the dollar fueled and not staunched by higher interest rates, dollar devaluation, austerity, and the other ususal policy moves, all hopes for global macro stability would disappear. A massive international rescue campaign would certainly be required, with worldwide implications impossible to foretell.[44]

Beyond these threats, it is also true most American communities would have much to gain from a world in which exchange rates were relatively stable, in which less American financial capital was funneled into speculative activities and more into real productive activities, in which the world's leading economies effectively coordinated macroeconomic policy so as to guarantee strong levels of aggregate demand and in which living standards, conditions of production, and social and democratic rights in the developing world were effectively ratcheted upward over time

In the meantime, we agree with American University economist Robin Hahnel and many other writers who—while lending at least qualified support to new "international Keynesian" measures of the sort discussed in this chapter—stress the importance of continued development of a bottom-up, international grassroots movement aimed at shifting both discourse and policy regarding the global economy. Observing that "it takes a democratic movement to successfully combat the preemption of economic decision-making at the core of the reactionary globalization agenda," Hahnel urges building on events such as the Seattle 1999 challenges to the WTO, with an explicit focus on measures to combat inequality in the global economy. Such a redistributive agenda, in addition to obvious measures such as debt relief, could draw on some of the ideas of the 1970s New International Economic Order movement, (such as price stability for commodity exports, technology transfer from developed to undeveloped countries, and substantial aid).[45]

Efforts to stabilize the world economy, and to undertake meaningful efforts to narrow global inequality, are surely important for their own sake. From our perspective, they are also important as a basic strategy to stabilize the overall context for democratic development in American communities. Until the United States is successfully urged by its own citizens (and its neighbors abroad)—or compelled by the force of international economic chaos—to take a leadership role in rewriting the rules of the global economy in ways favoring economic stability and giving priority to the gradual, steady increase of living standards, globalization will remain a potential source of destabilizing pressures on American communities. There is also, as always, the lingering threat of truly catastrophic, wrecking-ball-type global instabilities.

CHAPTER 13

ALTERNATIVE APPROACHES TO TRADE

W hile prospects for major institutional changes in the current structure of global financial institutions may appear dim in the near term, serious debate about appropriate trade policy has been at the heart of American political discussion for the past decade. We turn now to the question of what posture toward trade a community-sustaining economic policy aimed at establishing a solid framework for democratic development should assume.

Proponents of unrestricted "free trade" commonly label critics "protectionist," capping their arguments with the assertion that the economic logic guiding free trade policy is "unassailable." In fact, the arguments against free trade —and counterproposals—are a good deal more sophisticated than the "protectionist" label would imply. Equally important, there is also a philosophical divide between one strand of criticism of free trade (as, for instance, articulated by Pat Buchanan and Ross Perot) that is explicitly nationalist and protectionist and a second strand (associated with progressive activists) that is not opposed to trade per se but instead is concerned with ensuring that trade takes place under rules that promote healthy social and economic development for all trading partners.

It will be useful, before directly considering alternative trade policy measures, to briefly reconsider the range of arguments commonly made in everyday debate about trade.

TRADE TALK: A REVIEW OF THE ARGUMENTS

First, and most common in American political discourse, are arguments for free trade based on its positive economic consequences for the United States. Free trade is said to promote maximum economic efficiency (as each country specializes in its area of expertise), to cut prices for consumers, and to provide export markets for American goods—all gains that in the long run more than compensate for any short-term losses. The 1997 annual report of the United States Trade Representative (USTR) further argues:

> Exports are more important in our economy than ever. Since 1993, more than a third of our economic growth has come directly from exports, and the number of export-related jobs has increased by an estimated 2.2 million. A total of some 12.1 million U.S. jobs depend on exports, and U.S. jobs supported by goods exports pay an average of 13%–16% more than the overall U.S. average.

According to the USTR, the appropriate policy stance is clear: "There remain too many barriers to U.S. goods and services exports throughout the world. Because increasing trade has become an important part of our strong economic growth and global leadership, it is of great importance to our prosperity and prestige that we continue our push to remove these remaining barriers."[1] These are instrumental arguments for free trade: More trade is good not simply on its own terms but specifically because it helps the American economy, as measured by data on jobs, wages, and growth in national income.

Arguments employed in challenging free trade on instrumental grounds take the opposite tack, emphasizing its negative economic consequences within the United States: Free trade undermines the security of American workers and communities and leads to negative effects such as job loss, unsustainable trade deficits, and capital flight to lower-wage countries. As we noted in Chapter 1, some 3.2 million net jobs were lost due to trade in the United States between 1992 and 1999, according to Robert Scott of the Economic Policy Institute. Between 1993 and 1998, trade with Mexico and Canada led to a net loss of 440,000 U.S. jobs.[2] Analysts who emphasize these facts again are making instrumental arguments: Free trade is not bad in itself, but bad because it produces undesirable consequences for the American economy.

A third set of arguments, analytically distinct from but often used concomitantly with the first set of arguments, is essentially a moral argument for free trade. Free trade, it is said, promotes other important desirable outcomes, such as international interdependence (which, it is held, makes war less likely) and international development. The classic statement of the presumed linkage between trade, peace, and freedom comes from the nineteenth-century English reformer Richard Cobden, who was instrumental in ushering in free trade policies in England in the 1840s: "The progress of freedom depends more upon the maintenance of peace, the spread of commerce, and the diffusion of education, than upon the labours of cabinets and foreign offices."[3] In modern terms, this sort of view assumes that opening America's markets to imports from low-wage countries will improve the lot of some of the world's poorest people and provide Third World countries with a plausible development path. Seeking to directly protect one group of relatively well-off workers who happen to live within the United States from incursions by less well-off workers working in overseas industries is morally unjustified, according to this view.

A fourth set of arguments makes precisely the opposite claim: that the purpose of a nation's economy is to benefit the people who live in that country, and that workers who live within America's borders have a legitimate right to receive protection from overseas competition even if this raises prices for consumers. Underlying this position is the notion that international free trade agreements amount to a forfeiture of sovereignty, which in turn implies that sovereign nations have the right to restrict flows of goods, capital, and people as they see fit. There is a higher good than economic efficiency, and it is the well-being of the people who live in a particular country. It has also been claimed by some free trade critics (such as Buchanan) that buying products from within the country strengthens national bonds and feelings of patriotism.

Finally, a fifth set of arguments suggests that what is most destructive about free trade is not so much changes in aggregate job totals or a dilution of nations' sovereign powers but damage to American communities from avoidable economic dislocations. Such destruction is of importance because communities serve as the loci of civic participation and moral formation for the American citizenry and as the fundamental building blocks of American democracy. Those taking this view also often echo the points made in the sovereignty argument, especially regarding the deleterious impact of shifting authority over how goods are treated from local communities to distant inter-

---

*   These characteristic positions, of course, refer to commonly held stances on trade within the United States. Taking stock of the various perspectives held in developing countries would complicate the issue further, as trade advocates in the developing world emphasize the importance of access to affluent markets while critics worry about the destabilizing impact of trade and investment liberalization on developing countries, particularly on agricultural populations, and the expansion of foreign economic power into their nations. As we have seen in Chapter 1, the economic theory of free trade and the doctrine of comparative advantage have also been critiqued as incoherent or out of date in an era in which capital is highly mobile.

national bureaucracies, as specific restraints on trade or biases toward local production are made illegal or subject to legal challenge by other countries.* As legal scholar Mark Gordon of Columbia University has pointed out, state governors wishing to toughen environmental standards, introduce new industry regulations, or promote local enterprises through purchasing policies—"the types of policy decisions that States use to define some of their most basic beliefs"—now must consider not only the policy impact of such initiatives, but whether or not the measure might be challenged under an international trade agreement.[4]

OUR VIEW: AN EXPOSITION AND DEFENSE

Our position emphasizes, primarily but not exclusively, the final set of arguments. In this volume we are centrally concerned with how unrestricted trade can undercut a community's capacity for self-governance, either through erosion of a community's capacity to regulate its economic life or through direct economic shocks that destabilize local economies. "Races to the bottom," which give producers who can evade social and ecological standards a competitive advantage, are also clearly antithetical to community self-governance, as are formal rules encoded in trade and investment treaties aimed at restricting many types of community-building economic policies, from preferences for local goods in government purchasing to aid to worker-owned firms. Moreover, since—as we have argued throughout this book—community economic stability is a requirement of meaningful local-level democracy, to the extent that trade destroys the material security of a community, it damages democracy in general. Political theorist David Moore of the University of Maryland has developed this point:

> The democratic community, and not just the individual citizen . . . must have the material security and autonomy to be meaningfully self-governing as a collective association. Therefore structural conditions which constrain the range of options among which a community can choose, or which reduce the capacity of its citizens to engage in making those decisions, threaten the potential for good democratic politics both locally and beyond.[5]

This community democracy approach to trade policy stands in sharp contrast to nationalist antitrade arguments. To illustrate the critical distinction, let us first consider the core trade policy proposal of a representative nationalist, Pat Buchanan. Central to this policy are tariffs based on wage differentials between nations, through which goods from poor countries would be penalized at a rate equivalent to the difference between the prevailing industry wage in the United States and the prevailing industry wage in the exporting nation.

There are two major problems with such a proposal. The first is that it ignores the fact that even within manufacturing—to say nothing of other sectors—American workers are much more productive than Third World workers. A 1999 study published by the Bureau of Labor Statistics found that in 1996 on average Latin American manufacturing workers produced 29 percent as much output (measured as contributions to GDP) per hour as American workers. For Asia, excluding Japan, the figure is 10 percent as much per hour. Even in the newly industrialized countries of Hong Kong, Singapore, South Korea, and Taiwan, output per hour is only 43 percent of the output produced by American manufacturing workers.[6]

To be sure, multinational corporations can often achieve unit cost advantages by using Third World labor. In the case of Mexico, in 1997 average manufacturing compensation totaled 10 percent of U.S. compensation, even though in 1996 Mexican manufacturing workers were 23 percent as productive as American workers.[7] Moreover, as Harley Shaiken of the University of California at Berkeley has shown in the case of export plants in Mexico owned by American automakers, in many specific cases the productivity of Mexican plants is comparable to American levels. But by looking only at the wage difference between workers in poorer nations and those in the United States and not at the comparative productivity of each worker, a Buchanan-type tariff exaggerates the competitive advantage that poorer nations obtain from low wages. Firms care about labor cost per unit of output, not labor costs per se.[8] Thus, any blanket wage tariff that does not at least distinguish between products made in higher-tech, foreign-owned export plants and those made in locally owned plants, or between high-productivity and low-productivity sectors, would be economically questionable even on its own terms.

The second problem with a Buchanan-type proposal is of a moral and philosophical nature. Consider the hypothetical case of a Brazilian clothing cooperative with twenty-five employee-owners, where decisions are made democratically, innovative ecological practices are employed, and child care is provided. This firm meets the social standards encoded in United States law regarding labor and ecological practices and is a model of what a just economic enterprise might look like. Suppose the firm also makes one-third of its sales in the United States to affluent liberal consumers, and suppose that workers in the cooperative pay themselves one-third of what American textile workers making analogous clothing products earn—enough for a decent, above-poverty-level lifestyle but not enough for an automobile in the garage.

Under a Buchanan-type policy, this firm would be subject to a punitive tariff equivalent to the wage differential between the two nations; its products would be treated no differently than goods produced at a nonunionized, pollution-spewing maquiladora.[9]

In Buchanan's conception, then, America should enact protectionist measures not primarily because they are just in the sense of meeting norms of safe production, minimal ecological damage, democratic civil liberties (i.e., right to organize unions, free political speech), and equitable distribution, but because the jobs such measures protect are our own—they are American. In this position, Buchanan enjoys the support of numerous other economic nationalists, both historical and contemporary. In 1837 the German-American economist Friedrich List, for instance, wrote:

> At present a nation may be regarded from two distinct points of view with regard to its relations with other countries:
>
> (i) First, a nation is a sovereign political body. Its destiny is to safeguard and to maintain its independence by its own efforts. Its duty is to preserve and to develop its prosperity, culture, nationality, language, and freedom—in short, its entire social and political position in the world.
>
> (ii) Secondly, a nation is a branch of human society. It is the duty of a nation—as far as its own special interests permit—to join with other countries in the task of promoting the welfare and prosperity of the whole world.[10]

List went on to strenuously defend the first conception, which in his view implied the need for mercantilist policies to protect and enhance the development of industries, termed by List "the foundations upon which national independence can be built."[11]

Similarly, two contemporary liberal writers, Michael Lind and John B. Judis, urge a new economic nationalism for America based on the following principle: "Ultimately American economic policy must meet a single test: Does it, in the long run, tend to raise or depress the incomes of most Americans? A policy that tends to impoverish ordinary Americans is a failure, no matter what its alleged benefits are for U.S. corporations or for humanity as a whole."[12] For Lind and Judis, this conception implies a pragmatic approach to trade questions, concrete steps to slow the flow of capital out of the United States—and, too, domestic policies to reduce inequality. However, the argument tends to beg a number of critical questions: Is any policy that enriches Americans while hurting poorer nations (i.e., "humanity as a whole") justifiable, no matter how extreme? Ought not America then pursue a foreign policy aimed at total American control, colonial-style, over important foreign resources (such as oil), perhaps even resorting to war to achieve this goal? Is there not a point at which America's pursuit of the sole goal of enriching its own citizens might conflict, perhaps violently, with other nations' similarly constituted objectives? What, precisely, are the appropriate limits of any policy?

TRADE AND THE JUST COMMUNITY

An alternative to the nationalist view of the state's proper stance is the principle that a primary aim of the state in regard to trade policy should be to seek to nurture just, sustainable, and secure communities within its own borders—and simultaneously give due consideration to the nurturance of such communities elsewhere. This is not to disregard all (alleged) economic efficiency arguments for trade; it is to put the central issue of democracy explicitly into the debate. If democracy is a fundamental goal of long-term importance—and if this requires a foundation in democratic communities—then certain policies follow: A democratic community should provide sufficient material provision for all its members, minimally, and must ultimately be able to exercise meaningful self-determination over its economic and social life. Civil liberties for workers, workers' right to exercise collective action, and a minimum wage set above the poverty level would all be ground rules for production in just communities. Such communities need to rest on a secure economic base to practice active self-governance, and they should be able to take active steps to ensure that production is organized in a manner that upholds the dignity, civil liberties, and self-respect of those who engage in production. (Ideally, production should also be organized in a manner that tends to cultivate democratic virtues that would be transferable from the workplace to the public arena.)

In addition to these qualities—which mainly speak to the justice half of the equation—the conception of a just community also values the particularities, traditions, history, institutions, and other distinct qualities of place that characterize and constitute community, and thus tends to view skeptically policies that ignore or run roughshod over these particularities, especially policies that jeopardize the accumulated civic and social networks through which local-level democratic politics finds its expression.[13] (Of course, these community particularities must respect norms regarding human rights and democratic fairness established and enforced by larger political units.) While we do not believe that many (if any) existing communities in the United States adequately embody the notion of a just community, the country as a whole has achieved important elements of the concept, particularly in regard to establishing basic standards of decency in the production process—even if that achievement is fragile and not always observed.

We believe it is reasonable, then, to consider restrictions on goods whose entry into America would tend to undercut the principle of nurturing just, sustainable, and secure communities. On the other hand, this conception of the just community does not in most circumstances justify restrictions on commodities made in just conditions simply because they come from abroad. Our conception of community largely accepts localist conceptions of what a just community should look like, while at the same time balancing this against a global view of the moral importance of all communities. Our concern is to foster just communities both abroad and at home, and hence we are loath to levy punitive tariffs on a firm's products for the sole reason that its workers are poorer than American workers.[14]

Still, it needs to be said why exactly we should care about fostering just communities in other nations and not simply those in the United States. Five basic arguments in support of this position may be cited.

1. *Fostering just communities elsewhere can prevent a "race to the bottom."* As living standards and conditions of production rise in other countries that trade with the United States, American workers and communities also will benefit, since capital flight to those countries will become less attractive and because fewer goods will be entering the United States that have been made under substandard working conditions.

2. *America has a moral responsibility to promote just and democratic communities throughout the world.* We believe the United States and its citizens have a positive moral obligation to assist in improving the well-being of poorer nations. There are numerous, overlapping normative considerations that persuasively support the idea that the world's richest nation should recognize this obligation: principles of economic justice and charity to neighbors found in religious traditions; conceptions of moral duty and obligation; utilitarian calculations suggesting that the redistribution of economic resources would increase total human utility; philosophical concepts of distributive justice, applied to a global scale; and the view that the United States owes historical debts to many Third World nations for unjust activities in the past and/or present (including military, covert, and diplomatic interventions into other nations' politics).

3. *Positive examples of just communities are a good in themselves.* Even if

Americans had no positive moral obligation to help poorer nations achieve just communities, and even if they stood little to gain from it, achieving just communities wherever this is possible is worthwhile in itself—for the sake of the people and communities themselves, as well as for the example such communities set for others.

4. *Just communities contribute to democracy and to global peace.* Democracies rarely go to war with each other. The United States has a positive interest in fostering the conditions which build democracy from the ground up. Economic and political instability pose a danger to the security and well-being of both new and established democracies.

5. *International competition in product markets under certain circumstances is legitimate and desirable.* A fifth relevant argument is that economic competition between communities that have roughly equivalent labor and ecological standards is legitimate and ultimately to the benefit of both. We believe this is true under certain (but not all) conditions. In particular, fair trade governed by rules promoting harmonization of production and environmental standards between countries with roughly equal levels of social and economic development is likely to be desirable for both countries. However, there are good reasons why less developed countries should not be expected to offer completely reciprocal trade openness as a precondition of access to American markets. Indeed, while the policy suggested here would allow American market access to exports from the developing world that were made in reasonably just conditions, this does not necessarily mean that we see export-based growth as the most desirable primary development strategy for the developing world.

ADDITIONAL CONSIDERATIONS

Several additional observations are in order before moving on to consider what a community democracy approach to trade might look like. For instance, it is important in all this, especially for the nonspecialist economist, to remember that there is no gain in efficiency—understood here as how much labor and how many resources it takes to produce a product—when we simply import products made at subpoverty wages (although such imports may provide a modest positive benefit to American consumers). Cheap imports often simply represent the exploitation of poor people who cannot command a higher price for their labor and cannot engage in collective bargaining with employers to improve their wages.

It is also important to remember that most U.S. trade is with other advanced nations, not poor countries. In 2000 nearly three-fifths (57 percent) of American exports were sold to other industrialized nations, and 52 percent of imports came from those same nations. Over one-fifth of American trade (measured at prevailing exchange rates) is with Canada alone. It is true that there has been a substantial increase in the overall volume of trade with non-OPEC Third World nations and also in such trade as a percentage of America's overall trade—imports from non-OPEC nations in the Third World were 41 percent of total imports in 2000, up from 32 percent in 1989, and exports to such countries were 40 percent of total exports in 2000, up from 30 percent in 1989. However, the bulk of America's overall trade continues to be with its historical trading partners: Canada, Western Europe, and Japan.[15]

Finally, it is important to recall—and emphasize—that it is by no means clear (to say the least) that free trade brings with it all the purely economic benefits its advocates claim for it. First, the evidence is mixed in connection with growth: Many protectionist nations, like the United States for much of its history, do or have done as well or better than free trade nations. Perhaps the most impressive capitalist success story of most of the postwar era, Japan, restricted imports and openly practiced favoritism for domestic industries, as did export-oriented successful East Asian "tigers" such as South Korea. As noted earlier, Dani Rodrik has demonstrated that while at least slight increases in exports relative to GDP between 1975 and 1994 characterized twenty-three of the twenty-five fastest-growing countries in the developing world as a whole, export growth alone hardly guarantees successful development: In fact, the twenty-five developing nations with the fastest increases in exports between 1975 and 1994 had a decidedly mixed growth record over that same time period, with five countries actually losing ground.[16]

Second, in large countries, competition within the country can achieve many of the efficiency-enhancing effects trade produces in smaller countries. The United States is not Belgium: The vast size of the U.S. economy means that local monopolists only rarely control markets in key goods and that the United States is capable of providing for itself at reasonable cost a very high proportion of the goods and resources needed in an advanced economy.

Third, as we have seen, the available evidence indicates that the effects of more open trade under NAFTA on job creation in the United States have been mixed, possibly even negative. Recall that existing government data show a net loss of 440,000 American jobs due to NAFTA alone between 1993 and 1998.[17] Meanwhile in Mexico, as Sarah Anderson and John Cavanagh have reported, "direct US investment jumped from $16.9 billion to $25.3 billion in the first four years of NAFTA . . . but real manufacturing wages have dropped 23 percent. Moreover, overall employment has declined, as locally owned firms are crippled by high interest rates set by the government to attract foreign investors."[18]

Fourth, the costs of thrown-away communities and thrown-away workers generated by unrestricted trade must also be included in any full accounting. A total of 1.58 million Americans are estimated to have lost their jobs due to NAFTA alone between 1993 and 1998. Even though 1.14 million other jobs were created as a result of the treaty, the human costs on people and their families who lost jobs must be taken into consideration even when such costs are merely "frictional," as in the case of those who find new jobs in a reasonable time frame. As previously noted, the Economic Policy Institute estimates that a total of 7.3 million American workers lost their jobs due to imports between 1992 and 1999.[19]

Fifth, trade across vast distances often imposes hidden costs, which tend to be borne by the public—for instance, through subsidies to transportation. Journalist Jeff Gersh notes that air cargo shipments by Boeing nearly tripled between 1985 and 1997, to some 123 billion ton-kilometers (one ton of goods shipped one kilometer). "In practical terms, that means that transporting 1 kilogram of tomatoes from, say, Spain to Stockholm produces 1.7 kilograms of carbon dioxide emissions and 5 grams of nitrogen oxide. . . . As long as fossil fuels and their pollutants continue to be highly subsidized around the world, the environmental costs of trade will not show up in the price of the goods."[20]

Sixth, the benefits to consumers that are said to flow from free trade are not always realized, particularly when large firms with a dominant position in a given market are involved. As noted in Chapter 1, a multinational corporation that imports goods produced cheaply by an overseas subsidiary may pocket the cost savings rather than pass the savings on to consumers in the form of lower prices.

Seventh, following the logic of John Maynard Keynes, if managed trade policy can help permit all countries to reach higher levels of overall aggregate internal growth—above all by reducing instabilities from the global market—then the average sustained volume of world trade might actually increase even if some restrictions are in place.

Eighth, and related to Keynes' concerns, is the issue of community stability and imbalances in trade. In some cases (such as steel and semiconductors) rapid loss of jobs due to such factors as shifting currency values can hinder the long-term competitiveness of domestic industries, even after financial conditions (such as the strength of the dollar) have normalized. Also, as economist Robert Scott of the Economic Policy Institute observes, trade deficits have specific negative effects on the American economy, the most obvious of which is job loss, particularly in manufacturing.

Trade deficits have also been linked to reduced expenditures on research and development. Economist Peter Morici estimates that eliminating the trade deficit would increase annual research spending by 3 percent a year.[21] Most important, continued large-scale trade deficits such as those run by the United States create a major risk of severe financial instability if the dollar becomes less attractive to overseas investors and financial investors pull capital out of the United States and sell holdings of U.S. currency. Scott noted in 1998 that if, the trade deficit continued to grow, "the deficit will come perilously close to 5 percent of GDP, a widely accepted trigger point for currency instability." The trade deficit in 2000, in fact, exceeded 4.5 percent of the GDP.[22]

ALTERNATIVE STRATEGIES

If, as we believe, a primary goal of trade policy should be to sustain economically secure communities in the United States while also contributing to democratic social and economic development abroad, what specific mechanisms must be adopted? Below we review three alternative approaches to trade and investment that hold some promise for meeting these objectives: the Hemispheric Social Alliance's (HSA) "Alternatives for the Americas", the Global Sustainable Development Resolution proposed by Vermont representative Bernard Sanders, and the "social tariff" suggested by journalist William Greider. Again, our primary focus is on the long-term development of democratic communities.

HSA's "Alternatives for the Americas," a document jointly produced by activist organizations in Canada, Chile, Mexico, and the United States, is intended to spell out in some detail the basis for a Peoples' Hemispheric Agreement aimed at raising living standards and international standards of productions and prioritizing ecological sustainability in North and South America. The document is based on the premise that expanded social and economic integration between the United States and its neighbors would be a desirable outcome if, and only if, it is done in the right way.[23]

The proposed People's Hemispheric Agreement is based on a multi-pronged development strategy that relies both on exports and on the development of internal markets. The HSA coalition calls for tariff cuts negotiated in trade agreements to be implemented through coordinated timetables that would give affected industries time to adjust to new competitive pressures.* Affected industries would also be given technical assistance, access to credit, and research and development support. The document declares: "For developing countries, trade liberalization without an industrial policy is suicidal." Additionally, it proposes that tariff reductions on end products be coordinated with simultaneous tariff reductions on inputs needed to produce the end product.[24]

Nontariff barriers ought to be approached judiciously, the HSA coalition urges. Simply put, there are "good" nontariff barriers, such as those protecting labor, ecological, and health standards, and "bad" nontariff barriers, aimed narrowly at benefiting private interests. A new approach to trade should vigilantly weed out the latter form of barrier while honoring legitimate rules that uphold the public interest. However, the HSA urges, even ecological and labor rules should not be allowed to act as an absolute, unilateral barrier to another nation's goods; instead, the content of such rules should be the subject of international agreement. Most important, countries that need to raise standards should be given assistance in doing so over time. At the same time, multinational corporations would be required to meet the same standards regarding environment, labor, and health (among others) that obtain in their home country.

A central aim of the HSA document is to ensure that trade and investment actually generate the social and economic benefits for a country promised by abstract economic theory. For instance, the Peoples' Hemispheric Agreement would permit countries to impose minimum content requirements if corporations wish to claim "designation of origin" for a particular good. Without such rules, corporations have incentives to use a given country (i.e., Mexico under NAFTA) to produce a small part of a given product, then claim free trade privileges for the entire product without any need to buy other inputs from the platform nation. For instance, a German corporation might open a factory in Mexico, have few linkages with Mexican firms and hence generate a relatively small multiplier effect within Mexico, but be able to export the finished product to the United States tariff-free as a "Mexican" product.

The HSA group also proposes a set of regulations governing foreign direct investments. Investors' rights would be subordinated to internationally ratified treaties and national conventions regarding human rights, labor practices, and ecological standards and would also be subjected to additional

---

* On this point the agreement follows the advice of Adam Smith: "The undertaker of a great manufacturer, who, by the home markets suddenly laid open to the competition of foreigners, should be obliged to abandon his trade, would no doubt suffer very considerably. . . . The equitable regard, therefore, to his interest requires that changes of this kind should never be introduced suddenly, but slowly, gradually, and after a very long warning" (*The Wealth of Nations,* Book IV, Chapter II).

internationally agreed regulations. Signatories to international agreements on, for instance, labor or ecological standards would not be permitted to unilaterally enact laxer regulations in order to attract investment.

Additionally, nations would be permitted to enforce an extensive set of performance requirements on multinationals operating within their borders. These would be roughly analogous to stipulations commonly set by individual states in the United States as a precondition to receiving state subsidies (i.e., clawback provisions). Such performance requirements might include requirements that a percentage of inputs be purchased locally, preferences for hiring local workers, giving local or national investors an equity stake in investments, minimum requirements for investment duration (perhaps by requiring the deposit of a percentage of the investment for the first year), limits on how much money can be repatriated at a given time, and abiding by ecological standards (including gaining permission to use local natural resources) and fair labor practices (including provision of pensions, health benefits, and a early warning of shutdowns or layoffs). The intent of such provisions is to ensure that foreign investments produce positive ripple and spin-off effects on local living standards. Under the HSA proposal, corporations not meeting these requirements could be sued either by governmental entities or by citizen groups and organizations.

As can be seen, the overall goal of the HSA document is to ensure that neither international trade nor cross-national investment significantly damages national and local autonomy in policy making. This approach would extend to many other policy areas as well—including, for instance, intellectual property rights and the state role in the economy. States would be permitted to give preferences to local businesses, women-owned businesses, cooperatives, and the like in awarding government contracts.

The long-term goal of the HSA approach is to facilitate the upward harmonization of social standards while at the same time capturing the economic benefits associated with trade and cross-border investment. It is not assumed that such harmonization can take place instantaneously. On certain issues, such as whether corporations and governments must respect the right to organize unions and the rights of free association, the HSA group urges that a universal, unbending standard be applied. But appropriate minimum wages, on the other hand, would vary from country to country, depending on what might constitute a livable wage in a given country at a given time. That is to say, developing countries would still be able to claim a competitive advantage in attracting investment associated with lower wages than, say, American workers receive—but not if such wages were depressed below a minimum living standard. On other issues, such as ecological standards, an evolutionary approach is also suggested by the HSA. This would require that relatively stern standards be applied universally, but with allowances made for those countries that need additional resources, technological assistance, and time to upgrade to internationally agreed standards.[25]

A broadly similar ideal paradigm is articulated in the Global Sustainable Development Resolution proposed by Vermont representative Bernie Sanders (as discussed in greater detail in Chapter 12). The bill's section on trade policy urges the need to "reorient trade and investment to be means to carrying out just and sustainable development rather than ends to be maximized for their own sake."[26] Sanders proposes that all trade agreements ensure that international conventions regarding labor, the environment, and human rights are enforced, that minimum standards of production are observed, and that local and national governments retain the right to set labor and ecological standards at higher levels than these conventions.

Critically, Sanders argues that trade agreements should not infringe on prospects for local- and national-level policies to support community economic stability and economic democracy: Any trade agreement, the bill states, must preserve the "right of nations and localities to plan for local economic development objectives such as raising employment levels, enhancing employment opportunities for targeted populations, raising wage levels in specific industries, dignified work, and healthy communities" as well as "the right of countries to take legal measures that require public or state ownership in some sectors, exclusive national ownership in some sectors, and national participation in the ownership of some sectors." Like the HSA document, the Sanders bill permits countries to enforce performance requirements and antispeculation rules on foreign investors. The bill also calls for steps to stabilize commodity prices, give preferential market access to the world's poorest nations, and to place a Tobin tax on capital flows (the proceeds of which would be used to fund environmental cleanup and job insurance funds).[27]

A third approach to trade policy consistent with the goal of promoting community economic security at home and healthy social and economic development abroad, as suggested by journalist William Greider, involves the implementation of a "social tariff" on goods from certain other countries.[28] Under a social tariff, goods produced in countries that do not respect labor rights, have poor environmental regulations, or show little regard for health and safety would be subject to a tariff on entering the United States. This would be designed to offset the estimated cost savings of such low standards. Imports would be permitted to compete with American-made goods on the basis of quality and even price savings generated by lower labor costs (so long as such labor costs provide workers in the exporting country a living wage), but not on the basis of cost advantages derived from substandard conditions of production. Such a tariff would give incentives to developing countries to raise their standards over time in order to gain unfettered access to American markets. A social tariff might be introduced by a single nation unilaterally or by a number of nations acting in concert (and conceivably could be overseen by a radically reworked WTO-type organization).

The social tariff is radically different from the wage tariff proposed by Pat Buchanan—which, as discussed earlier, would impose a tax equivalent to the difference between the American wage in a given industry and the wage in the exporting country. The social tariff approach would permit developing countries to make use of the comparative advantage produced by cheaper labor—an advantage, as we have seen, that can easily be exaggerated if we fail to consider the superior productivity of American workers compared to those in low-wage nations.

Implementing a social tariff would be administratively complex, and estimating the cost savings from substandard production processes and setting social tariff levels for each of America's trading partners would be a politically charged and inevitably controversial process—not least because this tariff would undoubtedly lead to price increases for American consumers on many imported goods (such as Nike running shoes). Refined proposals for how to best administer such a tariff—including provisions for frequent adjustment of tariff levels as conditions change—are needed if the idea is to get off the ground. But it should also be noted that the controversy such a tariff would entail should be welcomed, not shunned. The embarrassment of being hit with a relatively high social tariff by the United States could be a spur to improvements in labor, environmental, and safety conditions in developing countries.

APPROACHES TO TRADE IN PERSPECTIVE

From the standpoint of community economic stability and community democracy, the emphasis by critics of free trade on maintaining and strengthening labor, health, safety, and ecological standards in international agreements is well placed. When trade rules allow mobile capital to play off one community against another on the basis of differentials in standards of production, the long-term economic and social stability of communities in both rich and poorer nations is threatened. Still, most progressive critics of free trade are also willing to permit goods from developing countries made by lower-wage workers to compete with American-made goods if such goods are produced in ways that meet international standards. Accordingly, even if a program of upward harmonization of standards was implemented, some American workers and communities would continue to face trade-related layoffs.

In our view, the response to those challenges that a community democracy approach must give over the long haul is clear. A dramatically expanded program of trade adjustment assistance for both workers and firms—compensation for those who would lose even under economic integration carried out on relatively just terms—must be a vital component of any trade policy that also aims to promote community economic stability. If Flint, Michigan, loses jobs because it cannot make quality cars as cheaply as Guadalajara, Mexico (even when cars are made under comparable conditions of production with respect to labor practices, workers' rights, and ecological standards), the result should not simply be that factories close and workers scramble for service-sector jobs or leave town. Instead, government assistance should be provided to Flint to help convert productive facilities to new production, and workers should receive ample retraining to fill new jobs. Alternatively, government assistance could be provided to help workers and communities purchase the facility so they could choose whether to keep producing the same good, albeit with lower profits and perhaps lower wages, than under the previous proprietors. (Often corporations close an inherently profitable plant because it cannot meet an exceedingly high profit margin demanded of each company plant—even though the general value to the workers and community of keeping it open might make a lower profit margin acceptable.)[29]

FREE TRADE AND THE DEVELOPING WORLD RECONSIDERED: THE "THERE IS NO ALTERNATIVE" ARGUMENT

Will not restrictions on free trade, even those imposed for the purpose of fostering high standards of production, have the effect of damaging the economic prospects of some of the world's poorest people? This position has been stated eloquently by Princeton economist and *New York Times* columnist Paul Krugman. Speaking with respect to recent controversies over the employment of sweatshop labor by affluent American corporations, Krugman forcefully charges critics of open trade and the global economy with ignoring the real-world problem of poverty:

> Workers in those shirt and sneaker factories are, inevitably, paid very little and are expected to endure terrible working conditions. I say "inevitably" because their employers are not in business for their (or their workers') health; they pay as little as possible, and that minimum is determined by the other opportunities available to workers. And these are still extremely poor countries, where living on a garbage heap is attractive compared with the alternatives. And yet, wherever the new export industries have grown, there has been measurable improvement in the lives of ordinary people.[30]

Krugman cites the increase in per capita daily calorie intake in Indonesia from less than 2,100 in 1970 to 2,800 today—a significant, measurable increase in human welfare that has accompanied what Krugman admits is the exploitation of desperate labor by multinational corporations.[31] He emphasizes that he sees no feasible alternative to this process:

> As long as you have no realistic alternative to industrialization based on low wages, to oppose it means that you are willing to deny desperately poor people the best chance they have of progress for the sake of what amounts to an aesthetic standard—that is the fact that you don't like the idea of workers being paid a pittance to supply rich Westerners with fashion items."[32]

What response can be offered? First, it must be admitted that in the broadest sense, Krugman in many instances is probably right: Low-wage industrialization is likely the most effective motor for economic development in a number of poor countries. But this does not necessarily mean that free trade and unregulated foreign investment are the sole recipe for improving social and economic well-being. Take the example of Mexico after NAFTA. As we have noted previously, while foreign direct investment in Mexico has tripled from 1980s levels to some $11 billion in 1998, real wages have declined over the same period, with the real value of the minimum wage declining dramatically.[33] Poverty rates also have increased in Mexico since the mid-1990s, and living standards have not rebounded from the collapse of the peso in 1994.[34]

Moreover, while it is true that many countries in Asia in particular have raised living standards—using Krugman's measure of calorie intake as a barometer—since 1970, many other countries have not. Twenty-eight countries in the developing world have seen per capita calorie intake increase by 500 or more since 1970, but twenty-four other countries (mostly in Africa but also some Latin American and Caribbean nations such as Paraguay, Nicaragua, and Haiti) have seen declines over the same period. Total calorie intake has declined in sub-Saharan Africa as a whole as well as in countries deemed by the United Nations Development Program to be "least developed countries."[35] This finding in part confirms Krugman's claim that nations (such as Indonesia and China) engaged in low-wage industrialization have a better chance of achieving increased living standards than nations left behind —but it also illustrates that globalization so far has done little or nothing for the poorest countries in Africa and Latin America. Furthermore, recall that industrializing countries experiencing the most spectacular gains in living standards in the past thirty years (such as China and South Korea) have not done so by adhering to a neoliberal, free trade policy agenda.

The real question, then, is whether the process of low-wage industrialization must unfold without any conscious intervention to shape it in a direction fostering the creation of just communities as rapidly as possible. Many defenders of sweatshops seem to assume that the creation of relatively wealthy, relatively just communities is the result only of the natural workings of economic forces and economic development and that social struggle and political intervention are not required. The historical experience of the United States, Britain, and other countries shows that social struggle is indeed required to achieve basic regulatory standards such as the eight-hour day, safety procedures, the right to organize, and so on.[36] Market forces do not automatically generate the standards of human decency in the process of production with which progressive critics of free trade are most concerned. A study of wage and employment trends in Latin America from 1970 to 1998 by John Weeks of the University of London found that "most workers in most Latin American countries have not shared in the benefits of economic growth, either in terms of reduced unemployment or in terms of rising real wages," despite increases in capital investment in most countries. Weeks concluded that strengthening unions and worker's rights vis-à-vis capital, as well as establishing minimum workplace standards, are required if future economic growth is to lead to wider prosperity in developing countries.[37]

If this is the case, the question is whether restrictions on trade of the kind advocates of the just community urge represent a reasonable intervention into the rules of the world economy. While the answer to this question is open to reasonable debate, implementing restrictions on goods produced under dictatorships, or where ecological standards are ignored, or where workers toil fourteen hours a day with forced overtime, or where the legal minimum wage is below even the producing country's own poverty line is important in and of itself.[38] Trade penalties tied to working conditions and respect for human rights would give poorer nations significant economic incentives to improve or upgrade their conditions of production—and producers would no longer be able to relocate from one poor nation to the next simply to avoid humane regulation. There are other possible mechanisms for actively encouraging a rise in production standards; recall that Bernie Sanders' Global Sustainable Development Resolution calls for making World Bank and IMF financing for poor countries contingent on respecting basic labor rights.

Over the long haul, a new approach must also increase domestic investments in basic education and economic infrastructure in developing nations—investments that cannot be financed via market processes (i.e., by foreign direct investment). This requires other means of transferring capital to the developing world, whether via international aid or international financial institutions. In short, a full-fledged long-term alternative to the free trade regime that is both economically and morally coherent must combine careful restrictions on trade aimed at encouraging developing nations to respect basic rights and improve working conditions with mechanisms to provide sustained, substantial assistance to help fund community-oriented development in poorer nations. And it must be part and parcel of an overall financial and trade strategy to reduce global economic instabilities.

THE POLITICS OF TRADE AND THE FUTURE

Few issues in American politics at the dawn of the twenty-first century exhibit a clearer divide between the views of the majority of the populace and the views of elites than the question of trade. Polls consistently show that most Americans are skeptical of claims made by free traders, yet most academic economists, pundits, and Washington politicians remain firmly wedded to free trade orthodoxy.[39]

Even so, the political climate regarding trade and investment issues has changed dramatically in the past decade. As Mark Weisbrot points out, for decades before the 1993 fight over passage of NAFTA, American presidents were free to negotiate bilateral and multilateral trade agreements with minimal public debate. But in 1993 a powerful coalition of trade unions, public interest organizations, and some environmental groups formed to challenge NAFTA, forcing President Clinton to make numerous promises to recalcitrant lawmakers (such as those representing sugar growers in Florida) in order to secure approval of the bill by a narrow margin. Since NAFTA passed, free trade critics have demonstrated increased political clout, blocking both the attempt to give Clinton fast-track authority to negotiate a free trade agreement with Chile in the fall of 1997, which failed, and the OECD proposal for a Multilateral Agreement on Investments (MAI), which had to be tabled at the end of 1998 under the glare of intense public scrutiny in response to widespread anti-MAI activism. (Two exceptions to this trend are congressional approval of the Uruguay Round trade negotiations, which led to the creation of the WTO in 1994, and legislation passed in 2000 to give China most-favored-nation status as a trading partner.) Finally, the Seattle protests against the WTO in December 1999 and subsequent protests against mainstream global economic institutions in Washington and Prague have afforded free trade opponents a new level of public visibility.

We believe public opposition to unrestrained free trade is likely to continue to grow—especially if the American economy weakens. On the other hand, defenders of traditional free trade will not go down without a fight;

powerful and determined interests remain behind the free trade lobby. Indeed, in the spring of 2001 George W. Bush requested fast-track authority to negotiate the proposed Free Trade in the Americas Agreement (FTAA), which would encompass most countries in North and South America. The proposed FTAA, like past trade agreements, is again constructed on the model of prioritizing "investors' rights" and the prerogatives of business, stripping the state of its capacity to shape markets and development. The same progressive coalitions that contested NAFTA and the MAI and criticized the WTO have again mobilized to challenge the FTAA.[40] The power of free trade critics was again evident when Democrats and sympathetic Republicans succeeded in forcing the new Bush administration to initially put off its own request for fast-track authority, and, as of this writing, to offer substantial trade adjustments and environmental concessions to try to win its passage.

In the upcoming debates over the FTAA and other trade issues in coming years, critics of unfettered free trade will have many chances to articulate alternative principles to guide American international trade and investment policy. We believe it critically important—for intellectual, moral, and political reasons—to distinguish a progressive approach designed to sustain just communities, at home and abroad, from abstract theoretical approaches, on one hand, and nationalist, chauvinistic approaches to trade, on the other.

Some measure of economic disruption from trade is inevitable, just as some measure of economic disruption from shifts in market conditions caused by changes in technology and product development is also inevitable. Within the context of a comprehensive community-sustaining economic policy, disruptions can be cushioned and minimized. If, on the other hand, disruptions resulting from fair trade are exacerbated by disruptions resulting from unfair, regulation-avoiding trade, and if global rules codifying the inviolable "rights" of global corporations are enacted, then trade and investment flows will become a major, perhaps *the* major, source of community destruction in the new century. It will also become, inevitably, a major source of political resentment and backlashes, which may be expressed in the kind of xenophobia hinted at by current nationalist critics of free trade.

CONCLUSION

POLITICAL-ECONOMIC POLICIES FOR THE NEXT STAGE OF DEMOCRATIC DEVELOPMENT

his "primer" has focused on the problem of how to anchor capital in geographically defined communities —in other words, how to give substance to the idea of a place respecting political-economy in the face of the triple threat of sprawl, internal capital mobility, and globalization. Such a place-respecting political economy would dramatically strengthen local American democracy in two fundamental ways. First, it would ensure that local communities have the capacity to exercise meaningful governance over their own economic fortunes. Second, it would open up new possibilities for more egalitarian, inclusive politics and policies at the local levels as communities are no longer held hostage to the exigencies of attracting and retaining mobile capital to keep their economic ship afloat. Strengthening local democracy in both ways, we hold, is critically important for the revitalization of American democracy in general.

Our call to restore the substantive basis of community democracy in America through community-centered, place-stabilizing policies is intended to be a starting place, not an ending point. The challenge is to move from high-minded rhetoric about the decay of community in America to real action. Simply defining community economic stability as a critical frame of reference for thinking about the decline of community life, community-spiritedness, and local democracy is an important step. We have little doubt that if this fundamental goal were to gain wide acceptance, creative minds, committed activists, and courageous policy makers would find countless ways to further the goal—perhaps drawing on the ideas and initiatives detailed in this primer, perhaps through new innovations. Even in a climate of ideological hostility to the notion of preserving places and respecting communities, Americans in all walks of life have already played a role in developing a wide range of economic alternatives with community-stabilizing potential, from community credit unions to worker-owned firms to community land trusts to CDCs and beyond. If local- and state-level initiatives can ultimately be married to higher-order activism and policy making on the federal and international levels, we believe there is a real, not chimerical, chance of making serious headway in reconstructing community in America over the coming decade.

Our review of the key elements in a comprehensive, community-stabilizing policy agenda has covered a broad array of issues, data, and description. A serious place-supporting agenda would require an expansion of existing but often little-noted policies at the state and local level to assist place-based firms. It would entail strengthening a series of federal programs that, though currently inadequate in scale, already honor the principle of place-based development. And it would entail new long-term strategies to seriously alter global governance—strategies that in some cases would require unprecedented levels of international policy coordination. The detailed information presented in this volume regarding many of these programs, policies, and proposals is obviously subject to change: Budgets will fluctuate, new grassroots innovations will emerge while others fail, and policy proposals will become more nuanced and sophisticated to take account of changing circumstances and lessons learned from previous efforts. What is unlikely to change, however, is the underlying rationale for a broad-based, comprehensive policy agenda in support of community stabilization.

There are many additional issues bearing on the future of community life and democracy in America that we have not directly addressed. Most prominent among these are economic inequality, racial inequality, gender inequality, cultural tolerance, and the ecological requirements of a sustainable society. Many other writers have addressed these various issues in depth, and each of us has addressed them in earlier writings.[1]

Still, the many issues associated with community stabilization strategies intersect in interesting and not always recognized ways with questions of inequality, race, gender, and the environment. For instance, the growth of sprawl is connected to the persistence of spatial racial segregation, and persistent economic inequality is related to the degree to which both individuals and communities enjoy economic security. Similarly, ecological problems will usually be given (at best) second priority by state and local policy makers facing pressing economic problems or the loss of local jobs. Beyond this, we believe that the rehabilitation of local-level democratic practice is a necessary (but certainly not sufficient) precondition for rebuilding the sense of community and shared goals that is required to sustain a larger policy program aimed at reducing inequalities, prioritizing community needs over private interests, and renewing American democracy in general.

COMMUNITY AND DEMOCRACY

It is worth recalling that the very word *politics*—derived from the Greek word *polis,* "city-state"—implies an intrinsic concern with the health and governance of particular localities. Classical political thinkers like Aristotle and Cicero assumed that a healthy, secure economic base must underpin any stable political regime. Nineteenth-century democratic theorists like Mill and Tocqueville pointed to the quality of local democratic experience as important in itself and critical to the health of larger-order democratic institutions. John Dewey in the twentieth century held that "fraternity, liberty and equality isolated from communal life are hopeless abstractions. . . . Democracy must begin at home, and its home is the neighborly community."[2] And recent analysts of the state of American civil society and American democratic process such as Robert Putnam draw a picture of an increasingly hollowed-out body politic, in which fewer and fewer citizens participate locally in face-to-face political activity and where the substance of democratic decision making has been largely reduced to periodic plebiscites between candidates who are selected on the basis of fund-raising acumen rather than grassroots political organization.[3]

We have argued that something critical is missing from the picture commonly drawn by academic and journalistic critics of American democracy regarding the decline of civic and community life in America. That something is a clear recognition that the question of how to reinvigorate local-level participation in the processes of democratic governance cannot be abstracted from the question of how to stabilize geographic communities economically.[4] In the most dramatic cases economic dislocation entails the wholesale destruction of civic networks. But even in less dramatic instances, community economic insecurity inevitably tilts local politics in the direction of business elites and orients local policy toward attracting outside investment, no matter what the costs. In such cases, local politics tends to consist of deal making between elected officials and the most powerful local business interests, with sporadic resistance from neighborhood-based groups fighting an uphill battle while the vast majority of residents sit on the sidelines.[5] The result in both instances is the undermining, economically and politically, of the very notion of democracy as citizen self-rule.

Although a wide range of federal and state policies already aim, piecemeal, at achieving place-based economic stability, for decades it has been assumed that a serious place-based economic policy would involve massive economic irrationalities. Both before and after "A National Agenda for the Eighties"— the 1980 Carter administration report lambasting place-based development —the refrain of most economists and many policy makers has been that government should aim to help only people, not places.

That argument no longer holds water. Four central observations underlie our view of the inherent viability of community-stabilizing policies. First, given the massive ongoing public intervention in the economy and the huge subsidies given by all levels of government to private firms to encourage the relocation of capital, it is (and in most cases always has been) implausible to argue that the decline and growth of particular places in the American economy is simply a result of market efficiencies working themselves out. Second, by refusing to consider the costs of place-destroying policies from a public (or community) balance sheet perspective, most economists and policy makers have simply ignored the economic waste involved in throwing away existing places and the decades-long public investment they embody. Third, vast technological leaps in transportation and especially communication mean that purely geographic reasons (e.g., access to water transportation) for why a given firm must be located in one place and not another have declined in importance. Fourth, manufacturing plants producing goods for export beyond the immediate locality now occupy an ever-smaller share of the American economy. A mere 14 percent of all jobs are manufacturing jobs today; within two decades, 90 percent of Americans will likely work in other sectors. Most productive activities in the new service and knowledge-based economy can operate relatively efficiently in many locations—and *this* is fast becoming the economy of the new century.

Simply put, there are no overriding technical or efficiency reasons why each community in the United States could not be home to productive, community-stabilizing enterprises. Moreover, those who choose between helping individuals and helping communities present a false dichotomy. We believe both should be done—and that often they work best if done together. The real question now is how to implement workable strategies to achieve community stability. To help answer that question, in Part II we highlighted many traditional, place-based policies already being pursued by the state and federal governments that could be expanded.

Our review of national-level public policy precedents stressed the many ways the federal government already attempts to support community stability—albeit usually in an inadequate, after-the-fact fashion. Relevant current policies of particular importance include job training programs, Community Development Block Grants, trade adjustment assistance, regionally oriented economic assistance provided by such agencies as the Economic Development Administration and the Appalachian Regional Commission, policies targeting federal contracts to depressed areas, Empowerment Zones and Enterprise Communities, assistance to small businesses and to rural communities, the EPA-led Brownfields Initiative, and assistance to communities affected by military base closures. Several suggestions for expanding such policies at relatively little cost are noted below.

In both Parts II and III we highlighted the development over the past thirty years of an array of place-based economic institutions such as worker-owned firms, community land trusts, community development corporations, municipal enterprises, and nonprofit enterprises as well as new financial and investment mechanisms (such as community credit unions and economically targeted pension investments) directly aimed at promoting community stability. Many of these institutions also have the potential (often not yet fully realized) to give ordinary Americans a stronger say in the workplace and more control over their own working lives, and they offer new avenues for making enterprises more responsive to community concerns. To the extent that more participatory, job-anchoring institutions continue to expand, place-stabilizing strategies can go hand in hand with the extension of meaningful local-level democracy both at work and in the community. Beyond this, in localities where community-based enterprises are well developed, such enterprises and their workers and supporters could join together—in alliance with other community organizations—to help form a credible political force capable of challenging existing governing coalitions and local politics as usual.[6] A community stability strategy focused on building inherently place-based, democratically structured firms might ultimately help push the structure of local politics, slowly but steadily, in a more inclusive, egalitarian direction over time.

Although the number of existing place-based economic institutions is growing and some are beginning to operate at significant scale, community development corporations, city-owned enterprises, majority worker-owned firms, and the like together still make up only a small portion of the economy. On the other hand, the developmental work of the past three decades has generated enough experience, competence, and knowledge that a new framework of explicit policy support could permit a major advance in the coming period. We believe that with adequate policy support, these institutions can and should expand in the next two decades, both to provide increased direct employment and to help leverage other private employment rooted in local communities. Many community development corporations, targeted pension fund investments, and community development financial institutions are already doing exactly that. Continued development and refinement of these institutional forms, combined with intelligent use of existing public financial flows, and policy steps to increase multiplier effects (as discussed in Chapter 7), could in time provide many communities not already anchored by public institutions a far greater capacity to stabilize their local employment base.

Launching a development strategy of this kind, we believe, would be demonstrably more efficient and less wasteful than many existing development practices, which, as we have seen, often consist of giving massive incentives to corporations to induce local investment. As noted in Chapter 4, numerous recent estimates of various forms of corporate subsidies place the bill at at least $125 billion a year (equivalent to about 6 percent of the total federal budget in recent years). There are no reliable studies of the cost of state and local corporate incentives, but a reasonable estimate would be at least another $50 billion a year (equivalent to just over 4 percent of total state and local government expenditures). Finally, there are the billions of dollars wasted, as noted, by current policies that "throw away" cities and entail building unnecessary new capital facilities. Such policies result in lost tax revenue, increased social welfare costs, and related social problems borne by declining communities that experience capital flight.

Economic instability at the international level also has the potential to severely damage community-level economic stability. Medium-term international economic policies that could help minimize the risk of global economic instability include Tobin taxes to limit speculation on international currency transactions, debt forgiveness for developing countries saddled by long-term interest payments, and new regulations to stabilize international capital flows.

Longer-term structural changes that could further stabilize the international economy include creating a new clearinghouse for international financial transactions along the lines proposed by Jane D'Arista (with the aim of radically reducing currency speculation), the creation of both private and public investment funds aimed at generating long-term investment in developing countries, and an overhaul of the International Monetary Fund and the World Bank to put an end to structural adjustment policies that inappropriately impose a one-size-fits-all policy agenda on developing countries. International economic institutions should implement policies that recognize that strengthening infrastructure and human capital is essential to long-term healthy development, that the development of healthy domestic sectors must not be sacrificed to export-led development, and that maintaining economic stability at both the national and international levels is an overriding aim.

Our overall proposals also included reversing policies which subsidize companies that move plants abroad and strategies to stop proposed treaties that would codify a set of "investors' rights" that limit the capacities of local, state, and national bodies to regulate economic activities or to promote locally oriented enterprise. We also discussed several related proposals designed to reshape trade agreements so that domestic U.S. producers are not undercut by imports made in grossly substandard environmental and labor conditions abroad. At the same time we have suggested providing incentives for developing nations to improve production standards over time. Such proposals reflect a balanced, community-oriented approach to trade policy—one that holds that the goal should be to promote and sustain communities that have fair working conditions and that respect the environment, both in the United States and abroad. Unlike completely unrestricted free trade, such an approach would not allow countries to compete on the basis of exploiting workers in grossly substandard conditions or by wantonly disrespecting the environment. Unlike nationalist approaches to trade, our proposed strategy would in appropriate circumstances permit developing nations to compete with countries such as the United States on the basis of lower wages. We pointed out that the net benefits of trade to the American economy are often exaggerated—and that the costs of adjusting our trade policies to a community-based approach would not be prohibitive.

TOWARD A NEW AGENDA

We noted above that federal subsidies of business alone cost at least $125 billion a year. A portion of that spending could wisely be placed in the service of a comprehensive policy agenda aimed at stabilizing communities. We have reviewed dozens of policy proposals and existing government programs that promote this aim. Many—such as adjustments in trade policy—involve few or no short-term fiscal costs. Other proposals involve more substantial costs, but even these are relatively small in overall budget terms in what is now a

$10 trillion economy. Here is a partial list of initial federal-level policy steps that might be taken to implement a new approach:

- *Providing federal funding to establish state centers to assist and support worker-owned firms based on the successful Ohio Employee Ownership Center.* Allocating $100 million a year would permit all fifty states to establish centers at over twice the scale of the Ohio program. To recall, one striking finding from the experience in Ohio and elsewhere is that in numerous cases worker-ownership feasibility studies have persuaded the original owner to keep the facility open—a finding that suggests many plant closings today may be unnecessary. An additional $100 million in federal funding to help states to carry out feasibility studies prior to plant shutdowns—combined with a strengthening of the current sixty-day-notice law so as to require firms planning significant shutdowns to participate in a feasibility study—could help prevent thousands of jobs from being needlessly eliminated due to imperfect information about a facility's market prospects. Such funding should increase, step by step, to $1 billion a year. We also support California Republican Dana Rohrabacher's proposal to provide significant tax breaks to majority worker-owned firms that permit substantial worker control over management decisions. A program twice the scale of the current ESOP tax benefit would amount to roughly $3 billion a year.

- *Increasing annual funding for the federal Community Development Finance Institution Fund.* An increase from $118 million (2001) to $1 billion annually would allow the fund to respond to current demand for assistance (now over twice as high as what the fund can support) as well as to initiate new programs. An additional $15 billion would allow the federal government to directly capitalize new CDFIs in some 300 metropolitan areas nationwide on roughly the same scale as North Carolina's successful Center for Community Self-Help.

- *Restoring CDBG funding and other direct federal assistance for community and regional development.* Between 1980 and 2002 the value of total federal assistance for community and regional development (excluding disaster relief)—including principally federal Community Development Block Grants—declined in real terms by over 50 percent.[7] Such funding often directly assists community development corporations, among other efforts. Restoring federal community development spending to 1980 levels would involve increasing spending from roughly $9 billion to $20 billion. These additional funds would allow CDCs and other community development agencies to undertake more ambitious, comprehensive development strategies—and reduce their financial dependence on foundations and private actors (such as banks and corporations). Given that the economy in real terms has grown by roughly 90 percent since 1980, a further increase in funding to a total of $37 billion would restore federal spending for community development to roughly the same percentage of GDP it had at the end of the Carter administration. We support such an increase—and indeed, in time, even more dramatic increases—although we recognize that a restoration to previous levels of funding should be implemented in stages, so as not to overwhelm the absorptive capacity of current community development actors.

- *Providing federal support to states that create funds to buy undeveloped land and place such land in conservation reserves.* As part of a strategy to contain urban sprawl, the federal government should provide states with matching funds for land conservation efforts, using as a guide New Jersey's current expenditure of $100 million a year to buy undeveloped land. Federal antisprawl matching funds to support state efforts at the same scale as the New Jersey initiative would total approximately $5 billion a year—and, importantly, would encourage more states to follow New Jersey's lead.

- *Expanding the Federal Trade Adjustment Assistance program.* This program should be expanded to cover persons who lose their jobs due to the secondary impact of trade (i.e., via the multiplier effect), liberalize requirements that workers must prove that their job loss was directly related to trade, and extend the duration of financial benefits so that workers can more easily take advantage of educational opportunities. A sixfold increase in current TAA expenditure would cost $3 billion a year.

We estimate that less than $75 billion in new federal spending would be more than adequate to launch an ambitious first-stage agenda that included the above steps as well as increased federal aid to counter urban sprawl, promote urban land trusts and affordable urban housing, and provide aid to communities affected by deindustrialization. This is far less than the costs of current policies that degrade and destabilize communities. Indeed, $75 billion is less than 4 percent of projected federal spending for fiscal 2003—and only slightly more than the *initial* estimated costs of the Pentagon's proposed missile defense system.[8]

It is important to recognize that making substantial progress on this agenda does not require directly confronting and overcoming powerful vested interests and passing massive new legislation (as would be the case with a new national health care program and many other oft-proposed progressive policies). To be sure, many of the existing subsidies to corporations we propose cutting or reducing are long entrenched. But no untested, massive new federal bureaucracy needs to be constructed to implement our agenda; in fact, almost all the relevant programs are in place already. What is needed is refinement and expansion. We believe it is important to articulate how the federal government could move—with a relatively minor shift of priorities that builds upon prior precedent—to dramatically expand support for community economic stability. On the other hand, we recognize that in the immediate future, most new innovation and experimentation in stabilizing communities economically are likely to develop—and should be supported—at the state and local levels.

TOWARD A NEW POLITICS OF PLACE

Moving a new policy agenda to the next level of development is not simply a question of providing rational arguments or pointing out (as so many have done) the flaws and waste inherent in current policies. A place-based agenda can move forward only if there is visible, vocal political support on behalf of using a modest portion of the extraordinary wealth of this country to secure the underpinnings of the neighborhoods, towns, cities, and regions where people live. While this agenda violates extreme free market dogma, we believe the goal of stabilizing communities has a commonsense appeal that cuts across traditional ideological divisions. In fact, many of the most promising institutional developments we have documented in this volume, from the emergence of large-scale employee ownership to the establishment of city-owned enterprises, have garnered support from conservative leaders and elected officials, as well as those on the political left and center.

Although the war on terror has temporarily clouded politics, we believe that there is a long term basis for a broad-based and steadily expanding political coalition focused on issues of community economic stability.

The last five years have seen increasing opposition to state- and local-level job chasing (and corporate welfare in general), local-level mobilization against sprawl and the Wal-Martization of America nationwide, and mass protest and sustained activism against corporate- led globalization and its representative institutions (the WTO, World Bank, etc.). Each of the movements involved in such efforts has aimed to exercise civic control to shape political-economic policies and institutions in a manner that respects local communities and their residents. The triple threat to American communities, in other words, also points to the possibility of a triple alliance on behalf of community economic stability. Members of such an alliance could include not only antisprawl, antisubsidy, and anticorporate globalization activists but also many local business people and the hundreds of thousands of Americans now directly involved in building place-based economic institutions. We believe an alliance aimed at promoting community economic stability could also attract the attention and participation of some of the millions of Americans who, while concerned about the loss of community and excessive corporate power, have nonetheless remained on the sidelines because they have not as yet seen a way to make a constructive political response to the threats facing American communities.[9]

Indeed, a place-based economic policy agenda offers multiple ways for citizens to get involved in bringing economic change to life. Implementing such an agenda would surely require support and activity by advocacy groups and traditional citizens' organizations as well as support from top elected officials. But it also would benefit from the direct participation of citizens who wish not only to lobby for change but also to take steps themselves to build place-based economic institutions in their own locality. Citizens who push for employee takeovers of firms that threaten to leave, support the efforts of a community development corporation to create local jobs, join a community-supported agriculture organization, help form a land trust, or participate in any number of related activities all make a concrete contribution to the long-term goal of making economic stability a reality in America's communities. In short, citizens can participate in constructing economically secure communities not only through traditional means of strictly political participation, but also through their own *direct* participation in place-based economic institutions (participation that would, not incidentally, also help build or rebuild networks of social capital and stronger feelings of community and place in general).

In some instances, moreover, first steps toward a general community stability agenda can be taken even in the absence of local institutional change. This is because community stability policies often provide an opportunity to capture resources that are literally being wasted, such as abandoned buildings, unused public facilities, and vacant land in deteriorated urban neighborhoods. Policies to put such resources to use offer opportunities for a payoff to community-based groups as well as business-oriented groups, making possible a broad-based local political coalition on behalf of specific measures that bring uncaptured resources into use. Michigan State University political scientist B. Jeffrey Reno has pointed to a telling example of this phenomenon: the Michigan Urban Homestead Act, signed by Republican governor John Engler in July 1999, as well as companion legislation altering Michigan's "tax reversion" process. The two bills accelerated the process by which abandoned properties on which no taxes have been paid revert to the state, and then allowed low-income households to obtain the unused land for just $1. The intended result is more affordable housing, a positive impact on real estate values in neighborhoods less scarred by dilapidated structures (thereby helping local real estate groups), and an increase in tax revenues for the state; the final bill passed overwhelmingly in the Michigan legislature.[10] While there are limits to how far strategies for capturing wasted resources can be pushed, the Michigan example shows that commonsense measures to make use of currently wasted infrastructure are capable of gaining broad-based political support, starting now.

As we look to the future, the possibility of direct—not simply political—participation in building place-based economic institutions is, we believe, critical. The common depiction of Americans now in their twenties and early thirties is that of a generation uniquely apolitical, a generation overwhelmingly consumed with their private lives and skeptical about involvement in public life. But one striking fact consistently borne out by research into the civic and social habits of Americans cuts strongly against that picture: Volunteerism among young Americans has increased sharply in recent years. The number of college freshmen volunteering at least an hour a week increased by over fifty percent between 1987 and 1998.[11]

That simple fact—like the outpouring of civic support in response to the September 11, 2001, World Trade Center attack—should remind us that Americans, young and old, are not devoid of social conscience or the capacity to care about their communities. What has been missing are ways to translate the wish to help others into a coherent community-building agenda. National political parties no longer even attempt to offer such a translation or pretend that their policy agendas will solve substantial community problems.

In our view, working to achieve community economic stability—and at the same time reconstructing the basis for a vigorous democracy, starting at the local level—is a purpose that may one day be capable of helping build the basis of a far more powerful, broader social movement.

A social movement committed to valuing place and community necessarily would encompass both locally minded action to root jobs in particular geo-graphic locations as well as advocacy on behalf of broader state and federal policies and redesigning the rules of the international economy. The agenda we have proposed also connects local institutional seeds planted and nurtured by over thirty years of development at the grassroots level with the powerful critique of corporate-led globalization espoused by many important public groups. Our goal has been to sketch a constructive set of policies aimed, on one hand, at containing the triple threat to American communities posed by globalization, internal capital mobility, and suburban sprawl and, on the other hand, at taking a range of positive steps to strengthen community stability directly. Our hope is that those concerned with community, strengthening particular communities, and a reenergized vision of democracy in the United States will find this primer a useful guide as the next generation of policy development, institutional innovation, and movement building goes forward in the first, foundational quarter of the twenty-first century.

APPENDIX: RESOURCES FOR REBUILDING

COMMUNITY-BASED AGRICULTURE

AMERICAN COMMUNITY GARDENING ASSOCIATION

100 N. 20th St., 5th Floor
Philadelphia, PA 19103
(215) 988-8785
Fax: (215) 988-8810
E-mail: smccabe@pennhort.org
Web: http://www.communitygarden.org

The American Community Gardening Association is a nonprofit membership organization that supports community gardening practices through technical assistance, outreach, and state and local-level networking.

COMMITTEE FOR SUSTAINABLE AGRICULTURE

406 Main St., #313
Watsonville, CA 95076
(831) 763-2111
Fax: (831) 763-2112
Web: http://www.csa-efc.org
The Committee for Sustainable Agriculture is a nonprofit educational organization that seeks to promote ecologically sound agriculture through the exchange of ideas at conferences and agricultural fairs.

CSA OF NORTH AMERICA

Indian Line Farm, Box 57
Jug End Rd.
Great Barrington, MA 01230
(413) 528-4374
Web: http://www.umass.edu/umext/csa

CSA of North America is one of the nation's leading supporters of community-supported agriculture, the practice of linking local farmers with consumers in their area in support of local food production and self-sufficiency.

COMMUNITY ALLIANCE WITH FAMILY FARMERS

P.O. Box 363
Davis, CA 95617-0363
(530) 756-8518
Fax: (530) 756-7857
Web: http://www.caff.org

The Community Alliance with Family Farmers is a nonprofit member/activist organization promoting family-scale and community-based agriculture through political, educational, and grassroots activist campaigns.

COMMUNITY FOOD SECURITY COALITION

P.O. Box 209
Venice, CA 90294
(310) 822-5410
Fax: (310) 822-1440
E-mail: asfisher@aol.com
Web: http://www.foodsecurity.org

The Community Food Security Coalition works to ensure the nutrition of those in need through community-based agriculture.

NATIONAL COOPERATIVE BUSINESS ASSOCIATION

1401 New York Ave., NW, Suite 1100
Washington, DC 20005
(202) 638-6222
Fax: (202) 638-1374
E-mail: ncba@ncba.org
Web: http://www.cooperative.org

The National Cooperative Business Association is a trade association that represents cooperatives in a wide variety of fields, including agricultural cooperatives, through education, training, technical assistance, and advocacy.

ROCKY MOUNTAIN FARMERS UNION

10800 East Bethany Dr.
Aurora, CO 80014
(303) 752-5800
Fax: (303) 752-5810
Web: http://www.rmfu.org

The Rocky Mountain Farmers Union is a grassroots advocacy organization dedicated to strengthening diverse rural economies in the Rocky Mountain region. Representing both farmers and rural citizens, RMFU provides market research and technical assistance to producer-owned cooperatives and supports the development of value-added agricultural-based products.

THE URBAN AGRICULTURE NETWORK
1711 Lamont St., NW
Washington, DC 20010
(202) 483-8130
Fax: (202) 986-6732
Web: http://www.cityfarmer.org/tuan.html

TUAN is a nonprofit corporation founded in response to the increase in persistent hunger in urban areas in both poor and rich countries. The network focuses on research and the promotion of urban farming, with an emphasis on low-income communities.

COMMUNITY DEVELOPMENT CORPORATIONS

COASTAL ENTERPRISES, INC.
36 Water St., P.O. Box 268
Wiscasset, ME 04578
(207) 882-7552
Fax: (207) 882-7308
Web: http://www.ceimaine.org

Coastal Enterprises is a nonprofit organization dedicated to helping residents of Maine and nearby communities, particularly those with low incomes, reach an adequate and equitable standard of living, learning, and working. The organization works to accomplish its goals through policy research and development, mobilizing public and private resources, and increasing public awareness.

ENTERPRISE FOUNDATION
10227 Wincopin Cir., Suite 500
Columbia, MD 21044
(410) 964-1230
Fax: (410) 964-1918
E-mail: mail@enterprisefoundation.org
Web: http://www.enterprisefoundation.org

The Enterprise Foundation is a nonprofit community development and housing organization that works through a national network of more than 1,200 organizations to provide community development in areas such as employment and housing for low-income individuals and neighborhoods.

LOCAL INITIATIVES SUPPORT CORPORATION
773 3rd Ave, 8th Floor
New York, NY 10017
(212) 455-9800
Fax: (212) 682-5929
E-mail: josh@liscnet.org
Web: http://www.liscnet.org

The Local Initiatives Support Coalition works to foster the growth and development of community development corporations (CDCs) with public, private, and nonprofit organizations by helping to channel grants and technical support to some of the nation's most distressed areas.

MOUNTAIN ASSOCIATION FOR COMMUNITY ECONOMIC DEVELOPMENT
433 Chestnut St.
Berea, KY 40403
(606) 986-2373
E-mail: breed@maced.org
Web: http://www.maced.org

MACED is a regional organization serving communities in Kentucky and the Central Appalachian region. Services offered include the Business Development Program, which helps to finance job-creating enterprises, particularly for those at lower income levels. Other programs are designed to promote entrepreneurial activity and sustainable development throughout the region.

NATIONAL COMMUNITY DEVELOPMENT INITIATIVE

330 West 108th St., Suite 1
New York, NY 10025
(212) 662-6650
Fax: (212) 662-1369
E-mail: ncdi@ncdi.org
Web: http://www.ncdi.org

NCDI provides financial and technical support to nonprofit CDCs to improve economically distressed inner-city neighborhoods. It creates a mechanism through which major corporations, foundations, and the federal government can invest in the revitalization of urban neighborhoods.

NATIONAL CONGRESS FOR COMMUNITY ECONOMIC DEVELOPMENT

1030 15th St., NW, Suite 325
Washington, DC 20005
(202) 289-9020
Fax: (202) 289-7051
Web: http://www.ncced.org

The National Congress for Community Economic Development is the trade association for the Community Development Corporation industry, representing more than 3,600 CDCs nationally through research, policy analysis, and advocacy.

COMMUNITY DEVELOPMENT, MAINSTREAM: INFORMATION SOURCES

COMMITTEE FOR ECONOMIC DEVELOPMENT

2000 L St., NW, Suite 700
Washington, DC 20036
(202) 296-5860
Fax: (202) 223-0776
E-mail: charlie.kolb@ced.org
Web: http://www.ced.org

The Committee for Economic Development (CED) is a nonpartisan organization that provides business and educational leaders with research and policy recommendations in the areas of economic and social issues such as budget reform, school reform, and global markets.

THE FANNIE MAE FOUNDATION

4000 Wisconsin Ave., NW
North Tower, Suite 1
Washington, DC 20016
(202) 274-8000
Web: http://www.fanniemaefoundation.org/

The Fannie Mae Foundation publishes numerous journals and periodicals on the subjects of affordable housing and community development.

INTERNATIONAL CITY/COUNTY MANAGEMENT ASSOCIATION

777 North Capitol St., NE, Suite 500
Washington, DC 20002
(202) 289-4262
Fax: (202) 962-3500
Web: http://www.icma.org

The International City/County Management Association is a professional and educational organization that represents local government administrators throughout the United States and the world. Membership services include policy research and analysis, networking, workshops, and symposiums as well as online research services.

INTERNATIONAL ECONOMIC DEVELOPMENT COUNCIL

734 15th St., NW, Suite 900
Washington, DC 20005
(202) 223-7800
E-mail: mail@urbandevelopment.com
Web: http://iedconline.org

Established via a merger of the Council of Urban Economic Development (CUED) and the American Economic Development Association (AEDC), the International Economic Development Council (IEDC) is a large membership organization for economic and community development professionals. It provides resources such as information, research, and technical assistance to local development specialists in both the public and private sectors.

NATIONAL ASSOCIATION OF COUNTIES

440 1st St, NW, Suite 800
Washington, DC 20001
(202) 393-6226
Fax: (202) 393-2630
Web: http://www.naco.org

The National Association of Counties is a national organization that represents county governments. Services for participating counties include legislative analysis and research, technical and public affairs assistance, and advocacy.

NATIONAL ASSOCIATION OF DEVELOPMENT ORGANIZATIONS

400 North Capitol St., NW, Suite 390
Washington, DC 20001
(202) 624-7806
Fax: (202) 624-8813
E-mail: nado@sso.org
Web: http://www.nado.org

The National Association of Development Organizations is a public interest group that provides a variety of services for regional development organizations across the United States, including training, advocacy, and research in support of a regional approach to economic development.

NATIONAL ASSOCIATION OF STATE DEVELOPMENT AGENCIES

750 1st St., NE, #710
Washington, DC 20002
(202) 408-7014
Fax: (202) 898-1312
E-mail: mconte@nasda.com
Web: http://www.nasda.com

The National Association of State Development Agencies (NASDA) is a national, nonprofit trade association that provides members with a wide variety of training services, workshops, technical assistance, and data analysis in the area of

economic development. Members come from economic development agencies across the country as well as from public, private, and nonprofit enterprises.

NATIONAL DEVELOPMENT COUNCIL

51 East 42nd St.
New York, NY 10017
(212) 682-1106
Web: http://www.ndc-online.org

The National Development Council is a nonprofit organization that provides training and development services to the public, private, and nonprofit sectors to design economic development and affordable housing programs throughout the country.

NATIONAL LEAGUE OF CITIES

1301 Pennsylvania Ave., NW, Suite 550
Washington, DC 20004-1763
(202) 626-3000
E-mail: pa@nlc.org
Web: http://www.nlc.org

The National League of Cities was founded in 1924 as a representative organization for America's cities. The NLC has since expanded to include over 18,000 municipal members. Through a variety of programs NLC works to educate and assist both government officials and public servants in their capacity as policymakers.

U.S. CONFERENCE OF MAYORS

1620 I St., NW
Washington, DC 20006
(202) 293-7330
E-mail: info@usmayors.org
Web: http://www.usmayors.org

As the official organization of cities with over 30,000 inhabitants, the U.S. Conference of Mayors contributes to the development of national urban policy. Each of the more than 1,000 member-municipalities is represented by its mayor. In adopting policy positions, the conference helps make federal officials aware of the concerns and needs of urban areas.

U.S. DEPARTMENT OF HOUSING AND URBAN DEVELOPMENT (PD&R)

P.O. Box 6091
Rockville, MD 20849
(800) 483-2209
E-mail: huduser@aspensys.com
Web: http://www.huduser.org

The Office of Policy Development and Research (PD&R) of the U.S. Department of Housing and Urban Development (HUD) sponsors HUD USER, an information service that provides data, research reports, and policy analysis relating to issues of housing and community development.

COMMUNITY DEVELOPMENT, PROGRESSIVE: INFORMATION SOURCES

CENTER FOR COMMUNITY CHANGE

1000 Wisconsin Ave., NW
Washington, DC 20007
(202) 342-0567
Fax: (202) 333-5462
Web: http://www.communitychange.org

The Center for Community Change provides research, technical assistance, networking, and coalition building in an effort to support grassroots organizations that foster community development.

CENTER FOR NEIGHBORHOOD TECHNOLOGY

2125 W. North Ave.
Chicago, IL 60647
(773) 278-4800
Fax: (773) 278-3840
E-mail: info@cnt.org
Web: http://www.cnt.org

The Center for Neighborhood Technology is a nonprofit organization that promotes ecologically responsible economic development practices through research, advocacy, publications, and education in areas such as transportation, sprawl, and community ownership.

CENTER FOR POLICY ALTERNATIVES

1875 Connecticut Ave., NW
Washington, DC 20009
(202) 387-6030
Fax: (202) 387-8529
E-mail: cfpa@capaccess.org
Web: http://www.cfpa.org

The CPA is a nonprofit, nonpartisan public policy and leadership development organization dedicated to arriving at community-based solutions to problems facing family and community. Areas of research focus include sustainable economic and community-based development, increased civic participation, and resource preservation and renewal.

COMMUNITY INFORMATION EXCHANGE

1029 Vermont Ave., NW, Suite 710
Washington, D.C.
(202) 628-2981
Fax: (202) 783-1485
E-mail: cie@comminfoexch.org
Web: http://www.igc.org/ifps/casestud/banking/cie.htm

The Community Information Exchange provides research for community-based organizations to foster local revitalization in many areas including community business development, environmental concerns, and low-income housing.

CORPORATION FOR ENTERPRISE DEVELOPMENT

777 North Capitol St., NE
Washington, DC 20036
(202) 408-9788
Web: http://www.cfed.org

The Corporation for Enterprise Development works to promote asset-building strategies for both distressed individuals and communities as a way to ensure a sustainable economy accessible to all segments of the community. CED provides economic policy design, research, and analysis services as well.

ECONOMIC POLICY INSTITUTE
1660 L St., NW, Suite 1200
Washington, DC 20036
(202) 775-8810
Fax: (202) 775-0819
E-mail: economic@cais.com
Web: http://www.epinet.org

EPI is a nonpartisan think tank that fosters discussion in economic policy matters and aims to strengthen political participation. EPI provides analysis and research in areas such as economics, globalization, sustainable economies, labor markets, and living standards, with a focus on low- and middle-income families. Findings are made available to lawmakers and the public alike.

INSTITUTE FOR LOCAL SELF-RELIANCE
2425 18th St., NW
Washington, DC 20009
(202) 232-4108
Web: http://www.ilsr.org

The Institute for Local Self-Reliance provides research, information, and resources for those interested in the promotion of environmentally responsible fiscal and economic practices. Emphasis is placed on maximization of available local resources in the development of sustainable, local economies. (Also see the ILSR's New Rules Project under "Local Ownership Category.")

INSTITUTE FOR POLICY STUDIES
733 15th St., NW, Suite 1020
Washington, DC 20005
(202) 234-9382
Web: http://www.ips-dc.org

The Institute for Policy Studies (IPS) is a progressive think tank working to create a more responsible society centered around the values social and economic justice and peace. IPS runs four programs in support of this goal: Global Economy, Paths for the 21st Century, Sustainable Communities, and Peace & Security.

NATIONAL ECONOMIC DEVELOPMENT AND LAW CENTER
2201 Broadway, Suite 815
Oakland, CA 94612
(510) 251-2600
Fax: (510) 251-0600
E-mail: nedlcsearch@igc.org
Web: http://www.nedlc.org

The National Economic Development and Law Center (NEDLC) is a resource organization dedicated to addressing the needs of low-income persons. NEDLC's three branches focus on the needs of children and families, jobs and income, and community infrastructure. Through collaborations with outside organizations, NEDLC provides both legal and economic research and resources for those local groups working for the economic and social advancement of their respective communities.

NEIGHBORHOOD REINVESTMENT CORPORATION
1325 G St., NW, Suite 800
Washington, DC 20005
(202) 220-2300
Fax: (202) 376-2600
E-mail: nrti@nw.org
Web: http://www.nw.org

The Neighborhood Reinvestment Corporation is a nonprofit organization that builds and supports networks of residents and public, private, and nonprofit organizations to revitalize declining neighborhoods.

PLANNERS NETWORK
Pratt Graduate Center for Planning and the Environment
379 DeKalb Ave.
Brooklyn, NY 11205
(718) 636-3461
Fax: (718) 636-3709
E-mail: pr-net@pratt.edu
Web: http://www.plannersnetwork.org

The Planners Network is an association of planning professionals, academics, and students interested in achieving ecological sustainability and economic and social justice through responsible rural and urban planning policies.

PREAMBLE CENTER
2040 S St., NW
Washington, DC 20009
(202) 265-3263
Fax: (202) 265-3647
E-mail: preamble@rtk.net
Web:.http://www.preamble.org/

The Preamble Center, a public policy think tank, seeks to expand democracy by opposing the power of multinational corporations and the ideology of the market, working with organizations to build a movement toward this end.

RESOURCE RENEWAL INSTITUTE
Fort Mason Center, Bldg. A
San Francisco, CA 94123
(415) 928-3774
Fax: (415) 928-6529
E-mail: info@rri.org
Web: http://www.rri.org

RRI provides research, analysis and technical assistance to those communities seeking to develop plans to promote long-term environmental sustainability (Green Plans) that rely on a multi-faceted collaboration of private, public and non-profit entities.

ROCKY MOUNTAIN INSTITUTE
1739 Snowmass Creek Rd.
Snowmass, CO 81654-9199
(970) 927-3851
Fax: (970) 927-3420
E-mail: simon@rmi.org
Web: http://www.rmi.org

The Rocky Mountain Institute is a research foundation that focuses on sustainable resource policy in areas such as energy, transportation, green development, economic renewal, and forest management.

E. F. SCHUMACHER SOCIETY
140 Jug End Rd.
Great Barrington, MA 01230
(413) 528-1737
E-mail: efssociety@aol.com
Web: http://www.schumachersociety.org

The E. F. Schumacher Society is dedicated to achieving the goals of economic and ecological sustainability through the principle of decentralism. In support of these aims, the Schumacher Society offers lectures, educational programs, and extensive research resources.

COMMUNITY DEVELOPMENT: UNIVERSITY-BASED INFORMATION SOURCES

CENTER ON WISCONSIN STRATEGY
University of Wisconsin, Madison
1180 Observatory Dr.
Madison, WI 53706
(608) 263-3889
Fax: (608) 262-9046
E-mail: cows-info@cows.org
Web: http://www.cows.org

The Center on Wisconsin Strategy is a research and policy analysis program at the University of Wisconsin of Madison. COWS provides research, policy analysis, feasibility studies, and technical assistance in the area of high-road economic alternatives that provide for worker-friendly, high-wage jobs in the state of Wisconsin.

COMMUNITY DEVELOPMENT PROGRAM
225 Gentry Hall
University of Missouri, Columbia
Columbia, MO 65201
(573) 882-8393
Fax: (573) 882-5127
E-mail: wadej@missouri.edu
Web: http://ssu.agri.missouri.edu/commdev

The Community Development Program at the University of Missouri at Columbia combines outreach, education and research, both within and outside of the university, to promote community viability throughout Missouri. CDP services are available to public, private, and nonprofit organizations interested in promoting community development.

COMMUNITY DEVELOPMENT RESEARCH CENTER

Graduate School of Management and Urban Policy
New School for Social Research
72 5th Ave., 7th Floor
New York, NY 10011
(212) 229-5415
www.newschool.edu/milano/cdrc.htm

The Community Development Research Center provides research, analysis, evaluation, and publications about community-revitalizing practices and policies and their effect on urban neighborhoods. A wide range of topics are evaluated, including local and federal policies and community development corporations.

COMMUNITY AND ECONOMIC DEVELOPMENT PROGRAM

Center for Urban Affairs
Michigan State University
1801 West Main St.
Lansing, MI 48915-1097
(517) 353-9555
Fax: (517) 484-0068
Web: http://www.msu.edu/~cua/

The Community and Economic Development Program at Michigan State University provides research, training, and technical assistance to community-based organizations throughout Michigan. Among other activities, CEDP has developed the Community Income and Expenditure Model, which allows communities to track income and expenditure flows.

THE DEMOCRACY COLLABORATIVE

1241 Tydings Hall
University of Maryland
College Park, MD 20742
(301) 405-9266
Fax: (301) 314-2533
Web: http://www.democracycollaborative.org

The Democracy Collaborative brings together an international consortium of more than twenty of the world's leading academic centers and citizen engagement organizations, hosted and sponsored by the University of Maryland. Through programs of theoretical and practical research, teachings, training, and community action, the collaborative works to strengthen democracy and civil society locally, nationally, and globally.

GREAT CITIES INSTITUTE

University of Illinois, Chicago
412 South Peoria St., Suite 400
Chicago, IL 60607-7067
(312) 996-8700
Fax: (312) 996-8933
E-mail: gcities@uic.edu
Web: http://www.uic.edu/cuppa/gci

The Great Cities Institute is a program of the University of Illinois at Chicago. GCI is an interdisciplinary research program designed to disseminate information on urban development. Areas of research focus include metropolitan sustainability and community/human development.

RURAL POLICY RESEARCH INSTITUTE

135 Mumford Hall
University of Missouri, Columbia
Columbia, MO 65211
(573) 882-0316
E-mail: lchristopher@rupri.org
Web: http://www.rupri.org/

The Rural Policy Research Institute conducts research and facilitates public dialogue with a focus on the effects of policy on rural areas. RUPRI involves researchers, practitioners, and analysts from numerous other universities, research institutes, governmental units, and other organizations.

COMMUNITY FINANCE

CATHOLIC CAMPAIGN FOR HUMAN DEVELOPMENT
3211 4th St., NE
Washington, DC 20017
(202) 541-3000
E-mail: nccbuscc.org@cchd.org
Web: http://www.nccbuscc.org/cchd.org

The Catholic Campaign for Human Development, the social justice program of the US Catholic bishops, is a loan organization designed to fund low-income groups working for institutional change and providing assistance to worker-ownership enterprises, as well as other economic development projects within low-income communities.

COALITION OF COMMUNITY DEVELOPMENT FINANCIAL INSTITUTIONS
Public Ledger Bldg., Suite 572
620 Chestnut St.
Philadelphia, PA 19106-3405
(215) 923-5363
Fax: (215) 923-4755
E-mail: cdfi@cdfi.org
Web: http://www.cdfi.org

The Coalition of Community Development Financial Institutions represents more than 350 CDFIs throughout the United States, providing networking and information to the CDFI industry. The coalition also serves as an advocate for community development financial institutions by providing information and resources to lawmakers, media, and the general public in order to increase financial and public support of CDFIs.

COMMUNITY DEVELOPMENT VENTURE CAPITAL ALLIANCE
330 7th Avenue, 19th Floor
New York, NY 10001
(212) 594-6747
E-mail: cmayo@cdvca.org
Web: http://www.cdvca.org

The CDVCA is a membership organization that works to provide members with technical assistance, information, and resources to maximize the implementation of community development venture capital funds in distressed communities throughout the world.

FINANCIAL MARKETS CENTER
P.O. Box 334
Philmont, VA 20131
(540) 338-7754
Fax: (540) 338-7757
Web: http://www.fmcenter.org

The Financial Markets Center is a nonprofit organization that provides research, information, and analysis on the financial markets, the Federal Reserve System, and the impact of their policies. Information provided by the FM Center is available for use by the public, private, and nonprofit sectors alike in an effort to increase the Federal Reserve System's level of accountability to the public.

FOUNDATION FOR INTERNATIONAL COMMUNITY ASSISTANCE
1101 14th St., NW, 11th Floor
Washington, DC 20005
(202) 682-1510
Fax: (202) 682-1535
E-mail: finca@villagebanking.org
Web: http://www.villagebanking.org

The Foundation for International Community Assistance is an organization dedicated to fighting poverty through the creation of microcredit programs known as "village banks," or peer groups of approximately fifty persons who receive capital loans for self-employment.

NATIONAL COMMUNITY CAPITAL ASSOCIATION

620 Chestnut St., Suite 572
Philadelphia, PA 19106
(215) 923-4754
Fax: (215) 923-4755
E-mail: ncca@communitycapital.org
Web: http://www.communitycapital.org

The National Community Capital Association is a membership organization comprised of CDFIs, CDCs, community development loan funds, microenterprise funds, and community development venture capital funds from across the United States. NCCA provides members with a variety of resources, including networking services, workshops, training, and publications.

NATIONAL COMMUNITY REINVESTMENT COALITION

733 15th St., NW, Suite 540
Washington, DC 20005
(202) 628-8866
Fax: (202) 628-9800
E-mail: hn1748@handsnet.org
Web: http://www.ffhsj.com/fairlend/ncrc.htm

The National Community Reinvestment Coalition is a membership organization that promotes community reinvestment and the necessary public and financial support to increase capital flow to underserved areas. Members participate in workshops, lectures, conferences, and a variety of outreach activities designed to realize these objectives.

NATIONAL COOPERATIVE BANK

1725 I St., NW, Suite 600
Washington, DC 20006
(800) 955-9622
E-mail: webmaster@ncb.org
Web: http://www.ncb.com

The National Cooperative Bank provides financial services to cooperative organizations. Services offered include real estate, small business, and commercial lending programs as well as a variety of community development services.

NATIONAL FEDERATION OF COMMUNITY DEVELOPMENT CREDIT UNIONS

120 Wall St., 10th Floor
New York, NY 10005-3902
(212) 809-1850
E-mail: nfcdcu@pipeline.com
Web: http://www.natfed.org

The National Federation of Community Development Credit Unions serves as an advocacy organization on behalf of CDCUs. Through outreach and training, NFCDCU actively promotes the advancement of community development credit unions throughout the nation.

JESSE SMITH NOYES FOUNDATION

6 East 39th St., 12th Floor
New York, NY 10016
(212) 684-6577
Fax: (212) 689-6549
E-mail: noyes@noyes.org
Web: http://www.noyes.org

The Jesse Smith Noyes Foundation is dedicated to promoting sustainable communities and individuals by making grants primarily in the fields of environmental and reproductive rights as well as to those individuals and organizations seeking to promote community-sustaining, economically and environmentally just practices in their communities.

SELF-HELP
(Center for Community Self-Help)

301 Main St.
Durham, NC 27701
(919) 956-4400
Web: http://www.self-help.org

Self Help is a model of development banking that provides direct lending to low-income communities and individuals, particularly women, minorities, and rural residents, throughout North Carolina.

SELF HELP ASSOCIATION FOR A REGIONAL ECONOMY
140 Jug End Rd.
Great Barrington, MA 01230
(413) 528-1737

The Self Help Association for a Regional Economy is a nonprofit organization that promotes local self-reliance by helping local businesses secure loans to ensure a more economically sustainable community through the SHARE credit fund.

SHOREBANK CORPORATION
7054 S. Jeffrey Blvd.
Chicago, IL 60649
(773) 288-1000
Fax: (773) 493-6609
E-mail: info@shorebankcorp.com
Web: http://www.shorebankcorp.com

The Shorebank Corporation is the parent corporation of South Shore Bank, the flagship community development bank in Chicago. Today it also operates development banks in Cleveland, Detroit, the Upper Peninsula of Michigan, and the Pacific Northwest.

WOODSTOCK INSTITUTE
407 S. Dearborn St., Suite 550
Chicago, IL 60605
(312) 427-8070
E-mail: woodstck@wwa.com
Web: http://www.woodstockinst.org

The Chicago-based Woodstock Institute works at both the grassroots and national levels to promote community reinvestment and economic sustainability through technical assistance, education, and research in areas such as CRA, fair lending policies, financial and insurance services, CDFIs, and small-business lending.

WORKING CAPITAL
56 Roland St., Suite 300
Boston, MA 02129
(866) 245-0783
E-mail: wcapmgelb@aol.com
Web: http://www.workingcapital.org

Working Capital is a nonprofit microlending organization that provides direct aid in the form of loans, as well as business and technical support for microenterprise development.

WORLD COUNCIL OF CREDIT UNIONS
805 15th St., NW, Suite 300
Washington, DC 20005-2207
(202) 682-5990
Web: http://www.woccu.org

The World Council of Credit Unions is a representative organization for credit unions around the world. Through publications, meetings, and technical assistance, WCCU works to extend credit unions as viable tools of economic development.

COMMUNITY LAND

INSTITUTE FOR COMMUNITY ECONOMICS
57 School St.
Springfield, MA 01105-1331
(413) 746-8660
Fax: (413) 746-8862
E-mail: iceconomics@aol.com
Web: http://www.iceclt.org

The Institute for Community Economics is a nonprofit organization that promotes community land trusts as a tool to support sustainable economic development through its revolving loan fund.

THE LAND INSTITUTE
2440 E. Water Well Rd.
Salina, KS 67401
(785) 823-5376
Fax: (785) 823-8728
E-mail: theland@landinstitute.org
Web: http://www.landinstitute.org

The Land Institute is a nonprofit research organization that provides research in natural-systems agriculture as well as educational opportunities and research in the area of ecologically responsible agricultural practices.

THE LAND TRUST ALLIANCE
1331 H St., NW, Suite 400
Washington, DC 20005
(202) 638-4725
Fax (202) 638-4730
Web: http://www.lta.org

The Land Trust Alliance promotes voluntary land conservation, assisting the efforts of over a thousand land trusts to protect open spaces via direct grants, training, and technical assistance.

LINCOLN INSTITUTE OF LAND POLICY
113 Brattle St.
Cambridge, MA 02138
(617) 661-3016
E-mail: seanc@lincolninst.edu
Web: http://www.lincolninst.edu

The Lincoln Institute of Land Policy is a nonprofit educational organization that provides research, analysis, and education in the areas of land taxation, land markets, and land as common property.

COMMUNITY ORGANIZING, POLITICAL EDUCATION, AND POLITICAL ACTIVISM

ACORN
739 8th St., SE
Washington, DC 20003
(202) 547-2500
Fax: (202) 546-2483
E-mail: dcn@acorn.org/community
Web: http://www.acorn.org

ACORN is a national grassroots organization that seeks to empower low-income communities and individuals by working toward economic and social justice on the local and national levels through community organizing.

CAMPAIGN FOR AMERICA'S FUTURE
1025 Connecticut Ave., NW, Suite 205
Washington, DC 20036
(202) 955-5665
Fax: (202) 955-5606
Email: info@ourfuture.org
Web: http://www.ourfuture.org

The Campaign for America's Future is an organization dedicated to revitalizing a progressive policy agenda, opposing the policy agenda of big-money corporations, and encouraging Americans to debate and discuss economic alternatives. The organization engages citizens, activists, and political leaders through publications, the dissemination of political information, and other innovative activities at the grassroots level.

HIGHLANDER CENTER
1959 Highlander Way
New Market, TN 37820
(423) 933-3443
Fax: (423) 933-3424
E-mail: hrec@igc.apc.org
Web: http://www.hrec.org

The Highlander Center provides resources and assistance, including research, education, and workshops to community organizations struggling with a variety of problems, economic and social, throughout Appalachia and the South.

INDUSTRIAL AREAS FOUNDATION
220 West Kinzie St., 5th Floor
Chicago, IL 60610
(312) 245-9211
Fax: (312) 245-9744
Web: http://www.tresser.com/IAF.htm

The Industrial Areas Foundation was built on the principles and practices of legendary community activist Saul Alinsky. The IAF provides progressive leadership training in organizing and coalition building with faith-based, private, public, and nonprofit institutions.

INTERCOMMUNITY JUSTICE AND PEACE CENTER

215 E. 14th St.
Cincinnati, OH 45210
(513) 579-8547
Fax: (513) 579-0674
Web: http://ijpc-cincinnati.com

The Intercommunity Justice and Peace Center is a faith-based organization dedicated to promoting economic and social justice on a local, national, and global scale. IJPC supports a wide variety of workshops, lectures, and educational and community outreach programs that deal with matters such as women's issues, racial equality, peace, ecology, and economic/social justice.

JOBS WITH JUSTICE

501 3rd St., NW
Washington, DC 20001-2797
(202) 434-1106
Fax: (202) 434-1477
Web: http://www.jwj.org

Jobs with Justice is a national membership coalition of activists and unions seeking to uphold basic worker rights and working conditions across the country through amalgamating individual unions and civic groups on a nationwide scale to empower like-minded activist organizations.

180 MOVEMENT FOR DEMOCRACY AND EDUCATION

31 University Sq.
Madison, WI 53715
(608) 256-7081
Fax: (608) 265-1131
E-mail: clearinghouse@tao.ca
Web: http://www.corporations.org/democracy

180 Movement for Democracy and Education is an organization dedicated to promoting campus activism, equitable education policies, the political empowerment of the student body, and opposition to corporate control of universities through education, networking, organizing, and coordination of direct action campaigns.

PROGRESSIVE CAUCUS, US HOUSE OF REPRESENTATIVES

Bill Goold, Staff Coordinator
213 Cannon HOB
Washington, DC 20515
(202) 225-4115
Web: http://www.bernie.house.gov/pc

The Progressive Caucus of the US House of Representatives is the representative organization of the progressive members of Congress, working to promote progressive views and policies in the House.

CORPORATE SUBSIDIES/ ACCOUNTABILITY

CO-OP AMERICA

1612 K St., NW, Suite 600
Washington, DC 20006
(800) 58-GREEN
E-mail: info@coopamerica.org
Web: http://www.coopamerica.org

Co-op America is a nonprofit organization dedicated to addressing social and environmental problems through a variety of programs, research, and education. Co-op initiatives focus on a wide range of issues including fostering small, environmentally responsible and socially conscious start-up businesses, directing purchasing power toward those enterprises engaging in responsible business and environmental practices, and encouraging corporate responsibility.

GRASSROOTS POLICY PROJECT

2040 S St., NW, Suite 203
Washington, DC 20009
(202) 387-2933
Fax: (202) 234-0891
E-mail: hinsons@rtk.net
Web: http://www.grassrootspolicy.org
Using education, research, and analysis, the Grassroots Policy Project works with activist organizations on both the state and local level to increase grassroots activity and participation in the political process in an effort to promote social and economic justice in the areas of community building, education, government oversight and reform, and corporate accountability.

INSTITUTE ON TAXATION AND ECONOMIC POLICY/GOOD JOBS FIRST

1311 L St., NW
Washington, DC 20005
E-mail: mattg@ctj.org
Web: http://www.ctj.org/itep/index.htm

The Institute on Taxation and Economic Policy is a research and educational organization that focuses on government spending priorities and taxation policies, including corporate subsidies and the effects of current/proposed tax law on various income levels. One of their initiatives, the Good Jobs First Program, serves as a clearinghouse for grassroots organizations across the United States that work to hold corporations receiving economic development incentives accountable for the provision of family-wage jobs.

SUGAR LAW CENTER FOR ECONOMIC AND SOCIAL JUSTICE

645 Griswold St., Suite 1800
Detroit, MI 48226
(313) 962-6540
Fax: (313) 962-4492
Web: http://www.surgarlaw.org

The Sugar Law Center is a national, nonprofit public interest law center founded on the principle that economic and civil rights are inseparable and one cannot exist without the other. The center promotes a concern for economic justice and the rights of the economically disenfranchised through publications and a variety of legal projects.

THE STAKEHOLDER ALLIANCE

733 15th St., NW, Suite 1020
Washington, DC 20005
(202) 234-9382
Fax: (202) 387-7915
E-mail: stakeholder@essential.org
Web: http://www.stakeholderalliance.org

The Stakeholder Alliance is a grassroots organization dedicated to the concept of economic justice by making business accountable to all stakeholders in society.

STUDENT ALLIANCE TO REFORM CORPORATIONS

Dwight Hall
P.O. Box 206253
New Haven, CT 06520
E-mail: starc@corpreform.org
Web: http://www.corpreform.org

The Student Alliance to Reform Corporations is a student movement designed to make corporate policy more socially, economically and environmentally responsible. STARC is a member of 180 Movement for Democracy and Education. (See description under "Community Organizing.")

EMPLOYEE OWNERSHIP

CAPITAL OWNERSHIP GROUP

E-mail: cog@kent.edu
Web: http://cog.kent.edu

The Capital Ownership Group (COG) is an on-line think tank that works to promote the advancement of broad-ownership systems, specifically employee ownership, and the raising of social and wage standards on an international level through policy proposals and advocacy.

**CENTER FOR ECONOMIC AND SOCIAL
JUSTICE**
P.O. Box 40711
Washington, DC 20016
(703) 243-5155
E-mail: thirdway@cesj.org
Web: http://www.cesj.org

The Center for Economic and Social Justice
is a nonprofit, nonpartisan education and
research organization dedicated to promoting economic justice on a global scale by
expanding capital ownership to a broader
segment of society.

**EMPLOYEE STOCK OWNERSHIP PLANS
ASSOCIATION**
1726 M St., NW, Suite 501
Washington, D.C. 20036
(202) 293-2971
Fax: (202) 293-7568
Web: http://www.the-esop-emplowner.org

The ESOP Association is a membership organization composed of companies with
employee ownership and those transitioning
to employee ownership status. This nonprofit organization provides educational
materials and training seminars necessary
for the successful management of
employee-owned companies.

**FOUNDATION FOR ENTERPRISE
DEVELOPMENT**
2020 K St., NW
Washington, DC 20036
(202) 530-8920
Fax: (202) 520-5702
Web: http://www.fed.org

The Foundation for Enterprise Development
is a nonprofit organization that provides
strategies for employee ownership and
equity compensation through research and
technical assistance.

**INDUSTRIAL COOPERATIVE ASSOCIATION
(ICA GROUP)**
1 Harvard St., Suite 200
Brookline, MA 02445
(617) 232-8765
Web: http://www.ica-group.org

The Industrial Cooperative Association (ICA
Group) is a nonprofit organization that
seeks to promote economic stability by providing education and technical assistance to
those organizations seeking to start a
community-based or worker-owned business.

INSTITUTE FOR PUBLIC GOOD
3930 Ivyhill Ave.
Las Vegas, NV 89121
E-mail: ipgmail@aol.com
Web: http://www.publicgood.org

The Institute for Public Good is a nonprofit
organization established to promote civic
participation and responsible citizenship.
Areas of research focus include economic
reform proposals in pursuit of social/eco-
nomic justice and the democratization of
capital ownership.

**NATIONAL CENTER FOR EMPLOYEE
OWNERSHIP**
1736 Franklin St., 8th Floor
Oakland, CA 94612
(510) 208-1300
E-mail: nceo@nceo.org
Web: http://www.nceo.org

NCEO is a research organization dedicated
to advancing worker ownership by providing
information, publications, and research on
employee stock ownership plans (ESOPs).

OHIO EMPLOYEE OWNERSHIP CENTER
Kent State University
309 Franklin Hall
Kent, OH 44242
(330) 672-3028
Fax: (330) 672-4063
E-mail: OEOC@kent.edu
Web: http://www.kent.edu/oeoc/

The Ohio Employee Ownership Center is a nonprofit organization that provides research and technical assistance to those interested in employee ownership, as well as ownership training to established employee-owned businesses.

THE SHARED CAPITALISM INSTITUTE

1266 West Paces Ferry Rd., Suite 284
Atlanta, GA 30327
(404) 386-6643
Fax: (770) 451-4985
E-mail: jeffgates@mindspring.com
Web: http://www.sharedcapitalism.org

The Shared Capitalism Institute prepares policy papers and educational materials to inform public debates about the role of economic inclusion in addressing key social issues, with a heavy focus on promoting employee ownership.

WORKER OWNERSHIP INSTITUTE

5 Gateway Center, 7th Floor
Pittsburgh, PA 15522
(412) 562-2254/55
Fax: (412) 562-6978
E-mail: webmaster@workerownership.org
Web: http://www.workerownership.org

The Worker Ownership Institute provides a forum for both management and labor from worker-owned firms to educate and interact with one another, as well as training programs in areas such as collective bargaining, financial training, and labor-management committees.

FEDERAL SPENDING

CENTER ON BUDGET AND POLICY PRIORITIES

820 1st St., NE, Suite 510
Washington, DC 20002
(202) 408-1080
Fax: (202) 408-1056
E-mail: bazie@cbpp.org
Web: http://www.cbpp.org

The Center on Budget and Policy Priorities is a research organization that provides analysis on a wide range of policy issues including state and federal fiscal policy and its effects on low- and middle-income citizens.

GREEN SCISSORS CAMPAIGN

c/o Friends of the Earth
1025 Vermont Ave., NW, Suite 300
Washington, DC 20005
(202) 783-7400
Fax: (202) 783-0444
Web: http://www.foe.org

Through their annual report, the Green Scissors Campaign serves as an advocacy organization designed to eliminate irresponsible government spending by targeting those federal spending programs that are environmentally harmful.

OMB WATCH

1742 Connecticut Ave., NW
Washington, DC 20009
(202) 234-8494
Fax: (202) 234-8584
E-mail: ombwatch@rtk.net
Web: http://www.ombwatch.org

OMB Watch tracks the activities of the White House Office of Budget and Management (OMB). In particular, OMB Watch focuses on policy that deals with nonprofits, nonprofit advocacy, budget performance evaluations, and regulatory accountability.

GLOBALIZATION

CENTER FOR ECONOMIC AND POLICY RESEARCH

1015 18th St., NW
Washington, DC 20036
(202) 822-1180
Fax: (202) 822-1199
E-mail: cepr@cepr.net
Web: http://www.cepr.net

The Center for Economic and Policy Research specializes in globalization and international trade and finance, Social Security, and other issues related to the federal budget. The CEPR strives to present information surrounding these issues in an accurate and understandable manner (primarily through publications) so that the public can decide on policy options.

ECONOMIC POLICY INSTITUTE
See description under "Community Development, Progressive: Information Sources."

GLOBAL PUBLIC POLICY PROJECT
1610 Crittenden St., NW
Washington, DC 20036
(202) 291-7521
E-mail: GPP@globalpublicpolicy.net
Web: http://globalpublicpolicy.net

The Global Public Policy Project is part of "Visioning the UN," a four-part program sponsored by the United Nations. The goal of the GPPP is to prepare a report focusing on the implementation of global economic policy networks and how such networks, including participants from the public, private, and nonprofit sectors, can provide solutions to the wide variety of challenges that globalization presents.

INTERNATIONAL FORUM ON GLOBALIZATION
The Thoreau Center for Sustainability
1009 General Kennedy Ave., #2
San Francisco, CA 94129
(415) 561-7650
E-mail: ifg@ifg.org
Web: http://www.ifg.org

The International Forum on Globalization (IFG) was founded in response to the passage of NAFTA in 1994. In an effort to curb the negative effects of globalization, the IFG supports community-stabilizing economic policies through education, programs, publications, and events.

INTERNATIONAL LABOR RIGHTS EDUCATION AND RESEARCH FUND
733 15th St., NW, Suite 920
Washington, DC 20005
(202) 347-4885
E-mail: laborrights@igc.org
Web: http://www.laborrights.org

The International Labor Rights Education and Research Fund is a nonprofit advocacy organization that works to both further international labor rights and ensure compliance of existing labor standards.

THE INSTITUTE FOR POLICY STUDIES
See description under "Community Development, Progressive: Information Sources."

IMPORT SUBSTITUTION

ACENET
See description under "Small Business."

ASSET-BASED COMMUNITY DEVELOPMENT INSTITUTE
Institute for Policy Research
Northwestern University
2040 Sheridan Rd.
Evanston, IL 60208
(847) 491-8711
Fax: (847) 467-4140
Web: http://www.nwu.edu/IPR/abcd.html

The Asset-Based Community Development Institute provides research, training videos, workshops, publications, and consultation services for those interested in capacity-building community development and neighborhood asset mobilization. The institute's work is based on the premise that through mobilizing their own assets, neighborhoods can substitute for imports and become more self-sufficient.

E. F. SCHUMACHER SOCIETY
See description under "Community Development, Progressive: Information Sources."

INTERNATIONAL ECONOMIC INSTITUTIONS AND TRADE REFORM

ALLIANCE FOR RESPONSIBLE TRADE
927 15th St., NW, 4th Floor
Washington, DC 20005
(202) 898-1566
Fax: (202) 898-1612
E-mail: dgap@igc.org
Web: http://www.art-us.org

The Alliance for Responsible Trade is a national coalition that advocates sustainable trade policies in which furthering the cause of human rights, locally rooting capital, and strengthening both environmental and labor rights policies are promoted.

BRETTON WOODS PROJECT
Hamlyn House
Macdonald Rd.
London N19 5PG, United Kingdom
(44) (20) 7561 7546
E-mail: bwref@gn.apc.org
Web: http://www.brettonwoodsproject.org

Through briefings, reports, and a quarterly digest, the Breton Woods Project monitors and critiques IMF and World Bank policies to facilitate the work of nongovernmental organizations concerned with the social, economic, and ecological ramifications of IMF/World Bank practices.

GLOBAL TRADE WATCH
215 Pennsylvania Ave., SE
Washington, DC 20003
(202) 546-4996
Fax: (202) 547-7392
E-mail: lgrund@citizen.org
Web: http://www.tradewatch.org

A division of Public Citizen, Global Trade Watch works to promote the pursuit of environmentally and socially responsible policies by international financial institutions in the areas of government accountability, ecological responsibility, and public health.

50 YEARS IS ENOUGH
3628 12th St., NE
Washington, DC 20017
(202) 463-2265
Fax: (202) 544-9359
E-mail: wb50years@igc.org
Web: http://www.50years.org

50 Years Is Enough is a coalition of over 200 women's, faith-based, policy, justice, youth, labor and development organizations dedicated to reforming international financial institutions to increase their accountability.

HALIFAX INITIATIVE
153 rue Chapel St., Suite 104
Ottawa, Ontario
Canada K1N 7H5
(613) 789-4447
E-mail: halifax@web.net
Web: http://www.halifaxinitiative.org

The Halifax Initiative is a coalition of more than fifty organizations concerned with the practices of international financial institutions. Through advocacy and research, the Halifax Initiative seeks the fundamental reform of international financial institutions in areas such as the development of sustainable economic/environmental policy, the promotion of decentralized decision-making processes, and the cancellation of multilateral debt.

INSTITUTE FOR AGRICULTURE AND TRADE POLICY
2105 1st Ave. S
Minneapolis, MN 55404
(612) 870-0453
Fax: (612) 870-4846
E-mail: iatp-info@iatp.org
Web: http://www.iatp.org

Through coalition building, education, research, and analysis, the Institute for Agriculture and Trade Policy works to promote conservation-based agricultural/trade policies, such as regional trade integration treaties, that support economic sustainability in rural communities.

LOCAL CURRENCY/TIME DOLLARS

ITHACA HOURS
Box 6731
Ithaca, NY 14851
(607) 273-8025
E-mail: ithacahour@aol.com
Web: http://www.ithacahours.org

Ithaca Hours is a long-running local currency program. IthacaHOURS online offers a variety of services for those looking to start their own local currency system.

LANDSMAN COMMUNITY SERVICES
1600 Embleton Crescent
Courtenay, BC V9N 6N8, Canada
Phone (604) 338-0213
E-mail: lcs@mars.ark.com
Web: http://www.gmlets.u-net.com

Landsman Community Services specializes in the creation and implementation of systems of local currency known as LETSystems.

TIME DOLLAR INSTITUTE
5500 39th St., NW
Washington, DC 20015
(202) 686-5200
Fax: (202) 537-5033
E-mail: yeswecan@aol.com
Web: http://www.timedollar.org

Established in 1995, the Time Dollar Institute is a nonprofit organization that helps to foster implementation of Time Dollars initiatives, a volunteer-based system of service exchange.

WOMANSHARE
680 West End Ave.
New York, NY 10002
(212) 662-9746
E-mail: wshare@aol.com

Womanshare is a system of exchange in which the skills and time of the members are used as currency. Members can deposit hours into the Womanshare "bank" and redeem them for the services of other members.

LOCAL OWNERSHIP

BOULDER INDEPENDENT BUSINESS ALLIANCE
1202 Folsom St.
Boulder, CO 80302
(720) 565-3854
E-mail: jeff@boulder-iba.org
Web: http://www.boulder-iba.org

The Boulder Independent Business Alliance (BIBA) is a nonprofit membership organization consisting of locally owned businesses in the Boulder area. Through advocacy, shared advertising, and group purchasing, BIBA is working to strengthen the bond between local business and the community to promote local ownership in Boulder.

NEW RULES PROJECT
Institute for Local Self Reliance
1313 5th St., SE
Minneapolis, MN 55414
(612) 379-3815
E-mail: simona@islr.org
Web: http://www.newrules.org

The New Rules Project, a program of the Institute for Local Self Reliance (see description under "Community Development, Progressive: Information Sources"), provides research, analysis, and education about those factors and policies that support economically sustainable communities, local ownership, and local control in order to promote procommunity policies that reverse the negative effects of globalization.

MICROENTERPRISE

ACCION INTERNATIONAL
56 Roland St., Suite 300
Boston, MA 02129
(617) 625-7080
Fax: (617) 625-7020
E-mail: info@accion.org
Web: http://www.accion.org

Acción International is the nonprofit umbrella organization for microfinance institutions across the United States and Latin America, providing technical assistance, planning, policy research and analysis, and publications to their international network of microfinance affiliates.

ALLIANCE FOR PUBLIC TECHNOLOGY
919 18th St., NW, Suite 900
Washington, DC 20006
(202) 263-2970
Fax: (202)-263-2960
Web: http://www.apt.org

The Alliance for Public Technology is a membership organization composed of various nonprofit groups and individuals concerned with access to affordable and useful information and communication services and technology. Of particular concern to APT is access for those historically left out of the information age, including the elderly, minorities, low-income groups, and people with disabilities.

THE ASPEN INSTITUTE
Economic Opportunity Program
1 Dupont Cir., NW, Suite 700
Washington, DC 20036
(202) 736-5807
Fax: (202) 467-0790
Web: http://www.aspeninstitute.org

The Aspen Institute is a nonprofit organization that, among its many initiatives, facilitates the development of microenterprise in order to generate income and employment in disadvantaged communities through financing and education.

GRAMEEN FOUNDATION, USA
1709 New York Ave., NW, Suite 101
Washington, DC 20006
(202) 543-2636
Fax: (202) 543-7512
E-mail: grameen_foundation@msn.com
Web: http://www.grameenfoundation.org

The Grameen Foundation, USA is a nonprofit organization taking its name from the microcredit movement started in the village of Grameen, Bangladesh. It aims to eliminate poverty in the United States through the creation of microcredit-related institutions and programs.

INSTITUTE FOR SOCIAL AND ECONOMIC DEVELOPMENT
1901 Broadway, Suite 313
Iowa City, IA 52240
(319) 338-2331
Fax: (319) 338-5824
Web: http://www.ised.org

The Institute for Social and Economic Development is a nonprofit organization that seeks to alleviate poverty by providing research, consulting, and technical assistance in the development of microenterprise.

WOMEN'S SELF-EMPLOYMENT PROJECT
20 North Clark St., Suite 400
Chicago, IL 60602
(312) 606-8255
Fax: (312) 606-9215
E-mail: hn1578@handsnet.org
Web: http://www.fieldus.org/directory/records/332.htm

The Women's Self-Employment Project is a community development financial institution designed to promote the economic self-sufficiency of low- and moderate-income women. WSEP services include peer lending networks, entrepreneurial training, and educational seminars.

MUNICIPAL ENTERPRISE

AMERICAN PUBLIC POWER ASSOCIATION
2301 M St., NW
Washington, DC 20037
(202) 467-2900
Fax: (202) 467-2910
Web: http://www.appanet.org

The American Public Power Association is the trade association for publicly owned electric utilities. APPA serves to help keep publicly owned utilities competitive in today's market through publications, networking, and information services.

GLASGOW ELECTRIC PLANT SERVICE DIVISION
P.O. Box 1809
Glasgow, KY 42142
(270) 651-8341
Fax: (270) 651-7572
Web: http://www.glasgow-ky.com/epb/

The Glasgow Electric Plant Board Service Division is a division of the municipally owned power plant in Glasgow, Kentucky. The service division provides consulting services and viability studies to those communities interested in starting a municipally owned utility, the acquisition of a privately operated facility, or the diversification of existing services.

NONPROFITS IN BUSINESS

COMMUNITY WEALTH VENTURES
733 15th St., NW, Suite 6
Washington, DC 20005
(202) 393-1945
Web: http://www.communitywealth.com

Community Wealth Ventures is a for-profit subsidiary of Share Our Strength dedicated to expanding the resources generated by profitable enterprise for the purpose of promoting social change, especially by assist-ing and documenting the efforts of non-profit organizations to create businesses.

NATIONAL CENTER FOR SOCIAL ENTREPRENEURS
5801 Duluth St., Suite 310
Minneapolis, MN 55422
(612) 595-0890
Fax: (612) 595-0232
Web: http://www.socialentrepreneurs.org

The National Center for Social Entrepreneurs is a nonprofit organization that seeks to encourage entrepreneurship throughout the nonprofit sector through education and consulting services.

ROBERTS ENTERPRISE DEVELOPMENT FUND
P.O. Box 29266
San Francisco, CA 94129-0906
(415) 561-6677
Fax: (415) 561-6685
E-mail: info@redf.org
Web: http://www.redf.org

The Roberts Enterprise Development Fund provides technical assistance and philanthropic investments to help nonprofit organizations in the San Francisco area attain marketplace sustainability in their enterprise ventures. REDF also works with organizations across the United States who engage in nonprofit enterprise strategies.

PENSION FUNDS AND TARGETED INVESTMENTS

AFL-CIO HOUSING INVESTMENT TRUST
1717 K St., NW, Suite 707
Washington, DC 20006
(202) 331-8055
Fax: (202) 331-8190
Web: http://www.aflcio-hit.com

The AFL-CIO Housing Investment Trust (HIT) is one of the nation's largest pension investment programs specializing in housing investment.

**CALIFORNIA PUBLIC EMPLOYEES RETIRE-
MENT SYSTEM (CalPERS)**
Lincoln Plaza
400 P St.
Sacramento, CA 95814
(916) 326-3000
Web: http://www.calpers.ca.gov

The California Public Employees' Retirement System pension fund is actively engaged in targeted investment and serves as a resource for information on the policy issues surrounding this practice.

CENTER FOR WORKING CAPITAL
c/o AFL-CIO
815 16th St., NW
Washington, DC 20006
(202) 637-5000
Fax: (202) 637-5058

The Center for Working Capital is an independent, nonprofit organization formed by the AFL- CIO. The center serves to organize workers' assets in order to promote capital stewardship practices by providing technical assistance and training to pension fund trustees.

HEARTLAND LABOR CAPITAL NETWORK
One Library Pl., Suite 201
Duquesne, PA 15110
(412) 460-0488
Fax: (412) 460-0487
E-mail: t.w.croft@att.net
Web: http://www.heartland.network.org

The Heartland Labor Capital Network works to implement jobs-creating economic development investment strategies that utilized the capital held by labor in pension funds and other institutions in order to create high road workplaces and build sustainable regional economies.

INSTITUTE FOR FIDUCIARY EDUCATION
350 University Ave., Suite 707
Sacramento, CA 95825
(916) 922-1100
Fax: (916) 922-9688
E-mail: jprinzi@ifecorp.com
Web: http://www.ifecorp.com

The Institute for Fiduciary Education is an educational organization that provides workshops and seminars for private, public, and nonprofit executives in the area of economically targeted investments (ETIs.)

RETIREMENT SYSTEMS OF ALABAMA
135 South Union St.
Montgomery, AL 36104
(800) 214-2158
Fax: (334) 240-3032
Email: info@rsa.State.al.us
Web: http://www.rsa.state.al.us/news.html

Retirement Systems of Alabama (RSA) manages the state's pension funds. It has been a leader and innovator among state pension funds in the area of economically targeted investments (ETIs).

UNION LABOR LIFE INSURANCE COMPANY
111 Massachusetts Ave., NW
Washington, DC 20001
(202) 682-0900
Web: http://www.ullico.com

One of the nation's leading union-friendly investors, the Union Labor Life Insurance Company is working to support sustainable development through labor-based pension activism such as the J for Jobs program, a tax-exempt pension plan that invests in income-producing properties that are exclusively union-built.

SMALL BUSINESSES

ACENET
94 N. Columbus Rd.
Athens, OH 45701
(614) 592-3854
Fax: (614) 593-5451
E-mail: jholley@tmn.com
Web: http://www.seorf.ohiou.edu/~xx001

ACENET promotes local economic sustainability by assisting those local businesses seeking to manufacture complex goods on a regional level through the creation of informal networks with other local businesses.

NATIONAL BUSINESS INCUBATORS ASSOCIATION
20 East Circle Dr.
Athens, OH 45701-3751
(740) 593-4331
Fax: (740) 593-1996
E-mail: straxler@nbia.org
Web: http://www.nbia.org

The National Business Incubators Association is a nonprofit membership organization that provides technical assistance, hands-on management assistance, and access to financing opportunities to help ensure the long-term viability of participating member-businesses in incubators.

URBAN SPRAWL

AMERICAN FARMLAND TRUST
1200 18th St., NW
Washington, DC 20036
(202) 331-7300
Fax: (202) 659-8339
E-mail: info@farmland.org
Web: http://www.farmland.org

The American Farmland Trust is a nonprofit organization dedicated to the preservation of America's farmland. Through advocacy, research, and education, ATF works to promote sustainable farming and development practices.

CENTER FOR LIVABLE COMMUNITIES
Local Government Commission
1414 K St., Suite 250
Sacramento, CA 95814
(916) 448-1198
Fax: (916) 448-8246
Hotline: (800) 290-8202
Web: http://www.lgc.org

The Center for Livable Communities is a local initiative that assists local governments and community leaders in their use of land and transportation planning. The center works with local governments and community leaders to adopt policies and programs to expand transportation alternatives, reduce infrastructure costs, create more affordable housing, improve air quality, and restore local and social vitality.

COMMUNITY AND ENVIRONMENTAL DEFENSE SERVICES
8100 Greenspring Valley Rd
Owings Mills, MD 21117
(800) 773-4571
E-mail: info@ceds.org
Web: http://www.ceds.org

Community and Environmental Defense Services (CEDS) is a combination of nonprofit, law clinic, and consulting firm. CEDS offers research and resources to measure the impact of proposed development projects such as landfills, highways, strip malls, and sprawl to ensure responsible community growth.

CONGRESS FOR NEW URBANISM
The Hearst Buildings
5 Third St., Suite 500A
San Francisco, CA 94103
(415) 495-2255
Fax: (415) 495-1731
Web: http://www.cnu.org

The Congress for New Urbanism seeks to restructure public policy to support the restoration of existing urban centers and outlying towns within a metropolitan area.

The CNU works to reconfigure sprawling suburbs into communities of real neighborhoods and diverse districts, conserve natural environments, and preserve the legacy of the built environment.

NATIONAL TRUST FOR HISTORIC PRESERVATION

1785 Massachusetts Ave., NW
Washington, DC 20036
(800) 944-6847
Web: http://www.nationaltrust.org

The National Trust for Historic Preservation is a nonprofit advocacy and education-based organization that fights to preserve historic buildings and locales and prevent sprawl through a network of regional offices and local community groups across the United States.

NATURAL RESOURCES DEFENSE COUNCIL

40 West 20th St.
New York, NY 10011
(212) 727-2700
E-mail: nrdcinfo@nrdc.org
Web: http://www.nrdc.org

The Natural Resources Defense Council is a nationwide organization dedicated to the protection of natural resources, the environment, ecologically responsible growth, and the prevention of sprawl through education, research, and advocacy.

PLANNERSWEB

Planning Commissioners Journal's Sprawl Resource Guide
Web: http://www.plannersweb.com

PlannersWeb's Sprawl Resource Guide is a comprehensive on-line resource on the causes of urban sprawl, problems associated with it, and resources for combating and curtailing it in local communities.

SIERRA CLUB CHALLENGE TO SPRAWL WEB SITE

Web: http://www.sierraclub.org/sprawl

An on-line resource that provides reports, fact sheets, and resources designed to combat the effects and spread of urban sprawl.

SPRAWL-BUSTERS

21 Grinnell St.
Greenfield, MA 01301
(413) 772-6289
E-mail: info@sprawl-busters.com
Web: http://www.sprawl-busters.com

Sprawl-Busters provides consultation, research, and organizational strategies for those concerned about urban sprawl in America's communities.

SURFACE TRANSPORTATION POLICY PROJECT

1100 17th St., NW, 10th Floor
Washington, DC 20036
(202) 466-2636
Fax: (202) 466-2247
E-mail: stpp@transact.org
Web: http://www.transact.org

The Surface Transportation Policy Project (STPP) provides a variety of resources, including publications and strategies for supporting transportation policies that promote sustainable community and economic growth, not sprawl.

WORLD RESOURCES INSTITUTE

10 G St., NW, Suite 800
Washington, DC 20002
(202) 729-7600
Fax: (202) 729-7610
Web: http://www.wri.org

World Resources Institute provides information, ideas, and solutions to global environmental problems, including the problem of urban sprawl. The institute works to reverse damage to ecosystems, expand participation in environmental decisions, avert dangerous climate change, and increase prosperity while improving the environment.

NOTES

Some of the information in this book was directly obtained via interviews with government and nongovermental organization officials conducted by the research staff of the National Center for Economic and Security Alternatives (NCESA) in Washington, as indicated in the notes. Gar Alperovitz is President of NCESA, and David Imbroscio and Thad Williamson have each been affiliated with the center.

FOREWORD

1. Charles Lindblom. *the Market System: What It Is, How It Works, and What to Make of It* (New Haven: Yale University Press, 2001), 235.

PREFACE

1. Marc Miringoff and Maria-Louise Miringoff, *The Social Health of the Nation: How America is Really Doing.* (New York: Oxford University Press), 1999, 25, 39–42.
2. Michael Sandel, "Reply to Critics," in Anita L. Allen and Michael C. Regan, eds., *Debating Democracy's Discontent* (New York: Oxford University Press, 1999), 335.
3. For a critical academic examination of the "social capital" debate which aims to connect declining civic engagement with changes in the American political economy, see Bob Edwards, Michael W. Foley, and Mario Diani, eds., *Beyond Tocqueville: Civil Society and the Social Capital Debate in Comparative Perspective* (Hanover: University Press of New England, 2001).
4. There is, however, a long tradition focusing on "place prosperity" (a phrase coined by Louis Winnick in a 1966 essay) in urban economic development and regional planning circles. See Roger Bolton, "Place Prosperity Versus People Prosperity Revisited: An Old Issue With a New Angle," *Research in Urban Economics* 9 (1993): 79–97.

INTRODUCTION

1. To be sure, the agenda for promoting community stability laid out in this book will involve specific costs: the costs of new policy initiatives, and possibly price increases for some goods. But such costs must be measured against the costs of the current policy of throwing away communities.

2. In referring to the need to reconstruct local democracy and stabilize local communities, we are not referring primarily to neighborhood-sized units or to each particular town. Our primary concern is with stabilizing the economic bases and altering the political practices of significant population centers. We believe that civic and political institutions that encourage neighborhood-level participation and engagement are extremely important, and we welcome the further development of formal neighborhood-level organizations which act as both decision-makers on local problems and as advocates for neighborhood interests. But addressing inequalities among neighborhoods (such as in the provision of public goods and access to economic opportunities) and facing up to land-use and environmental issues are extremely difficult in the absence of community stability. Similarly, while we strongly advocate institutional forms (such as community development corporations) which target job development to particular neighborhoods, even the most successful efforts will not suffice to turn the tide if the economic prospects of the larger unit in which a neighborhood is located are poor. Simply put, a comprehensive policy needs to ensure that sufficient rooted capital has stabilized the larger community context—*and* that vibrant neighborhood-based organizations and supporting policies are in place to ensure that each neighborhood can capture the economic benefits of larger-order economic stability.

3. For a useful recent discussion of the distinction between "community" and "association", see the discussion of the thought of English thinker G. D. H. Cole in Mark E. Warren, *Democracy and Association*. (Princeton: Princeton University Press, 2001), 43–48.

4. Robert Putnam, *Making Democracy Work* (Princeton: Princeton University Press, 1993); Robert Putnam, *Bowling Alone* (New York: Simon and Schuster, 2000).

5. Sidney Verba, Kay Lehman Schlozman, and Henry E. Brady. *Voice and Equality: Civic Voluntarism in American Politics* (Cambridge: Harvard University Press, 1995), 452–55. See also Putnam, *Bowling Alone*, 204–5 and related citations.

6. Social Capital Community Benchmark Survey of the Saguaro Seminar On Civic Engagement at Harvard University. Based on bivariate correlations between years lived in the community and expecting to live in one's community in five years with number of group memberships, an index of civic participation, and an index of social trust. Survey data is available via http://www.ksg.harvard.edu/saguaro.

7. For an interesting paper presenting data on residential stability in different types of neighborhoods in Chicago, see Jeffrey Morenoff and Marta Tienda, "Underclass Neighborhoods in Temporal and Ecological Perspective," *Annals of the American Academy of Political and Social Science*, May 1997, 59ff, Table 1. See also Scott Hacker, "Regional Mobility and Economic Downturns," *Journal of Regional Science*, 40 (2000): 45–65, for evidence that in the immediate wake of an economic downturn mobility rates may slow in affected regions since individuals feel less secure. (Long term economic downturns, however, will lead to reduced population in localities.)

Some studies also show that very poor neighborhoods can have residential stability rates comparable to secure middle class neighborhoods, presumably because the residents' economic disadvantages and limited job prospects inhibits moving. A recent study of the effects of residential stability on rich and poor neighborhoods in Illinois found, however, that "In affluent neighborhoods, stability is associated with low levels of distress; under conditions of poverty the opposite is true. In part this occurs because residents of poor, stable neighborhoods face high levels of disorder in their neighborhoods. Stability does not reduce perceived disorder under conditions of poverty, as it does in more affluent neighborhoods, which leaves residents feeling powerless to leave a dangerous place." See Catherine Ross, John Reynolds, and Karlyn Geis, "The Contingent Meaning of Neighborhood Stability for Residents' Psychological Well Being," in *American Sociological Review* 65 (August 2000) 581–97. Quote from abstract.

8. After controlling for standard demographic factors such as age, income, race, education, number of children in household, and homeownership status. Without controlling for such factors, the relationship between public/nonprofit sector employment and years lived in community is present but much weaker. In general, well-educated and higher income people are more likely to move than others. See Thad Williamson, "The Impact of Local-Level Public Sector Employment Upon Social Capital," unpublished working paper, Department of Government, Harvard University, January 2002.

9. See Robert J. Sampson, "Local Friendship Ties and Community Attachment in Mass Society: A Multilevel Systemic Model," *American Sociological Review* 53 (October 1988): 766–79, on the link between residential stability and "community social integration."

10. According to U.S. Census Data. See Jason Schachter, "Why People Move: Exploring the March 2000 Current Population Survey," http://www.census.gov/prod/2001pubs/p23-204.pdf.

11. Bluestone and Harrison, "Jobs, Income and Health", in Paul D. Staudohar and Holly E. Brown, *Deindustrialization and Plant Closure* (Lexington, MA: Lexington Books, 1987). Also see Thomas S. Moore, *The Disposable Work Force: Worker Displacement and Employment Instability in America* (New York, NY: Aldine de Gruyter, 1996), 44–48.

12. Kathryn Marie Dudley, *The End of the Line: Lost Jobs, New Lives in Postindustrial America* (Chicago: University of Chicago Press, 1994), 134.

13. The New York Times, *The Downsizing of America* (New York, NY: Times Books, 1996), 113.

14. "Extended Mass Layoffs in 2000," Bureau of Labor Statistics, Report 951, July 2001; See also "Displaced Workers Summary," August 2000, available at www.bls.gov/news.release/disp.nro.htm.

15. See, for example, Paul Peterson, *City Limits* (Chicago: University of Chicago Press, 1981); Todd Swanstrom, *The Crisis of Growth Politics* (Philadelphia: Temple University Press, 1995); John Logan and Harvey Molotch, *Urban Fortunes* (Berkeley: University of California Press, 1987); Paul Kantor, *The Dependent City* (Boulder: Westview Press, 1995); Martin Shefter, *Political Crisis/Fiscal Crisis* (New York: Basic Books, 1985); Bryan Jones and Lynn Bachelor, *The Sustaining Hand* (Lawrence: University Press of Kansas, 1993).

16. See David Imbroscio, *Reconstructing City Politics* (Thousand Oaks, CA: Sage, 1997).

17. Stephen Elkin, "Business-State Relations in the Commercial Republic," *Journal of Political Philosophy*, 135, 2 (1994): 115–39. See also Stephen Elkin, *City and Regime in the American Republic* (Chicago: University of Chicago Press, 1987).

18. John Jakle and David Wilson, *Derelict Landscapes* (Savage, MD: Rowman and Littlefield, 1992), 261.

19. Gordon Clark, *Interregional Migration, National Policy, and Social Justice* (Totowa, NJ: Rowman and Allenheld, 1983). See 139–40.

20. Judith Skhlar, *American Citizenship* (Cambridge: Harvard University Press, 1991), 101.

21. As noted with respect to Swedish regional policy by Douglas Yuill et al in *European Regional Incentives*, 19th Edition. London: Bowker Saur, 1999, p. 19. As Yuill documents, Finland and Norway also have had regional policies strongly oriented toward balanced development in all areas of the country with special emphasis on stemming population loss from remote areas.

22. J. Eric Oliver. *Democracy in Suburbia*, Princeton: Princeton University Press, 2001.

23. Lewis Mumford, *The Culture of Cities*. Harcourt, Brace and Company, 1938, 336.

24. Alexis de Tocqueville, *Democracy in America*, vol. 1, Trans. George Lawrence, ed. J. P. Mayer (New York: Harper Collins, 2000), 63.

25. Dewey, *The Public and Its Problems* (Athens: Ohio University Press, 1959), 219.

26. *A National Agenda for the Eighties* (Washington, DC: Government Printing Office, 1980). 166–67.

27. See Richard Thaler, *The Winner's Curse* (New York: The Free Press, 1992). See Thaler's Chapter Six.

28. Jakle and Wilson, *Derelict Landscapes*, 78–79.

29. Scott Bernstein, *Using The Hidden Assets of America's Cities and Regions to Ensure Sustainable Communities*, Chicago: Center for Neighborhood Technology, 1999, pt. 1. Available at www.cnt.org/hidden-assets.

30. The Sierra Club, *How Sprawl Costs Us All*, 1999. Quoted material from 4, 8. Available at www.sierra.org.

31. See Deirdre A. Gaquin and Katherine A. Debrandt, eds. *2000 County and City Extra: Annual Metro, City, and County Data Book*, 9th ed. (Lanham, MD: Bernan Press, 2000) We recognize that population declines in some very large cities can be carried out in ways that enhance the well-being of both those who leave and those who stay behind (as noted in Chapter 3). We do not think, however, that the actual decline of so many towns and cities in the latter part of the twentieth century had this beneficial effect.

32. See also the discussion of capital cost estimates in Fodor, *Better Not Bigger* (Gabriola, BC: New Society Publishers, 1999), 77–103. Eben Fodor, "The Costs of Growth in Oregon," Eugene: Fodor and Associates, 1998, Table 2.

33. As Richard Carson has pointed out in critical commentary on Fodor's work, a substantial portion of this public infrastructure cost is often in practice borne by developers, depending on local context. We are not here primarily concerned here with the issue of who pays these infrastructure costs, but with the larger efficiency issue involved in building new infrastructure to accommodate movers from declining localities, whether this tab is picked up by private or public actors. Carson also cites work by Sonny Conder on the costs of new infrastructure in Oregon producing results roughly similar to Fodor's estimate. See Richard H. Carson, "Paying for Our Growth In Oregon," report published by New Oregon Meridian Press, October 1998.

34. We do not mean to imply that cities experiencing actual population losses are the only cities experiencing severe economic distress. Some thirty of the seventy-four central cities listed by the Federal Housing and Urban Development Department in 1999 as "doubly distressed cities"—experiencing unemployment 50 percent or more above the national average and either high poverty rates (20 percent or higher of the local population) or population losses of at least 5 percent—actually gained residents between 1980 and 1996. Over three-quarters of these cities are in the fast-growing states of Florida, Texas and California. See the important HUD report, "Now Is the Time: Places Left Behind in the New Economy," 1999, available at www.hud.gov. See Table 12.

35. Tom Ricker, "Estimating the Capital Costs of Community Destabilization: A Preliminary Report." National Center for Economic and Security Alternatives working paper, Washington, DC: May 1998.

36. Ibid. The basis for Ricker's (highly preliminary) estimate is a comparison of private residential and nonresidential capital costs with public capital costs in twelve fast-growing cities between 1980 and 1990, drawing on census data.

37. Had this migration *not* taken place, maintenance costs in declining cities might have been slightly higher.

38. Bernstein, *Using The Hidden Assets,* pt. 2.

39. David Smith, *The Public Balance Sheet* (Washington, DC: National Center for Economic Alternatives, 1979). See also Gar Alperovitz and Jeff Faux, *Rebuilding America* (New York: Pantheon, 1984), 147–50; and David L. Imbroscio. "The Local Public Balance Sheet: An Alternative Evaluation Methodology for Local Economic Development," in Laura Reese and David Fasenfest, eds., *Critical Evaluations of Economic Development Policies* (Detroit: Wayne State University Press, 2002).

40. Imbroscio, "The Local Public Balance Sheet."

41. *Economic Report of the President 2000* (Washington: Government Printing Office, 2000); *Regional Projections to 2045: Volume 1, States* (Washington, DC: Bureau of Economic Analysis, 1995). Even much of traditional manufacturing is shifting towards a service-manufacturing hybrid, which can also allow for more localized economic activity. See Patricia Panchak, "The Future of Manufacturing" (Interview with Peter Drucker), *Industry Week* 247, No. 17 (1998): 96–105.

42. Edward Glaeser, "Demand for Density? The Functions of the City in the 21st Century," *Brookings Review,* Summer 2000, 10–13.

43. Peter Dreier, "Putting Cities on the National Agenda," *Urban Affairs Review* 30 (1995): 645–56. (quote from 648).

44. Jeffrey Lustig, "The Politics of Shutdown," *Journal of Economic Issues* 19 (1985): 123–53 (quote from 133).

45. Gaquin and Debrandt, *2000 County and City Extra,* Table D, item 64.

46. "A Town Link Its Fate With Doomed Hospital," *New York Times,* March 2, 1992.

47. *Statistical Abstract of the United States 2000* (Washington, DC: Government Printing Office, 2000. Table 494, "All Governments-Detailed Finances, 1996," and Table 717, "Gross Domestic Product in Current and Real (1996) Dollars."

48. David Korten, *When Corporations Rule the World* (West Hartford, CT: Kumarian Press, 1995); Herman Daly and John Cobb, *For the Common Good* (Boston: Beacon Press, 1989); Michael Shuman, *Going Local* (New York: Free Press, 1998).

49. *Congressional Record,* February 27, 1978, 4718–20.

CHAPTER 1

1. Thomas Michael Power, *Lost Landscapes and Failed Economies* (Washington, DC: Island Press, 1996), 37.
2. Ibid., 49.
3. Wim Wiewel and Joseph Persky, "The Growing Localness of the Global City," *Economic Geography* 70, 2 (1994): 129.
4. Ibid.
5. *Economic Report of the President 2000* (Washington, DC: Government Printing Office, 2000).
6. Dunn cites a 1999 United States International Trade Commission study showing that "the complete removal of existing U.S. barriers to trade would produce welfare gains of less than 0.5 percent of U.S. GDP." On the other hand, removing those barriers, Dunn, estimates would cost just 135,000 jobs. These figures, however, do not tell the whole story of the *current* costs of trade—only that such costs are not likely to dramatically *increase* in the future due to further liberalization. See Robert Dunn, Jr. Review of Thomas Friedman's *The Lexus and the Olive Tree,* in *Challenge,* January-February 2000, 129.
7. Dean Baker, "Gaining With Trade?" Center for Economic Policy Research working paper, March 2001. Available via www.cepr.net.
8. John S. Dryzek, *Democracy in Capitalist Times* (New York: Oxford University Press, 1996), 79.
9. Quoted in David Morris, "A Bad Big Idea," in Ralph Nader et al, *The Case Against Free Trade* (San Francisco: Earth Island Press, 1993), 140–41.
10. David Ricardo, *Principles of Political Economy and Taxation* (Cambridge: Sraffa Edition, 1951), 136–37. Cited in Herman Daly and John Cobb, *For the Common Good.* Boston: Beacon Press, 1989, 214.
11. See also Robert E. Prasch, "Reassessing Comparative Advantage: The Impact of Capital Flows on the Argument for Laissez-Faire," *Journal of Economic Issues* 29, 2 (1995).
12. Smith adds: "This would not give the monopoly of the home market to domestic industry, nor turn towards a particular employment a greater share of the stock and labour, than what would naturally go to it. It would only hinder any part of what would naturally go to it from being turned away by the tax into a less natural direction, and would leave the competition between foreign and domestic industry, after the tax, as nearly as possible upon the same footing as before it." Adam Smith, *The Wealth of Nations* (1776), Book IV, Chapter II, "Of Restraints Upon the Importation From Foreign Countries of Such Goods As Can Be Produced At Home."
13. Morris, op. cit., p. 146.
14. David Moore of the University of Maryland emphasizes two further critiques of the comparative advantage model. Conventional accounts of the benefits of trade commonly avoid discussion of the effects of large firms with substantial market power. Such firms need not necessarily pass the cost savings from trade-related cheapened production onto consumers, can instead use the cost savings to pad profits. As Moore notes, "Even if we take as given mainstream economics' contention that trade yields aggregate benefits in most cases, market power makes a big difference in the distribution of those impacts, especially to consumers, whose benefit is the main justification

for free trade." Likewise, most discussion of free trade ignores the politically constructed nature of comparative advantage. That certain places become particularly adept at particular forms of production is not simply a product of the accidents of geography and climate. Rather, the ability of places to produce depends heavily on public policies of all types—from educational provision to subsidies and protections for infant industries to government investments in research and technological development. See David Moore, "Thinking and Acting Locally in the Face of Globalization," *The Good Society,* 10.2 (2001), 52–56.

15. Eckes adds: "Today most economists and pundits associate free trade with rapid economic growth. This assertion, frankly, is incompatible with American economic history. The most rapid growth occurred during period of high protectionism, not free trade. From 1889 to 1929, a forty-year period ending in the Great Depression, U.S. growth averaged 3.6 percent, significantly above the 3 percentage point average real growth for the twentieth century." Alfred E. Eckes, Jr., "U.S. Trade History," in William A. Lovett, Alfred E. Eckers, JR, and Richard L. Brinkman, *U.S. Trade Policy: History, Theory and the WTO* (Armonk, NY: M.E. Sharpe Inc., 1999), 51–105. See especially 58–61, quoted material 60–61. Tariff data noted by Eckes are derived from *Historical Statistics of the United States* (Washington, DC: Bureau of the Census, 1976).

16. Eckes, op.cit., 78–97, 100–5.

17. Robert E. Scott, "The Facts About Trade and Job Creation," *Economic Policy Institute Issue Brief,* March 24, 2000.

18. Public Citizen and Global Trade Watch, "NAFTA at 5," December 1998. Available at www.citizen.org/pctrade/nafta/reports/5years.htm.

19. Robert E. Scott, "NAFTA's Pain Deepens: Job Destruction Accelerates in 1999 With Losses in Every State," *Economic Policy Institute Briefing Paper,* December 1999.

20. David Firestone, "A Chief Exporter, and Not At All Pleased About It," *The New York Times,* February 23, 2001.

21. For one careful study, see Lori G. Kletzer, "International Trade and Job Displacement in U.S. Manufacturing, 1979–1991," in Susan Collins, ed., *Imports, Exports, and the American Worker* (Washington, DC: Brookings Institution, 1998), 423–72.

22. Jeffrey D. Sachs and Howard J. Shatz, "Trade and Jobs in U.S. Manufacturing," *Brookings Papers on Economic Activity,* 1994, vol. 1, 1–84.

23. Lori G. Kletzer, "Trade and Job Loss in U.S. Manufacturing, 1979–1994," in Robert C. Feenstra, ed., *The Impact of International Trade on Wages* (Chicago: The University of Chicago Press, 2000), 349–93, quote from 382.

24. Cited by David Gordon, *Fat and Mean* (New York: Basic Books, 1996), 194.

25. See *Economic Report of the President 1999* (Washington, DC: Government Printing Office, 1999). Table B-105.

26. Krugman has recently revised his view that technological shifts account for most of growth in wage inequality, admitting that much of the evidence for this thesis is indirect and rests on theoretical assumptions. Krugman has instead developed the hypothesis that growing wage inequality in the most recent period may be the result of a ongoing process in which external shocks, perhaps caused by trade or perhaps by techonological changes, have caused the labor market to move from one relatively "egalitarian" equilibrium to a second, much less egalitarian equilibrium. See Krugman, "And Now For

Something Completely Different: An Alternative Model of Trade, Education, and Inequality," in Feenstra, ed. *The Impact of International Trade on Wages,* 15–36.

27. William Cline, *Trade and Wage Inequality* (Washington, DC: Institute for International Economics, 1997). Cited by Rodrik, *Has Globalization Gone Too Far?* (Washington, DC: Institute for International Economics, 1998), 15.

28. See Jagdish Bhagwati, "Fear Not," *The New Republic,* May 22, 1997, 39.

29. Adrian Wood, "How Trade Hurt Unskilled Workers," *Journal of Economic Perspective,* 9, 3 (1995): 72–73.

30. Rodrik, *Has Globalization Gone Too Far?* 17.

31. Thomas Palley, *Plenty of Nothing* (Princeton: Princeton University Press, 1998), 169–70 and throughout.

32. Richard Freeman. *When Earnings Diverge: Causes, Consequences, and Cures for the New Inequality in the U.S.* (Washington, DC: National Policy Association, 1997), 41.

33. See Adrian Wood, *North-South Trade, Employment, and Inequality: Changing Fortunes in a Skill-Driven World* (Oxford: Clarendon Press, 1994), and Adrian Wood, "How Trade Hurt Unskilled Workers," *Journal of Economic Perspectives* 9, 3 (1995): 57–80.

34. Andrew B. Bernard and J. Bradford Jensen, "Understanding Increasing and Decreasing Wage Inequality," in Robert C. Feenstra, ed. *The Impact of International Trade on Wages* (Chicago: University of Chicago Press, 2000), 227–68.

35. Thomas Palley, "The Economics of Globalization: Problems and Policy Responses," AFL-CIO working paper, Washington, DC, 1999, 8.

36. Kate Bronfenbrenner, "Final Report: The Effects of Plant Closing or Threat of Plant Closing on the Right of Workers to Organize," 1996, cited in Mark Weisbrot, "Globalization for Whom," *Cornell International Law Journal,* 1998. Weisbrot also cites a 1992 *Wall Street Journal* poll of corporate executives in which 40 percent of the business leaders said they would at least partially move to Mexico if NAFTA were passed and 24 percent would threaten to move in order to keep wages in check in the U.S. Bob Davis, "One America," *Wall Street Journal,* September 24, 1992, R1.

37. Kate Bronfenbrenner, "Raw Power: Plant-Closing Threats and the Threat to Union Organizing," *Multinational Monitor,* December 2000.

38. Rodrik, *Has Globalization Gone Too Far?,* 25.

39. Ibid., 16–25.

40. Cited in ibid., 21. See also Peter Gottschalk and Robert Moffit. "The Growth of Earnings Instability in the U.S. Labor Market," *Brookings Paper on Economic Activity,* 1994: vol. 2: 217–54.

41. Many economists now speak of a "policy trilemma" in which countries cannot simultaneously maintain control over exchange rates, maintain independent monetary policies (via control over interest rates), and also permit open flow of capital across borders, without inviting economic disaster. In Chapter 12, we discuss in further detail this "trilemma" and possible ways to deal with it.

42. "In the United States, between 1966 and 1995, exports and imports as a share of GDP increased from 7.4 percent to 18.7 percent; in the United Kingdom, they increased from 29.0 percent to 45.9 percent; in Canada they increased from 18.3 percent to 28.3 percent. If a country now expands its level of economic activity, consumer demand leaks out through imports, potentially creating an unsustainable balance-of-payments

deficit. This has afflicted almost all the industrialized countries except the United States, which has been protected by the fact that the dollar is the international reserve currency and by foreigners' desire to build up their portfolio holdings of US assets." Thomas I. Palley, "Working the Supply Side," *Boston Review,* December-January 1997–1998, 13.

43. Palley, "The Economics of Globalization," 7.

44. John Maynard Keynes, "Mitigation by Tariff," (1930) in *Essays in Persuasion* (New York: W. W. Norton, 1963), 279.

45. Barry Eichengreen, *Globalizing Capital* (Princeton: Princeton University Press, 1996), 96.

46. Rodrik, *Has Globalization Gone Too Far?* 63–64; quote in previous paragraph from 53.

47. For a recent overview, see Paul Pierson, ed. *The New Politics of the Welfare State* (New York: Oxford University Press, 2001).

48. Helen V. Milner and Robert Keohane, "Internationalization and Domestic Politics: An Introduction," in Keohane and Milner, eds. *Internationalization and Domestic Politics* (Cambridge: Cambridge University Press, 1996), 17–18. See also Jeffry Frieden, "Invested Interests: The Politics of National Economic Policies in a World of Global Finance," *International Organization* 45, 4 (1991): 428; and Fritz W. Scharpf, "The Viability of Advanced Welfare States in the International Economy: Vulnerabilities and Options," *Journal of European Public Policy* 7, 2 (2000): 190–228.

49. Paul Pierson, "Post-industrial Pressures on Mature Welfare States," in Pierson, ed. *The New Politics of the Welfare State* (New York: Oxford Universrity Press, 2001), 80–104. See also Torben Iversen and Christopher Wren, "Equality, Employment, and Budgetary Restraint: The Trilemma of the Service Economy," *World Politics* 50 (1998): 507ff.

50. Robert Wade, "Globalization and Its Limits," in Suzanne Berger and Ronald Dore, eds., *National Diversity and Global Capitalism* (Ithaca, NY: Cornell University Press, 1996), 86–87.

51. Andrew Glyn, "Internal and External Constraints on Egalitarian Policies," in Robert Pollin, ed., *Globalization and Progressive Economic Policy* (Cambridge: Cambridge University Press, 1998), 391–408. See also Paul Hirst and Grahme Thompson, *Globalization in Question* (Cambridge: Polity Press, 1996).

52. Paul R. Krugman, *The Accidental Theorist* (New York: W. W. Norton, 1998), 79.

53. Dunn, Jr. review of *The Lexus and the Olive Tree,* 126.

54. Floyd Norris, "Does the U.S. Trade Deficit Matter? This Year it Will," *New York Times,* February 23, 2001, C1.

55. A third way trade may affect domestic norms is by effectively weakening or destroying a particular sector or community with special social or cultural import (for instance, French agriculture or non-American cultural products.)

56. State Department study cited by Sarah Anderson and John Cavanagh (with Thea Lee), *Field Guide to the Global Economy* (New York: The Free Press, 2000), 62.

57. Wallach, "Hidden Danger of GATT and NAFTA" in Nader et al., *The Case Against Free Trade,* 46.

58. Mark Weisbrot, "Globalization For Whom?" *Cornell International Law Journal* 31 (1998): 631ff.

59. A June 2001 WTO ruling upheld the U.S. law, finding that the United States had taken

adequate steps to comply with a 1998 WTO ruling that the United States had implemented the law in a discriminatory manner.

60. See Chris Mooney, "Localizing Globalization," *American Prospect,* July 2–16, 2001.

61. Mark C. Gordon, "Democracy's New Challenge: Globalization, Governance, and the Future of American Federalism," report for the Demos organization, July 2001, 34–46, available at www.demos.org. Quote from 36.

62. William Schweke, "The Importance of the WTO Subsidy Discipline For U.S. Economic Development Policy," Corporation for Enterprise Development working paper, May 1999, available via www.cfed.org.

63. Given the character of international economic governance institutions, however, we are not persuaded by Schweke's suggestion that international mechanisms can (or even should) be used to rein in state-level subsidies to mobile capital firms while simultaneously upholding subsidies which benefit community-oriented firms and local small businesses. The basic principle of democratic subsidiarity—that is allowing decisions to be made at the lowest feasible level of organization—strongly suggests that the case for or against state-level subsidies to mobile firms, like the case for or against state and local subsidies to community-rooted firms, should rest or fall on the merits of the case as judged by local and state electorates and their representatives, not on the dictates of an international trade agreement.

64. William Drozdiak, "EU May Hit U.S. With $4 Billion in Penalties; Commission Calls Tax Credits Illegal," *Washington Post,* August 21, 2001, E1.

65. Robert Kuttner, "The End of Citizenship?" *American Prospect,* December 20, 1999, 4.

66. See, for instance, Krugman, *The Accidental Theorist,* as well as his numerous other writings.

67. Jay Mandle, "The Problem With Thinking Locally," *Boston Review,* summer 1998, 54.

68. Jay Mandle, "Reforming Globalization," *Challenge,* March-April 2001, 28ff.

69. Anderson and Cavanagh, *Field Guide to the Global Economy,* 47.

70. Dani Rodrik, "Trading in Illusions," *Foreign Policy,* March-April 2001, 54–62.

71. Dani Rodrik, *The New Global Economy and Developing Countries: Making Openness Work* (Washington: John Hopkins University Press, 1999), 33–35, Tables 2.1 and 2.2.

72. Rodrik, "Trading in Illusions," 54–62.

73. Rodrik, *The New Global economy and Developing Countries.*

74. Indeed, as Rodrik, shows, many nations (especially in Latin America) which practiced import substitution industrialization policies during the 1960s and early 1970s enjoyed much, much higher growth rates than the export-oriented policies of the past two decades have been able to produce.

75. Robin Hahnel, *Panic Rules: Everything You Need to Know About the Global Economy* (Boston: South End Press, 1999), 17. On the asian crisis, see Frank Ching "Social Impact of the Regional Financial Crisis," available at www.asiasociety.org.

76. Ibid., 19.

77. Benjamin Barber, *Jihad vs. McWorld* (New York: Times Books, 1995); Samuel Huntington, *The Clash of Civilizations* (New York: Simon and Schuster, 1996). See also the essays on "The Fate of National Culture," in David Held and Anthony McGrew, eds., *The Global Transformations Reader* (Cambridge: Polity Press, 2000).

78. Rosabeth Moss Kanter, *World Class: Thriving Locally in a Global Economy* (New York:

Simon and Schuster, 1995). Kanter's emphasis on taking stock of local capabilities and local resources is well-placed, as is her emphasis on constructing a coordinated local-level economic strategy.

CHAPTER 2

1. "Boeing, Jolting Seattle, Will Move Headquarters," *New York Times*, March 22, 2001, A16.

2. "Chicago: Boeing Workers' Kind of Town? Employees Worry About Housing, Family Upheaval," *Seattle Times*, May 11, 2001.

3. "A Rude Awakening for Lincoln: Gallup's Decision to Leave Exposes the City's Shortcomings," *Omaha World-Herald*, August 10, 2000.

4. "With Merger, Winston-Salem, N.C., Would Lose Wachovia Bank's Headquarters," *Charlotte Observer*, April 17, 2001; "First Union-Wachovia Merger a Tale of Two Cities," *AP Wire Story*, April 7, 2001.

5. "Fidelity Raises Profile of Westlake, Texas, as Haven for Company Campuses," *Fort Worth Star-Telegram*, June 3, 2001.

6. Louis Uchitelle, "Shifting Workplace: Renewed Corporate Wanderlust Puts a Quiet Brake on Salaries," *The New York Times*, July 24, 2000, A1.

7. Ibid.

8. Ibid.

9. Jay H. Walder and Herman B. Leonard, *The Federal Budget and the States*, 22nd edition. Cambridge: JFK School of Government, 1998, 4, Table 1; *The Federal Budget and the States*, 23rd ed., Table C-6.

10. In *Industrial Incentives: Competition Among American States and Cities* (Kalamazoo, MI: W. E. Upjohn Institute for Employment Research, 1998), 203–11, Peter S. Fisher and Alan H. Peters estimate that the nominal public costs associated with these subsidies are about twice as high as the actual post-tax value of the subsidies. Even so, the costs in these cases are huge. See also James Barlett and Donald Steele, "Corporate Welfare," *Time*, November 9, 1998, 36ff; Greg LeRoy, "The Terrible Ten: Corporate Candy Store Deals of 1998," *The Progressive*, May 1999; Ron Starner, "The Top 10 Deals of 2000: Chip Plants Deliver Big Bucks," *Site Selection Magazine*, May 2001, 273ff; and Graham S. Toft, "Industrial Development in the New Economy," *Journal of Applied Manufacturing Systems*, vol. 8, no. 1, 1995–1996.

11. Greg LeRoy, "The Terrible Ten: Corporate Candy Store Deals of 1998." Starner, The Top 10 Deals of 2000."

12. In his study of the political economy of North Carolina in the postwar era, for instance, Philip Wood demonstrated how the state attracted investments in manufacturing from the North, using low wages and the political repression of organized labor the basis of a development strategy. Philip Wood, *Southern Capitalism: The Political Economy of North Carolina, 1900–1980* (Durham: Duke University Press, 1986).

13. James Laughlin and Graham Toft, "The New Art of War," *Economic Development Commentary*, Spring 1995.

14. Peter S. Fisher and Alan H. Peters, "Tax and Spending Incentives and Enterprise Zones," *New England Economic Review*, March-April 1997, 128.

15. Robert M. Ady, "Discussion," *New England Economic Review,* March-April 1997, 77–82.

16. Fisher and Peters, *Industrial Incentives.*

17. Scott Loveridge, "On the Continuing Popularity of Industrial Recruitment" *Economic Development Quarterly,* 10, 2 (1996): 151–58.

18. Joseph Persky, Daniel Felsenstein, Wim Wiewel, "How Do We Know That 'But For the Incentives' The Development Would Not Have Occurred," in Richard D. Bingham and Robert Mier, eds., *Dilemmas of Urban Economic Development.* (Thousand Oaks: Sage, 1997), 28–45.

19. Mark Schneider, "Undermining the Growth Machine: The Missing Link Between Local Economic Development and Fiscal Payoffs," *Journal of Politics* 54, 1 (1992): 226–27.

20. Fisher and Peters, *Industrial Incentives,* 219. The academic research on industrial incentives is voluminous. For an overview of a range of positions in the literature in addition to the works cited here, see Keith R. Ihlandfeldt, "Ten Principles for State Tax Incentives," *Economic Development Quarterly,* 9, 4 (1995): 339–355; Herbert J. Rubin, "Shoot Anything That Flies, Claim Anything That Falls: Conversations With Economic Development Practitioners," *Economic Development Quarterly* 2, 3 (1988): 236–51; William Schweke, Brian Dobson, and Carl Rist, "Making Development Incentives More Accountable," in *Improving Your Business Climate* (Washington, DC: Corporation for Enterprise Development, 1995), 19–44; and Robert G. Lynch, *Do State and Local Tax Incentives Work?* (Washington, DC: Economic Policy Institute, 1996).

21. See Loveridge, "On the Continuing Popularity of Industrial Recruitment," for a rundown of eleven hypotheses about why job-chasing strategies remain so pervasive.

22. Harold Wolman with David Spitzley, "The Politics of Local Economic Development," *Economic Development Quarterly* 10, 2 (1996), 132.

23. Ibid., 131.

24. Ibid.

25. Rubin, "Shoot Anything That Flies."

26. Timothy Barnekov, Robin Boyle, and Daniel Rich, *Privatism and Urban Policy in Britain and the United States* (New York: Oxford University Press, 1989).

27. John Rennie Short, "Urban Imagineers: Boosterism and the Representation of Cities," in Andrew E. G. Jonas and David Wilson, eds., *The Urban Growth Machine: Critical Perspectives Two Decades Later* (Albany: State University of New York Press, 1999), Table 3.3, 49.

28. Harvey Molotch, "Growth Machine Links," in Jonas and Wilson, eds., *The Urban Growth Machine,* 258.

29. Greg LeRoy et al., *No More Candy Store* (Washington, DC: Grassroots Policy Project, 1994); Jeremy Brecher, *50 Proposals to Counter Downsizing* (Washington, DC: Preamble Collaborative, 1997).

30. Ann Markusen, P. Hall, S. Campbell and S. Deitrick, *The Rise of The Gun Belt* (New York: Oxford University Press, 1991), 25.

31. For an elegant theory of industrial agglomeration in the Midwest and Mid-Atlantic states in the late nineteenth and early twentieth centuries, see Paul Krugman, *Geography and Trade* (Cambridge, MA: MIT Press, 1991).

32. Saskia Sassen, "The State and the Global City: Notes Toward A Conception of Place-Centered Governance," in *Globalization and Its Discontents: Essays on the New Mobility of People and Money* (New York: The New Press, 1998), 195–219.

33. Michael Piore and Charles Sabel, *The Second Industrial Divide* (New York: Basic Books, 1984).

34. Anna Lee Saxenian, *Regional Advantage: Culture and Competition in Silicon Valley and Route 128* (Cambridge, MA: Harvard University Press, 1994).

35. Peter B. Doerringer and David G. Terkla, "Business Strategy and Cross-Industry Clusters," *Economic Development Quarterly,* 9 3 (1995): 225–37.

36. Ann Markusen, "Four Structures for Second Tier Cities," in Markusen, Yong-Sook Lee, and Sean DiGiovanna, eds., *Second Tier Cities: Rapid Growth Beyond the Metropolis* (Minneapolis: University of Minnesota Press, 1999), 21–41; see especially Table 2.1, 23–26. See also Markusen, "Studying Regions by Studying Firms," same volume, 58–59, on how investment decisions are made.

37. David Harvey, "The Geography of Capitalist Accumulation: A Reconstruction of the Marxian Therory," in Richard Peet, ed., *Radical Geography* (Chicago: Maaroufa Press, 1977), 273.

38. See Bennett Harrison, "Regional Restructuring and 'Good Business Climates,'" in Larry Sawers and William Tabb, eds., *Sunbelt/Snowbelt: Urban Development and Regional Restructuring* (New York: Oxford University Press, 1984).

39. See, for instance, Michael Storper and Richard Walker, *The Capitalist Imperative* (London: Basil Blackwell, 1989).

40. Ronald Ferguson lectures on state and local economic development, Kennedy School of Government, Harvard University, Spring 1999, attended by Thad Williamson.

41. Robert Reich, *The Work of Nations* (New York: Knopf, 1991).

CHAPTER 3

1. William Fulton, Rolf Pendall, Mai Nguyen, and Alicia Harrison. "Who Sprawls Most? How Growth Patterns Differ Across the United States," July 12, 2001. Report available from the Brookings Institution at www.brookings.edu/es/urban/urban.htm.

2. Ibid.

3. For a well-stated critique, see Betty Friedan, *The Second Stage* (New York: Summit Books, 1981), 282–87. See also Dolores Hayden, *Redesigning the American Dream* (New York: W. W. Norton, 1984). Hayden is an important representative figure in a large literature on the relationship between gender inequality and city and land use planning. See also Leslie Weisman, *Discrimination by Design* (Urbana: University of Illinois, 1992), and Marsha Ritzdorf, "A Feminist Analysis of Gender and Residential Zoning in the United States," in Irwin Altman and Arza Churchman, eds., *Women and the Environment* (New York: Plenum Press, 1994). For a more positive recent assessment of suburban life from a feminist standpoint see Rosalyn Baxendall and Elizabeth Ewen, *Picture Windows: How the Suburbs Happened* (New York: Basic Books, 2000).

4. Richard Applebaum, *Size, Growth, and U.S. Cities* (New York: Praeger Publishers, 1978), 100–1.

5. J. Eric Oliver, *Democracy in Suburbia* (Princeton: Princeton University Press, 2001).

6. Ebenezer Howard, *Garden Cities of To-Morrow*, ed. with a preface by F. J. Osborn, with an introductory essay by Lewis Mumford (Cambridge, MA: MIT Press, 1965), 142.

7. Peter Hall and Colin Ward, *Sociable Cities: The Legacy of Ebenezer Howard* (Chichester, England: John Wiley and Sons, 1998), 67.

8. Kenneth Jackson, *Crabgrass Frontier* (New York: Oxford University Press, 1985).

9. *Federal Budget of the United States 2003—Analytical Tables* (Washington, DC: Government Printing Office, 2002).

10. Jackson, *Crabgrass Frontier*, 205.

11. Richard Moe and Carter Wilkie, *Changing Places* (New York: Henry Holt & Co, 1997), 48.

12. As Melvin Oliver and Thomas Shapiro have helped show, this in turn limited African-American's accumulation of economic assets in the postwar era. See Oliver and Shapiro, *Black Wealth/White Wealth: A New Perspective on Racial Inequality* (New York: Routledge, 1995).

13. David Rusk, *Inside Game/Outside Game* (Washington, DC: Brookings Institution, 1989). 88–89.

14. Moe and Wilkie, *Changing Places,* 57.

15. Rusk, *Inside Game/Outside Game,* 90–91.

16. Pietro S. Nivola, *Laws of the Landscape: How Policies Shape Cities in Europe and America* (Washington, DC: Brookings Institution, 1999), 13–14.

17. Nivola, op. cit., 15; *Ten Years of Progress* (Washington, DC: Surface Transportation Policy Project, 2001), 11.

18. David M. Roodman, *Paying the Piper: Subsidies, Politics, and the Environment* (Washington, DC: Worldwatch Institute, December 1996), 42.

19. Nivola, *Laws of the Landscape,* 18, Figure 3-3.

20. Ibid., 26, citing John Pucher, "Urban Travel Behavior as the Outcome of Public Policy," *Journal of the American Planning Association* 54 (1988): 513.

21. Nivola, *Laws of the Landscape,* 25.

22. *Federal Budget of the United States 2003—Analytical Tables* (Washington, DC: Government Printing Office, 2002), 100.

23. Moe and Wilkie, *Changing Places,* 258.

24. James Kunstler, *Home from Nowhere* (New York: Simon and Schuster, 1996), 196–97.

25. Nivola, *Laws of the Landscape,* 26–27.

26. Bruce Katz and Joel Rogers, "The Next Urban Agenda," in Robert Borosage and Roger Hickey, eds., *The Next Agenda: Blueprint for a New Progressive Movement* (Boulder: Westview Press, 2001), 191.

27. Robert A. Beauregard, "Federal Policy and Postwar Decline: A Case of Government Complicity?" *Housing Policy Debate* 12, 1 (2001): 129–51.

28. Jennifer Preston, "Battling Sprawl, States Buy Land for Open Space," *New York Times,* June 9, 1998, A1.

29. Rob Gurwitt, "The Quest for Common Ground," *Governing,* June 1998, 21, 22.

30. Kaid Benfield, Matthew Raimi, and Donald Chen, *Once There Were Greenfields* (Washington, DC: Natural Resources Defense Council, 1999), 35.

31. See William Shore, "Recentralization: The Single Answer to More than a Dozen United

States Problems and a Major Answer to Poverty," *Journal of the American Planning Association* 61 (1995): 496–503.

32. Jack Nasar and David Julian, "The Psychological Sense of Community in the Neighborhood," *Journal of the American Planning Association* 61 (1995): 178–84.

33. Robert Putnam, *Bowling Alone* (New York: Knopf, 2000), 204–15. Quoted material from 213, 215.

34. Timothy Beatley, *Green Urbanism: Learning from European Cities* (Washington, DC: Island Press, 2000).

35. For interesting discussions along these lines, see Juliet Schor, *The Overspent American* (New York: Basic Books, 1998), and Jerome Segal, *Graceful Simplicity* (New York: Henry Holt & Co., 1999).

36. Ann Sorenson, Richard Greene, and Karen Russ, *Farming on the Edge,* published by the American Farmland Trust, March 1997, available at www.farmlandinfo.org. See Table 7.

37. Benfield, Raimi, and Chen, *Once There Were Greenfields,* 64–72.

38. HUD Report, *The State of Our Cities* (Washington, DC: Government Printing Office, 1999), iv.

39. Benfield, Raimi, and Chen, *Once There Were Greenfields,* 55, 58.

40. United States Bureau of the Census, "Private Vehicle Occupancy for the United States: 1990 and 1980 Census," undated, cited in Benfield, Raimi and Chen, *Once There Were Greenfields,* 34, Table 2–1.

41. Benfield, Raimi, and Chen, *Once There Were Greenfields,* 51; citing Clay Chandler, "The 60 Watt Mind-Set," *Washington Post,* November 14, 1997, A20, and Warren Brown, "Trucks Are Putting Cars Out of Commission," *Washington Post,* October 7, 1998.

42. Benfield, Raimi, and Chen, *Once There Were Greenfields,* 51. Marc Breslow, "Two Cheers for OPEC," *Dollars and Sense,* May-June 2000, 8.

43. Benfield, Raimi, and Chen, *Once There Were Greenfields,* 78–84.

44. Myron Orfield, *Metropolitics,* rev. ed. (Washington, DC: Brookings Institution, 1998), 72.

45. James E. Frank, *The Costs of Alternative Development Patterns* (Washington, DC: Urban Land Institute, 1989). Cited in Benfield, Raimi, and Chen, *Once There Were Greenfields,* 97–98.

46. James Duncan and Associates, *The Search for Efficient Urban Growth Patterns* (Tallahassee: Florida Department of Community Affairs, July 1989). Cited in Benfield, Raimi, and Chen, *Once There Were Greenfields,* 98–100.

47. Robert Burchell et al., *Impact Assessment of the New Jersey Interim State Development And Redevelopment Plan. Report II: Research Findings* (Trenton: New Jersey Office of State Planning, 1992). Cited in Benfield, Raimi, and Chen, *Once There Were Greenfields,* 101–2.

48. Alan Altshuler and José Gómez-Ibáñez, *Regulation for Revenue* (Washington, DC: Brookings Institution, 1993), 62–76.

49. For a comprehensive literature review on this topic, see Robert Burchell et al., *The Costs of Sprawl—Revisited,* Transit Cooperative Research Program Report 39 (Washington, DC: National Academy Press, 1998).

50. See William Julius Wilson, *When Jobs Disappear* (New York: Knopf, 1996).

51. For further analysis, see Chapters 2 and 3 of Peter Dreier, John Mollenkopf, and Todd Swanstrom, *Place Matters* (Lawrence: University Press of Kansas, 2001).

52. Joseph Persky and Wim Wiewel, *When Corporations Leave Town* (Detroit: Wayne State University Press, 2000), 23–72.

53. Ibid, 72.

54. Joseph J. Persky and Wim Wiewel, "Economic Development and Metropolitan Sprawl," in Max Sawicky, ed., *The End of Welfare?* (Washington, DC: Economic Policy Institute, 1999), 141–42.

55. Moe and Wilkie, *Changing Places,* 144; a solid general discussion of this issue can be found in their book on pages 142–77.

56. Stacy Mitchell, *The Hometown Advantage: How To Defend Your Main Street Against Chain Stores . . . and Why It Matters* (Minneapolis: Institute for Local Self-Reliance, 2000), 5–9. See also Mitchell's excellent discussion of why local ownership is more beneficial than chain stores for local communities, 11–17. Also on this issue, see Christopher and Hazel Dayton Gunn, *Reclaiming Capital* (Ithaca: Cornell University Press, 1991).

57. See Gunn and Gunn, *Reclaiming Capital;* David Morris, *Self-Reliant Cities* (San Francisco: Sierra Club Books, 1982); David Imbroscio, *Reconstructing City Politics* (Thousand Oaks: Sage Publications, 1997).

58. Kenneth E. Stone, "Impact of the Wal-Mart Phenomenon on Rural Communities," paper presented at National Public Policy Education Conference, Charleston, South Carolina, September 24, 1997.

59. Annette Bernhardt, "The Wal-Mart Trap," *Dollars and Sense,* September-October 2000.

60. See Thomas and Mary Edsall, *Chain Reaction* (New York: Norton, 1991).

61. Andres Duany, Elizabeth Plater-Zyberk, and Jeff Speck, *Suburban Nation: The Rise of Sprawl and the Decline of the American Dream* (New York: North Point Press, 2000), 45–46.

62. Juliet F. Gainsborough, *Fenced Off: The Suburbanization of American Politics* (Washington, DC: Georgetown University Press, 2001). See Appendix for summary tables, 143–69.

63. For an important recent analysis of the consequences of suburban privilege in metropolitan contexts from a political theory point of view, see Iris Marion Young, *Inclusion and Democracy* (New York: Oxford University Press, 2001).

64. Timothy Egan, "Dreams of Fields: The New Politics of Urban Sprawl," *New York Times,* November 15, 1998; Peter S. Goodman and Dan Eggen, "A Vote to Keep Sprawl at Bay," *Washington Post,* November 5, 1998, B1.

65. Robert Geddes, "Metropolis Unbound," *American Prospect,* November-December 1997, 44.

66. Jennifer Preston, "New Jersey Legislature Puts Plan To Conserve Open Land on Ballot," *New York Times,* July 31, 1998, A1; Goodman and Eggen, "A Vote to Keep Sprawl at Bay."

67. Neal Peirce, "Sprawl Control: Now Key Political Issue," *Baltimore Sun,* November 15, 1998.

68. Egan, "Dreams of Fields"; see also Peirce, "Sprawl Control," and "'Growing Smarter' offers millions to preserve open space," *AP Wire Story,* November 4, 1998.

69. Egan, "Dreams of Fields"; Peirce, "Sprawl Control"; Jennifer Preston, "Battling Sprawl, States Buy Land for Open Space," *New York Times,* June 9, 1998, A1. Quote from Peirce.

70. Egan, "Dreams of Fields."

71. Peter S. Goodman, "Glendening vs. Suburban Sprawl," *Washington Post,* Oct. 6, 1998, B1.

72. Ibid.

73. "Governor Puts Md. Money on Smart Growth," *Washington Post,* August 20, 2000, C1.

74. "Maryland Farmland a Focus In Suburban Sprawl Battle," *New York Times,* June 25, 2001, 10.

75. "Maryland Going 'Beyond the Pavement'; State Shifting Focus From Roads to Pedestrians and Transit," *Washington Post,* September 15, 2000, A1.

76. Alan Ehrenhalt, "New Recruits in the War on Sprawl," *New York Times,* April 13, 1999, A23.

77. John Hughes, "Study: Businesses Fight Urban Sprawl," AP news item, June 14, 1999.

78. See www.smvg.org for an overview of SMVG's activities.

79. Judith Havemann, "Gore Calls For Smart Growth," *Washington Post,* September 3, 1998, A17.

80. 2000 Democratic Party Platform Committee Report, 16, available at www.democrats.org.

81. Peter Grant, "Raising Arizona: A Sprawling Battle Nears Vote—Polls Show Strong Support For Measure to Limit Growth Around Cities," *Wall Street Journal,* September 20, 2000, B2.

82. For a solid discussion of the issue in Portland from an activist perspective, see Tasha Harmon "Portland, Oregon: Who Pays the Price for Regional Planning? How To Link Growth Management and Affordable Housing," in *Planners Network* 128 (March-April 1998).

83. See Justin Phillips and Eban Goodstein, "Growth Management and Housing Prices: The Case of Portland, Oregon," *Contemporary Economic Policy* 18, 3 (2000): 334–44; See, also, the discussion of Oregon planning consultant Eben Fodor in *Better Not Bigger* (Gabriela, BC: New Society Publishers, 1999), 60–76.

84. Wim Wiewel, Joseph Persky, and Mark Sendzik of the University of Illinois at Chicago have helpfully reviewed a wide range of antisprawl policies in "Private Benefits and Public Costs: Policies to Address Suburban Sprawl," *Policy Studies Journal,* 27, 1 (1999): 96–114.

85. But Wiewel and Persky suggest that this windfall is offset by the public costs averted when a central city household chooses to remain in place rather than move to the suburbs.

86. Wiewel, Persky and Sendzik, "Private Benefits and Public Costs."

87. Ibid.

88. Ibid, 129.

89. Peter Dreier, John Mollenkopf and Todd Swanstrom, *Place Matters* (Lawrence: University Press of Kansas, 2001), 211–12.

CHAPTER 4

1. Alice O'Connor, "Swimming Against the Tide: A Brief History of Federal Policy in Poor Communities," in Ronald Ferguson and William Dickens, eds. *Urban Problems and Community* Development. Washington: Brookings, 1999, 79–80.

2. "The government is a major part of the problem; it is also central to the remedy." John Kenneth Galbraith, *Economics and the Public Purpose.* Boston: Houghton Mifflin, 1972, 242.

3. Ethan Kapstein, "Trade Liberalization and the Politics of Trade Adjustment Assistance" in *International Labour Review* Vol. 137 (1998), No. 4, 511.

4. Thomas Friedman, *The Lexus and The Olive Tree.* New York: Farrar, Strauss and Giroux, 1999, 358–60; Howard D. Samuel, Lawrence Chimerine and Marvin Fooks, "Strengthening Trade Adjustment Assistance," manuscript available from the Economic Strategy Institute at www.econstrat.org/taa.htm; I.M. Destler, "Trade Politics and Labor Issues, 1953–1995," in Susan Collins, ed. *Imports, Exports, and the American Worker.* Washington: Brookings, 1998, 389–408.

5. *Budget of the United States Fiscal Year 2003: Appendix* (Washington: Government Printing Office, 2002), 659, 209.

6. Gary Clyde Hufbauer and Howard F. Rosen: *Trade Policy for Troubled Industries* (Washington, DC: Institute for International Economics, 1986), 34; Destler, "Trade Politics and Labor Issues," 392.

7. Department of Labor fact sheet on TAA available at www.doleta.gov/programs/fact-sht/taa.htm

8. Leah Marcal, "Does Trade Adjustment Assistance Help Trade Displaced Workers?" *Contemporary Economic Policy,* 19, 1 (2001), 59–72.

9. Department of Labor fact sheet on TAA.

10. See statement of Loren Yager, Director, International Affairs and Trade, General Accounting Office, "Trade Adjustment Assistance: Improvements Necessary, but Programs Cannot Solve Communities' Long Term Problems," testimony to Senate Subcommittee on International Trade, Committee of Finance. July 20, 2001. GAO-01-988T. See Appendix of Yoger's statement.

11. "Nabisco Workers in Falls to Get Trade-Related Benefits," *The Buffalo News,* August 25, 2001, C7

12. Louis Jacobson, "Compensation Programs," in Susan Collins, ed. *Imports, Exports, and the American Worker* (Washington, DC: Brookings Institution, 1998), 486.

13. "Dislocated Workers: Comparison of Assistance Programs." GAO/HRD-92-153BR.

14. "Trade Adjustment Assistance: Experiences of Six Trade-Impacted Communities." August 2001. GAO-01-838, m 3–4.

15. *Budget of the United States Fiscal Year 2003: Appendix,* 209.

16. Quote from Economic Development Administration website, summer 2000 (page now defunct). For the current (October 2001) EDA page on Trade Adjustment Assistance for firms, see http://www.doc.gov/eda/html/2B4_6_tradeadjustment.htm.

17. "Effective Aid to Trade-Impacted Manufacturers: An Evaluation of the Trade Adjustment Assistance Program," report prepared for the Economic Development Administration by the Urban Institute, 1998.

18. See the website of the Trade Adjustment Assistance Centers, www.taacenters.org, for an overview of the TAA for firms program: re Trager, see www.taacenters.org/wceol.html.

19. "Effective Aid to Trade-Impacted Manufacturers: An Evaluation of the Trade Adjustment Assistance Program."

20. "Trade Adjustment Assistance: Impact of Federal Assistance to Firms is Unclear," letter report, December 15, 2000, GAO/GAO-01-12.

21. Description used in Solomon Moore, "Loan Pool Targets Pacoima Job Losses," *Los Angeles Times,* January 28, 1998, B1. On Torres and the creation of the NADBank, see John R. MacArthur, *The Selling of "Free Trade",* (New York: Hill and Wang, 2000) 258–59.

22. Ibid., 305–6.

23. Joint Status Report, Border Environment Cooperation Commission and the North American Development Bank, June 30, 2001. These quarterly status reports are available from the Web site of the North American Development Bank, www.nadbank.org.

24. North American Development Bank Web site, www.nadbank.org.

25. SBA press release, "SBA Offers Loans to Businesses in Areas Locally Affected by NAFTA," August 5, 1997.

26. Joint Status Report, BECC and NADBank, June 30, 2001; "Trade Adjustment Assistance: Opportunities to Improve the Community Adjustment and Investment Program," letter report, September 29, 2000, GAO/NSIAD-00-229.

27. Moore, "Loan Pool Targets Pacoima Job Losses."

28. Border Environment Cooperation Commission and the North American Development Bank, Joint Status Report, March 31, 2001. See also the NADB Web site, www.nadbank-caip.org for details on CAIP projects.

29. "Employment Training: Successful Projects Share Common Strategy," GAO, 1996, T-HEHS-96-127, 1.

30. *Budget of the United States, Fiscal Year 2003: Appendix* (Washington, DC: Government Printing Office, 2002), 657. See also the Catalog of Domestic Financial Assistance, www.cfda.gov/static/p17260.htm.

31. *Budget of the United States, Government, Fiscal Year 2003: Appendix,* 660. For more information, see the AFL-CIO's guide to the WIA at www.workingforamerica.org/documents/Factsheets/factsht10.htm.

32. See, for example, Gordon Lafer, "The Politics of Job Training: Urban Poverty and the False Hope of JTPA," *Politics and Society,* 22, 2 (1994).

33. O'Connor, "Swimming Against the Tide," 113.

34. *The Budget of the United States Government, Fiscal Year 2003: Appendix,* 485.

35. That is, for each activity, 51 percent of the beneficiaries must have a low or moderate income for that activity to count towards the 70 percent quota.

36. *Federal Funds, Local Choices: An Evaluation of the Community Development Block Grant Program* (Washington, DC: Urban Institute, 1994), 6:13.

37. Ibid., p. 6:14, 30.

38. Ibid., p. 3:39.

39. Ibid., p. 3:43.

40. "An Assessment of the Nation's First Block Grants," *The Urban Institute Policy and Research Report,* 25, 1, (1995): 3.

41. *Housing and Urban Development: Use and Oversight of the Economic Development Loan Fund* (GAO/RCED-97-195), 1.
42. *Budget of the United States, Fiscal Year 2003: Appendix,* 492.
43. *Federal Register,* vol. 64, no. 38, February 26, 1999, 9791.
44. *Budget of the United States Fiscal Year 2001: Appendix* (Washington, DC: Government Printing Office, 2000), 493.
45. *Budget of the United States Fiscal Year 2003: Appendix,* 485.
46. For a complete list of labor surplus areas in one recent year, fiscal 2000, see the following Department of Labor web page, doletawdsc.org/newsroom/press/labor.htm.
47. *Department of Energy Annual Procurement and Financial Assistance Report,* Fiscal 1996 (Washington, DC: Department of Energy, 1997).
48. NCESA interview with Tony Diamond, small-business advisor, NASA.
49. From information provided by the Fact Sheet and Program Summary available at the HUBZone program website, www.sba.gov/hubzone.
50. Bruce K. Mulock, "Economic Development Administration: Issues in the 105th Congress," Congressional Research Service issue brief for Congress, October 7, 1997.
51. *Budget of the United States Government 2003: Appendix,* 209. The EDA has had its share of critics over the years. For a defense of the federal role in community economic development in general and that of the EDA in particular by two EDA officials, see Chester J. Straub and Kelly Robinson, "Response to Thornburgh and Hill: The Federal Role in Economic Development," *Economic Development Quarterly* 14, 3 (2000): 255–64.
52. *Budget of the United States Government 2001* (Washington, DC: Government Printing Office, 2000), 229.
53. Bruce K. Mulock, "Economic Development Administration: Issues in the 105th Congress," Congressional Research Service issue brief for Congress, October 7, 1997.
54. *Budget of the United States Government, Fiscal Year 2001,* 229.
55. *Budget of the United States Government, Fiscal Year 1999,* 202.
56. *Budget of the United States Government, Fiscal Year 2001,* 230–31; *Budget of the United States Government, Fiscal Year 2003,* 391.
57. *Budget of the United States Government, Fiscal Year 2003,* 391; see also the National Association of Development organization's web page www.nado.org/legaffair/delfa_/htm.
58. *Budget of the United States Fiscal Year 2003: Appendix,* 487; *Analytical Perspectives, Budget of the United States 2003* (Washington, DC: Government Printing Office, 2000), 100. The total value of EZ/EC/Renewal Community tax expenditures is expected to exceed $1.1 billion in fiscal 2003.
59. "Introduction to the RC/EZ/EC Initiative," www.hud.gov/offices/cpd/ezec/about/ezecinit.cfm.
60. Information adapted from Gov. Doc. # HUD-1443-CPD, Department of Housing and Urban Development and Office of Community Planning, *Guidebook: Strategic Planning,* HUD-1443-CPD (Washington, DC: HUD, 1994). Quote from 13.
61. A qualified zone business is one where at least 50 percent of gross income is from a business within the zone, a substantial portion of the employer's services are performed within the zone, and at least 35 percent of its employees are residents of the empowerment zone. See "Tax Incentives for Empowerment Zones and Other Distressed Communities," Internal Revenue Service Publication 954, June 2001.

62. U.S. Department of Housing and Urban Development, "Opportunities for Business in EZ/EC Urban Communities," 1995, HUD-1552-CPD: 9–10.

63. *Guidebook: Federal Programs from Housing and Urban Development,* HUD-1533-CPD (Washington, DC: Government Printing Office, 1995), 92.

64. Executive Order 12072, Federal Space Management, August 16, 1978.

65. "Clinton Signs New Directive on Agency Location, But Battle Brews in Congress," *Economic Developments* 21, 11 (1996). Quotes are from article. See also Executive Order 13006, May 21, 1996; and goodneighbor.gsa.gov.

66. *Guidebook: Federal Programs from Housing and Urban Development*

67. See Alan Peters and Peter Fisher, "Tax and Spending Incentives and Enterprise Zones," *New England Economic Review,* March 1997, for an analysis of the advantages firms are likely to derive from locating in an Enterprise Zone community. Peters and Fisher plan to publish a more complete analysis in book form in 2002.

68. O'Connor, "Swimming Against the Tide," 117.

69. "Fact Sheet: President Clinton's New Markets Initiative: Revitalizing America's Underserved Communities," press release issued by the White House Press Office, December 15, 2000.

70. "How HUD's APIC Program Will Work," HUD document, October 1999. For a description of the original New Markets Initiative proposal, see See "SBA's New Markets Initiatives," Small Business Administration document, 2000.

71. *Military Bases: Status of Prior Base Realignment and Closure Rounds,* GAO/NSIAD-99-36 (Washington, DC: GAO, 1998), 85, Appendix I.

72. *Military Bases: Lessons Learned From Prior Base Closure Rounds,* GAO/NSIAD-97-151 (Washington, DC: GAO, 1997), 32–33.

73. "Economic Renewal: Community Reuse of Former Military Bases," Department of Defense report released April 21, 1999, available at www.defenselink.mil/pubs/reuse042199.html.

74. Peter L. Stenberg, "Rural Communities and Military Base Closures," *Rural Development Perspectives* 13, 2 (1998): 18.

75. Joshua Gotbaum (former Assistant Secretary of Defense for economic security), "Closing Bases Tough but Necessary" *Defense Issues* 10, 23 (1995). Text available online at http://www.defenselink.mil/speeches/1995/di1023.html.

76. *Military Bases: Status of Prior Base Realignment and Closure Rounds,* 85, Appendix I.

77. David Sorenson, *Shutting Down the Cold War: The Politics of Military Base Closures* (New York: St. Martin's Press, 1998), 65.

78. "Economic Renewal: Community Reuse of Former Military Bases."

79. John Lynch, George Schlossberg and William Bopf, "Acquiring Base Closure Property," in Karl F. Seidman, ed., *Best Practices in Defense Conversion: A Practitioner's Guide to Successful Strategies and Programs* (Washington, DC: National Council for Urban Economic Development, 1995).

80. Sorenson, *Shutting Down the Cold War,* 63.

81. "Economic Renewal: Community Reuse of Former Military Bases."

82. *The Upside of Base Closure: Tools for Reinvesting in Communities,* report of the East Bay Conversion and Reinvestment Commission (Oakland, CA: East Bay Conversion and Reinvestment Commission, 2000), 6. This report is an excellent overview of the military base conversion process.

83. Kay B. Podagrosi, "Leadership in Economic Development: The Case of the Closing of Chanute Air Force Base in Rantoul, Illinois," *Economic Development Review* 14, 1, Baker (1996): 39ff.

84. Sorenson, *Shutting Down the Cold War,* 65.

85. See Scott M. Reznick, *Defense Adjustment Infrastructure Bonds: Credit Enhancement Grants Make Affordable Capital Available* (Washington, DC: Economic Development Administration, Dept. of Commerce, 1998).

86. *Military Bases: Status of Prior Base Realignment and Closure Rounds,* 42.

87. Department of Defense sources. See, for instance, Raymond DuBois, Jr., deputy under secretary of defense for installations and environment, remarks to the National Association of Installation Developers Annual Conference, San Antonio, TX, August 7, 2001, available at www.acq.osd.mil/docs/DuBois-NAID_8%20Aug%2001.htm.

88. *The Report of the Department of Defense on Base Realignment and Closure* (Washington, DC: Department of Defense) April 1998, 56. Available at www.defenselink.mil/pubs/archive.html.

89. For a critical examination of prior experience with converting military bases closed in the 1960s, see Catherine Hill, "Measuring Success in the Redevelopment of Former Military Bases: Evidence From a Case Study of the Truman Complex in Key West, Florida," *Economic Development Quarterly* 14, 3 (2000): 265–75.

90. *Budget of the United States Government, Fiscal 2003, Appendix,* 135–37.

91. See the following Department of Agriculture Web site: www.rurdev.usda.gov/rbs/busp/b&i_dir.htm.

92. See the following Department of Agriculture Web site: www.rurdev.usda.gov/rbs/busp/b&i_gar.htm.

93. See the following Department of Agriculture Web site: www.rurdev.usda.gov/rbs/busp/rbeg.htm.

94. *Budget of the United States Government, Fiscal Year 2003: Appendix,* 146–147.

95. Ibid., 140. See also this Department of Agriculture Web site: www.rurdev.usda.gov/agency/rhs/cf/cf.htm.

96. *Budget of the United States Government, Fiscal Year 2003: Appendix,* 129. -See also rcdnet.org, web site of the National Association of Resource and Conservation Development Councils.

97. "Rural Utilities Service: Opportunities to Operate Electricity and Telecommunications Loan Programs More Effectively," GAO/RCED-98-42, 3–4.

98. *Budget of the United States Government, Fiscal Year 2003: Appendix,* 154.

99. David Imbroscio, *Reconstructing City Politics* (Thousand Oaks, CA: Sage, 1997).

100. *Budget of the United States Government, Fiscal 2003: Appendix,* 1056.

101. Ibid., 1055, 1060.

102. See the following Small Business Administration Web page: www.sba.gov/budget/sum3.html.

103. See the following Small Business Administration Web page: wwwsba.gov/sbir/indexsbir-sttr.html.

104. For the USDA's contract goals in 1998, see www.gov/da/smallbus/goals.htm

105. See Mark Solof, "The History of MPOs," 1997, available from the North Jersey Transit Planning Authority at njtpanjit.edu/hist_mpo1.htm.

106. *Budget of the United States Government, Fiscal 2003: Appendix,* 768.

107. John Swanson, "In the Spotlight: MPO Best Practices," March 1998, available from the Association of Metropolitan Planning Organizations.

108. See the Web site of the Association of Metropolitan Planning Organizations, www.ampo.org, for an overview.

109. "Super Fund: EPA's Use of Funds for Brownfield Revitalization," GAO/RCED-98-87, 3.

110. *The Brownfields Economic Redevelopment Initiative: Proposal Guidelines for Brownfields Job Training and Development Demonstration Pilots* (Washington, DC: EPA, 2000).

111. "Brownfields Economic Redevelopment Initiative Fact Sheet," 2000, available at http://www.epa.gov/swerosps/bf/pdf/econinit.pdf.

112. Ibid.

113. Ibid; "Federal Interagency Working Group on Brownfields Fact Sheet," April 1999, EPA.

114. "Brownfields Tax Incentive," EPA fact sheet, August 1997.

115. *The Brownfields Economic Redevelopment Initiative: Proposal Guidelines for Brownfields Cleanup Revolving Loan Fund Demonstration Program* (Washington, DC: EPA, 1999).

116. "Brownfields Cleanup Revolving Loan Fund Pilot Program Fact Sheet," September 2001, EPA.

117. "Brownfields Showcase Communities Fact Sheet," October 2000, EPA.

118. "EPA Administrator Carol M. Browner Announces the Selection of 12 New Brownfields Showcase Communities," EPA press release, October 11, 2000.

119. For academic views of Brownfield efforts to date, see Ken M. Chilton, "Community Reinvestment and Brownfields: The Missing Corporate Link" and Peter Meyer, "Looking at State 'Smart Growth' Efforts in Living Color: Can Brownfield Generation Really Protect Greenfields from Urbanization," papers delivered at 2001 meetings of the Urban Affairs Association, Detroit, MI, 2001. Chilton is at Jackson State University and Meyer is at the University of Louisville.

120. Janice Shields, "Aid For Dependent Foreign and U.S. Corporations," Center for Study of Responsive Law policy brief, Washington, DC, 1997.

121. Donald Bartlett and James Steele, "Fantasy Islands and Other Perfectly Legal Ways That Big Companies Manage to Avoid Billions in Federal Taxes," *Time,* November 16, 1998, 78ff.

122. *Budget of the United States Government, Fiscal 2003: Analytical Tables* (Washington, DC: Government Printing Office, 2002), 100.

123. "John McCain vs. the Internet," *National Review Washington Bulletin,* February 14, 2000.

124. Robert Benson, "Getting Business Off the Public Dole: State and Local Model Laws to Curb Corporate Welfare Abuse," National Lawyers Guild of Los Angeles, 1995. See also Robert McIntyre, ed., *Tax Expenditures: The Hidden Entitlements* (Washington, DC: Citizens for Tax Justice, 1996), available at www.ctj.org.

125. Ralph Nader, testimony before the House Committee on the Budget, June 30, 1999. See this testimony for a stellar, comprehensive overview of the various forms of "corporate welfare." Available at www.nader.org. See Donald Bartlett and James Steele, "Corporate Welfare," *Time,* November 9, 1998, 36ff for the estimate of $125 billion in annual corporate support.

126. Ralph Nader, testimony before the House Committee on the Budget, June 30, 1999.

127. Numerous proposals have been offered from both the left and the right to confront "corporate welfare" expenditures; in 1997, for instance, conservative Congressional leader John Kasich spearheaded an alliance of conservative and libertarian lawmakers named the "Stop Corporate Welfare Coalition." Perhaps the most comprehensive plan to date to reduce corporate welfare is Ralph Nader's twenty-five-point legislation (which would eliminate tax breaks and most forms of market promotion and export assistance, as well as put an end to the free corporate use of public resources), outlined in his testimony before the House Committee on the Budget, June 30, 1999. For a fine analysis of how one form of welfare, to corporations, remains largely invisible whereas poor people with pressing economic problems are demonized for accepting federal grants, see Paulette Olson and Dell Champlin, "Ending Corporate Welfare As We Know It: An Institutional Analysis of the Dual Structure of Welfare," *Journal of Economic Issues* 32, 3 (1998): 759–71.

CHAPTER 5

1. James Heckman, "Policies to Foster Human Capital," *Research in Economics* 54 (2000), 3–56.

2. *Directory of Incentives for Business Investment and Development in the United States: A State by State Guide* (Washington, DC: National Association of State Development Agencies, 1998). See also these state web sites for further information: www.ecodev.state.mo.us; www.state.ia.us; www.ctdol.state.ct.us; www.state.nd.us/jsnd.

3. For a variety of perspectives on job training programs in the United States, see Gordon Lafer, "The Politics of Job Training," *Politics and Society* 22, 3 (1994), and W. N. Grubb, *Learning to Work* (New York: Russell Sage Foundation, 1996). See also Nathan Glazer, "A Human Capital Policy for Cities," *The Public Interest* 112 (1993): 36, and R. LaLonde, "The Promise of Public Sector-Sponsored Training Programs," *Journal of Economic Perspectives* 9, 2 (1995).

4. As quoted in Glazer, "A Human Capital Policy for Cities," 40.

5. E. Mueller and A. Schwartz, "Leaving Poverty Through Work," *Economic Development Quarterly* 12, 2, (1998), 169; Brenda A. Lautsch and Paul Osterman, "Changing the Constraints: A Successful Employment and Training Strategy," in R. P. Giloth, ed., *Jobs and Economic Development* (Thousand Oaks, CA: Sage, 1998), 214–33.

6. Mueller and Schwartz, "Leaving Poverty Through Work," 169.

7. Steven L. Dawson, "Start-Ups and Replication," in Giloth, ed., *Jobs and Economic Development,* 123.

8. Ibid., 132.

9. William T. Dickens, "Rebuilding Urban Labor Markets," in Ronald F. Ferguson and William T. Dickens, eds., *Community Development and Urban Problems* (Washington, DC: Brookings, 1999), 406–8.

10. Bennett Harrison and Marcus Weiss, *Workforce Development Networks* (Thousand Oaks, CA: Sage, 1998), 39.

11. Ibid., 2–3.

12. Edwin Melendez and Bennett Harrison, "Matching the Disadvantaged to Job Opportunities," *Economic Development Quarterly* 12, 1 (1998): 3–11; Harrison and Weiss, *Workforce Development Networks.*
13. Dickens, "Rebuilding Urban Labor Markets," 413.
14. Harrison and Weiss, *Workforce Development Networks.* See also Heckman, "Policies to Foster Human Capital," 43.
15. Laura Dresser and Joel Rogers, "Networks, Sectors, and Workforce Learning," in Giloth, ed., *Jobs and Economic Development,* 75.
16. Ibid. See also the Center on Wisconsin Strategy web site, www.cows.org.
17. Ibid., 71–72.
18. Lautsch and Osterman, "Changing the Constraints," 215.
19. Dawson, "Start-Ups and Replication," 133; Dresser and Rogers, "Networks, Sectors, and Workforce Learning," 72.
20. Dresser and Rogers, "Networks, Sectors, and Workforce Learning," 72.
21. John Howe and Mark Vallianatos "Making Corporations Accountable Through Legislative Initiatives," in *Public Subsidies, Public Accountability* (Washington, DC: Grassroots Policy Project, 1998), 43–44.
22. Greg LeRoy, Fiona Hsu, and Sara Hinkley, "The Policy Shift to Good Jobs," report released by Good Jobs First, Washington, DC, May 2000, available at www.goodjobsfirst.org.
23. Howe and Vallianatos, "Making Corporations Accountable," 50.
24. According to an estimate made by the director of economic-development incentives at Coopers and Lybrand. See Michael M. Phillips, "Localities Force Firms to Keep Promises," *Wall Street Journal,* June 26, 1996.
25. Alan H. Peters, "Clawbacks and the Administration of Economic Development Policy in the Midwest," *Economic Development Quarterly,* 7, 4 (1993): 328.
26. Howe and Vallianatos, "Making Corporations Accountable," 50–52.
27. Greg Leroy, *No More Candy Store* (Chicago, IL: Federation for Industrial Retention and Renewal, 1994), 43–46.
28. Peters, "Clawbacks," 339.
29. Phillips, "Localities Force Firms to Keep Promises."
30. Ibid.
31. Howe and Vallianatos, "Making Corporations Accountable," 51. For a brief recent overview of proposals to establish multi-state compacts to stop job raiding, see Leslie Parrish, "Can State Incentive Compacts Work?" *Accountability: The Newsletter of the Business Incentives Clearinghouse,* March 2001, available at www.cfedorg/sustainable_economies/business_incentives/BI_newsletters/3_01.html.
32. Howe and Vallianatos, "Making Corporations Accountable," 51.
33. Jay Hancock, "Resolving the War Between the States," *The Baltimore Sun,* October 17, 1999.
34. Howe and Vallianatos, "Making Corporations Accountable," 52.
35. Charles Mahtesian "A Non-Poaching Peace Pact Is Under Fire in Florida," *Governing,* May 2000, 90.
36. Ralph Nader, testimony before the House Committee on the Budget, June 30, 1999.

37. Hancock, "Resolving the War Between the States."

38. Ibid.; Mahtesian, "A Non-Poaching Peace Pact."

39. Howe and Vallianatos, "Making Corporations Accountable," 48.

40. In a clever move, the Employment Policies Institute registered the domain name www.livingwage.org for their site tracking the campaign. The Institute argues that studies favoring the living wage are biased and that the movement threatens to hurt low-income workers by reducing the number of low-income jobs (parroting arguments made against the minimum wage more broadly). No evidence yet exists to support that conclusion.

41. Living wage provisions also can be included as a condition imposed on businesses receiving public subsidies (see discussion of corporate accountability measures above). See Howe and Vallianatos, "Making Corporations Accountable," 47–48. Also see LeRoy et al, "The Policy Shift to Good Jobs."

42. See www.livingwageresearch.org, maintained by the Employment Policy Foundation.

43. David Moberg, "Martha Jernegons's New Shoes," *The American Prospect,* June 19–July 3, 2000, 50–53.

44. See ACORN's website, www.livingwagecampaign.org, for updates.

45. Marc V. Levine. "The Politics of Partnership," in G. D. Squires, ed., *Unequal Partnerships: The Political Economy of Urban Redevelopment in Postwar America* (New Brunswick, NJ: Rutgers University Press, 1989), 30.

46. Clarence N. Stone, "Summing Up," in C. Stone and H. Sanders, eds., *The Politics of Urban Development* (Lawrence, KS: University Press of Kansas, 1987), 279.

47. T. Herrero, "Housing Linkage," *Journal of Urban Affairs* 13 (1991): 4–7.

48. M. P. Smith, "The Uses of Linked-Development Policies in U.S. Cities," in M. Parkinson, B. Foley, and D. Judd, eds., *Regenerating the Cities* (Glenview, IL: Scott, Foresman, 1989), 173–96.

49. Edward G. Goetz, "Type II Policy and Mandated Benefits in Economic Development," *Urban Affairs Quarterly* 25 (1990): 170–90; Laura Reese, "Sharing the Benefits of Economic Development: What Cities Use Type II Policies," *Urban Affairs Review* 33, 5 (1998). The work of Reese and Goetz surveys cities' use of what they call "type II policies," not simply their use of "linkage," although linkage is a prominent example of type II policies. Type II policies include a variety of measures that obligate private developers "to provide a service or public benefit in exchange for development rights." See Goetz, "Type II Policy," 171.

50. Wim Wiewel et al., "Private Benefits and Public Costs," *Policy Studies Journal* 27, 1 (1999): 104–5.

51. David L Imbroscio."Overcoming the Economic Dependence of Urban America," *Journal of Urban Affairs* 15 (1993): 175–76.

52. Wiewel et al., "Private Benefits and Public Costs," 104–5.

53. Ibid., 104.

54. Ibid.,104–5.

55. David Rusk, foreword to Myron Orfield, *MetroPolitics* (Washington, DC: Brookings Institution, 1998), xi.

56. Wiewel et al., "Private Benefits and Public Costs," 105; see also Orfield, *MetroPolitics,* 167–71.

CHAPTER 6

1. Theodore J Stumm, "Municipal Enterprise Activities as Revenue Generators," *American Review of Public Administration,* December 26, 1996, 477–88.

2. Theodore J. Stumm, "Revenue Generation and Expenditure Implications of Municipal Non-Utility Enterprises," *Journal of Public Budgeting, Accounting, and Financial Management* 8 (1997): 498–515.

3. David Osborne and Ted Gaebler, *Reinventing Government* (New York: Addison-Wesley, 1992); Michael Silverstein, *The Public Entrepreneurship Manual* (Collingdale, PA: Diane Publishing, 1996).

4. Gary Paul, "Measuring the Effects of Municipal Enterprise on the Budgets of Local Governments," *Western Journal of Black Studies,* winter 1999, 217–28.

5. For all statistics quoted here, see the data on power statistics available from the American Public Power Association at www.appanet.org. Data cited are for 1999.

6. Bureau of the Census, 1999 Public Employment Data, accessed at www.census.gov/govs/www/apes.html; "Public Power: An American Tradition That Works," from American Public Power Association, www.appanet.org.

7. Jeff Stansbury, "The State: How Kilowatt Socialism Saved L.A. from the Energy Crisis," *Los Angeles Times,* April 29, 2001.

8. "Public Power Costs Less," *2001 Annual Directory and Statistical Report of the American Public Power Association,* available at www.appanet.org.

9. See "Straight Answers to False Charges Against Public Power," at www.appanet.org.

10. Sacramento Municipal Utility District web page, www.smud.org, fact sheet on "Public Goods" updated June 2001.

11. See www.smud.org/info/profile.html (dated August 2001).

12. Ibid.

13. See the Sacramento Municipal Utility District Web site, www.smud.org; and NCESA interviews.

14. Seattle City Light, 1999 Annual Report, available at www.cityofseattle.net/light/aboutus.

15. NCESA interview.

16. Agis Salpukas, "The Rebellion in 'Pole City,'" *The New York Times,* October 10, 1995.

17. NCESA interview.

18. M. Van Wart et al., 2000. "Economic Development and Public Enterprise: The Case of Rural Iowa's Telecommunication Utilities," *Economic Development Quarterly* 14, 2 (2000): 131–45.

19. Jim Booth and R. W. Beck, "Municipal Utilities Can Thrive Under Deregulation," *The American City & County* 114, 2 (1999): 16–17.

20. Earl Hazan, "City Utilities Build Upon their Strengths to Compete," *Transmission & Distribution World* 51, 1 (1999): 50–54.

21. Booth and Beck, "Municipal Utilities."

22. *Public Power Weekly,* January 5, 1998, 4.

23. Burnaby J. Feeder, "Some Local Cheers for 'Creeping Socialism,'" *New York Times,* October 4, 1997; Van Wart et al., "Economic Development and Public Enterprise"; Jan Youtie, "Field of Dreams Revisited: Economic Development and Telecommunications in LaGrange, Georgia, *Economic Development Quarterly* 14, 2 (2000): 146–53; Susan E.

Clarke and Gary L. Gaile, "Local Politics in a Global Era: Thinking Locally, Acting Globally," *AAPSS Annals* 551 (1997): 38.

24. Youtie, "Field of Dreams," 146.

25. See city of Glasgow Web site, www.glasgow-ky.com. The following account also draws on Kristin Rusch, *The Emerging New Society,* (Washington, DC: National Center for Economic and Security Alternatives, 2001), 133–37.

26. "Purchase of Comcast by Glasgow EPB Now Complete," press release of Glasgow Electronic Plant Board, April 2, 2001 Available at www.glasgow-ky.com/releases.

27. See Glasgow Electric Power Board online FAQ, at http://www.glasgow-ky.com/epb.

28. See city of Tacoma Web site, www.ci.tacoma.wa.us, and www.click-network.com.

29. Ron Starner, "Tacoma: Wired for Growth," *Site Selection Magazine* online, September 25, 2000, available at www.conway.com/ssinsider/special/000925tacoma.htm.

30. David Armstrong and Dennis K. Berman. "High in Fiber: Telecom Companies Confront New Rival: The Municipal Network," *The Wall Street Journal,* August 17, 2001.

31. Ibid.

32. Wisconsin State Life Insurance Fund Web site, badger.state.wi.us/agencies/oci/slif.htm.

33. Annual Statement of the State Life Insurance Fund, State of Wisconsin, 1998. See also M. Carnoy and D. Shearer, *Economic Democracy* (New York, NY: M. E. Sharpe, 1980), 68–69.

34. David L. Imbroscio, *Reconstructing City Politics* (Thousand Oaks, CA: Sage Publications, 1997), 152.

35. Bank of North Dakota, 2000 Annual Report, available at www.banknd.com.

36. Bank of North Dakota, 1998 Annual Report (Bismarck, ND: Bank of North Dakota, 1999), 4.

37. Ibid., 8.

38. Ibid., 3.

39. See Imbroscio, *Reconstructing City Politics,* 156–58.

40. Ibid., 158, 169.

41. Robert G. Heard and John Sibert, *Growing New Businesses with Seed and Venture Capital: State Experiences and Options* (Washington, DC: National Governors Association, 2000), 49.

42. Chris Silva, "Biotech Firms Near Funding," *Baltimore Business Journal,* August 31, 2001; Dana Hedgpeth, "Fund for Start-Up Firms Yields Big Payoff for Md.," *Washington Post,* March 6, 2000.

43. Dana Hedgpeth, "Fund for Start-Up Firms Yields Big Payoff for Md.," *Washington Post,* March 6, 2000.

44. "Investments in Firms Pay Off for State," *Baltimore Sun,* October 26, 1997

45. Hedgpeth, "Fund for Start-Up Firms."

46. P. K. Eisinger, "State Venture Capitalism, State Politics, and the World of High-Risk Investment," *Economic Development Quarterly* 7 (1993): 131–39.

47. Hedgpeth, "Fund for Start-Up Firms."

48. A. O'M. Bowman, *Tools and Targets* (Washington, DC: National League of Cities, 1987), 4.

49. Susan E. Clarke and Gary L. Gaile, *The Work of Cities* (Minneapolis: University of Minnesota Press, 1998), 84.

50. Imbroscio, *Recontructing City Politics*, 144; also see Scott Cummings et al., "Redevelopment in Downtown Louisville: Public Investments, Private Profits, and Shared Risks," in Squires, ed., *Unequal Partnerships*.

51. T. Barnekov and D. Rich, "Privatism and the Limits of Local Economic Development Policy," *Urban Affairs Quarterly* 25 (1989): 212–38; G. D. Squires, "Public-Private Partnerships: Who Gets What and Why," in Squires, ed., *Unequal Partnerships*, 1–11.

52. David Imbroscio, "Nontraditional Public Enterprise as Local Economic Development Policy," *Policy Studies Journal* 23 (1995): 218–30.

53. B. J. Frieden and L. B. Sagalyn, *Downtown, Inc.* (Boston, MA: MIT Press, 1989), 169.

54. Consultant Allen Katin, as quoted in R. F. Babcock, "The City as Entrepreneur," In T. Lassar, ed. *City Deal Making* (Washington, DC: Urban Land Institute, 1990), 14.

55. NCESA interviews, See also *Moving Toward Joint Development Transit Partnership*, (Washington: National Council for Urban Economic Development, 1989.)

56. NCESA interview; City of San Diego 2001 Comprehensive Annual Financial ReportPort of Los Angeles documents.

57. NCESA interviews; city of Portland 2001 Comprehensive Annual Financial Report; Part of Los Angeles documents.

58. Imbroscio, *Reconstructing City Politics*, 219; See also Osborne and Gaebler, Reinventing Government, 200–01.

59. Penelope Lemov, "Billboards & Souvenirs," *Governing*, October, 1994, 46–50; NCESA interviews; City of San Diego 2001 Comprehensive Annual Financial Report.

60. NCESA interviews. According to city budget documents, the CENTRE did not make a contribution to the city's general fund in fiscal 2001.

61. Michael Silverstein, *The Public Entrepreneurship Manual* (Upland, PA: DIANE Publishing Co.), 1996. NCESA interviews; www.metro-region.org/drc

62. David Morris and Daniel Kraker, "Rooting the Home Team," *The American Prospect* 40 (1998).

63. Charles Mahtesian, "Memo to the Cities: If You Can't Bribe the Owner, Maybe You Can Buy the Team," *Governing*, March 1996, 45.

64. Charles Mahtesian, "Memo to the Cities," 42.

65. David Imbroscio, "Reformulating Urban Regime Theory: The Division of Labor Between State and Market Reconsidered," *Journal of Urban Affairs*, 20 (1998): 239–40.

66. Andrew Zimbalist, *Baseball and Billions* (New York: Basic Books, 1992), 140.

67. Morris and Kraker, "Rooting the Home Team," 42.

68. Charles Mahtesian, "Reinventing the Rec Department," *Governing*, November 1996.

69. *Operating and Financial Performance Profiles of 18-Hole Golf Facilities in the U.S.-Municipal Facilities*, 1998 edition. Jupiter, FL: National Golf Foundation, 1999, 121; "Bethpage: America's Golf Mecca," *Parks & Recreation*, April 1996, 96–97. See also "Bethpage State Park: The People's Country Club," United States Golf Association press release available at www.usga.org.

70. NCESA interviews. Sludge-to-fertilizer operations such as Milwaukee's have been criticized by some environmentalists on health grounds. According to the Milwaukee Metropolitan Sewage District, the city's fertilizer exceeds EPA standards; the fertilizer program also has been defended by independent scientists with no industry ties. Critics

of the program acknowledge that the city has succeeded in sharply reducing the metals content of the fertilizer in the past two decades.

71. NCESA interviews; see also www.eren.doc.gov and "Tomorrow's Energy Today," Department of Energy Publication, 1994.

72. Imbroscio, *Reconstructing City Politics,* 156; Sam Howe Verhovek, "It's Wet. It's Bottled. It Sort of Tastes Like Water," *New York Times,* August 10, 1997, 72.

73. "North Carolina Rail Plan 2001," available at www.bytrain.org/quicklinks/reports/rail2001.

74. Ellen Perlman, "Rail's Resurgence," *Governing,* September 1999.

CHAPTER 7

1. Thomas Michael Power, *Lost Landscapes and Failed Economies* (Washington, DC: Island Press, 1996), 11

2. The seminal work of Jane Jacobs on city economies demonstrates the underlying conceptual dynamics at work. As Jacobs explains, the key process driving local economic expansion is what she calls "import replacement," where businesses begin to produce goods and services locally that were before imported. This process strengthens the linkages among local businesses, as they form a kind of symbiotic relation to one another, and each fill niches within the local economic system. See Jane Jacobs, *Cities and the Wealth of Nations: Principles of Economic Life* (New York: Random House, 1985).

3. Power, *Lost Landscapes,* 11.

4. "Community Income and Expenditure Model," Michigan State University, Center for Urban Affairs, Lansing, Michigan For more information, see the Center for Urban Affairs Web page, http://www.msu.edu/~cua/projects/CIEM%20Project.htm.

5. Sam Cole, "A Community Accounting Matrix for Buffalo's East Side Neighborhood," *Economic Development Quarterly* 8 (1994): 107–24. Jordan Yin, "Toward an Economic Base Study Method for Community Economic Development," paper presented at the annual meeting of the Urban Affairs Association, Fort Worth, Texas, 1998; C. Gunn and H. D. Gunn, *Reclaiming Capital* (Ithaca, NY: Cornell University Press, 1991), 37–45.

6. Yin, "Toward an Economic Base Study Method."

7. Power, *Lost Landscapes,* 11.

8. Thomas Michael Power, *Environmental Protection and Economic Well-Being* (Armonk: M. E. Sharpe, 1996), 134, 195.

9. Jane Jacobs, *Cities and the Wealth of Nations* (New York: Random House, 1984).

10. Joseph Persky et al., "Import Substitution and Local Economic Development," *Economic Development Quarterly* 7 (1993): 21.

11. "Local-to-Local Buying Programs Aid Rural Economies," *Economic Development Digest* 4, 11 (1995): 1, 6.

12. Persky et al., "Import Substitition," 21; "Information Resources for Oregon Businesses," fact sheet provided by Oregon Legislature Policy Research and Committee Services, September 15, 1998.

13. NCESA interview; Bradley County, Arkansas web site, warren.dina.org/incentives; and Patrick Stafford, "Arkansas' Match Maker Program," *State Innovations Briefs,* August 1996, available from the Council of State Governments, Lexington, Kentucky.

14. NCESA interviews.
15. UIC Center for Urban Economic Development, *Community Economic Development Strategies: A Manual for Local Action* (Chicago, IL: UIC Center for Economic Development, 1987), 37.
16. National Institute of Governmental Purchasing (NIGP), *NIGP 1998 Preference Report* (Herndon, VA: NIGP, 1998).
17. Ibid.
18. Persky et al., "Import Substitution," 25.
19. Ibid., 21.
20. Harry Black, *Achieving Economic Development Success: Tools That Work* (Washington, DC: ICMA, 1991), 104.
21. Ibid.
22. "Local to Local Buying Programs Aid Rural Economies," *Economic Development Digest* 4, 11 (1995): 6.
23. Paul Sommers, "Rural Networks in the United States," *Economic Development Quarterly* 12 (1998): 54–67.
24. Joel Rast, *Remaking Chicago* (DeKalb, IL: Northern Illinois Press,1999), 15.
25. Ibid., 15.
26. Martin Perry, *Small Firms and Network Economies* (London: Routledge, 1999), 81.
27. NCESA interview.
28. "Northeast Kingdom Business Networks," Pamphlet Published by the Northeastern Vermont Development Association, Newport, VT; no date.
29. From the Vermont Sustainable Jobs Fund Web site, www.vsjf.org/projects.
30. Quotes from Rast, *Remaking Chicago,* 92–93.
31. Ibid., 147–48.
32. David L. Imbroscio, *Reconstructing City Politics* (Thousand Oaks, CA: Sage Publications, 1997), 81.
33. Ibid., 68.
34. Imbroscio, *Reconstructing City Politics,* 89.
35. Deborah M. Markley and Kevin T. McNamara, "Economic and Fiscal Impacts of a Business Incubator," *Economic Development Quarterly* 9 (1995): 273.
36. See the Web site of the National Business Incubator Association, www.nbia.org.
37. Ibid.
38. Michael Shuman, *Going Local* (New York: The Free Press, 1998), 50.
39. David Morris, *The New City States* (Washington, DC: Institute for Local Self-Reliance, 1982); Gar Alperovitz and Jeff Faux, *Rebuilding America* (New York: Pantheon, 1984); Imbroscio, *Reconstructing City Politics;* Stacy Mitchell, *The Home Town Advantage* (Washington, DC: The Institute for Local Self-Reliance, 2000).
40. "Boulder Considers Community Vitality Act," *The New Rules,* winter 2000.
41. Mitchell, *The Home Town Advantage,* 86.
42. Ibid., 35.
43. Ibid., 39–45.
44. *The Home Town Advantage Bulletin* 1 (2000), available from the Institute for Local Self-Reliance at www.ilsr.org; Mitchell, *The Home Town Advantage,* 50.
45. *The Home Town Advantage Bulletin* 1 (2000).

46. Mitchell, *The Home Town Advantage,* 60.

47. Ibid., 81–84.

48. Although we have focused this discussion on the business sector, the ownership structure of a community's housing stock also can impact the magnitude of its multiplier
substantially. For example, a significant source of economic leakage, especially in poorer
inner-city areas, comes from the flow of rental payments to absentee landlords (see
Gunn and Gunn, 1991, *Reclaiming Capital,* 39). Promoting the local or community
ownership of housing—either through individual home ownership or community-
based institutions such as community development corporations and community cooperatives—can help stem this outward tide of resources, enhancing local multipliers.

49. Susan Meeker-Lowry, "Community Money: The Potential of Local Currency," in Jerry
Mander and Edward Goldsmith, eds., *The Case Against the Global Economy And For a
Turn Toward the Local* (San Francisco: Sierra Club Books, 1996), 448, 458.

50. NCESA interview.

51. Shuman, *Going Local,* 138.

52. NCESA interview.

53. Monica Hargraves, "The Multiplier Effect of Local Currency," from the Ithaca
HOURS Web page, www.lightlinkcom/hours/ithacahours/archive/9812.html; www.
ithacahours.org.

54. Shuman, *Going Local,* 136, quoting Paul Glover.

55. List Serve communication on cooperative-bus@relaydoit.wisc.edu, by John Hanratty,
re: Local Currency, January 16, 1997; available at csf.colorado.edu/co-op/coop-bus/
winter97/0034.html.

56. According to comprehensive listing by Ithaca HOURS founder Paul Glover at
www.lightlink.com/hours/ithacahours.

57. See the Time Dollars Web site for more information: www.timedollar.org.

58. Nonpublic pension funds (such as those held by labor and church organizations)
also have significant experience with targeted community investments. For example,
the AFL-CIO Housing Investment Trust (HIT), with over $2 billion in assets, has
created 40,000 union jobs and 65,000 housing units over the past few decades by
investing directly in affordable housing construction; it also has a Building
Investment Trust (BIT) with over $1.3 billion invested in commercial real estate.
The AFL-CIO's latest initiative, dubbed Urban Investment 2000, plans to mobilize
some $1 billion in investments from the HIT and BIT over a five-year period. The
investments promote home ownership, new rental housing, permanent housing for
the homeless, economic development, and neighborhood stabilization (Housing
Trust Fund information, AFL-CIO, Washington, DC, 1999). The Interfaith Center
on Corporate Responsibility estimates that religious denominations had invested
roughly $900 million in community development initiatives by late 1999. (NCESA
Interview).

59. Isamu Watson, *Investment Intermediaries: Model State Programs* (Washington, DC:
Center for Policy Alternatives, June, 1995), 2.

60. General Accounting Office, "Public Pension Funds: Evaluation of Economically
Targeted Investment Programs," March 1995, GAO/PEMD-95-13, 2.

61. I. Watson, *Investment Intermediaries,* 5.

62. Ibid.
63. I. Watson, *Investment Intermediaries*, 5–6.
64. Pat Griffith, "AFL-CIO Pension Money May Fund City Housing," *Pittsburgh Post-Gazette,* January 16, 1994.
65. Monique Morrissey, "The Case Not Made," article published by the Financial Open Markets Center, available at www.fmcenter.org/fmc_superpage.asp?ID=189.
66. Ibid.
67. Ronald D Watson."Does Targeted Investing Make Sense," *Financial Management* 23 (1994): 68–72.
68. Michael Calabrese, "Would Economically Targeted Investments Trigger a Pension Crisis," *Insight on the News,* September 16, 1996, 25.
69. Watson, "Does Targeted Investing Make Sense," 69–70.
70. Ibid., 69–70.
71. Calabrese, "Would Economically Targeted Investments Trigger a Pension Crisis."
72. General Accounting Office, "Public Pension Funds: Evaluation of Economically Targeted Investment Programs," March 1995, GAO/PEMD-95-13, 28.
73. Ibid., 15, 27.
74. Richard Ferlauto and Jeffrey Clabourn, *Economically Targeted Investments by State-Wide Public Pension Funds* (Washington, DC: Center for Policy Alternatives), 1993.
75. Retirement Systems of Alabama, Annual Report 2000.
76. Interview with David Bronner; "Work Ethic of Community's Martin Caught Right Eye," *Birmingham Business Journal,* August 8, 1998; Retirement Systems of Alabama, Annual Report, 1999.
77. "CalPers Invests $475 Million in 11 California Private Equity Firms," press release by CalPers, May 14, 2001, available at www.calpers.ca.gov/whatsnew/press/2001/0514a.htm.
78. Neal R. Peirce, Renee A. Berger, Farley M. Peters, and Carol F. Steinbach, *Market Standards, Community Dividends,* National Academy of Public Administration, 1994.
79. "Economically Targeted Investments: Rebuilding America's Communities," conference report, Center for Policy Alternatives, Washington, DC, 1994, 10.
80. CalPers Invests $475 Million in 11 California Private Equity Firms."
81. "Economically Targeted Investments," 32; NYCERS 2000 Annual Report, available at www.nyc.gov/html/nycers; and Ira Goldfine, "New York City Pension Funds—Economically Targeted Investment Program," presentation at Canadian Labor and Business Centre "Capital That Works" conference, January 2002. Available at www.clbc.ca.
82. See the Colorado Public Employee Retirement System Web page, www.copera.org/pera/about/investments.stm.
83. Some states have created investment intermediaries to help direct institutional investors (such as state pension funds) to ETI investment opportunities of high fiduciary quality. These intermediaries provide institutional investors with ETI investment expertise, reduce the transaction costs of smaller sized ETI investments, and manage the risks associated with some kinds of ETIs. The Colorado Housing and Finance Agency (CHFA) is one such intermediary; the Texas Growth Fund is another prominent intermediary. See I. Watson, *Investment Intermediaries,* 3.
84. Peirce et al., *Market Standards, Community Dividends,* 33.
85. "Economically Targeted Investments," 18.

86. Neal Peirce, "Investing our Billions in California," *The San Diego Union-Tribune,* July 26, 1999. Quote is from Peirce.

87. Ibid. Quote is from Angelides.

88. General Accounting Office, "Public Pension Funds: Evaluation of Economically Targeted Investment Programs," March 1995, GAO/PEMD-95-13, 4–5; I. Watson, *Investment Intermediaries,* 6–7.

CHAPTER 8

1. John Stuart Mill, *Principles of Political Economy* (London: Longmans, Green, 1923), Book V, Chapter XI, 791.

2. Ibid., 789–90.

3. See, for instance, Robert Dahl, *A Preface to Economic Democracy* (Berkeley: University of California Press, 1985), Chapter 4.

4. See Derek C. Jones and Donald J. Schneider, "Self-Help Production Cooperatives: Government-Administered Cooperatives During the Depression," in Robert Jackall and Henry M. Levin, eds., *Worker Cooperatives in America* (Berkeley: University of California Press, 1984), 57–84.

5. Staff of the Grassroots Economic Organizing (GEO) Newsletter, *An Economy of Hope* (New York: GEO, 2000), 127.

6. About eighty of these non-ESOP worker cooperatives are listed in *An Economy of Hope,* the excellent sourcebook published by the Grassroots Economic Organizing Newsletter.

7. See Tim Huet, "Can Coops Go Global? Mondragon is Trying," in *Dollars and Sense,* November–December 1997. For a critical analysis of the Mondragon cooperatives that argues that the experience of workers at Mondragon is analogous to those in conventional capitalist firms, see Sharryn Kasmir, *The Myth of Mondragon: Cooperatives, Politics, and Working-Class Life in a Basque Town.* (Albany: State University of New York Press, 1996). A more sympathetic critical analysis of Mondragon is provided by George Cheney in *Values at Work: Employee Participation Meets Market Pressures at Mondragon* (Ithaca, NY: Cornell University Press, 1999).

8. For recent discussions of the kibbutzim, see Uriel Leviatan, Hugh Oliver, and Jack Quarter, eds., *Crisis in the Israeli Kibbutz: Meeting the Challenge of Changing Times* (Westport, CT: Praeger, 1998), and Christopher Warhurst, *Between Market, State, and Kibbutz: The Management and Transformation of Socialist Industry* (London: Mansell, 1999).

9. Piero Ammirato, *La Lega: The Making of a Successful Cooperative Network* (Aldershot, UK: Dartmouth Publishing, 1996), 2. Data is for 1989.

10. "The path to higher income per worker-member for cooperatives," Booth writes, "is to reduce nonlabor input costs. Investments that cut energy and materials needs per unit of output will clearly lift income per worker. If less must be paid out for such inputs, more income will be available to worker-members. For the corporation, scale-expanding investments that cooperatives would reject may well be more profitable than investments reducing the use of nonlabor inputs. Since the scale expansion option is unattractive to cooperatives [since expansion may reduce income per worker], they will be more inclined to choose investments that economize on nonlabor

inputs. This will mean that cooperatives are likely to be more efficient users of natural resource inputs than corporations." Douglas Booth, *The Environmental Consequences of Growth: Steady-State Economics as An Alternative to Ecological Decline* (New York: Routledge, 1998), 179.

11. "A Statistical Overview of Employee Ownership," available from the National Center for Employee Ownership at www.nceo.org/library/eo_stat.html.

12. "An Overview of ESOPs, Stock Options, and Employee Ownership, " National Center for Employee Ownership, Oakland, CA, available at www.nceo.org/library/overview.html.

13. See Louis Kelso and Patricia Hetter, *Two Factor Theory* (New York: Random House, 1967).

14. See the Small Business Administration Web page, www.sba.gov/financing/frqet.html for a description of Qualified Employee Trusts Loan Program.

15. John Logue, Richard Glass, and John Grummel "State Use of JTPA Funds for Preliminary ESOP Feasibility Studies," *Journal of Employee Ownership, Law, and Finance* 11, 2 (1999): 41–59.

16. Ibid.

17. Available from the National Center for Employee Ownership, at www.nceo.org/library/esop_tax_law.html. See also "Tax Advantages for Business Planning," an ESOP Association publication available at at www.the-esop-emplowner.org.

18. "Should C ESOP Corporations Convert to S?" in *Employee Ownership Report,* January-February 1998. *Employee Ownership Report* is a publication of the National Center for Employee Ownership.

19. "New Data on Employee Ownership in 401(k) Plans," in *Employee Ownership Report,* March–April 1996.

20. "Legislature Renews Ohio Employee Ownership Assistance Program," *Owners at Work,* winter 2001. *Owners at Work* is a publication of the Ohio Employee Ownership Center.

21. As noted by John Grummel and John Logue, "Employee and Ownership: Trends, Characteristics, and Policy Implications of State Employees Ownership Legislation," 2000. This is the definitive study to date of state-level programs to aid employee ownership, available from the Capital Ownership Group Web site, www.cog.kent.edu/lib/grummel.htm.

22. See *Employee Ownership Handbook* and *Employee Ownership Resource Guide* (Oakland: National Center for Employee Ownership), 1997.

23. Interview by Tom Ricker of NCESA/University of Maryland with Jon Grant of Ownership Transition Services in New York, 1998.

24. Interview by Tom Ricker of NCESA/University of Maryland with June Sekera of the Corporation for Work, Business, and Learning, 1998.

25. Employee Involvement and Ownership Program, "Employee Stock Ownership Plans: The Untold Story of Wealth Sharing in Massachusetts" (Boston: Corporation for Business Work and Learning, 2000).

26. Grummel and Logue, "Employees and Ownership."

27. John Logue, "Thinking Globally, Acting Locally: Subnational Strategies to Promote Employee Ownership," *Owners at Work,* Summer 2001.

28. For a useful, short summary of previous research on employee ownership and productivity,

see Corey Rosen, "A Guide to Doing Research on Employee Ownership," available from the National Center for Employee Ownership www.nceo.org/library/research.html.

29. *Theory O: Creating an Ownership Style of Management* Oakland: National Center for Employee Ownership, 1999.

30. From information provided by Ownership Associates, Cambridge, MA. Ownership Associates is closely consulting with Carris on their efforts to broaden democracy within the firm.

31. From information provided by Ownership Associates; see also Mobile Tool's website, www.mobiletool.com, and Parametrix's web site, www.parametrix.com.

32. See Seymour Melman, *After Capitalism* (New York: Alfred A. Knopf, 2001.)

33. See www.nceo.org/library/research.html.

34. See John Logue and Jacequelyn Yates, *The Real World of Employee Ownership* Ithaca: ILR Press, 2001, 32-33.

35. Peter Kardas, Adria Scharf, and Jim Keogh *Wealth and Income Consequences of Employee Ownership,* 1998. Study available through the National Center for Employee Ownership, at www.nceo.org

36. Source of case: NCESA interviews with the staff of Krause Publications as well as company documents. Information dates from 1998.

37. See the company web site, www.krause.com for an overview.

38. Source; NCEO; Jeff Gates, *The Ownership Solution* (Reading, MA; Addison-Wesley, 1998), 161.

39. Dan Swinney, "Building the Bridge to the High Road", July 1998, paper available at the Center for Labor and Community Research web site, www.clcr.org.

40. Information provided by Ownership Associates, Cambridge, MA.

41. Adria Scharf, "Unions and ESOPs: Building A Better Employee Stock Ownership Plan," *Dollars and Sense,* September-October 1999, 48–50. Mackin quote in previous paragraph taken from this article.

42. "CXT Sells Operations to Pittsburgh Firm," *Spokane Spokesman-Review,* July 1, 1999, A12.

43. "When Employee Owners Sell," *Owners at Work,* Winter 1995–96, available online at dept.kent.edu/oeoc/PublicationsResearch/Winter1995-6/SellWin1995-6.html.

44. See Charles S. Varano, *Forced Choices: Class, Community, and Worker Ownership* (Albany: State University Press of New York, 1999), for an excellent critical study of the impact of the ESOP at Weirton on the workplace experience of employees.

45. "Bypassed by the Boom," *Wall Street Journal,* December 29, 1999.

46. Ibid.; Weirton Steel Corporation, 2000 Annual Report, available at www.weirton.com.

47. "The Steel Crisis and Employee Ownership," *Owners at Work,* Summer 2001.

48. "Employees Win! Brainard Rivet Re-Opens," *Owners at Work,* Summer 1998, 1.

49. For more information, see Brainard Rivet's Web site at www.brainardrivet.com.

50. Joseph Blasi, "Memorandum to Clinton Administration on Employee Ownership," December 1992, copy provided by Blasi to Gar Alperovitz.

51. John Logue, "Rustbelt Buyouts: Why Ohio Leads in Worker Ownership," *Dollars and Sense,* September-October 1998, 37; John Logue and Jacqueline Yates, *The Real World of Employee Ownership* (Ithaca, NY: Cornell University Press, 2001), 176.

52. Gates, *The Ownership Solution,* 214–20.

53. Ibid.

54. "Will America Be 30% Employee Owned in 2010," *Owners at Work*, Summer 1999, 4.

55. See Corey Rosen, "Questions and Answers About Enron, 401(k)s, and ESOPs," February 2002, available at www.nceo.org, and Douglas Kruse, "Research Evidence on Prevalence and Effects of Employee Ownership," Testimony before the Subcommittee on Employer-Employee Relations Committee on Education and the Workforce, U.S. House of Representatives, February 13, 2002.

56. See Samuel Bowles and Herbert Gintis, "Efficient Redistribution: New Rules for Markets, States and Communities," in Bowles and Gintis, *Recasting Egalitarianism* (New York: Verso Books, 1998).

CHAPTER 9

1. Kennedy quoted in David Rusk, *Inside Game, Outside Game* (Washington, DC: Brookings Institution, 1999), 25.

2. *Coming of Age: Trends and Achievements of Community-Based Development Organizations* (Washington, DC: National Congress for Community Economic Development, 1999).

3. Ronald Ferguson and William Dickens, "Introduction," in Ferguson and Dickens, eds., *Urban Problems and Community Development* (Washington, DC: Brookings Institution, 1999), 4.

4. See Mark A Pinsky, "CDFIs: Bridges to Opportunity," *The Neighborhood Works*, July/August, 1998, 9.

5. See the web site of the National Community Credit Association, www.communitycapital.org/community_development/finance/statistics.html.

6. For a largely upbeat account of CDCs and community credit's role in reviving inner cities, see Paul S. Grogan and Tony Proscio, *Comeback Cities: A Blueprint for Urban Neighborhood Revival* (Boulder: Westview Press, 2000).

7. *Coming of Age: Trends and Achievements of Community-based Development Organizations* (Washington, DC: National Congress for Community Economic Development, 1999).

8. Local Initiatives Support Corporation Annual Report, 1994.

9. Local Initiatives Support Corporation Annual Report, 1997.

10. "LISC Facts At a Glance," available at www.liscnet.org/whatwedo/facts.

11. Pierce Clavel, Jessica Pitt and Jordan Yin, "The Community Option in Urban Policy," *Urban Affairs Review* 32 (1997), 446.

12. Dan Swinney, "Building the Bridge to the High Road," July 1998, paper available from the Center for Labor and Community Research, www.clcr.org.

13. Sigmund Shipp, "The Road Not Taken: Alternative Strategies for Black Economic Development in the United States." *Journal of Economic Issues* 30 (1996), 85.

14. See Randy Stoecker, "The CDC Model of Urban Development: A Critique and an Alternative," *Journal of Urban Affairs* 19 (1997): 1–21; Herbert Rubin, "Renewing Hope in the Inner City: Conversations with Community-Based Practitioners," *Administration & Society* 27 (1995): 127–60; Benjamin Marquez, "Mexican American Community Development Corporations and the Limits of Directed Capitalism," *Economic Development Quarterly* 7 (1993): 287–95; David Imbroscio, *Reconstructing City Politics* (Thousand Oaks, CA: Sage, 1997), esp. 126–33.

15. Except where otherwise noted, all information from this section comes from materials provided by the organizations or NCESA interviews.

16. See Asian Neighborhood Design's Web site, www.andnet.org, for more information.

17. See the Pathway Supermarket project Web site, www.restorationplaza.org/jv/rsc/index.html, for more details.

18. See the profile of Bickerdike at the Nonprofit pathfinder Web site, www.independentsector.org.

19. See the Rural Local Initiatives Support Corporation page on Dineh, www.ruralisc.org/dineh.htm, for more information.

20. See the Esperanza Unida Web site, www.esperanzaunida.org, for more information.

21. See the Ganados de Valle Web site, www.ganados.org, for more information.

22. See the New Community Corporation Web site, www.newcommunity.org; also NCC's 1999 Annual Report.

23. See also the profile of the Quitman County Development Organization at www.ruralisc.org/qcdo.htm, for more information, as well as the QCDO Web site at www.qcdo.org.

24. See also TELACU Annual Report 1999.

25. See Coastal Enterprises' Web site, www.ceimaine.org, for more information.

26. See www.khic.org; and testimony of Jerry Ricketts, President and CEO of KHIC to Subcommittee on Early Childhood Youth and Families, Committee on Education and the Workforce, U.S. House of Representatives, June 5, 1998.

27. NCESA staff interview with Raymond Codey.

28. J. Philip Thompson, "A Political and Practical Approach to Building Urban Political Coalitions," talk given at Kennedy School of Government, March 12, 2001.

29. See Sirianni and Friedland's interesting account of community development and community organizing in the United States in *Civic Innovation in America* (Berkeley: University of California Press, 2001). As Sirianni and Friedland note with regard to St. Paul, however, there is also the possibility of unhealthy competition between CDCs and community organizing efforts over who best represents community interests—a possibility which makes the need for close cooperation between the two activities all the more important.

30. Shorebank Corporation 2000 Annual Report, available at www.shorebankcorp.com.

31. For more information, see the profile of the Southern Development Bank at the CDFI Coalition Web site, www.cdfi.org/sdb.html.

32. NCESA research; interview with Ed Voris, Community Bank of the Bay (Oakland), August 25, 1997. See also www.communitybankbay.com.

33. See the National Credit Union Association Web page, www.ncua.gov, and Charles D. Tansey, "Community Development Credit Unions: An Emerging Player in Low Income Communities," September 2001, available at www.brookings.edu.

34. See the Web sites of NCCSH and the Coalition for Responsible Lending, www.self-help.org and www.responsiblelending.org for more details. See also Jeanette Bradley and Peter Skillern, "Predatory Lending: Banks Trick Poor into Expensive Loans," in *Dollars and Sense,* January-February 2000.

35. See the Web site of the Santa Cruz Credit Union, www.scruzccu.org, for details.

36. See the Web site of the Alternatives Federal Credit Union, www.alternatives.org, for more details.

37. National Credit Union Association Press Release, January 13, 2000, available at www.ncua.gov/news/press_releases/pr011300.html.

38. See the National Community Capital Association Web page www.community capital.org/community_development/finance/statistics.html.

39. Material provided by Institute for Community Economics (Springfield, MA), June 30, 1999 and March 31, 1997; see also ICE Web page www.iceclt.org/loanfund for the most recent information, including short profiles of recent loan recipients.

40. See www.grameen-info.org, official Web site of the Grameen Bank, for more information.

41. *1999 Directory of US. Microenterprise Programs* (Aspen, CO: Aspen Institute, 1999). As Lisa Servon notes in *Bootstrap Capital: Microenterprise and the American Poor* (Washington, DC: The Brookings Institution, 1999), 3, this figure probably understates the number of programs under way, since the Aspen Institute relies on survey responses to generate its directory.

42. Servon, *Bootstrap Capital,* 3.

43. "Acción USA and Working Capital Join Forces," press release, July 27, 2001, available at www.accionusa.org/pressreleases.asp#46.

44. Acción International Web site, www.accion.org; *San Antonio Express-News,* September 14, 1996.

45. Study released by Working Capital, 2000.

46. "CDVC Profiles," June 1999, available at the Community Development Venture Capital Alliance Web site, www.cdvca.org. See also Julia Sass Rubin, "Case Studies of Nontraditional Venture Capital Institutions," July 2001, available from the Rural Policy Research Institute.

47. Avis Vidal, *Rebuilding Communities: A National Study of Urban Community Development* (New York: New School University, 1992), 53.

48. Christopher Walker and Mark Weinheimer, *Community Development in the 1990s* (Washington, DC: The Urban Institute, 1998), 21.

49. *Implementing Block Grants: A First Year Evaluation of HOME* (Washington, DC: The Urban Institute, 1996), as described in Christopher Walker and Mark Weinheimer, *Community Development in the 1990s,* 19.

50. *Budget of the United States Government, Fiscal Year 2003: Appendix* (Washington, DC: Government Printing Office, 2002), 488.

51. From information at the Federal Housing Finance Board, www.fhfb.gov. See also the FHLB Web site, www.fhlbanks.com.

52. Ibid.

53. See the discussion in Paul S. Grogan and Tony Proscio, *Comeback Cities: A Blueprint for Urban Neighborhood Revival* (Boulder: Westview Press, 2000), 94–95. See also the National Equity Fund, Inc. web site, www.nefinc.org; and *Budget of the United States Government Fiscal Year 2003: Analytical Tables,* 99.

54. Department of Health and Human Services, "Administration for Children and Families Request for Applications Under the Office of Community Services," Fiscal Year 1999 Combined Program Announcement No. OCS.99.01.

55. See the Department of Health and Human Services' Web page www.acf.dhhs.gov/programs/ocs/01comply/urrural.htm for a breakdown of the program's spending.

56. See the New Community Corporation Technologies, Inc Web site, www.newcommu-

nity.org/ncctech/index.html, for more details; and "Urban/Downtown Development," available at www.doc.gov/eda.

57. "HUD Helps Create Jobs and Revitalize SE Washington," HUD press release, March 12, 1997.

58. See the New York Division of Housing and Community Renewal web page www.dhcr.state.ny.us/ocd/progs/npp/ocdprgnp.htm for more information. See also www.dhcr.state.ny.us/ocd/progs/rpp/ocdprgrp.htm; see also National Congress for Community Economic Development, *States and Community Development Model Programs,* 1996, 8–10.

59. National Congress for Community Economic Development, *Model Programs,* 9.

60. Ibid., 11.

61. For more information, see the North Carolina Community Development Initiative web site, www.ncinitiative.org.

62. National Congress for Communtiy Economic Development, *Model Programs,* 13–14.

63. "The Community Enterprise Economic Development Program Fact Sheet," available at www.state.ma.us/dhcd/publications/fact_sheets/ceed.pdf;Fiscal 2000 Annual Report of the Massachusetts Department of Housing and Community Development, available at www.state.ma.us/dhcd/publications/annual_report/default.htm.

64. NCESA interview. See also www.financefund.org, website of the Ohio Community Development Finance Fund.

65. Christopher Walker and Mark Weinheimer, "Community Development in the 1990s," The Urban Institute, September 1998, 90–93.

66. *Budget of the United States Government, Fiscal Year 2003: Appendix,* 807.

67. "CDFI Act," available at the Coalition's of Community Development Financial Institutions' Web site, www.cdfi.org. Exceptions to the matching requirement, can be made when the CDFI has severe constraints such as: total assets of less than $100,000; is serving rural or non-metropolitan areas; or requesting $25,000 or less. In such cases the matching requirement can be reduced to 50 percent, or flexible matching requirements can be imposed.

68. Another 200 CDFI organizations have received assistance ($15 million) through the Fund's Intermediary component. Statistics from 2000 Annual Report of the CDFI Fund, available at http://www.ustreas.gov/cdfi/news/index.html.

69. CDFI position paper, "FHLB Reform," available at www.cdfi.org/popaper.html.

70. Alex Schwartz, "The Past and Future of Community Reinvestment Agreements," *Housing Facts & Findings,* spring 2000, 3.

71. The National Community Reinvestment Coalition, "The New Community Reinvestment Act (CRA) Regulation" (Washington, DC: National Community Reinvestment Coalition, 1997); E. L. Baldinucci, "The Community Reinvestment Act: New Standards Provide New Hope," *Fordham Urban Law Journal* 23 (1996): 831.

72. Ibid.

73. Schwartz, "The Past and Future of Community Reinvestment Agreements," 3; emphasis added.

74. Grogan and Proscio, *Comeback Cities,* 126.

75. Christopher Heisen, "Community Development Lite: An Economic Analysis of the

Community Development Financial Institutions Act," *Howard Law Journal* 39 (1995): 359.

76. Immergluck's comments explained in Linda Lutton, "CDFIs Essential Partners in Making CRA Work," *The Neighborhood Works,* July-August 1998, 18.

77. See U.S. Department of Treasury, *Capital Access Programs: A Summary of Nationwide Performance,* October 1999.

78. Michael Shuman *Going Local* (New York: The Free Press, 1998), 114.

79. Interview with Judy Meima published in *Trust Fund News,* Winter 2000; this is a publication of Illinois's Statewide Housing Action Coalition.

CHAPTER 10

1. *A Day in the Life of Co-operative America* (Washington, DC: National Co-operative Bank, 1998), 7.

2. USDA, *Farmer Cooperative Statistics,* RBS Service Report 56, 1997; Charles Kraenzle, "Coops Share of Farm Marketings Up Slightly in 1998," *Rural Cooperatives,* January/February 2000.

3. Paul Hazen, "Together We Stand: Employee Ownership and the Cooperative Sector," *Owners at Work,* Summer 2001. See the Grassroots Economic Organizing Newsletter's *An Economy of Hope* (New York: GEO, 2000) for brief profiles of many worker cooperatives.

4. Christoper Gunn and Hazel Dayton Gunn, *Reclaiming Capital* (Ithaca, NY: Cornell University Press, 1991), 101.

5. Jean Hammond, "Consumer Cooperatives," in S. Bruyn and J. Meehan, eds., *Beyond the Market and the State* (Philadelphia, PA: Temple University Press, 1987), 100.

6. Ibid., 98.

7. National Rural Electric Co-operative Association website, www.nreca.org.

8. See Walden Swanson, Peg Nolan and Dave Gutknecht, "Retail Operations Survey 2000," *Cooperative Grocer* 95 (2001), available at www.cooperativegrocer.com. See also Mike Bohmann, "Beyond Granola: Food Co-ops Come of Age," *Progressive Populist,* January 1999.

9. NCESA interview. See Park Slope Food Coop's Web site, www.foodcoop.com, for more detailed information.

10. See www.rei.com and www.co-op100.com for details.

11. Information in this section from "National Consumer Co-operative Bank: Oversight Adequate but Federal Loan Repayment Needs Monitoring," GAO/GGD-95-63; National Cooperative Bank Annual Report, 2000.

12. NCESA interview.

13. Information in this section from: Annual Report, Washington, DC: Co-operative Development Fund, 1998, and NCESA interview with Judy Ziewacz.

14. See www.coopdevelopment.org.

15. Northcountry Cooperative Development Fund Annual Report 1998; NCESA interviews.

16. Northcountry Cooperative Development Fund Annual Report 1999; available at www.ncdf.org.

17. Ellen Perlman "Taking Mom and Pop Public," *Governing,* January 1997, 17.

18. Ibid.

19. Pamela Ferdinand, "Town Rallies to Revive Locus of Life," *Washington Post,* December 16, 1999, A3.

20. Michael H. Shuman, "Community Corporations: Engines for a New Place-Based Economics," *The Responsive Community,* summer 1999, 52. See also Michael H. Shuman, *Going Local* (New York: The Free Press, 1998).

21. As quoted in Charles Mahtesian, "If You Can't Bribe the Owner, Maybe You Can Buy the Team," *Governing,* March 1996, 44. As Mahtesian adds, "It would be a lavish memorial indeed, since the team is now worth in excess of $100 million."

22. Daniel Kraker, "Keeping the Minors Home," *The New Rules,* winter, 2000, 14. See also the Web site www.newrules.org/sports.

23. Shuman, "Community Corporations," 52–53 (emphasis in original).

24. Ibid., 52.

25. Shuman, *Going Local,* 102–3.

26. Ibid, 101.

27. *The New Nonprofit Almanac in Brief* (Washington, DC: Independent Sector, 2001). Available at www.independentsector.org/PDFs/inbrief.pdf.

28. Ibid.

29. Ira Harkavy and Harmon Zuckerman, "Eds and Meds: Cities' Hidden Assets," The Brookings Institution Survey Series, Center on Urban and Metropolitan Policy, August 1, 1999.

30. Edward Skloot, *The Nonprofit Entrepreneur* (New York: The Foundation Center: 1989), 2.

31. Bill Shore, *The Cathedral Within* (New York: Random House, 1999), 127.

32. Tracy Thompson, "Profit with Honor," *The Washington Post Magazine,* December 16, 1999, 9.

33. Jed Emerson and Fay Twersky, eds., *The New Social Entrepreneurs* (San Francisco: The Roberts Foundation, 1996).

34. See www.buycake.com/bakery.html, home page of Greystone Bakery.

35. See www.mdi.org, homepage of Minnesota Diversified Industries.

36. Jerr Boschee, "Social Entrepreneurship," *Across the Board* (Publication of The Conference Board), March 1995. See also www.socialent.org, Web site of the Institute for Social Entrepreneurs.

37. See the web page of Housing Works at www.housingworks.org.

38. See the Rubicon Programs Web site, www.rubiconpgms.org.

39. See the Nonprofit Pathfinder, www.independentsector.org; see also PHS's Web site, www.pioneerhumanserv.com, and Kristin Rusch, *The Emerging New Society* (Washington, DC: National Center for Economic and Security Alternatives, 2002).

40. Shore, *Cathedral Within,* 131; see also the Nonprofit Pathfinder, www.independent sector.org.

41. See "Meshing the Sacred and the Secular, Floyd Flake Offers Community Development via Church and State," *New York Times,* November 22, 1995; "For God and Country," *Newsday,* August 10, 1997; "The Role Model," *Newsday,* August 12, 1999; and www.allencathedral.org, Allen A.M.E.'s home page.

42. NCESA interviews.

43. Emerson and Twersky, eds., *The New Social Entrepreneurs*, 8.

44. Thompson, "Profit with Honor," 22.

45. Shore, *Cathedral Within*, 132.

CHAPTER 11

1. Judith A. Garber. "Law and Possibilities for a Just Political Economy," *Journal of Urban Affairs* 12 (1990): 1–15; John R. Logan and Harvey Molotch, *Urban Fortunes* (Berkeley: University of California Press, 1987); Stephen L. Elkin, *City and Regime in the American Republic* (Chicago: University of Chicago Press, 1987).

2. Institute for Community Economics Web site, http://www.iceclt.org/clt/cltlist.html.

3. Robert Swann, "Peace, Civil Rights, and the Search for Community," available at www.schumachersociety.org.

4. Institute for Community Economics Annual Report 1995.

5. K. White and C. Matthei, "Community Land Trusts," in S. Bruyn and J. Meehan, *Beyond the Market and the State* (Philadelphia: Temple University Press, 1987), 41–42.

6. "Profiles of Community Land Trusts" (Springfield, MA: Institute for Community Economics, undated), 4; *Annual Report*. (Springfield, MA: ICE.)

7. NCESA Interview. BCLT has 140 conventional rental units, 32 special-needs units, 115 co-ops (with another 34 coming on line), and more than 200 homeownership units.

8. NCESA interview. See also the profile of BCLT at www.independentsector.org/pathfinder.

9. NCESA interview.

10. NCESA interview.

11. See the Association of Resident Controlled Housing Web page, www.weown.net/LimitedEquityCoops.htm, for more information.

12. See "National Land Trust Census," at www.lta.org (Web site of the Land Trust Alliance).

13. Robyn Van En, "Eating for your Community," *In Context* 42 (1995): 29.

14. See www.umass.edu/umext/csa/about.html.

15. NCESA Interview.

16. NCESA research; much of this account is drawn from the NCESA publication Kristin Rusch, *The Emerging New Society* (Washington, DC: National Center for Economic and Security Alternatives, 2000.) See also Roxburyfarm.com.

17. Don Villarejo, "Hired Farm Workers and Their Role in Community Food Systems," in Gail Feenstra, David Campbell, and David Chaney, eds., *Community Food Systems Sustaining Farms and People in the Emerging Economy: Conference Proceedings, Davis, California, University of California, October 2–3, 1996* (Davis, CA: University of California, Sustainable Agriculture Research and Education Program, 1997).

18. David W. Orr, "Prices and the Life Exchanged: Costs of the U.S. Food System," *EcoCity Cleveland*, September-October 1996, 8.

19. UNDP, *Urban Agriculture: Food, Jobs and Sustainable Cities*, United Nations Development Programme Publication Series for Habitat II, Vol. 1. (New York: UNDP, 1996), 189.

20. Environmental Protection Agency, "Pesticides Industry Sales and Usage 1994 and 1995 Market Estimates," EPA Office of Pesticide Programs, 1996, available at http://www.epa.gov/oppbead1/pestsales.

21. *After Silent Spring: The Unsolved Problem of Pesticide Use in the United States,* Washington: Natural Resources Defense Council, 1993.

22. 1997 National Resources Inventory, conducted by the U.S. Department of Agriculture.

23. "More Than One-Fourth of U.S. Food Wasted," Department of Agriculture press release, July 1, 1997.

24. See www.foodsecurity.org/exec_summ.html for details of the Community Food Security Coalition's policy agenda.

25. "Sudden Deals Saves Gardens Set for Auction," *New York Times,* May 13, 1999, B1.

26. Karl Linn, "Reclaiming the Sacred Commons," *New Village Journal* 1 (1999): 42.

27. See Patricia Hynes, *A Patch of Eden: America's Inner-City Gardeners* (White River Junction, VT: Chelsea Green Publishing). See the Philadelphia Green Web site, www.pennsylvaniahorticulturalsociety.org/pg/pg_home.html; Philadelphia Green Brochure, Philadelphia, PA, 1996.

28. See the BUG Web site, www.greenfornewengland.org/members/bug.html.

29. NCESA Interview; and www.greenthumbnyc.org.

30. NCESA Interview; *SLUG Update,* summer 1997, 11–13; Nina Siegal, "Fruits of their Labor," *San Francisco Bay Guardian,* October 30, 1996, 11. See also www.slug-sf.org.

31. Homeless Garden Project Web site, www.infopoint.com/sc/orgs/garden; "What Everyone Wants To Know," Homeless Garden Project fact sheet. (Undated.) The project employed 43 homeless men in 1999.

32. NCESA Interview; see also www.gla.med.va.gov/vetsgarden.

33. See The Garden Project's Web site, at www.gardenproject.org.

34. Chris Lazarus, "Urban Agriculture: Join the Revolution," *New Village Journal* 2000, issue 2, 66.

CHAPTER 12

1. See John Eatwell and Lance Taylor, *Global Finance at Risk: The Case for International Regulation* (New York: New Press, 1999); and Eatwell and Taylor, "International Capital Markets and the Future of Economic Policy." Center for Economic Policy Analysis working paper, September 1998.

2. Eatwell and Taylor, *Global Financial Risk,* 1–53.

3. Thomas Palley, "The Economics of Globalization: Problems and Policy Responses," AFL-CIO working paper, 1998, Washington, DC, 18–22. See also Thomas Palley, "International Finance and Global Deflation: There is an Alternative," in Jonathan Michie, and John Grieve Smith, eds., *Global Instability: The Political Economy of World Economic Governance* (London: Routledge, 1999); Thomas Palley, *Plenty of Nothing* (Princeton: Princeton University Press, 1998), 174–75.

4. Palley, "The Economics of Globalization," 18–22.

5. Bernie Sanders, "Global Sustainable Development Resolution," drafted March 1999, available via www.netprogress.org. See also Jeremy Brecher and Brendan Smith, "In Focus: The Global Sustainable Development Resolution," *Foreign Policy in Focus* 4, 12

(1999). The Sanders proposal is also recapitulated in Jeremy Brecher, Tim Costello, and Brendan Smith, *Globalization from Below: The Power of Solidarity* (Cambridge: South End Press, 2000), 67–80.

6. Sanders, "Global Sustainable Development Resolution," Section 8, Article H (iv).

7. Ibid.

8. Byron Dorgan, "Global Shell Games: How Corporations Operate Tax Free," *Washington Monthly,* July-August 2000, 33–36.

9. For additional literature, see, among others, the Hemispheric Social Alliance's "Alternatives for the America," available through the Institute for Policy Studies at www.ips-dc.org (and discussed at length in Chapter 13); Robert Borosage and William Greider, "Global Fairness: The Historic Debate," in Borosage and Roger Hickey, eds., *The Next Agenda: Blueprint for A New Progressive Movement* (Boulder: Westview Press, 2001), 49–72; Walden Bello, Nicola Bullard, and Kamal Mallhorta, eds., *Global Finance: New Thinking on Regulating Speculative Capital Markets* (London: Zed Books, 2000); Brecher, Costello, and Smith, *Globalization from Below: The Power of Solidarity;* and Ellen Frank, David Levy, and Alejandro Reuss, eds., *Real World Globalization,* 6th ed. (Cambridge: Economic Affairs Bureau, 2001).

10. See for instance, *Economic Report of the President 1999* (Washington, DC: Government Printing Office), 1999, esp. the Council of Economic Advisers' view on international financial reform, 267–305.

11. Robert A. Blecker, *Taming Global Finance: A Better Architecture for Better Growth And Equity* (Washington, DC: Economic Policy Institute, 1999), 89–95.

12. Ibid., 97–98.

13. For a detailed analysis of this widely acknowledged trilemma, see Jeffry Frieden, "Exchange Rate Politics," in Frieden and David Lake, eds., *International Political Economy: Perspectives on Global Power and Wealth,* 4th ed. (Boston: Bedford/St. Martin's, 2000).

14. See Robert A. Blecker, *Taming Global Finance* (Washington, DC: Economic Policy Institute, 1999), 21–25. Quote from 21.

15. Paul Krugman, "The Eternal Triangle," *Slate* (on-line magazine), October 1998.

16. Blecker, *Taming Global Finance,* 99–101.

17. "Investors Free of Capital Controls," *Country Monitor,* April 30, 2001; "A Mellowed Socialist for Free-Market Chile," *New York Times,* January 22, 2000.

18. Blecker, *Taming Global Finance,* 101–2.

19. Jane D'Arista, "Reforming International Financial Architecture," *Challenge,* May-June 2000, 44–82. See also Blecker, *Taming Global Finance,* 102–3.

20. Blecker, 93–94.

21. For a representative right-wing critique of the IMF, see Steve H. Hanke, "Abolish the IMF," April 14, 2000, column published on-line by the Cato Institute at www.cato.org/dailys/04-14-00.html (originally published in *Forbes* magazine, April 13, 2000).

22. Blecker, *Taming Global Finance,* 144–45.

23. Ibid., 117.

24. Ibid. 121–25.

25. Jeffrey E. Garten, "Needed: A Fed for the World," *New York Times,* September 23, 1998.

26. Blecker, Taming Global Finance, 112.

27. See "Ousting the Oligarchs," (Interview with Jane D'Arista), *The New Internationalist*, January-February 2000, 16–17. See also Jane D'Arista, "Reforming International Financial Architecture." The complex mechanics of how the clearinghouse bank mechanism would handle international transactions are explained by D'Arista as follows (in "Ousting the Oligarchs"): "Let's say I buy your magazine and send you a cheque in U.S. dollars. You would take my cheque and deposit it in your corner bank which would in turn pass a cheque on to your national central bank. Your local bank would receive in payment of the cheque an addition to its 'reserve account' at your central bank. That would allow it to create a deposit for you in your currency, Canadian dollars. . . . [Y]our national central bank would then take the U.S. dollar cheque to the International Clearing Bank, which would maintain a balance sheet of assets and liabilities for every country. In payment it would receive a credit to its international reserve account at ICB. So on a balance sheet your national central bank has more reserves at the International Clearing Bank. The ICB then returns that cheque to the US central bank (the Federal Reserve) and accepts payment for it by deducting from the Fed's international reserve account at the ICB. At that point the Federal Reserve takes the cheque back to my corner bank where it's paid for by deducing from my bank's reserve account with the Fed. My banks then cancels the cheque and returns it to me."

28. Robert Wade and Frank Veneroso, "The Resources Lie Within," *The Economist*, November 5, 1998, 19–21.

29. Blecker, *Taming Global Finance*, 127.

30. Ibid., 130–31.

31. John Williamson, "Estimates of FEERs," in Williamson, ed. *Estimating Equilibrium Exchange Rates* (Washington: Institute for International Economics, 1994); John Grieve Smith, *Full Employment: A Pledge Betrayed*, (London: MacMillan, 1994); Blecker, *Taming Global Finance*, 132–35.

32. Eatwell and Taylor, *Global Finance at Risk*, 215–16.

33. Arjun Makhijani, *From Global Capitalism to Economic Justice* (New York: Apex Press, 1992), 165.

34. Ibid., 153–75.

35. Blecker, *Taming Global Finance*, 137–40.

36. Ibid, 141.

37. Ibid., 142–43.

38. Quoted in Robert Wade, "The Coming Fight Over Capital Flows," *Foreign Policy*, winter 1998–99, 52.

39. Quoted in Daniel Henninger, "Trading Places," *The Wall Street Journal*, February 9, 1999, 22.

40. "The International Financial Crisis: Interview with George Soros," *Challenge*, March-April 1999, 61.

41. Krugman, "The Eternal Triangle."

42. See Robin Broad and John Cavanagh's useful essay, "Death of the Washington Consensus?" in Bello, Bullard, and Malhotta, eds., *Global Finance*, 83–95.

43. Wade, "The Coming Fight Over Capital Controls," 47.

44. Eatwell and Taylor, *Global Finance at Risk,* 135.

45. Robin Hahnel, *Panic Rules* (Cambridge: South End Press, 1999), quote from 103; see also 104–10 and 97–98. American and G-8 aid could obviously help: the United Nations estimates that just $40 billion a year in targeted spending—less than 0.5 percent of the American annual GDP—would suffice to provide some of the most basic social services universally to the world's population. *United Nations Development Report* (New York: UNDP, 1997, 1999).

CHAPTER 13

1. United States Trade Representative. *1998 Trade Policy Agenda and 1997 Annual Report* (Washington, DC: Government Printing Office, 1998), 1, 3.

2. See Robert E. Scott, "NAFTA's Pain Deepens: Job Destruction Accelerates in 1999 With Losses in Every State," *Economic Policy Institute Briefing Paper,* December 1999.

3. Quoted in John R. MacArthur, *The Selling of "Free Trade"* (New York: Hill and Wang, 2000), 70.

4. Mark C. Gordon, "Democracy's New Challenge," July 2001, report published by the Demos organization, 34, available at www.demos.org.

5. David K. Moore, "Rethinking Dependency Theory: Global Capitalism's Threat to Liberal Individuals and Democratic Communities," paper presented at the Northeast Political Science Association meetings, Boston, November 1998. For similar argumentation, see David L. Imbroscio, *Reconstructing City Politics* (Thousand Oaks, CA: Sage, 1997).

6. Bart Van Ark and Robert H. McGuckin, "International Comparisons of Labor Productivity and Per Capita Income," *Monthly Labor Review* 122, 7 (1999), Table 2.

7. The picture is roughly similar for the other developing or newly industrialized nations for which data is available. Taiwanese manufacturing workers, for instance, are 47 percent as productive as American workers but receive 28 percent of the compensation per hour American workers get; for South Korea the figures are 37 percent and 27 percent, respectively. (Compensation is measured in terms of American dollars, which is the most relevant basis for assessing what the actual terms of trade are, not on a purchasing power parity approach. Use of the PPP approach would show that in most cases, such as Mexico, workers are able to consume more local goods than the comparison in dollar terms with American compensation would indicate.) See Van Ark and McGuckin, "International Comparison of Labor Productivity"; "International Comparisons of Hourly Compensation Costs for Production Workers in Manufacturing," news release, Bureau of Labor Statistics, 2001, available from stats.bls.gov.

8. See Harley Shaiken, "Going South: Mexican Wages and U.S. Jobs After NAFTA," *American Prospect,* fall 1993, No. 15.

9. Patrick Buchanan, *The Great Betrayal* (Boston: Little, Brown, 1998), 302–3.

10. Quoted in Michael Lind, ed., *Hamilton's Republic* (New York: The Free Press, 1997), 239.

11. Ibid., 240.

12. John Judis and Michael Lind, "For a New Nationalism," in Lind., ed., *Hamilton's Republic,* 324.

13. Skepticism, in this instance, does not equate to *a priori* rejection of any federal policy to

overturn local particularities, but rather serves to underscore that the importance of the normative value being pursued by such a policy must be very high to justify allowing an *external* agent to overturn a community's traditions. (*Internal* community efforts to overturn tradition are a different story.) We believe, for instance, that intervention by the Federal Government in the American South to enforce civil rights norms in the 1950s and 1960s was justified, since the values at stake were so high, but allowing a community's downtown business district to die for the sake of a trade policy that is said to help the national economy, in an aggregate sense, would not receive the same moral sanction.

14. It is important to note, however, that from our perspective, developing countries acting with a concern to foster just communities do *not* have a reciprocal obligation to let in all foreign goods or investment. Rather, the conception would allow a pragmatic approach to trade and investment flows by developing countries, and hence would tolerate, and at times actively encourage, restrictions aimed at protecting local entrepreneurs, emerging industries, and agricultural populations in developing countries. In very few cases would such restrictions successfully harm the project of developing stable, just communities in countries like the United States (although they might close off some profit-making opportunities for American corporations and investors). It is obviously in the interest of American workers that real wages and living standards in developing countries increase, and trade and investment restrictions that can plausibly contribute to that goal, even if they deny benefits to American investors, should be welcomed.

15. *Economic Report of the President 1999* (Washington, DC: Government Printing Office, 1999), Table B-105, and *Economic Report of the President 2002*, Table B-105.

16. Rodrik, *Making Openness Work*, Tables 2.1 and 2.2, 34–35.

17. Robert Scott, "NAFTA's Pain Deepens," *Economic Policy Institute Policy Brief,* November 1999.

18. Sarah Anderson and John Cavanagh, "Ten Myths About Globalization," *The Nation,* December 6, 1999.

19. Robert E. Scott, "The Facts About Trade and Job Creation," *Economic Policy Institute Issue Brief,* March 24, 2000.

20. Jeff Gersh, "Seeds of Chaos," *The Amicus Journal,* summer 1999, 39.

21. Peter Morici "The Trade Deficit: Where Does It Come From and What Does It Do?" available from the Economic Strategy Institute at www.econstrat.org/tradedef.htm.

22. Robert Scott, Congressional Testimony before the Senate Finance Committee, June 11, 1998, available from the Economic Policy Institute (www.epinet.org). For a full discussion of the possibility of an economic crisis stimulated by the American trade deficit, see Robert Blecker, "The Ticking Debt Bomb," Economic Policy Institute working paper, July 1999, available from www.epinet.org. See also Eamonn Fingleton, "Unsustainable," in *The American Prospect,* August 14, 2000, 18–21. For 2000 trade deficit figures, see *Economic Report of the President 2002*, Tables B-1 and B-105.

23. Principal authors of the document include Sarah Anderson (Institute for Policy Studies in Washington, DC), Alberto Arroyo (RMALC, Mexico), Peter Bakvis (CSN, Quebec), Patty Barrera (Common Frontiers, Canada), John Dillon (Ecumenical Coalition for Economic Justice/Common Frontiers, Canada), Karen Hansen-Kuhn (Development GAP, Washington, DC), and David Ranney (University of Illinois at Chicago), Victor Baez (ORIT), and Renato Martins (REBRIP, Brazil).

24. Hemisphere Social Allicance et al., *Alternatives for the Americas,* Discussion draft #3. Institute for Policy Studies (www.ips-dc.org), April 2001, 61.

25. For a proposal similar in intent to the HSA proposal, see the description of Canadian Tony Clarke's Alternative Investment Treaty in "Rewriting the Rules," *New Internationalist,* January-February 2000, 22–23.

26. Sanders, Global Sustainable Development Resolution, Section 9, Article 1(A).

27. Sanders, Global Sustainable Development Resolution, Section 9, Article 2.

28. William Greider, *One World, Ready or Not* (New York: Simon and Schuster, 1999), 169.

29. For development of this idea, see Gar Alperovitz and Jeff Faux, *Rebuilding America* (New York: Pantheon, 1984), 150–54.

30. Paul Krugman, *The Accidental Theorist* (New York: W. W. Norton, 1998), 82–83.

31. UN figures cited below credit Indonesia with an increase from 1,842 calories per capita in 1970 to 2,886 calories in 1997.

32. Ibid., 85.

33. Sarah Anderson and John Cavanagh (with Thea Lee), *Field Guide to the Global Economy* (New York: Free Press, 2000), 47.

34. See discussion in MacArthur, *The Selling of "Free Trade",* 81–89.

35. *United Nations Development Report 2000* (New York: United Nations Development Program, 2000). Table 23, 237–40.

36. Indeed, one of the leading organizations in the contemporary movement to upgrade sweatshop conditions worldwide is the National Consumers League, which originated in 1899 for the purpose of fighting sweatshops in the United States. This same general point is also made by Anderson and Cavanagh, *Field Guide to the Global Economy,* 57.

37. John Weeks, "Wages, Employment, and Workers' Rights in Latin America, 1970–1998," *International Labour Review* 138, 2 (1999): 151–68. Quote at 165.

38. For further discussion, see Kimberly Ann Elliot, "International Labor Standards and Trade: What Should Be Done?" paper presented at the conference "The Future of the World Trading System," Institute for International Economics, Washington, DC, April 15, 1998; for detailed expression of a proposal similar to that presented in this text, see Pharis Harvey, Terry Collingsworth, and Bama Athreya, "Developing Effective Mechanisms for Implementing Labor Rights In the Global Economy," International Labor Rights Fund working paper, Washington, DC, August 1998.

39. For a succinct review of American public opinion on trade and free trade agreements, see "The Pulse on Trade," Economic Policy Institute, December 1999, available via www.epinet.org. Polls showed a majority of Americans opposed to extending NAFTA to the rest of Latin America (*Business Week*/Harris, September 1998) as well as granting fast-track negotiating authority for the President (*Business Week*/Harris September 1997), and that about two-thirds of Americans believe corporations are the primary beneficiaries of NAFTA (Hart/AFL-CIO, July 1997). Over 70 percent of Americans support tying labor and environmental standards to trade agreements (Hart/AFL-CIO, July 1997.)

40. For a critique of the FTAA, see Hemispheric Social Alliance, "NAFTA Investors' Rights Plus: An Analysis of the Draft Investment Chapter of the FTAA," released June 19, 2001, available via the Institute for Policy Studies in Washington; see the IPS Web site, www.ips-dc.org.

CONCLUSION

1. On economic inequality, see Gar Alperovitz, "Distributing Our Technological Inheritance," *Technology Review,* October 1994; on the political consequences of economic inequality, see David Imbroscio, *Reconstructing City Politics* (Thousand Oaks, CA: Sage, 1997); on ecology, see Gar Alperovitz "Sustainability and the System Problem," *PEGS Journal,* 1996; Thad Williamson, "What an Environmentally Sustainable Economy Looks Like," *Dollars and Sense,* July-August 1999; and Gar Alperovitz, Thad Williamson, and Alex Campbell, "Notes Toward an Ecologically Sustainable Society," in Fred P. Gale and Michael M'Gonigle, *Nature, Production, and Power* (Cheltenham: Edward Elgar, 2000); on race, see Thad Williamson, review of Nathan McCall's *Makes Me Wanna Holler: A Young Black Man in America, Monthly Review,* May 1996. On each of these issues in an integrated perspective, see Gar Alperovitz, "Speculative Theory and Vision" in Karol E. Soltan and Stephen L. Elkin, eds., *The Constitution of Good Societies* (University Park: Pennsylvania State University Press, 1996).

2. John Dewey, *The Public and Its Problems,* cited by Robert Putnam, *Bowling Alone* (New York: Simon and Schuster, 2000), 317.

3. Indeed, while Putnam focuses on social capital as a critical explanatory variable for a wide range of desirable social outcomes, the evidence he has assembled makes it clear that economic dislocations and deprivations—as well as transient neighborhoods in general—make building social capital and strong community bonds much more difficult. See *Bowling Alone,* Chapters 18 and 19, esp. 312–18. Putnam also hints at the overlap between the concerns he raises and the agenda laid out in this book by approvingly citing Tupelo, Mississippi as an example of place-based collective-led community economic development carried out over a period of decades that successfully created physical, financial, and social capital in Tupelo.

4. In this context it is worth taking note that Putnam has ruled out residential mobility as a causal factor in explaining the *decline* in social capital in the United States since the 1950s, pointing out that residential mobility actually declined slightly over this same period. (See *Bowling Alone,* 205.) Note, however, that Putnam in this instance is focused on trying to account for changes in social capital over time, not to examine what circumstances are amenable to social capital creation. It would therefore be wrong to conclude that community economic stability is unimportant in generating social capital in general—or that increasing the economic stability of neighborhoods and cities would not have an important "social capital" payoff in the future. Indeed, many of the strategies for place-based development noted in parts II and III of this book make the creation of social capital—that is, stronger bonds of community—either a primary or a secondary aim.

5. See, for example, Stephen Elkin, *City and Regime in the American Republic* (Chicago: University of Chicago Press, 1987); John Logan and Harvey Molotch, *Urban Fortunes* (Berkeley: University of California Press, 1987).

6. J. Phillip Thompson, "A Political and Practical Approach to Building Urban Political Coalitions," presentation given at Multidisciplinary Program on Inequality seminar series, Kennedy School of Government, Harvard University, March 12, 2001.

7. *Historical Tables: Budget of the United States Government, Fiscal Year 2003* (Washington, DC: Government Printing Office, 2002), Table 3:2.

8. *Budget of the United States Government, Fiscal Year 2003* (Washington, DC: Government Printing Office, 2002), 2.

9. On American attitudes towards corporate power, see Aaron Bernstein, "Too Much Corporate Power?" *Business Week*, September 11, 2000.

10. B. Jeffrey Reno, "A Floor Without A Ceiling: Redevelopment and the Social Production Model," paper presented at the annual meeting of the American Political Science Association, Washington, DC, August 31–September 3, 2000.

11. Putnam, *Bowling Alone*, 265.

INDEX